VICARIOUS WARFARE

VICARIOUS WARFARE

American Strategy and the Illusion
of War on the Cheap

Thomas Waldman

BRISTOL
UNIVERSITY
PRESS

First published in Great Britain in 2021 by

Bristol University Press
University of Bristol
1-9 Old Park Hill
Bristol
BS2 8BB
UK
t: +44 (0)117 954 5940
e: bup-info@bristol.ac.uk

Details of international sales and distribution partners are available at bristoluniversitypress.co.uk

British Library Cataloguing in Publication Data
A catalogue record for this book is available from the British Library

ISBN 978-1-5292-0699-9 hardcover
ISBN 978-1-5292-0703-3 ePub
ISBN 978-1-5292-0702-6 ePdf

Cover design: blu inc, Bristol
Front cover image: blu inc, Bristol

Bristol University Press uses environmentally responsible print partners.

Printed in Great Britain by CPI Group (UK) Ltd, Croydon, CR0 4YY

FSC
www.fsc.org
MIX
Paper from
responsible sources
FSC® C013604

For Caroline

If the political aims are small, the motives slight and tensions low, a prudent general may look for any way to avoid major crises and decisive actions.... If his assumptions are sound and promise success we are not entitled to criticise him. But he must never forget that he is moving on devious paths where the god of war may catch him unawares.

Carl von Clausewitz, *On War*, 1832

Contents

List of Abbreviations

AFRICOM	United States Africa Command
ALP	Afghan Local Police
AMISOM	African Union Mission in Somalia
ARVN	Army of the Republic of Vietnam
AUMF	Authorization for Use of Military Force
AVF	All-Volunteer Force
CIA	Central Intelligence Agency (US)
COIN	Counterinsurgency
GPS	Global Positioning System
ISAF	International Security Assistance Force (NATO)
JDAM	Joint Direct Attack Munition
JSOC	Joint Special Operations Center (US)
KLA	Kosovo Liberation Army
MACV	Military Assistance Command, Vietnam
NATO	North Atlantic Treaty Organization
NSC	National Security Council (US)
OSS	Office of Strategic Services (US)
PGM	Precision-guided munition
PMSC	Private military and security company
PRT	Provincial Reconstruction Team
RMA	Revolution in military affairs
RPG	Rocket-propelled grenade
SAC	Special Activities Center (CIA, US)
SAD	Special Activities Division (CIA, US)
SDF	Syrian Democratic Forces
SFA	Security force assistance
SOCOM	Special Operations Command (US)
SOF	Special operations forces
SOG	Special Operations Group (CIA, US)
UAV	Unmanned aerial vehicle
UNOSOM	United Nations Operation in Somalia
WMD	Weapons of mass destruction
YPG	People's Protection Units (Syria)

Acknowledgements

Any book is the outcome of a journey and this has been a long one, with many people I need to thank for helping me along the way. *Vicarious Warfare* brings together different streams of research I have been working on for a number of years and draws from my experiences working in and on Afghanistan in the early 2010s.

In a book chapter I co-authored with Caroline Kennedy-Pipe on 'Ways of War in the 21st Century' in 2013, we concluded that, for Western states such as America,[1] the coming years would likely constitute 'an age of vicarious war'.[2] I felt this concept captured important features of contemporary warfare and that it could serve as a useful basis for further study. Indeed, events throughout the 2010s seemed only to confirm our earlier prognosis. My own thinking evolved as US policy became increasingly enamoured with indirect, proxy and remote means of applying force. Meanwhile, academic clusters emerged researching issues associated with private military actors, special forces, covert operations, drones and related subjects. Earlier scholars had led the way with concepts such as 'virtual', 'bloodless' and 'risk-transfer' warfare, but developments in both theory and practice suggested there was a need for fresh approaches.

Amid the tumult of events and the swirl of new thinking, the ideas of Carl von Clausewitz (the focus of my earlier book, *War, Clausewitz and the Trinity*) always seemed to serve as a reliable anchor to ground my own thinking and a useful lens through which to make sense of complex issues. In fact, most core strategic problems seemed to lead inexorably back to his ideas, especially his foundational insights on the politics of war. As such, Clausewitz here serves as something of a background 'tour guide' throughout the book, but I felt compelled to rely more heavily on his work when discussing the prominent strategic consequences of vicarious warfare in Chapter 7. I was fortunate enough to have the opportunity to present my thoughts on this subject to staff and students of Harvard University's Belfer Center in 2013. Many thanks to Steven E. Miller for hosting, and to all those who attended for their helpful feedback.

Subsequently, my ideas on the core themes of the book have evolved and been shaped through discussion with colleagues and students at the University of York and Macquarie University. In this respect, I am particularly grateful to Jacob Eriksson, Sultan Barakat, Andrea Varisco, James Rogers and the brilliant Nick Rengger (who sadly passed away in 2018). I also presented earlier versions of the ideas contained in this book at a workshop facilitated by the Remote Warfare Programme on 'cost-free warfare' at the University of St Andrews, and at a number of conferences. Thanks to all who provided feedback at those events. I would also like to express my gratitude to Christopher Bassford, Andrew Mumford and Vladimir Rauta for supporting my work in various respects along the way.

I ultimately pulled my ideas together into a series of journal articles which, in different ways, feed into parts of this book, especially my 2018 article with the same main title. I am grateful to the editors of *Contemporary Security Policy*, *Defence Studies* and *Survival* – respectively Hylke Dykstra, Simon Smith and Jonathan Stevenson – for publishing those earlier articles and to Taylor & Francis for permitting me to reuse some of the material here.[3] My older and far more accomplished brother, Matt Waldman, provided extensive input into those earlier articles based on his own his path-breaking work on empathy in international affairs and tireless diplomatic efforts in Afghanistan, Syria, Somalia and Yemen. My sister-in-law Nicolette – a fearless and inspiring international human rights lawyer – provided me with extremely valuable if often harrowing first-hand insights from her in-depth field research in the Middle East. Thank you both immensely. Really quite useful family to have!

I am especially indebted to colleagues who kindly read all or parts of the manuscript: Yves-Heng Lim, Lise Waldek and Ben Schreer. Anonymous reviewers of the book proposal and the final manuscript also provided thorough and helpful comments for which I am very grateful. The team at Bristol University Press, especially Stephen Wenham and Caroline Astley, have provided professional and comprehensive oversight and guidance throughout – thank you so much. Dawn Rushen did a wonderful job copyediting the book, spotting errors with an eagle eye and greatly enhancing its readability. I would also like to thank Macquarie University for awarding funding that provided me with valuable time to complete the manuscript.

This book is dedicated to my amazing mentor and friend, Caroline Kennedy-Pipe. It is impossible to fully express my debt of gratitude to someone who has so steadfastly supported me through thick and thin from my Master's degree, through my PhD, and then ever since. None of this would have been possible without your help. Thank you again for your close review of the manuscript and more generally providing such invaluable guidance and advice from the book's inception to its completion. Your immense breadth of knowledge, penetrating intellect, and ability to see perspectives on issues that I hadn't even considered never ceases to astound and inspire me.

I am incredibly grateful to all those who have supported me in writing this book, but it goes without saying that any weaknesses or errors remain my own. My friends and extended family, however, have a lot to answer for. Fun-filled holidays, long walks and runs in the fells, riotous playfights with kids, and hilarious Zoom calls under lockdown kept me from my desk and meant much burning of the midnight oil to meet deadlines: how inconsiderate of you all! Seriously, though, I'm so incredibly lucky and grateful to be surrounded by such amazing and talented people. During the course of writing this book we welcomed my niece, the whip-smart and adorable Alex (who will no doubt soon be writing her own books), while the arrival of her sister will likely just pip publication. We also very sadly said goodbye to our 'Jack the lad' – we miss you sorely, but the memory of your warm-hearted character and wonderful singing will live on in all our memories. Rest in peace.

Mum and my 'adopted' dad Steve went beyond the call of duty to read and comment on the entire manuscript, making many improvements in the process. I am incredibly grateful to you both for that and so much more beyond! My wife Katya has had to endure more of my musings on American warfare than perhaps our marriage vows countenanced – thank you for your patience and encouragement throughout. I'm so proud of all you have achieved and everything you are. Your gentle soul, kind heart and playful spirit make every day a happy one. You are the love of my life.

Introduction:
The Alchemy of War

The notion of the philosopher's stone concerned the attempt by alchemists to discover a substance that could turn base metals into gold or silver. The equivalent of this in war has been the endeavour to achieve victory at minimal cost relative to one's ambition, to realize strategic objectives but without the high political, human or financial price tag that typically accompanies violent contest, or, at a wider societal level, to use war to achieve national ends but in a manner that does not place significant demands on the people. Indeed, a recurring theme throughout the history of war – although not necessarily always the most prominent one – concerns the efforts of belligerents to somehow limit, minimize or evade the various liabilities associated with its conduct. Vicarious warfare is an extreme form of this strategic alchemy, and contemporary America is its most enthusiastic guild, presently engaged in its own military *magnum opus* toward this end.

Of course, in principle, the most important cost of war to avoid is defeat. The prospect of this eventuality is a major factor causing actors to commit fully to the fight, however arduous it may prove and however great the energies, resources and sacrifices it may demand. Where a community's survival is at stake there may be a tendency to 'pay any price, bear any burden'.[1] But in wars fought for more limited objectives – the majority in history[2] – there is a greater tendency to engage in cost-benefit calculations.[3] The rewards that might be had from war are set against the possible consequences of failure and the potential price of the whole endeavour, typically measured in blood and treasure, even if objective measures are almost impossible to determine or predict accurately in advance.[4] The resistance that the adversary is able to mount and the costs that accrue will cause belligerents to reassess where the balance lies, but the basic logic behind this lethal ledger nevertheless retains its relevance. Accordingly, the more that costs can be reduced relative to the prospective gains, the better, especially if lowering the former does not entail any simultaneous scaling back of the latter. This is all perfectly understandable.

But what if costs and requirements could be cut still further, reduced in absolute terms, or essentially bypassed altogether? This surely is a preferable course and it is one that has led countless warring actors to search for that magic bullet, inspired stratagem, strategic shortcut, operational end-run or organizational fix that promises to deliver success on the cheap. It is the allure of easy war, of budget belligerency and value victories.

In alchemy, the symbol of the squared circle represented the elements that would combine to create the philosopher's stone. We might employ a similar idea to capture the way actors seek to 'produce' less burdensome wars through reduced costs and requirements, whether in terms of, among other things, blood, treasure, political capital or material resources. True to the alchemical image, these different spheres are all deeply intertwined. The ideal might be the minimization of requirements in all spheres simultaneously, but often sacrifices might be required in some in order to achieve desired reductions in others, depending on priorities. However, there is a missing element that must be added, which pertains to the mindset of the alchemists themselves: *faith*, that 'secret fire' of desire, or its more mundane cousin, wishful thinking.

In war, this translates into a form of denial with regard to the serious costs that might have to be incurred or the level of investments in material, social, political and even emotional capital required to realize objectives, resulting in a mismatch between ends and means.[5] This takes us away from rational prudence or balanced cost-benefit appraisal and into the realm of what the 19th-century Prussian theorist of war, Carl von Clausewitz, termed 'passion' or 'moral forces'. It is a phenomenon principally generated by emotional impulses and psychological fixations, nourished by prevailing norms, values and preoccupations existing in wider society. But it can also be provoked by the alluring possibilities presented by developments in material spheres – the confidence inspired by a new wonder weapon, the hubris generated by early victories or one's sense of superiority deriving from an advantage over the adversary in terms of troops and armaments.[6]

Actors may on occasion be able to evade important costs while still achieving important objectives in the short run. However, much like the apocryphal nature of the philosopher's stone, this often reveals itself to have been fool's gold. In time, the supposed achievements turn to dust while harmful repercussions materialize in other areas. War's nature tends to mean that evasive efforts – even those successful in their immediate effect – are usually punished in one way or another, either with respect to the outcome of war itself or costs incurred in other unexpected spheres. Clausewitz held that 'in war too small an effort can result not just in failure but in positive harm'.[7] The line between strategically sound limitation and the military mirage of unrealistic evasion is blurred and extremely difficult to determine, especially without the benefit of hindsight, but the distinction remains valid nonetheless, and strategists need to be acutely aware of its seductive appeal.[8] Vicarious warfare represents an extreme strain of this type of behaviour. It captures attempts by actors to distance themselves from the costs and requirements of their wars, but to fight and win them nonetheless.

The American alchemists

Modern American strategists have evolved the scope and methods of this alchemy in ways unimaginable to earlier generations. Over the last decade, and despite bitter warfighting and significant costs incurred in the Afghanistan and Iraq Wars during the 2000s, the US has not retreated from foreign military intervention but has instead settled on a low-level, persistent, remote and evasive mode of fighting firmly within the vicarious mould. Observations bearing similarities to the argument here have been presented by a number of scholars of strategy, and this book seeks to build on these existing contributions.

The headline messages emerging from this literature are consistent and stark. The reluctance to engage in large 'boots on the ground' deployments has, according to Demmers and Gould, been superseded by a preference for 'light-footprint military interventions' involving 'a combination of drone strikes and airstrikes, special forces, intelligence operatives, private contractors, and military-to-military (M2M) training teams on the ground.'[9] For Kiras, this all reflects the way policymakers today have sought 'shortcuts to victory. New means, including special operations and/or emerging technologies, purportedly allow users to avoid the difficulties posed by the nature of strategy.'[10] In outlining the contemporary characteristics of Western warfare, Levite and Shimshoni describe how states such as America 'have acted instinctively to diminish the domestic social footprint of often contentious foreign operations by exploiting stand-off systems, minimising ground-force operations, and using special operations forces and professional soldiers, as well as subcontractors and proxies, instead of conscripts or reservists wherever possible.'[11] So we see recurring themes pertaining to both motivation and operational implementation. In the aftermath of costly wars there has been a shift toward tech-enabled economization, limitation, specialization, privatization and distance.

Currently, America's general preference is to fight its wars by delegating fighting to proxies, limiting the exposure of its own military forces to danger, and operating in the shadows through the use of special forces, covert practices and evolving offensive cyber techniques. These features of contemporary American warfare can be captured in the shorthand designations of delegation, danger-proofing and darkness: throughout the book we will chart the emergence of these practices, and in Chapter 7 we explore in depth the prominent strategic consequences related to them. But these three 'Ds' are only operational-level reflections of distancing processes in politics and wider society beyond the visible face of American war – this perspective forms an important part of the story. The book also argues that vicarious warfare should not simply be understood as the immediate fallout from the bloody 2000s. It is shaped by deeper patterns and many decades of experience employing force in broadly similar ways. This history has contributed to the gradual and cumulative yet still partial emergence of a separate tradition of war, complete with its own evolving myths and narratives, and that competes against alternative strategic agendas for policy influence.

Traditions of American war

The question of whether there is a distinctive American way of war has long intrigued scholars, stimulating considerable debate and producing varying levels of consensus. Typologies have been proposed which seek to capture the manner in which America has thought about or employed force throughout its history. Some have claimed there is a single dominant and coherent national style observable over generations;[12] others highlight the existence of multiple paradigms. While differing in precise focus, historical period covered or terminology employed, these frameworks provide us with valuable insights, notwithstanding their often-partisan nature. It is not a central aim of this book to argue for a definitive categorization or really to enter directly into these long-running debates. However, as a backdrop to the subsequent discussion throughout the book, it is useful to think about American strategic history through the lens of prominent contrasting traditions. The concept of 'tradition' is preferred to that of 'way of war', where the latter carries strong connotations of singularity, rigidity and cultural determinism. Tradition is a looser, more inclusive term that arguably better captures evolving practices, strategic ideas and accompanying narratives simultaneously.

Traditions are expressed through the actual practice or historical record of US warfighting but simultaneously exist as influential ideas and beliefs about how America should employ military force. These may remain largely theoretical or at least latent insofar as they may guide planning and preparation but not actual warfighting. Or they may represent the views of certain esoteric segments within military and strategic communities, only rising to prominence in policy and practice due to changing circumstances. In reality, different traditions are neither entirely mutually exclusive nor completely comprehensive, covering all American military ideas or practices; they are simplifying analytical devices that nevertheless capture meaningful historical patterns and help clarify fundamental issues.[13] It is also important to note that traditions are not purely the preserve of the US military but rather reflect the preoccupations of the wider security establishment and ultimately the nation as a whole.

So, vicarious warfare is presented here as an emergent third tradition alongside the existing traditions of 'conventional battle' and 'small wars'. Although appearing in various guises, these latter two traditions represent familiar understandings – indeed, they are far from original.[14] They are also more 'mature' insofar as they exist in practice and doctrine as broadly coherent and well-established traditions with their own associated histories, myths, defining events, natural institutional homes and high-profile proponents. Vicarious warfare has emerged alongside but also, in some important respects, *out of* these two traditions, borrowing approaches and ideas at their margins but crafting them into an increasingly novel and largely independent tradition of American warfare supported by its own intellectual pedigree and justificatory narratives. The idea of a third broad category, moving us beyond the two tradition framework, allows for a fresh perspective on US military history, enhances our understanding of core aspects of contemporary American warfare, and provides us with a framework that can help us reflect on possible future military developments. Before we address this particular tradition in greater depth throughout the book, it is first necessary to briefly outline the major characteristics of the other two traditions, and this also usefully serves to highlight and foreground what is distinctive about vicarious warfare.

Conventional battle

The tradition of conventional battle offers us a strongly contrasting mode of American warfare compared with that of vicarious warfare in almost all respects. At the heart of this tradition is the presumption of large-scale operations involving regular American forces employing conventional weapons platforms arrayed against (typically) a state adversary possessing comparable capabilities. The destruction of the enemy in head-to-head battle is to be achieved by exploiting American offensive spirit, material preponderance and technological superiority. It is a model dominated by major high-intensity combat operations fought by 'big battalions' over a discrete battlefield guided by the commander's operational art. It has been described as an industrial style of war. The chief aim of such 'big battle' conflicts or 'major theatre' wars is final decision and total victory in pursuit of clear national interests, usually of a territorial or ideological nature.[15] Put bluntly, when America goes to war, it should 'go big or go home'.

This tradition is essentially synonymous with the archetypal popular notion of the 'American way of war', especially given the claim that it is especially well suited to and reflects wider American culture.[16] Mead suggests it derives from the strong streak of Jacksonian populism found in much of Middle America, which demands 'that you must hit them as hard as you can as fast as you can with as much as you can.'[17] Its enduring influence is manifested not only in the conduct of particular wars but also in the way America prepares for war: in the syllabuses of the war colleges where future leaders are trained and educated; in the doctrinal content of countless field manuals that guide commanders when designing their campaigns; and in the force structure and procurement decisions that shape the kind of military the nation has available to it.

Some have traced the origins of this way of war to America's emulation of Prussian military doctrine during the 19th century as well as the influence of the ideas of Baron Antoine Henri de Jomini, an interpreter of Napoleon's campaigns, whose ideas were especially prominent during the Civil War.[18] Jomini advocated 'destroying enemy forces regardless of where they were' by using 'freedom of manoeuvre to bring masses of one's own troops against fractions of the enemy's, and to strike in the most decisive direction.'[19] Even Clausewitz's ideas, or at least certain interpretations of them among senior politicians and officers toward the end of the 20th century (see Chapter 7), contributed to the notion that the enemy possesses a discrete centre of gravity that, once identified, should be attacked with overwhelming force.[20] Strachan relates how the commander leading the 2003 Iraq War, General Tommy Franks, believed Clausewitz had 'dictated that mass – concentrated formations of troops and guns – was the key to victory'.[21]

This tradition is popularly associated with major inter-state wars prominent in the nation's historical imagination, such as the Civil War, the First and Second World Wars, the Korean War and the Gulf War.[22] Indeed, success in two massive global conflicts in the first half of the 20th century has deeply embedded this thinking. The powerful resonance of the Second World War 'greatest generation' continues to influence military thought to this day.[23] These wars take up a disproportionate amount of shelf space in American history and culture concerning its record in war, producing its defining myths and tropes. Meanwhile, the famous generals who fought them are hailed as exemplary exponents of the art.[24] Tellingly, when contemplating decisions on war, presidents have been accused of having their 'Patton moments', seeing themselves as embodiments of the hard-hitting Second World War general. In this way, bolstered by celebratory books, powerful images and popular myths, these representations come to be seen as synonymous with victory and American best practice in war, thus reinforcing the overarching narrative. These representations, whatever their truth or inherent worth, exert a powerful influence on the attitudes of policymakers, officials and the wider public.

Small wars

In the ideal image of conventional war, the people are essentially absent from the battlefield. American forces roam the otherwise empty land, sea and air seeking to engage and destroy the enemy in battle through the application of superior firepower. Their defeat presages a return to peace and politicians can use the victory to promote their political objectives. Small wars represent a very different form of war because they are really all *about* the people, they are fought among the people or, to use contemporary terminology, they are 'population-centric.' They are about the people because they tend to emerge in situations of state collapse, popular uprisings, civilian victimization or communal violence. They are fought among the people because the enemy emerges from the civilian population, operates in their midst, and often conducts its primary actions against them. They are population-centric because any realistic solution tends to be less about eliminating adversary forces and more about winning popular legitimacy, fostering inter-communal peace, or preventing further repression. The small wars tradition begins from the assertion that America has, can and should engage in such wars.[25]

This tradition embraces a wide range of military contingencies,[26] but it is defined less by the specific nature of the situation at hand and more by the measures that its advocates claim are required to achieve success. They argue that effective approaches entail long-term and resource-intensive commitments demanding significant resolve and patience. Confronting violent actors and adversarial forces may be an important element of small wars (indeed, they can be extremely bloody affairs), but they tend not to be so narrowly oriented around the final defeat or overthrow of an enemy force. The overarching strategic objective is often more about establishing the conditions in which political processes such as peace talks, governmental reform or inter-communal reconciliation can make progress, as opposed to achieving 'victory' as conventionally understood.[27]

At the operational level, generally less emphasis is placed on offensive kinetic actions and the military posture is often defensive, with missions focused on population and infrastructure protection. Even where aggressive operations are deemed necessary, the orthodox view is that they should be carefully managed, using the minimum of force necessary and accompanied by extensive efforts in the political, administrative and social spheres. This has led some to designate such operations as a form of armed social work insofar as soldiers are expected to carry out a range of activities beyond simply targeting enemy forces.[28] Additional activities might involve implementing small-scale development projects, conducting meetings with local leaders or even establishing basic systems of governance and dispute resolution before the situation is safe enough for civilian specialists to take over. The 'provincial reconstruction teams' widely deployed in Iraq and Afghanistan (building on similar earlier models adopted during the Vietnam War) were designed to enable simultaneous military and civilian efforts in providing security and essential services to threatened communities.

Proponents of the conventional battle tradition tend to denigrate small wars.[29] And in the public imagination such wars do not garner the same kind of attention that the big battles and wars of the conventional tradition attract. Figures such as Edward Lansdale (a major figure promoting clandestine counter-guerrilla operations in the 1950s and 1960s)[30] have some specialist admirers, and more recent commanders like General David Petraeus have achieved near celebrity status. But they are no Pattons. The way the small wars tradition is widely associated with quagmire and costly commitments – especially through its (somewhat unfair) association with Vietnam and defeat[31] – partly explains its subordinate status, only fleetingly gaining widespread popular or official attention during discrete periods in American history. But supporters of this tradition argue that America has not only successfully fought many such small wars, but also that they will need to be fought in the future. They argue that American experience conducting complex small wars constitutes a long, rich and important aspect of the nation's military history and culture, which is unjustifiably emasculated by the attention devoted to the conventional tradition.[32]

The concept of counterinsurgency – arguably the most prominent form of small war – sometimes elicits images of a singular or uniform phenomenon, reinforced by its modern common shorthand designation as 'COIN'. Yet there has never been a single or constant interpretation of the concept.[33] In this book, COIN refers to the traditional understanding of the term as denoting large resource-intensive population-centric approaches involving some element of 'nation building'. However, counterinsurgency stripped bare of its assumed connotations is, in fact, a neutral term simply denoting efforts to tackle a protracted armed rebellion against state authority. As such, it can theoretically take any number of forms, whether of a predominantly conventional, population-centric or vicarious nature. Indeed, it is suggested here that the more indirect, smaller-scale and minimal footprint counterinsurgency campaigns that have been conducted on occasion are best understood as being situated within the vicarious warfare tradition.

Toward a tradition of vicarious warfare

Commentary on strategic affairs during the 2000s seemed to crystallize around the latest iteration of the long-standing rivalry between the rival COIN and conventional traditions, or, as it was memorably dubbed, between 'crusaders and conservatives'.[34] Such strategic debates were often presented as if large-scale COIN or conventional battle were the only options available to American policymakers. The crusaders dominated US security narratives over the latter half of the decade, to the extent that, according to some, COIN had become 'an end in-and-of-itself.'[35] But the rise of COIN had itself prompted a mounting rear-guard action by those asserting that the US military should get back to its primary mission and double down on its mastery of high-intensity conventional war.[36] Indeed, Freedman observed an emerging 'counterrevolution' in strategic affairs at this time.[37] The results of the Iraq surge were beginning to look less positive than initially supposed. In Afghanistan, commanders confidently asserting that the mission was 'turning a corner' in the fight against the Taliban were increasingly met with scepticism. There was a growing sense that COIN was already passé after its relatively short-lived time at the top. As a result, the conventional tradition, which had never really gone away, was once again being placed front and centre in doctrine and strategy documents, exerting huge influence over military plans and procurement.

Yet, for other analysts, the rejection of COIN led them neither to a simplistic return to orthodoxy nor to wholesale disengagement. Rather, it led them toward what they described as a compromise option involving methods such as delegation to militias, covert operations, expanded security force assistance programmes, discrete military interventions and indirect light-footprint counterinsurgency. As we see later in the book, such activities had been long underway in various peripheral theatres, but now such thinking found an ever more receptive audience among officials. After all, the exhausting and costly campaigns of the 2000s were still fresh in the memory. At a Pentagon news conference in May 2012, presenting the outcome of a strategic review, President Barack Obama declared 'the end of long-term nation-building with large military footprints.' The US would instead 'develop innovative, low-cost, small-footprint approaches to achieve our security objectives.'[38] The path thus lay open for an unprecedented expansion and intensification of vicarious warfare, which progressively inserted itself to occupy the policy space somewhere alongside the crusaders and conservatives as a cost-cutting third option. But before that story can be told, we need a clearer understanding of the meaning and parameters of the concept under study.

Use of the term 'vicarious' could be understood in a quite literal sense, suggesting that those responsible for prosecuting American war only engage in it indirectly from afar or experience it through the actions and exploits of others. This perspective might, for instance, encompass the way leaders oversee their wars from situation rooms in Washington via video link, such as captured in the image of President Obama and senior officials huddled together watching as Seal Team 6 eliminated Osama bin Laden in 2011 or the Trump team watching the raid against Islamic State leader Abu Bakr al-Baghdadi in 2019. In the aftermath of the latter mission, directly authorized by President Trump, he remarked that it was 'like watching a movie'.[39] The concept might also relate to a drone pilot launching Hellfire missiles against militants in Pakistan from a trailer in Nevada, a CIA officer remotely directing proxy militias against adversaries in Libya, or ordinary American citizens following the exploits of their nation's warriors through live news feeds beamed directly to their smartphones.[40]

All these kinds of distancing effects may be a practical consequence of this form of warfare for many, and this is certainly part of the puzzle. However, for the most part, the term is employed more as an overarching metaphor that seeks to capture the notion of war fought by a society at arm's length, at a remove. Of course, American military personnel continue to be engaged in intense, sometimes hand-to-hand combat in disparate theatres around the globe. Accordingly, the argument here is not that there is no direct engagement, but instead that we can observe a general attempt by actors to shield themselves from the costs, burdens and requirements of contemporary war in interrelated physical, political and psycho-social respects. The distancing at the core of this concept essentially concerns that between the two fundamental elements of strategy: ends and means. The intent of vicarious warfare is *to achieve one's ends with relatively minimal means* – the metaphorical distance implied is that between the respective scope and magnitude of requirements on the one hand and desired results on the other. Or, to put it in colloquial terms, war fought vicariously is about limiting what it takes relative to what it brings. It is also possible to identify an associated ethical distancing whereby actors may seek to evade moral responsibility for the consequences of their decisions, directly for political leaders or more indirectly for the wider electorate; nevertheless, the focus in this book is on strategic dynamics, although the two areas are by no means unrelated.

Some scholars have argued that contemporary American warfare approximates to a form of global risk management, consistent with broader developments in Western social and economic affairs.[41] In this light, drone strikes and surrogate operations are not designed to achieve 'victory' but rather simply to keep a lid on global threats and risks through minimalist global 'firefighting' methods: a form of strategic economization to manage non-existential risks. This might suggest US behaviour is not truly vicarious according to our definition: the means reflect only limited ends. There is perhaps much to recommend this view. However, it would be mistaken to push these claims too far. First, we should take American leaders at their word – whether the target is Bashar al-Assad, Islamic State, al-Shabaab or the Taliban, officials have repeatedly articulated far-reaching objectives in specific theatres. Second, viewed holistically, there is nothing restrained or unambitious about seeking to oversee protracted military campaigns across the globe. Third, it could well be that what in hindsight ends up looking like a deliberate strategy of risk management is in fact simply evidence of the failure of vicarious methods to achieve the desired defeat of adversaries.[42]

In its contemporary form, the vicarious epithet is employed to capture how certain approaches allow the US to prosecute permanent warfare around the globe but without the kind of direct involvement, visceral engagement, social contestation, rigorous accountability and meaningful investment of resources or political capital that traditionally applies when states go to war. As we will see, this is not entirely new under the sun; only modern conditions have served to amplify dynamics identifiable earlier in America's history and in other societies throughout history.

★ ★ ★

Clausewitz contrasted the core logic of war – which he asserted is always about political power (a key point that we will return to in Chapter 7) – with its grammar: the particular character and dynamics of combat.[43] As with language, this will be infinitely variable and culturally defined. The changeable language of combat will reflect the nature of the communities that conduct it and its prominent features will usually be as they are because, as Coker explains, they 'benefit a particular social order of the day'.[44] In this way, vicarious warfare is not only a product of, but also holds up a mirror to, contemporary American politics and society.

It is tempting to associate modern forms of vicariousness primarily with the military because naturally it is in theatres of war where its ultimate manifestations are most apparent. However, a central contention of this book is that many vicarious military practices derive from dynamics in the political sphere and are simultaneously enabled or encouraged by attitudes and dynamics in wider American society. In fact, a prominent feature of vicarious warfare is the way it shifts the burdens of war further away from the military on to others, and directs force against targets in countries that America is not even technically at war with. However, this does not mean that factors within the military itself play no role. The prosecution of vicarious warfare is generated by and sustained through the combined behaviour of government, the military and wider society – all are implicated in its perpetuation in one way or another, often in a mutually reinforcing manner. We might understand this as a kind of conspiracy of distance that suits all societal actors in a nation waging perpetual war. In short, vicarious warfare is a product of intersecting dynamics taking place within the modern American state, shaped also by external challenges and broader conditions.

As the preceding discussion would suggest, assigning 'responsibility' for the prosecution of vicarious war is almost impossible. The American people, many holding romanticized conceptions of war and the military, naturally demand security – which may have to be achieved through force – but want it provided in bloodless ways that do not require their own sacrifice or disrupt their comfort, wealth and prosperity. Democratically elected politicians, recognizing this, seek to confront threats but in a minimalist fashion, employing available shortcuts where possible, limiting societal involvement and adopting measures that evade political costs and keep war out of the media spotlight, except when it may be politically beneficial to showcase certain successful or heroic actions. The military, suffused with long-standing traditions of sacrifice and an aggressive warrior ethos, is keen to maintain its revered status as guardian of the nation. But senior defence officials and military commanders – conscious of changing societal norms, buffeted by political pressures from above and fearful of litigation – often seek ways to economize, minimize risks to the force or protect institutional interests. Taken together there are thus powerful societal incentives to fight, to confront threats with force, but also to do so in a vicarious fashion if possible. These issues will be explored further over subsequent chapters.

So the phenomenon of vicarious warfare is indicative of an emergent and increasingly homogenous American tradition of war. It embraces a diverse range of views, remains eclectic and adaptable in terms of the different actors and agencies that it brings together, and, as with the conventional battle and small war traditions, consensus is by no means apparent on all issues – it can be said to only loosely cohere. However, in practical and conceptual terms, it gravitates around a number of core operational approaches that provide it with a semblance of unity, and some key aspects and ideas are finding their way into doctrine, supported by influential voices in defence and security policymaking circles. Moreover, this tradition's centrality to the conduct of contemporary American war is only made more apparent by the recent emergence of critical perspectives directly contesting many of its central claims.

This evolving tradition of vicarious warfare has taken many forms over the years. Today it is arguably most discernible in a disparate array of concepts and ideas such as working 'by, with and through' local partners, 'light-footprint operations', 'small-scale counterinsurgency' (or 'little COIN'), 'minimalist stabilization', 'discrete strategies', 'war-lite' or 'coercive airpower'. Yet, as will be made clear, vicarious warfare should not be understood as a coherent doctrinal methodology that could be neatly outlined in a military field manual, suggesting institutionally established operational principles to guide its implementation in any particular scenario.[45]

Vicarious warfare spans tendencies that can be observed in the long history of war and, more concretely, builds on important precedents in wider Western and specifically American military engagement, especially since the middle of the 20th century. It cannot be properly understood without being placed in the context of deeper currents in US foreign policy, military history and society. While the central subject of this book is America – arguably its chief contemporary 'architect' and preeminent practitioner – there is no reason in theory why vicarious approaches could not be employed by any nation given the right conditions. As we will see, it generally presumes states possessing a certain level of wealth and power, global military reach and relative technological sophistication as well as conducive socio-political foundations. Other advanced Western nations display some of the associated warfighting characteristics and it can even be perceived in the operational approaches of large states such as Russia and China or regionally powerful players like Iran (although it should not be confused with concepts of 'hybrid warfare', 'ambiguous warfare' or 'grey zone' operations).

Existing studies

This is not another book about the wars in Iraq and Afghanistan. Those wars serve as important background and, in fact, ongoing operations in both theatres are central to the story of vicarious warfare over the last decade. At their height, the Iraq and Afghanistan Wars provided a kind of focus to the scholarly study and interrogation of American warfare. Those wars have been the subject of numerous journalistic accounts and in-depth scholarly studies.[46] Such works revealed how institutional, conceptual or even idiosyncratic shortcomings help to explain the difficulties Western states encountered in employing force to achieve national political objectives during the 2000s. Many of the issues they identified remain valid. However, since the dénouement or, rather, the transformation of the Iraq and Afghanistan Wars, it has been difficult from an analytical perspective to identify meaningful unifying themes connecting the global and disparate nature of modern American military operations, which are today almost overwhelming in their variety and geographical spread. The campaign against Islamic State, lethal drone strikes in numerous theatres, multiple operations throughout the continent of Africa and a lingering commitment in Afghanistan are only the most visible expressions of the globe-spanning penumbra of US military activity.

A number of other earlier works offered analyses of related conditions and dynamics apparent in preceding periods that hold close resemblances to the argument presented here.[47] Their ideas will be considered later in the book. Although their insights are now slightly outdated or have been overtaken or supplemented by important technological, political and strategic developments, they nevertheless form part of the story of the emergence and maturation of vicarious warfare. Recognized as influential intellectual precedents and conceptual forerunners, *Vicarious Warfare* seeks to take forward their ideas, apply them to the contemporary era, and offer a more strategically focused critique, employing new research and evidence that has since emerged.

Some existing accounts have explored country cases in detail and numerous studies have appeared on specific aspects of modern warfare. This specialized research tends to be quite narrow in focus, looking in depth at issues such as proxy warfare, armed drones, cyber warfare, special forces, covert operations or security force assistance. Important insights from all these works inform the argument of this book. However, we presently lack a means of analytically and conceptually weaving these disparate threads together to provide a coherent account of this complex reality – this study offers a wider argument beyond any one technology or military practice, seeking to assess their influence as a collective phenomenon. The aim here is to help make better sense of a range of closely related contemporary developments by seeking to survey core features across the landscape of contemporary American warfare, place these elements in proper conceptual and historical context, and assess them in a critical yet balanced manner. The concept of vicarious warfare thus provides a lens through which to survey, understand, explain and critique emerging patterns in US strategic practice.

★ ★ ★

The book is divided into three parts. Part I considers the historical background to vicarious warfare in world history. Part II turns the focus to the American experience, charting developments from its founding until the end of the Cold War. Together, Parts I and II identify themes and issues that extend throughout the remainder of the book and thus serve as a foundation for the in-depth analysis of contemporary dynamics presented in Part III. That final section explores the factors driving the phenomenon in modern times, the way it has emerged over the last three decades as a core feature of American wars, and the prominent consequences of these developments.

Four central and interconnected arguments unfold across the following chapters: first, that partial forms or prototypes of vicarious warfare can be observed in the long history of war (Chapters 1 and 2); second, that this form of war has evolved and emerged throughout American history to constitute one of three major traditions of US warfare (Chapters 3 and 4); third, driven by powerful dynamics (Chapter 5), the contemporary era, especially the last decade, has been one characterized by the dominance of vicarious warfare in terms of American strategic practice (Chapter 6); and fourth, that, contrary to the claims made by its most enthusiastic advocates, it suffers from serious weaknesses and flaws that generate harmful costs and consequences for American security (Chapter 7). A short epilogue suggests some possible implications of the analysis for American grand strategy and considers the extent to which vicarious warfare might be eclipsed by the demands of re-emerging great power rivalry.

PART I

Historical Background

1

A Vicarious Instinct

There has always been a core tension underlying the experience and understanding of war in human society. On the one hand, it has been deemed by many as necessary and even welcome – a thing to be accepted, pursued and embraced for both coldly instrumental and more complex existential reasons. On the other hand, and often simultaneously, it has been seen as hugely wasteful, disruptive and costly – a thing to be avoided or constrained where possible. War, for most involved, is a realm of loss, pain, privation, anguish, uncertainty and horror. And aside from the injury and ignominy of defeat, it is typically accompanied by many other costs and consequences, for victors as much as for vanquished.[1]

While war may be necessary and even desirable in some respects, holding out the prospect of personal and group gain through victory or the realization of life-affirming ends, the stakes are usually high and the potential costs extreme. Even in such highly militaristic societies as classical Greece and Rome (on which more later), this duality was not absent. The horrors of war were understood for what they were, as philosophers, dramatists and political thinkers routinely reminded their audiences, and only relatively recently has this tragic view of war come to be seriously challenged.[2]

These contradictions pervade the long human experience of war, accounting simultaneously for its perpetuation but also the myriad attempts to limit its effects and costs.

★ ★ ★

Before moving on to examine the emergence of vicarious warfare in the contemporary American experience, it is first necessary to explore the concept itself in terms of its deeper historical background in socio-political forms, material-technological developments and opportunities, as well as its basis in the evolution of military and strategic thought. Some of the elements apparent in the contemporary American practice of vicarious warfare are not entirely novel in historical terms – earlier periods have displayed, tentatively, and in related but differing ways, some of the broad features we are witnessing today. The purpose of Part I is not to present all those historical instances where vicarious military approaches appear to have been adopted, but rather to identify broader patterns and conditions that might assist our appreciation of the phenomenon and provide a rough framework for our analysis of contemporary American strategic practice.

As this chapter and Chapter 2 seek to show, the conduct of vicarious warfare in a holistic sense only becomes meaningful in certain historical conditions. The contextual foundations for vicariousness in war tend to be associated with the convergence of growing state power and wealth, expanding external imperial ambition, and evolving societal differentiation. Underlying processes of technological, political and normative change also play an important facilitating role over the *longue durée*, along with developments in military and strategic thought, which can inspire and prompt actors to adopt novel approaches.

In exploring these issues, the analysis does not unfold in a strict chronological fashion, but rather presents a necessarily impressionistic historical analysis centred around broad recurring patterns apparent at different times in different periods; it utilizes representative cases, drawn mainly from European history, to tease out dynamics that have been apparent across other cultures and periods. As such, Part I offers some initial clues as to those deep underlying factors that might predispose and permit societies, including contemporary America, to wage this form of war. It also presents partial evidence regarding likely consequences. Societies that have sought to minimize the burdens of war sometimes succeed in the short run, but war tends to catch up with them in one way or another; their evasive actions often rebound in unexpected ways over time with detrimental consequences in strategic, political and social spheres.

Observing such historical precedents, the point is certainly not to suggest a simplistic linearity in history leading inexorably to American warfare today. Far from it. Admittedly, in some respects – especially concerning technological developments – the processes appear cumulative, evolving arrow-like (a fitting metaphor, perhaps) in their risk-minimizing potential toward greater strategic distancing. But as Heuser has observed, even the use of military technology has not been one-directional: sophisticated weapons systems have been entirely forgotten by subsequent generations or abandoned for various cultural and ideological reasons.[3] In this respect, the use of military technology in warfare only ever makes sense when conceived within its political, social, economic, cultural and strategic contexts. Similarly, while earlier military thinkers may have developed operational schemes or strategic ideas reflecting vicarious impulses, this does not necessarily mean they were always implemented in practice or were accepted by contemporaries as valid approaches. In this sense, even where opportunities for vicariousness appeared to exist, other factors often pointed in different directions.

Linked to this, it is important to stress that while we might instinctively search for evidence of vicariousness on the battlefield as displayed through observable tactical and operational behaviour, this can be misleading. Rather, the phenomenon more accurately describes a strategic predisposition or mentality deriving from deeper factors and dynamics in society. Thus, there are many instances in history where we witness even ruthlessly warlike communities seeking to employ force in ways that promise to reduce the price of victory, and which superficially appear vicarious. Beyond the devastating clash of phalanx battle there was a long tradition in Greek warfare of privatized warfare, raiding, ambush and Odyssean stratagem.[4] The famously aggressive Romans would often avoid battle until circumstances were favourable or seek to coerce enemies through starvation and siege.[5] Despite a warrior code encouraging heedless heroism in combat, medieval knights and kings were not averse to foregoing a chivalric clash of arms if ravaging hostile lands would suffice.[6] In the midst of the total wars of the 20th century, belligerents repeatedly sought indirect means – by manoeuvre, surprise or technological invention – in the hope of delivering a war-winning blow.[7]

However, these are simply methods that might deliver military victory in more imaginative and efficient ways than frontal assault, and which any self-respecting commander would pursue in the right circumstances. It is perfectly logical and probably instinctive to seek tactical advantage in this way. While bloodthirsty commanders throughout history have displayed a remarkable nonchalance regarding losses within their ranks, this is not to say that they actively desired such an outcome, and most sought to display their martial virtuosity by achieving victory at little cost, for obvious reasons. But such approaches were adopted in the broader context of a distinctly non-vicarious normative embrace of war paralleled by a strategic mentality perfectly willing to accept direct and bloody battle should coercive threat, siege or manoeuvre fail. And arguably these latter seemingly evasive approaches were likely only effective on occasion due to the deeper aggressive ruthlessness that underpinned them.

Beyond this note of caution regarding potential historical red herrings, a master caveat pervades the discussion here: the simple fact is that few societies have ever been in a position to experience or pursue war in anything approaching a vicarious manner or, for that matter, have they necessarily viewed it as something they might want to do.

The long history of non-vicarious warfare

For most of history, war has overwhelmingly been experienced as an intensely immediate reality for individuals and communities as a whole, viscerally implicating and deeply shaping entire societies. War was generally regarded as an inescapable state of affairs, its practice integral to the safety and very often the survival of communities.[8] Intimately wound up with the evolution of the human experience from earliest times (Rousseau's imagined peaceful state of nature, most experts now agree, is a misleading fiction), it is an institution that powerfully shaped group cohesion, meaning and identity, and was central to determining an individual's sense of group belonging, worth and status in society. This explains why many philosophers have depicted war as the supreme test of individuals and nations, irreplaceable as the foundry out of which the highest of human qualities and emotions might be fashioned, brought forth and displayed.[9]

For countless generations of military-aged males – whether in prospect, preparation or conduct, whether voluntary or coerced – war was an ever-present reality throughout their lives. The rest of society was similarly geared to war in different ways – in particular, women were expected to bear, raise and feed future generations of a community's warriors. Naturally people engaged in numerous other activities; nevertheless the prospect of war loomed over all. The extent to which war touched different communities, or specific groups and individuals within them, would, of course, vary in different times and places. However, it is safe to generalize that for the vast majority of people throughout human history, to posit any notion of vicariousness in relation to the social experience of war would be more or less meaningless.

Early human warfare has been described as essentially unthinking: 'each round of fighting provides sufficient motivation for the next. They cannot imagine alternative solutions that would involve less suffering, or fewer casualties in any encounter.'[10] In a world characterized by pervasive inter-clan and inter-tribal violence, individual and kin survival depended on the community's organization for war, which was likely propelled by competition with other groups to ensure a reliable food supply.[11] All men were expected to fight in these proverbially egalitarian societies. Self-worth and group interest were closely intertwined with the voluntary and willing participation of group members in forms of collective violence. While there was a voluntarist and undisciplined element to participation in tribal warfare, status and social advancement within the community was largely achieved by gaining warrior prestige through bravery or booty through loot.

In such warrior societies, notions of sacrifice, honour and acceptance of personal risk were deeply culturally ingrained, often inculcated through defining epics of warfare emphasizing the warrior spirit, passed on over successive generations.[12] In short, 'the lives of our prehistoric ancestors were utterly immersed in war.'[13] Given these roots, it is hardly surprising that notions of service and sacrifice on behalf of the community have persisted as deep-seated features of societies down to the present day, emphasized in popular culture, national histories and social myths – even in very different social conditions. The bonds generated by mutual dependence in the face of shared dangers forged a sense of collective identity and promoted the organization and orientation of societies toward preparation for warfare.

In terms of its actual conduct, throughout much of human history war has chiefly been fought in a bloodily direct, often hand-to-hand, fashion by armed forces, typically involving large sections of the able-bodied male population of a community – even if 'battle' was often a decidedly loose and unstructured affair compared to modern standards. Reflecting this, military and strategic thought has tended to incline toward approaches involving the destruction of the enemy through overwhelming force in a decisive clash of arms – the climactic battle.[14] Even where forms of missile and later gunpowder weapons enabled force to be applied from some distance, this rarely afforded any kind of safety in combat when the enemy usually possessed similar means or otherwise quickly developed ways to offset what advantage such ranged weaponry provided.

The people's prerogative

These non-vicarious dynamics are especially apparent in those societies in which, however partially, the people had managed to preserve some of their old tribal freedoms or otherwise begun to wrest some political power away from aristocratic elites. Good examples are the early city-states of Mesopotamia, the republics of classical antiquity, and ultimately, modern mass democracies. Consideration of earlier more inclusive models of government is important as it offers an intriguing comparison in terms of contemporary states like America – a nation consciously built on the principles and lessons the Founding Fathers derived from their understanding of ancient democratic societies, especially the Roman Republic.[15]

It was generally in more socially complex and urbanized city-states, principalities and independent kingdoms where organized and politically aware populations had managed to win or retain some stake in public affairs. This applied to states that had retained vestiges of the old popular assemblies, such as in the third millennium BC Sumerian city-states of Ur and Lagash. In others, such as in classical Greece and Rome, the citizens of growing city-states had iteratively managed to wrest power away from rural aristocratic powerholders.[16] The result of this in terms of developing methods of warfare was community mobilization around organized infantry formations – the people's inclusion in politics entailed their conscription into the military and simultaneously sustained their motivation in war, and such armies were vital for resisting the attempted encroachments of noble elites. Indeed, an armed free populace, equipped with long spears or pikes, deployed as dense infantry 'hedgehogs' – the classic hoplite phalanx formation – could confidently outmatch mounted aristocratic formations in the right circumstances.[17] This communal way of war harked back to the traditions of the tribe but played out under different forms of rule in the growing city-states, all incorporating some level of popular involvement in public affairs, even in oligarchical Sparta.

Ideas of citizenship in ancient city-states such as Athens were closely tied to a presumption of military service.[18] Military preparedness and political inclusivity were thus closely intertwined and mutually supportive. The people's participation in war as citizens naturally led to demands for further political rights, contributing to the emergence in some cases of true republics. Moreover, the people's new political freedom was something deemed very much worth fighting for.[19] Such states came to cohere through and be largely defined by collective preparation for and participation in war, even if it is true that there was much more to life in ancient Greece.[20] Meanwhile, cultural themes reinforced ideals of military honour, heroism and sacrifice. As Coker notes, 'no other society gloried so much in war.… They practised it with a single-mindedness to such an extent that it became a defining quality of the culture as a whole.'[21]

The aggressive militaristic attitude is hardly surprising for city-states that were on a permanent war footing, surrounded by a multitude of similarly warlike competitive polities: 'when not at war they soon might be, and when not actually fighting they were often in a state of armed truce.'[22] As far as the evidence suggests, most of the hundreds of other Greek city-states were similarly structured and oriented for war. As a military society, Sparta took this to an extreme. Its constitution promoted 'egalitarian communalism and full-time military service among the citizens'.[23] The absence of defensive walls around their city emphasized the extent to which the Spartans embraced the prospect of open battle and 'trusted in their military prowess.'[24]

Thus, community leadership, political society and war were all tightly wound up together in a web of constitutionally enshrined laws, social obligations and expectations. Manifested in battle, the famous Greek hoplite phalanx perhaps represents the apotheosis of this form of individual–community–war interdependence: those propertied farmers and artisans of the citizen militia fighting side by side, shields overlapping, for the polity.[25] Strategically, the emphasis was on seeking out the enemy and engaging them directly in battle or otherwise laying siege to their city. In this context, it has been suggested that those who employed projectile weapons, such as archers and peltasts, were scorned as cowards or cheats,[26] and that the outsourcing of military responsibilities was essentially off-limits given that war was the exclusive business of the propertied citizen willing to accept the risks of combat. While this is an idealized image and seriously misleading if understood as representing the entirety of Greek warfare – which was, in fact, incredibly diverse in form[27] – this so-called 'agonal' contest-based model nevertheless captures core realities of the period.

The case of Athens during the Peloponnesian War, famously chronicled by Thucydides, highlights these ideas but also speaks to the temptations of imperial power (discussed further in the next chapter) which can encourage a turn to more vicarious approaches. So when at the outset of the war Pericles adopted his defensive strategy of refusing battle to the Spartans and instead retreating behind the city walls, this was so contrary to the Greek way of war that the bellicose faction led by Cleon strongly advocated for it to be abandoned.[28] In certain respects it was, but this defensive and cost-evasive mindset nevertheless persisted among Athenians throughout the war. The polity became fatally 'accustomed to war at low risk and low cost in lives' while recoiling at the losses suffered in the battles that they did fight.[29] This meant that they refrained from adopting a sufficiently offensive approach when it might have proved decisive (especially at Mantineia in 418): victory in a major land battle might have destroyed Spartan power. Wishful thinking caused the Athenians to rely on a low-risk strategy, seemingly at odds with its traditional way of war, which involved striking others 'without danger to their own city or population'.[30] This policy failed to coerce Sparta and required Athens to attend to multiple crises throughout its empire before it disastrously overreached in launching the Sicilian expedition in 415. That venture itself evolved out of earlier small-scale forays and commitments in the area which tempted the Athenians to overconfidently grasp at yet further gains. Parallels with contemporary American war are tempting in all of this.

The Roman Republic, which borrowed many of its practices from the Greeks and was similarly exposed to incessant external threats, constituted a community almost entirely geared toward war. As Josephus commented, Romans were 'born ready armed'. The legions were not standing armies but conscripted through yearly calls of all property-owning male citizens, and such service was considered not only a duty but also a privilege, as it was an essential precursor to any position of rank.[31] This entailed over half of the male citizenry serving in the military as young adults – an unprecedented proportion, rarely matched in history. The enormous armies this system allowed them to field produced an ambivalence toward casualties that few other states could afford to entertain.[32] The way the Roman constitution, fundamentally geared toward the conduct of war, mixed monarchical, aristocratic and popular authority meant that all sections of society were implicated in its prosecution.[33] Major political offices (such as the consuls, praetors and tribunes) were centred around leadership related to war, whether direct command or more general management of military affairs. With armies comprising large sections of society, commanded by aristocrats bred to seek glory in hand-to-hand combat, and led into battle by their elected magistrates, Roman society was primed to anticipate ongoing cycles of war on an almost yearly basis.[34]

The contrast in this respect with their foremost early enemy, Carthage, was stark. Consistent with the patterns outlined further later, this maritime trading empire relied less on its citizen militias and used its great wealth to hire foreign mercenaries which 'indulged the inclinations of a citizenry indifferent to martial values' – the commercial elite and sizable proletariat lacked the martial spirit of the free farmer.[35] Carthage was not unlike some later Renaissance states, and so it is unsurprising that Machiavelli, in his attempt to derive ancient solutions for contemporary problems, might see parallels here. Drawing heavily from the famous interpreter of Roman war, Vegetius, he rejected the idea of waging war with 'gold instead of iron', small forces or specialists in favour of an aggressive military strategy pursuing decisive victory involving massed foot soldiers engaging in a bloody process of close sustained combat.[36] Admiring the deep interconnections between the Roman public and the military, he scorned the widespread contemporary Renaissance practice of employing untrustworthy mercenaries, preferring a citizen militia with a serious stake in the outcome.

In short, in ancient republics such as Athens and Rome, membership of the political community and positions of leadership within it were intimately linked to war. Free-riding and defection were strongly discouraged by collective sanction, and the concept of delegation of warfighting to foreign mercenaries or extensive reliance on marginal sections of society (the poor, slaves or disenfranchised citizens) was at odds with the fundamental foundations of the polity and what it meant to be a citizen, and thus disapproved of. Adoption of such measures only occurred in exceptional circumstances or as the social and political basis of military institutions began to fundamentally change or erode. While ruses, ravaging and surprise attacks might be employed to achieve results with less sacrifice, in general the citizen-soldier was clear-sighted about the prospect of the brutal mass clash of arms in which death was a likely outcome.

These examples from the classical world established an early model capturing dynamics that would reappear and be taken to extremes in more recent times. After the late 1700s, popular mobilization in states composed of millions of politically aware citizens would be combined with the ideology of nationalism, accelerating industrialization, powerful new weaponry, radically improved communications and sophisticated bureaucracies to produce a fearsome new form of non-vicarious warfare. Clausewitz, observing these changes first-hand, described how a 'force appeared that beggared all imagination. Suddenly war again became the business of the people.... There seemed no end to the resources mobilized.... War, untrammelled by any conventional restraints, had broken loose in all its elemental fury.'[37] The 19th-century wars of nations would lead to the total wars of the 20th century. As Heuser notes, 'whole nations were militarised'.[38] Industrialized mass armies fired by patriotic fervour were sent into battle seeking not only the defeat but also the utter destruction of their adversaries. Beyond even what Clausewitz could have imagined, 'war intruded into economic life and social experience as it rarely had before.'[39]

Leadership and accountability

While leaders in the ancient republics might use all the rhetorical and persuasive tricks up their sleeves to get their way in internal political battles, there was nevertheless little opportunity for conducting war in the shadows or out of the light of public scrutiny. In Athens, decisions on war and military operations were openly debated, and leaders or generals (*strategoi*) held directly accountable for their consequences.[40] In Sparta, its armies were led into battle by its kings while the popular Assembly, the *Apella*, decided on matters of war and peace. Generals fought and sometimes died alongside their troops.[41] Of course, intrigues, political manoeuvring and shady deals were rife. However, closely monitored by a politically active citizenry, accountability for political and military leadership in war was direct and sometimes brutally efficient.

In the Roman Republic, the distinctly military office of consul (entailing command of armies in the field) was elective and subject to popular sanction. Likewise, the Athenian Assembly 'which feared as much as it rewarded success in its leaders'[42] would, at a whim, pronounce judgement on supposedly errant generals, subjecting them to harsh punishment or political exile through the procedure of ostracism – a punishment suffered by Thucydides in 424 BC. In the later days of the Peloponnesian War, the consequences for poor performance reached extremes when 10 generals were tried by the Assembly and sentenced to death.[43]

War was the prime responsibility for group leaders and warriors in almost all historical societies, republican or otherwise. This applied not only with respect to organizational and moral leadership, but also often in their capacity as a vanguard of the armed host. Where larger battle was joined in early warfare, the archetypal wedge-shape formation captures the idea of a warrior-leader advancing at the head of the force into the melee, embodying the collective and accepting all the risks of war. Although the social and political foundations of warfare would greatly evolve with the consolidation of larger kingships and emergent states, and tactical formations developed into more disciplined and multifaceted forms, political power and military prowess would long remain tightly fused. In highly bellicose feudal societies, such as medieval Europe and Japan, to fight and accept risk in combat was central to the knight's personal and political standing, and any thought of avoidance was unconscionable. In fact, when arrayed for battle, the king, as commander-in-chief, would place himself centrally, 'his location clearly marked by a banner larger than the rest and serving to attract danger to his person.'[44]

Well into the early modern period, political leadership was largely synonymous with military command. In the monarchical states that emerged in Europe after 1500, the structure of society was geared toward making war, and 'princes still saw themselves, and were seen by their subjects, essentially as warrior leaders', resulting in almost continuous warfare until the middle of the 17th century.[45] Even where the direct participation of political leadership or, for that matter, senior military command in combat no longer occurred, war remained their top priority and its consequences did much to determine the extent or continued enjoyment of their power.

Accountability for leadership in war would essentially be decided *in* war itself, and political legitimacy or authority was very closely tied to military command and achievements in war.[46] This image of political-military leadership in war is far removed from that implied by modern vicarious warfare, even if, for instance, the American president holds the title 'commander-in-chief'. But this is not to claim that the physical distance of military or political leaders from the battlefield is necessarily indicative of vicariousness. Such progressive command distancing has in general been a practical consequence of the evolving character of war (in particular, an expanding battlespace, making personalized strategic command and communication impossible) and changing political structures and constitutional norms (such as the gradual separation of political and military leadership and the democratic principle stipulating a clear separation between civilian and military spheres of responsibility). The real point is thus less about the direct avoidance of physical harm and more about evasion of accountability – modern leaders often not only seek to distance themselves from harm but also from responsibility for strategic failures.

This is an idea perhaps captured by the probably apocryphal image of wholly unaccountable *ancien regime* princes launching personal wars for glory from the comfort of their palaces, or the 'château generals' of the First World War living in luxury far from the trenches while they sent their men into the slaughter. According to some commentators, it persists in the form of 'buck passing', whereby politicians, generals or different services blame each other for strategic failure.[47] In properly functioning democracies, politicians and senior officers will be held to account for serious failures in war. Elections allow the people to remove leaders who drag them into costly military adventures. But in the face of the emerging edifice of vicarious war, democracies today struggle to carry out this core function. American wars are increasingly fought in the shadows, such that they barely register as blips on the radar of public attention. This serves to disassociate leaders from the harmful outcomes of their actions. Nonetheless, for much of history, political-military leaders could not conceive of any alternative to direct forms of command in war.

Toward vicarious warfare

As the preceding section has argued, in both prospect and conduct, war has tended to pervade politics, culture and social relations – the opportunities for vicarious distancing have been few and far between. From tribal chiefdom to feudal fief to princely realm, noble warrior leaders presided over societies 'whose structure was predicated on the assumption of permanent war'.[48] The lingering effects of this long history are not entirely absent in contemporary times. Even as war is pushed further to the margins of our lives, this inheritance is expressed through unconscious societal militarism and an abiding almost voyeuristic curiosity regarding the experience of war. As McNeill observes, 'old psychic aptitudes remain near the surface of our consciousness still, and fit men for war in far-reaching ways.'[49]

Yet, despite humankind's belligerent record, the complete subordination of social life to the demands of war is generally unsustainable, despite some societies coming close to realizing this (ancient Assyria, Sparta, the Lakota Sioux or Nazi Germany come to mind).[50] War is mostly unproductive, consumes precious resources, and diverts the labour force from production and other tasks essential to human livelihoods. Thus, it has rarely entailed the exclusive adoption of militaristic attitudes, the total mobilization of society, the belief that war should be an end in itself, or the embrace of risk for risk's sake. Evidence suggests the development of various societal 'dikes' that in some measure have prevented societies from being completely engulfed by the requirements and effects of war.

Coker has even suggested that the idea of 'war' itself – in the sense of a consciously defined human institution possessing structure and rules, first systematically 'discovered' by the ancient Greeks[51] – is a way humans have sought to limit Hobbes' unrelenting 'war of all against all' in the 'primal night' of the state of nature. War as an institution regulated serious social violence in certain ways, for instance by giving it a beginning and an end. It also established a clear victor that would emerge from the contest after demonstrating superior courage and intelligence beyond simple warlike savagery, their bellicosity directed toward some conscious end.[52] While bloody and brutal, war, in contrast to endemic pre-civilized warfare, was a specialized activity, controlled and fought by organized groups against other such groups, and for collective 'rational' purposes.[53] Thus, counterintuitively perhaps, war is one way humans have sought to limit the consequences of merciless intraspecific violence, and it is at least worth pondering whether contemporary vicarious 'forever wars' serve to weaken some of those barriers erected by our distant forebears.

From early times, even among the most warlike societies, the costs associated with war naturally prompted attempts to curtail its most obviously negative effects where possible, and to circumscribe the associated risks inherent in its prosecution, be it at a personal or group level. Individuals might seek physical protection through armour or psychological solace through faith, philosophy, magic or mind-numbing narcotics. Groups might construct community defences or develop social myths, stories and norms that give meaning to the bloodshed and suffering involved. The precautions early societies took to mitigate some of the obvious risks and costs associated with war are entirely to be expected – a function of brute necessity motivated by the basic human instinct for survival in situations of imminent mortal danger. Such measures are difficult to compare with the kind of institutionally ingrained cost-averse warmaking approaches evident today, which are often more politically motivated or driven by changing norms and attitudes toward war.

Even in highly bellicose warrior societies, most understood the experience of war to be a terrible thing characterized by death, destruction, rape and pillage. Tribal warfare was often characterized by the 'low-casualty, "ritualistic", stand-off battle, where the sides kept a distance from each other in order to minimise harm to themselves.'[54] For instance, the Amazonian Yanomami apparently regarded their 'perpetual warfare as dangerous and ultimately reprehensible.'[55] Even as stronger groups emerged, surpassing the military capacity of loosely organized and modestly equipped tribal war band, formal battles remained infrequent while surprise raids and single combat between group representatives served to limit casualties.[56] The Romans adhered to elaborate codes and customs – enshrined in fetial law – to justify and mark the onset of war (but which appeared to be designed more to ease their own consciences than appease the gods or satisfy universal moral principles).[57] It has been observed how, from the 4th century BC into the Hellenistic era, commanders began to employ more 'indirect approaches' in seeking to undermine their adversaries, moving away from the agonal model described earlier.[58] In feudal times, the whole edifice of chivalric rules and custom served a similar function and, at an individual level, practices emerged which allowed those disinclined to fight to commute their service for payment (*scutage*).

There are intriguing parallels to be drawn here: might we understand vicarious distancing as a form of modern ritual, enabling debellicized Western society to better accommodate itself to the force that continues to be employed in its name? This is an issue we will return to later. Meanwhile, as Dyer reminds us, such war-related practices, customs and institutions are perhaps to be expected where warriors dominate society, but that 'does not mean that the wars these cultures wage are meaningless rituals … people die in significant numbers, and in the end real things get decided.'[59]

Elite monopolization: distancing the political cost of war?

As noted earlier, chiefly aristocratic or feudal warfare was far from vicarious in its prosecution, both for those who fought and those who suffered as victims on its margins. Yet there is a sense in which it shares characteristics with certain contemporary patterns. This concerns the way the jealous restriction of warfare to the nobility – isolating war from popular participation – functioned as a means of preserving the status quo of aristocratic social and political domination (in other words, it mitigated a particular category of potential serious personal, almost existential, cost).

In a manner not too dissimilar from the way modern political elites seek to 'hide' or 'isolate'[60] the conduct of war from the people in order to minimize potential political costs, aristocratic elites sought to protect their monopoly on warfare as it was the fundamental basis of their dominant social position. War had progressively become the almost exclusive preserve of a relatively small professional aristocratic elite centred around the king's household, who accepted direct risk in warfare in return for the power, wealth and honour it granted them.[61] Strangely to our eyes (unlike political leaders today) this required their sustained exposure to the immediate risks of battle, where it was a matter of honour not to flinch from an adversary's direct assault.[62] There was thus a very real sense in which 'elites fought wars because that justified the armies that kept them in power at home.'[63] They feared that a self-conscious and organized populace, accustomed to the use of arms, might become a more effective force capable of supplanting the mounted knight on the battlefield, thus challenging their whole *raison d'être*.

Meanwhile, with the military specialization that accompanied the rise of powerful warrior nobles, whole groups of poorer military-aged males were increasingly excluded from the practice of war and rendered subservient clients, subjects and serfs. For whole stretches of history where such systems dominated, despite the decline of direct participation, any societal notion of vicariousness is essentially meaningless for large portions of the population who had next to no say or stake in public affairs. The peasant masses, the Third Estate, were almost totally disenfranchised and without voice.[64] Moreover, the mass of ordinary people were far from spared the effects of war – their food was requisitioned by passing armies, they were recruited as peasant militia when required and forced to perform varieties of war-related labour, or they suffered as the victims of the enemy, killed or sold into slavery. Beyond that, the manifold costs and consequences of war were experienced by just about everyone. Lacking education, literacy or political self-awareness, ordinary people did not conceive of having any role in determining how their communities waged war, which was almost completely a noble pursuit. In short, 'wars were essentially waged by a small aristocratic minority which alone shared in the spoils, with the peasant masses on both sides suffering from their depredations.'[65]

In various contexts throughout history, we have seen desperate attempts by the warrior nobility to prevent the opening up of war to the wider populace, especially where the socio-political and military-tactical foundations of aristocratic warfare were beginning to crumble and their traditional ways of waging war were being undercut. Thus, knightly armies would be more willing to hire mercenaries to augment their fighting capacity than to accept into their ranks poorer segments of their own societies. This was often also the preferred option for the centralizing princes of growing states, similarly reluctant to sanction popular involvement but lacking the resources to generate or sustain their own forces. As Kane notes, 15th-century princes favoured mercenaries as they 'feared that providing their subjects with weapons and military training might actually threaten their personal interests.'[66]

This curious practice of mitigating the political costs of war through its monopolization would persist in altered but essentially synonymous form as the feudal era of fragmented authority slowly gave way to monarchs presiding over increasingly powerful, centralized and culturally cohesive states. Far-reaching changes were not only radically altering society but also the conduct of warfare, which meant it no longer became possible to rely purely on the mounted knight as the core military instrument. Thus, princes had to oversee delicate balancing acts to subordinate powerful regional aristocrats and simultaneously build modern infantry-based forces capable of confronting threatening neighbours without inadvertently undermining the basis of their power. Nobles were progressively subordinated and transformed (through a gradual process of inducement, cooptation and coercion) into obedient state servants. As the senior ranks of diversifying royal militaries, they oversaw armies comprised of limited quotas of selective conscripts and mercenaries, many of whom were essentially unemployed knights.[67]

Financing the future

In such a manner, centralizing monarchs essentially wrested the monopoly of war from the aristocrats, even if most kings had to accept some limitations on their power through the workings of various representative proto-parliaments – such as the Spanish *Cortes*, German *Reichstag* or French *États Généraux* – whose main role was to mediate the scope and extent of taxation to finance royal war. Indeed, if the blood price of war was made manageable by employing mercenaries and destitute conscripts, it was the sheer cost in treasure that was most problematic for monarchs at this time, lacking sophisticated fiscal or administrative capacity, but attempting to fight long and increasingly expensive wars.[68] For instance, fired by religious enthusiasm, the pugnacious Phillip II of Spain, at war for all but six months of his 43-year reign during the 16th century, pursued endless costly military campaigns funded through vast unsustainable borrowing, primarily from a Genoese cartel.[69] Gaddis contrasts Phillip's profligacy with his more strategically astute rival, Elizabeth I, who just about managed to keep her ambitions within her means: exploiting England's 'splendid isolation' as an island power and eschewing a large standing army, she resisted unnecessary expenditure of effort or resources and managed to balance the books for most of her reign.[70] Most other monarchs (such as Elizabeth's father, Henry VIII) relied heavily on loans and accumulated enormous debts such that a central preoccupation became 'keeping at arm's length one's many creditors'.[71] It was this aspect of war that for them was most in need of vicarious distancing, seeking to evade or defer the financial cost of war. However, borrowing was a policy which 'brought short-term relief but long-term disadvantage.'[72]

Consistent with the larger argument of this book, where princes sought to pursue this financially evasive form of war, they struggled to escape the negative consequences that would often come back to haunt them. The desperate sale of commissions to wealthy nobles to raise funds increased the likelihood that armies would be led by a bloated, corrupt and incompetent officership. Poorly paid and poorly motivated soldiers cohered only through fearsome discipline, which greatly limited operational flexibility. These shortcuts were 'easy in the short term but disastrous for the long term good of the country' – as Clausewitz might have put it, 'they were pennywise and pound-foolish.'[73] Requisition had its limits, and as credit became more costly due to frequent defaults on loans, rulers inevitably resorted to higher taxes on populations that were typically unwilling to pay them.[74] Phillip II, seeking immediate military success (which he frequently achieved)[75] at the cost of future solvency, not only triggered ruinous bankruptcies and undermined ongoing operations (such as the Duke of Alba's campaign against Dutch rebels in the 1570s), but ultimately contributed to Spain's long decline and demotion to the second rank of European powers.[76]

Strategically, militaries built on such precarious fiscal foundations left monarchies extremely vulnerable to states that might be able to exploit the power of the people. Largely resulting from the combined effects of these processes, the costs could be total and indeed *final* for some kings: for similar reasons, Charles I of Britain and Louis XVI of France lost not only their power but also their heads.[77] There are parallels here with contemporary American wars, which are generally funded through massive borrowing – while the fiscal institutions are far more advanced and thus economically more sustainable, in essence the rationale is the same: leaders can afford to fight the wars they want now while limiting domestic opposition to their conduct by passing on the cost to future generations.

The case of Louis XIV of France, the exemplar of absolute monarchy, is instructive here. In important respects the embodiment of non-vicarious war, he lived to wage military campaigns, admitting on his death bed that he had perhaps loved war too much. His entire personal reign (1661–1715) was devoted to fulfilling the values that had been instilled in him from birth, centred on the noble ideal of earning glory

34

and prestige by displaying courage and achieving victory in war.[78] But his thirst for war, even if of a more defensive nature as time passed, always outpaced his capabilities and resources. Perfectly willing to accept just about all other costs, Louis nevertheless wilfully evaded the economic implications of feeding his martial addiction. He sought to resolve the issue of unaffordable wars by essentially getting others to bear the economic burden: hapless creditors, expendable fusiliers, unfortunate foreigners and future generations.

When the promise of decisive and short war proved predictably illusory and France's meagre tax base failed to cover the cost of extended campaigns, he did not stop to recalibrate his strategic objectives. Instead, he attempted to make his chronically underpaid vagabond army sustain themselves in foreign territories through devastating 'courses' of pillage and to squeeze coerced 'contributions' out of controlled populations. Above all, he turned to credit, but much to the chagrin of his lenders, he 'was more inclined to borrow than to repay.'[79] Thus, as much as he loved war, as time went on Louis increasingly looked for ways to achieve his desired *gloire* on the cheap. Indicative of the general trend toward leaders distancing themselves from the battlefield, Louis' presence in the field was increasingly for show and his personal command of a 'backstage' variety,[80] even if heroic artistic representations might suggest otherwise – and tellingly, his 'gloating triumphalism' did much to unite his adversaries against his aspiring hegemony.[81] Regardless, it was primarily the Sun King's vicarious financial distancing that ultimately led France to defeat in the field and a debilitating legacy of 'fiscal exhaustion and debt so profound that the monarchy never really recovered' – Louis had set France on the road to revolution.[82]

In sum, the generally bellicose and non-vicarious character of the late medieval and early modern period nevertheless masked the emergence of subtle forms of politically and financially motivated vicariousness among ruling elites with respect to how they sought to apply force in ways that offered least risk to the great wealth and power they had managed to amass. These tentative trends would become even clearer over the course of the 18th century.

Game of thrones: war as the plaything of kings

Much has been written about the supposedly 'limited warfare' of 18th-century Europe. Contrasted with the periods either side of it, the designation might well be appropriate. Some prominent limitations simply stemmed from material realities such as the parlous state of communications which imposed severe logistical constraints on military operations. The composition of armies, based on a narrow recruitment pool, meant they were difficult to replace and could leave a state seriously exposed if destroyed in battle. War aims were also usually of a restrained nature. Campaigns were fought for 'discrete advantages more than for hegemony',[83] and the intricate balance of power between states also arguably served to punish excessively ambitious princes. According to one contemporary observer, rulers would 'play for what is staked and not for all that they have in the world.'[84] Clausewitz mocked the way that 'laurels were to be reserved for those generals who knew how to conduct a war without bloodshed.'[85] Some have suggested that the civilized enlightenment values of the age served to limit excesses and that, in a mercantilist age, rationalist cost-benefit attitudes encouraged rulers to seek gains at the expense of competitors as long as it did not come at too great a cost.[86] Thus limitation – to the extent that it existed – was in many ways a product of the age rather than a unilaterally sought attribute suggestive of vicarious intent.

Yet war in this era has also been derided as a kind of personal game of kings – the plaything of princes – somewhat akin to a leisurely pursuit like hunting on a larger scale, only involving thousands of human casualties. Kant scorned monarchs for pursuing 'war as on a party of pleasure, for reasons most frivolous.'[87] The image is one in which monarchs, safe from harm in their grand palaces, would move their militaries around on the map, racking up 'glory points' through successful battles, sparring with other monarchs over endless inter-dynastic disputes, and adding to their royal domains with a province here and a duchy there. If there is truth to this, vicarious methods permitted such militaristic indulgencies.

Borrowing continued to fund their expensive campaigns and the fighting was delegated to politically inconsequential sections of society in ways that would limit potential public opposition. Given centralized control over most of society, large numbers of long-serving troops could be raised through forcible enlistment – the people would 'serve if required and on terms that they did not influence.'[88] These armies were essentially the personal possession of the monarch and were kept purposefully separated from society, described, for instance, as a state within a state in the Prussian context. Subservient nobles were placed in command of downtrodden long-serving troops made up of foreigners and peasants.[89] Meanwhile ordinary citizens were not expected to have any say 'in making the decisions out of which wars arose nor to take part in them once they broke out.'[90] Similarly, armies were directed to fight one another as opposed to turning their weapons on civilian populations, as had occurred extensively during the Thirty Years War (1618–48), for instance. Everyday life and intercourse between nations generally went on unhindered as the monarchs fought between themselves. The very nature of their absolute rule militated against any serious form of public accountability, even in the event of failing wars. This picture of war as a royal game has more than a few superficial resemblances with contemporary American warfare: fought away from home populations using narrowly recruited militaries to pursue ill-considered adventures abroad, they are financed in a way that has the least effect on the people and does not provoke their ire, while leaders and commanders are rarely held to account for outcomes.

We should be careful not to take this argument too far, as some major issues were decided in the wars of this age.[91] Moreover, the actual fighting conducted by armies was far from vicarious: ranks of soldiers lined up opposite one another to discharge their muskets at point-blank range in terrifying volleys of lead shot: war was still, for those directly involved in it, a 'brutal and terrifying affair.'[92] Operationally, extended sieges of fortresses were common, but many big battles were also fought involving tens of thousands of troops and resulting in horrendous casualties. As Strachan suggests, if during the 18th century 'the effects of battle were limited, this was due to the practical constraints of the times and not to design.'[93] A haughty aristocrat like Marshal de Saxe might have been able to boldly claim that great commanders could 'win a campaign without fighting a battle at all',[94] but as Black notes, there was certainly nothing cautious about generalship at this time.[95] Command was generally still performed either by the monarch or aristocratic generals who often continued to expose themselves to the dangers of the battlefield.[96] There are also signs of the growing involvement of wider society and tentative forms of conscription that would, in due course, radically transform warfare over the next two centuries.[97]

★ ★ ★

The analysis so far has suggested that, despite the pervasive reality of war, earlier societies, in their own way and within the parameters that circumstances allowed, sometimes sought to fight in a manner that might shield them from unwelcome social and political developments associated with its conduct or otherwise limit their exposure to its attendant risks and costs. The following chapter continues this discussion, developing the argument that it is predominantly in the context of growing state power and imperial expansion that more comprehensive forms of vicarious warfare truly emerge.

2

Perversions of Power

In the previous chapter, we saw how states that had begun to amass significant power often took advantage of opportunities to adopt forms of vicarious warfare and to evade, minimize or limit the costs and requirements of war (typically with harmful strategic effects in the long run). Vicariousness was apparent primarily in financial, organizational and political spheres as well as the growing disinclination among leaders and elites to expose themselves to immediate danger. Meanwhile, public accountability was negligible given absolute rule, except where monarchs seriously overstepped traditional restraints on their authority.[1] Even rudimentary forms of proxy war are apparent in the early modern period, such as the French bank-rolling of Gustavus Adolphus' armies during the Thirty Years War or the later extensive support Louis XVI provided to American Patriots during the Revolutionary War. Similar was Elizabeth I's support to Dutch rebels in their resistance against attempted Habsburg subjugation and the way some in her court, especially the naval leaders, sought to make war pay for war by conducting plundering 'descents' on enemy ports and authorizing privateers to loot Spanish treasure fleets.[2]

As rulers gradually became more powerful in their domains (at different times in different places), the money resulting from an enhanced capacity for resource extraction meant that they were able to afford rudimentary standing forces or the services of mercenaries.[3] Even feudal knightly armies employed light mercenary troops on their margins, such as at Hastings in 1066 and Crécy in 1346.[4] Some states opted to essentially hire armies outright, such as when early modern French kings hired Swiss infantry to serve as the main body of their army. During the Renaissance period, these floating warriors were largely unemployed knights from the crusades or the Hundred Years War. States like France or the wealthy trading republics of Italy were able to purchase military power from the *condotierri* Free Companies where they lacked citizen-militia capability.[5]

Yet the widespread use of mercenaries by rising centralizing states, such as the Habsburg hiring of *Landsknechte* infantry pikemen in the late 1400s, should perhaps not be confused with true vicarious outsourcing. Aside from shielding elites from unwelcome political developments, this was an unavoidable expedient, either to rectify some pressing emergency or to more generally plug manpower gaps as states transitioned from feudal military organization but lacked the administrative or fiscal capacity to stand up large home-grown infantry armies. Where territorial defence remained a first-order priority for states still struggling to consolidate power at home, and where wealth and resources were accumulating but remained difficult to exploit due to weak fiscal, financial and administrative institutions, such quasi-vicarious outsourcing measures would always be partial and halting, and never really pursued as part of a consistent and holistic mode of warfare.

In fact, these tentative developments appear to be a function of a transitional phase in European history. As noted briefly in the previous chapter, states were actually gradually moving toward more comprehensive forms of national mobilization whereby citizens were increasingly called upon to serve, and this was rapidly becoming a prerequisite for success in war – trends that would accelerate exponentially in the aftermath of the French Revolution of 1789.[6] Yet, even as events marched inexorably toward the total wars of the 20th century and seemingly further away from vicarious warfare, leading European powers were simultaneously embarking on their 'assault on the world'.[7] And empire would constitute a vast laboratory for vicarious experimentation, as it has done for most imperialist states in the past. At one level, the resort to methods of vicarious warfare by imperial powers reflected a seemingly sensible form of grand strategic force-economy as states continued to prepare for possible major continental contingencies. Similarly today, America's defence and strategic planning is fundamentally oriented around conventional war while in practice ongoing operations are predominantly of a vicarious nature. These are not mutually exclusive considerations. However, more factors are at work here than a simple desire to balance competing strategic requirements.

The wheel of empire

A peculiar trait of empire is its circularity. Imperial dominion can, of course, bring great rewards, in treasure, trade, prestige and security – regarding the latter, dangers are essentially pushed further away.[8] And each new conquest brings new opportunities and tempting targets for acquisition into view, thus encouraging a self-perpetuating dynamic of expansion. However, empire creates its own new strategic vulnerabilities, new interests to be protected and new threats, both real and perceived, to be countered. This all demands vast efforts, drains resources, and generates all manner of political travails at home. At the same time that it creates these problems it seems to provide the opportunities and answers to respond to them, typically through vicarious military means. Porter captures this curious trait of empire when he observes that 'on the one hand, if it had not been there it would not have been necessary for governments to protect it. On the other hand, however, it could provide the means by which intervention might be exercised.'[9]

In this section, broad insights from the Roman Empire and the 19th-century European empires (mainly the largest of these, the British Empire) will be used to shed light on the pressures and possibilities that foreign dominion brings. We have already encountered some of the relevant issues in our discussion of large strong nations. But where states accrue significant power, wealth and territory, and control relatively large areas in an imperial fashion, this produces a distinct mix of strategic requirements, motivating incentives, emerging opportunities and changing social and cultural patterns. These serve to promote the adoption of vicarious approaches. However, imperial factors are only conditioning rather than determinative in this respect. Deep normative factors such as military and strategic culture may largely preclude a drift toward vicariousness, as illustrated in the case of Rome which resisted many of the more extreme forms of distancing for hundreds of years.

These explorations are suggestive, if not determinative, in pointing to issues associated with the contemporary American experience. They perhaps provide whispers of warnings about the dangers that might threaten states that follow too closely in similar footsteps.

Saddled with superiority

Whether external domination results from more or less conspicuous cupidity (Rome), in a 'fit of absence of mind' (as supposedly was the case for the British), or 'reluctantly' (as apologetic Americans claim), the effect is usually to encourage a parsimonious approach to the conduct of war. This was the essence of Britain's mid-Victorian half-hearted imperial policy: minimalist force commitments, widespread delegation and rule by proxy.[10] Such measures enabled the unceasing management of disparate security threats, both small and large, across expansive geographies. Much of this might be seen as inevitable given the size of the task. But other features result from less obvious factors associated with the peculiar political and social dynamics of empire as well as a continuing, often misguided, faith in the presumed effectiveness of these approaches relative to the magnitude of the ambition.

Certainly the capacity of vicarious methods to put out fires while maintaining internal stability and growth over extended periods is impressive. Yet, in most cases, ultimately the outcomes are familiar and ominous: cumulatively multiplying emergencies, intermittent military disasters and escalating commitments abroad; factional division, bureaucratic calcification, popular nationalistic militarism and expanding executive powers at home. As we will see, the purportedly informal and liberal American 'empire-lite' of today is not immune from the harms that affect any state which seeks to exercise forms of control over foreign territories well beyond its own shores.[11]

Imperial projects by default entail forms of external force projection. This immediately places great demands on military establishments, not least in terms of the logistical feats required to protect imperial possessions. As Alexander the Great discovered, after each of his spectacular victories a new enemy presented itself until finally he was compelled to cease further expansion.[12] For continental empires defending extensive land frontiers through protracted expeditionary campaigns far from the imperial centre, or maritime empires guarding non-contiguous scattered outposts over expanses of ocean, the challenges for military operations are significant.[13] Carefully designed political arrangements might provide some temporary respite, but sooner or later military force will be required to police restive indigenous populations, plug porous borders and otherwise keep the barbarians from the gates.

The benefits of expansion can soon be outweighed by the many burdens it brings – the classic disease of imperial overstretch.[14] The control of extensive possessions is especially problematic for states with insufficient forces to adequately man the ramparts across expansive territories. This was barely an issue for the Roman Empire (at least until the 3rd century AD), which was able to recruit from an expanding population base due to its policy of enfranchising freshly conquered nations, allowing it to draw first-rate soldiers from assimilated 'allies' and other client satellites. But it was a serious problem for the Portuguese, Dutch and British imperialists who had only small home populations to draw upon.[15] Moreover, fighting at long distances from home placed untenable burdens on citizen-soldiers, and it was difficult to supply mass infantry forces over vast oceans.

For various reasons, sending large numbers of a nation's young men overseas for extended periods to fight in obscure frontier wars has long been a highly unpopular and politically unsustainable proposition.

Popular indifference toward foreign imperial adventures might easily slip into outright opposition where home populations can no longer see the purpose of empire, especially if costly (reflected in rising taxes) and understood to be benefiting only a small set of elites.[16] The late Roman Empire suffered from widespread popular anger at high taxes, elite corruption and coercive measures of control introduced by the state.[17] Domestic discontent is even more likely where controversial episodes and embarrassing defeats come to light,[18] or imperial defence necessitates the use of distasteful methods inconsistent with the nation's values or conception of itself – although Rome never seemed to develop serious compunctions about instrumentalizing massacre in the service of empire. This problem can emerge over time as norms evolve and new thinking emerges. For instance, in the British Empire, consequential normative change occurred in the way mercantilist theories were gradually eclipsed by *laissez faire* economics less dependent on the direct control of foreign territory. Also, the evolution of liberal democratic political systems at home made domination over other peoples appear increasingly hypocritical and unpalatable – a circle America has sought to square through its self-description as an 'empire of liberty'.[19]

The problem is the solution

But where empire creates problems for strategists, so it seemingly provides some of the solutions. Even the inescapable physical distance of empire is not all negative. The physical burdens of war, almost always severe, are essentially exported abroad. Rulers seeking glory, riches or real estate through war can do so at a distance from their own populations, devastating the lands of others rather than their own. Rarely a chief motivation, this distance is nevertheless a useful by-product of foreign expansion. In this way, imperial ventures offer a basic form of geographical vicariousness almost by definition. But further opportunities arise from the large influxes of wealth gained from monopolized trade, control of natural resources, internal economic growth, the tribute and booty of empire and new populations to tax.

Plentiful money and resources can allow imperial states to produce and amass more powerful armaments with which to conduct and win 'campaigns small in scope but spectacular in results'.[20] Indeed, superior technology might offset some of the shortfalls in personnel or logistical constraints described earlier. For instance, faced with a rebellion in the Indian Carnatic in the mid-1700s, the dispatch of a small British battalion was sufficient to tip the balance in that fight.[21] On land, mobile light artillery and machine guns gave Europeans a formidable advantage over natives in the late 19th century, while at sea their gunned ships outmatched anything their Arabic or Asian adversaries could send out against them.[22] The disproportionate losses in many such imperial wars could allow Kitchener at Omdurman in 1898 to rue the 'dreadful waste of ammunition' rather than the 11,000 dervishes killed.[23] Such seeming ambivalence regarding enemy deaths would be echoed over a century later by American strategists apparently more concerned about wasting expensive Hellfire missiles than the tens of thousands of militants (and many civilians) killed through their use in recurrent drone strikes.

Sometimes technological superiority was not even required. Recalling the example of medieval knights noted earlier, and foreshadowing our later discussion of American policy towards native Indians, imperialists would often evade direct battle altogether and simply ravage the lands on which their enemies were dependent for their livelihoods.[24] But more important than superior weapons or devastation tactics has been the ability of empires to rely on politically low-risk types of military organization or forms of mobilization that somehow distance the prosecution of imperial war from the mass of the home population. The way the British managed to almost inadvertently win control of the Indian continent thanks to the efforts of a militarized private trading firm, the East India Company, is perhaps an extreme case. More typical is a general reliance on a mix of professional forces, mercenaries, proxies and clients to protect and advance the empire's interests. Conscripted civilian militia have, it is true, been employed by empires throughout history but generally on a small scale and rarely over the long term.[25]

In the case of Rome, the requirement to garrison new provinces following significant conquests throughout the Mediterranean during the late Republic prompted Gaius Marius to institute the use of volunteers at the end of the 2nd century BC, moving away from the earlier property restrictions. This was the beginnings of a 'dependent, quasi-professional Roman army' with the legions increasingly tied to influential commanders, becoming, in effect, private armies.[26] Aside from speeding the end of the Republic, professionalization of the legions and a growing reliance on non-citizen auxiliary units would characterize the military system through the height of Rome's power under the principate.[27] (Interestingly, Goldich argues that American armed forces have in modern times essentially been turned into imperial 'legions', capable, unlike citizen-soldiers, of being sent to fight in distant lands without complaint; their deployment generating relatively little domestic disquiet.)[28] Also, after the devastating defeat at Teutoburg Forest in AD 9, Rome gradually moved to more indirect forms of rule to manage troublesome Germanic tribes, and by the time of the later Empire, the army became less Roman as border protection was increasingly transferred to foreign mercenaries in the form of barbarian *foederati* and *numeri* auxiliary units led by Roman officers.[29] This may, as Gibbon famously argued, have been one factor leading to the demise of the Western empire. The Roman military writer Vegetius criticized such auxiliary units for not being able to fight in a coordinated fashion. But they were required, because conscription had become deeply unpopular and the Roman people had become accustomed to affluence, as Vegetius had also warned.[30] Tellingly, his writings communicated a strong preference for ambushes and raids over costly set-piece battles.[31]

The late Roman model was not so different from that adopted by European imperialists in the 19th century. Imperial campaigns were usually led by small numbers of career military officers, who tended to be either ambitious adventurers or fading aristocrats. Indeed, Cobden once remarked that the British Empire enabled 'the English upper classes to find jobs for their younger sons as governors and generals'.[32] These men led small contingents of regular troops, often drawn from poor and marginalized sections of society, much like the American soldiers sent to fight the Indian wars on the plains at around the same time.[33] Such forces were typically complemented by specially formed foreign units.[34] Porch explains that 'to restrain costs and [avoid] the requirement to draw extensively on European garrisons, the French and British recruited large numbers of indigenous forces.'[35] Thousands of foreigners – such as Hindu sepoys, Nepalese Gurkhas or Algerian Berber Zouaves – were brought into service, either controlled as surrogate forces or officially incorporated into imperial armies (again, not unlike the way Indian scouts were integrated into the American military after the Civil War for use on the frontier).[36] Surplus funds could, of course, also be used to hire the services of outright mercenaries when required – a common measure in most empires (even in Rome, as the *foederati* were essentially mercenaries). In some extreme cases, conquered peoples might be compelled or press-ganged into service; on the whole, however, such wretched recruits make poor soldiers.

Power and wealth can also be used more indirectly to manipulate local leaders into fighting battles on the empire's behalf – essentially a form of proxy war – by providing largesse to client princes, tribes and groups to buy their loyalty.[37] Linked to this, other forms of indirect control are often employed, such as 'divide and rule' strategies or the related policy of investing chosen tribal chiefs with authority and power, often grandly christening them as kings. The latter approach allows imperial authorities to deal with a single leader rather than disparate warlords, and affords a measure of control given their dependency on foreign patronage.[38] (This is not all so different, for instance, from the way America's preferred warlord, Hamid Karzai was installed as President of Afghanistan at Bonn in 2001 behind the fig leaf of a national *loya jirga* [legal assembly].) In this way, if handled well, imperial wars could be low cost compared to the apparent benefits in wealth, resources and grandeur. And even more so when the burden for taxation to fund these efforts is shifted onto foreigners or marginalized sections of society.

These measures are especially apparent in the twilight of empires. This was certainly the case for an increasingly desperate Rome. Even Athens, which had so prided its citizen armies, had begun to extensively hire mercenaries in the early 4th century BC. Spain resorted more and more to mercenaries as the sun set on its imperial project during the 17th century. And after the First World War the British increasingly shifted to an 'imperial policing' model in places like Afghanistan, Somaliland and Iraq: this approach meant foregoing large manned garrisons and moving toward a reliance on airpower as an instrument to overawe recalcitrant subjects at a distance. Today, such 'light-footprint' approaches might allow imperialists to effectively maintain tolerable levels of security over extensive territories and even achieve impressive victories against adversaries by relying on technology and local lackeys. But they can also indicate, alongside other things, a collapse in imperial confidence, over-extended commitments and resources, or even internal decay. Whether the contemporary dominance of vicarious methods is indicative of the slow demise of American hegemony abroad or possibly even democracy at home is beyond this book's scope, although such developments do not augur well.

The paradoxes of imperium

All these methods serve to mitigate some of the prominent political and material costs of empire. And this tends to be a self-reinforcing process. Due to the reliance on professionals, privateers and proxies, citizens who are spared the burdens of fighting become increasingly sedentary and unwarlike.

Due to near complete professionalization, demilitarized Roman civilians had, by the late Empire, almost entirely lost their old warlike habits – being passive and no longer socialized for combat, they were of little military value.[39] Officials and merchants who have grown rich on the spoils of empire are especially 'reluctant to leave their business and good life behind.'[40] But this does not mean they are unwilling to support further aggrandizement. In fact, imperial expansion can fuel nationalistic jingoism and a civic militarism urging new conquests,[41] while the wealthy stand to profit greatly from the expansion of territory and control of new markets. The unwelcome consequence in Rome, however, as in other empires, was that this tended to fuel rising inequality as elites monopolized wealth and concentrated property in large estates while the impoverished masses huddled in the metropolitan centre.

One way the ruling class might seek to divert public attention from such issues is to provide them with new campaigns and victories to savour. While no longer inherently warlike, the people can nevertheless display a vicarious and voyeuristic fascination with demonstrations of national martial prowess or tales of heroism and daring-do.[42] This is apparent in empires across the ages, from the Roman gladiatorial shows, which often involved re-enactments of battles,[43] to the Victorian fascination with imperial heroes and famous battles. But, as powerfully argued by Porter in relation to the British case, this interest tends to be superficial and ephemeral, often only associated with notable events or uncommonly large wars.[44] Despite the seeming enormity of empire, the mass of the public can be surprisingly 'imperially ignorant' and display scant interest in their nation's behaviour abroad, and this kind of apathetic and uncritical attitude is unlikely to result in serious examination of the conduct of imperial wars.[45] So a late 19th-century British chancellor complained that 'our people hardly watch or listen unless some favourite officer falls dead'.[46]

Aggrandizing military campaigns far from home, which much of the population might not even realize are taking place, will likely be subject to minimal scrutiny. The generally low-cost manner of their prosecution further serves to limit domestic awareness or opposition.[47] Meanwhile, the growth of increasingly unaccountable centralized control is a product of the accumulation of extraordinary powers granted in order to tackle persistent emergencies and the more general accretion of elite prerogatives and moral authority due to the necessity of sustaining extensive military operations.[48] In this way, bolstered by narratives glorifying triumphs,[49] papering over failures or inflating threats, the leadership is able to distance itself from responsibility for the costs of empire or, for that matter, accountability for massacres like those committed by the British in Amritsar in 1919 or in Kenya during the 1950s.

In the European wars of empire, the fighting often involved a clash of extremes in terms of the models we have reviewed throughout Part I: a contest pitting vicarious against non-vicarious ways of war; between aristocratic officers sent to lead foreign forces armed with repeating rifles against warriors adopting old tribal or 'heroic' methods armed with spears; between imperialists fighting limited wars to satisfy avaricious or ideological ambition against native peoples fighting for their homelands, and in some cases, their survival. This foreshadowed the kinds of adversaries America would find itself fighting across the frontiers of its modern informal empire.

Indeed, the parallels between the interminable campaigns of European imperialism and modern American 'forever wars' are stark. Fighting partly to spread enlightened Western values – then the white man's burden and the *mission civilisatrice*, today forceful democracy promotion and the Freedom Agenda – the imperialists often ended up curtailing freedoms at home due to exigencies abroad while employing the same kinds of terrorizing tactics of which they accused their enemies. Meanwhile, the people at home would voraciously consume whitewashed tales of its heroes and generals, its proconsuls and proxies, largely unconcerned by the carnage wrought in foreign societies through the perpetual wars fought in their name. But the presumed distance can soon collapse in unexpected ways. Sometimes, the methods employed abroad eventually ended up being turned against domestic populations as militarized foreign policy morphs into forceful suppression of internal dissent – in mid-2020, the response to widespread protests in American cities worryingly reflects these patterns.[50]

Models of vicarious mobilization

Reviewing the preceding discussion across Part I, it is possible to offer some broad observations with respect to how societies have organized for war in ways that might somehow mitigate its burdens on society or minimize important financial or political costs for leaders.

All war requires some form of armed force capable of applying coercive means against potential enemies. Arguably the least vicarious model – that of community mobilization, whether of the tribal 'warrior society', freeman-farmer levy, militia or conscript variety[51] – entails, for many states, unacceptable sacrifices or political liabilities, and can drain precious human resources from the nation's productive capacity. Such forces have been judged by some as amateurish or unreliable military instruments, especially ill suited, as we have seen, for expeditionary imperial adventures. Outright coercive impressment or military slavery (such as the Egyptian Mamluk or Ottoman Janissary systems) might be employed by autocratic rulers, but such extreme measures tend to breed not only widespread discontent but also ineffective and unmotivated armies liable to desert, defect, rebel or usurp power at the first opportunity. Beyond this, from a military-sociological perspective, there are only a limited number of 'ideal-type' ways leaders may seek to minimize the political or economic costs and implications of waging war beyond community levies: that is, with regard to how the force is mobilized or from where it is to be found. All options entail opportunity costs, and none offer perfect solutions.

As we have seen, in chiefdoms, feudal systems and other types of autocratic princely states, elites may seek to monopolize the practice of war and, so with it, power. This 'DIY' approach, sustained and resourced through continual war and the spoils of victory, nevertheless entails huge personal danger and, over the long run, the innate conservatism of these systems prevents them from effectively adapting to changes in political conditions or dominant modes of warfare; changes that ultimately work to undermine the very basis of the warrior-elite's position.

One of the most common options allowing some measure of vicarious distancing has been to create permanent standing forces, often built around an original aristocratic elite and complemented with impressed peasants or temporary levies, but usually composed of a core of recruits joining up for material reward. The voluntarist nature of the latter's enlistment minimizes the potential fallout from their loss in battle and crucially, the mass of society is not required to fight. Some hold that this model might limit war in other ways: 'a war fought by professional soldiers, because they are more costly to train and maintain, will in all probability be a war between smaller armies, with fewer consequent casualties and less impact on society as a whole.'[52] But such forces can become political liabilities, especially if excessive demands are made on them, while the high taxes required to sustain large permanent armies can generate intense popular dissatisfaction. Meanwhile, there is no certainty of limitation in conduct as that will largely depend on what tasks professional forces are directed to achieve and against whom they are arrayed.

States may otherwise look beyond their borders and seek to essentially import their armies. Foreign contingents may be raised *en masse* and integrated into the official military chain of command or otherwise independent mercenary groups might be hired to make up the bulk of the force. These troops do not weaken domestic production, can be hired off the shelf then abandoned in peacetime, and generate minimal immediate domestic political ramifications given that they are detached from society. But mercenaries are also costly, they potentially have an interest in perpetuating conflict and can become an armed threat in themselves, especially if they come to form a state's main force. They can also serve to erode the home population's military preparedness, and critics such as Machiavelli have argued they lack the fighting spirit of a citizen army.[53]

In some circumstances, another option is to employ or sponsor proxy forces or obedient client states willing and capable of doing one's bidding – essentially getting others to fight on your behalf. As we will see, this is something easier said than done, and can have greater negative strategic consequences than at first assumed. Other independent allied states might be encouraged to take up some of the burden of campaigns, but they are unlikely to remain committed if the state demanding action does not display sufficient investment in or dedication to the fight – something arguably signalled by its adoption of vicarious methods.

The point here is not to suggest that these models are only adopted to evade costs (presumed strategic effectiveness, military necessity or political acceptability may be critical factors in many cases), nor that they can simply be chosen at will – available options will be heavily constrained by prevailing conditions. Yet they do represent a simplified representation of the broad models that actors have employed in various combinations and that are all indicative at some level of increasingly vicarious measures that allow leaders (or nations as a whole) to offset various costs and risks associated with societal mobilization for war. As we move toward more vicarious models, the historical record suggests that these forms of mobilization require a significant measure of power and wealth to employ *on a sustained basis* and are prominent in large, and especially, imperial states. This does not mean all states that are powerful and rich will seek to use them – as we have seen, political, geographical and cultural conditions may preclude their adoption. Nevertheless, with growing power and the burdens of imperial control, there would be a tendency toward adoption of vicarious approaches.

In the light of this discussion, it may be useful to briefly reflect on how this all might apply to modern America. In fact, it is possible to observe how these models, often layered on top of one another, have been progressively adopted by the United States as we have moved further toward the contemporary vicarious era (albeit with periodical retreats, such as the mass conscription introduced in response to the world wars; this was not unlike the way the Roman Empire under Diocletian reintroduced conscription to tackle major barbarian incursions in the late third century AD). In broad terms there has been a drift toward increasing vicarious mobilization, from a reliance on citizen-soldiers, to professionals, to elite professionals and secretive paramilitary operators, to proxies and mercenaries, and now even potentially to autonomous warfighting machines and military robots. These changes have marched in step with America's growing power in service of its expanding imperial project.

Conclusion to Part I

This broad historical survey, while inevitably impressionistic and selective, provides us with some initial clues as to the factors and conditions that might cause states to adopt vicarious methods of warfare. The discussion has focused primarily on the kinds of social, political and economic distancing that can be observed in various contexts. This applies to issues around the nature, composition and command of militaries; opportunities for delegation of fighting to others; measures that might allow leaders to evade accountability for failure or abuses; and various practices that might lessen or at least defer the huge financial cost of war. But in casting our eye over previous historical eras we should be careful not to confuse approaches that we today might associate with an intent to minimize the direct costs and sacrifices of war (such as the widespread recruitment of foreign mercenaries throughout almost all historical periods) with measures that were often, in fact, driven by either weakness, necessity or otherwise sound logic given prevailing circumstances. As noted at the start of the book, the line between wise limitation or economization and misguided vicariousness is very difficult to draw. The historical record also suggests that such behaviour should not be understood as necessarily wholly inspired by the cynical machinations of the powerful, and nor should it be nonchalantly condemned without seeking to understand the dilemmas practitioners face. In many respects, rather than a consciously willed policy, it emerges as an almost organic response to the inherent brutality of war or the complex influence of changing conditions in all spheres of human affairs.

Technology has not been a major aspect in the story so far, largely because the means for effective or unilateral long-range distance warfare did not appear until relatively recently – such issues will be taken up in subsequent chapters. Of course, various new technologies emerged which extended the range at which force could be effectively applied, but rarely in strategically, as opposed to (often short-lived) tactically, decisive ways. The powerful longbow famously gave the English a critical advantage at Agincourt, but this did not enable them to prevail in the Hundred Years War.[54] And linked to this, we have encountered only a handful of thinkers who had begun to seriously conceive of practicable means to achieve victories requiring little sacrifice while others, such as Machiavelli, actively resisted such notions. Of course, thinking along vicarious lines goes back at least as far as Sun Tzu, who provided one of the most influential, if cryptic, contributions. Some writers on war – such as Vegetius or the Byzantine Emperor Maurice[55] – continued to place faith in the ability of inspired stratagems or cunning manoeuvres to deliver victory on the cheap. But most military and strategic works concentrated on narrow tactical or technical matters, detailing the armaments and arrangements that would enable forces to triumph in what almost always turned out to be direct, decisive and bloody campaigns.[56]

Taking a broad view, underlying the continuous unfolding of history there does appear to be an iterative and progressive (in the sense of being cumulative rather than positive) element to the evolution of vicarious warfare. This applies to the extent that we can detect large-scale changes that have produced conditions that make the vicarious prosecution of war ever more likely, if still not preordained. Also, an idea that we will pick up again specifically in relation to the American context concerns the way that future generations, reflecting on past experiences, become more attuned to the alluring (but generally illusive) idea that bloodless, low-cost roads to victory might exist. However, we must be extremely careful not to rush to conclusions in this respect. As noted at the start of Part I, rather than any sense of linearity in history leading inexorably toward the present day, such methods appear sporadically in an irregular manner at different times in different places, and are especially associated with those wars waged by certain states that happen to have amassed significant levels of power, wealth and capability.

However, power alone is insufficient to explain the adoption of vicarious warfare. Socio-political conditions and prevailing norms (such as political ideals, social myths or the status of military thought and ethical attitudes toward the use of force) can play an important role in either promoting or precluding it. So, too, can the nature of the strategic context, in terms of the real or perceived threats and challenges faced by states. In short, forms of warfare will always be shaped by the complex and changeable nature of societies that conduct them and the circumstances they find themselves in. America is no exception in this respect. Building on the historical foundation presented in Part I, the remaining two Parts of the book develop the analysis in relation to the United States.

PART II
American Experiences

3

Ambivalent Beginnings

Contemporary American vicarious warfare has no simple or clear-cut origins. As we have seen, taking a wide global historical perspective it is even possible to trace elements of vicariousness in war to much earlier times, well before America's emergence on the global scene. This tradition seemingly stands in stark contrast to the presumed 'American way of war' centred around large-scale conventional battles, and suffers from an awkward fit with dominant American professional military cultures, especially that of the US Army. It nevertheless feeds off long-standing forms of foreign intervention, ongoing developments in the technical dimensions of warfare, and decades of experimentation in more esoteric areas of American strategic behaviour such as frontier campaigns, gunboat diplomacy, special warfare, covert paramilitary action, discrete operations and various forms of military outsourcing and delegation to proxies.

The genealogy of American vicarious warfare is arguably only properly capable of being perceived retrospectively, with the benefit of hindsight and in the light of contemporary practice. That said, we need to be careful not to arbitrarily or anachronistically apply the model in a decontextualized Whiggish manner, forcing earlier periods to conform with how it appears to us today. That is not the intention here. Rather, the purpose of this chapter and the next is to explain how vicarious warfare has iteratively emerged and evolved in an American context. In doing so, the analysis brings into view episodes and events that traditional narratives or popular accounts often leave out. So, contemplating this diverse 'alternative' history of American warfare, Echevarria, for instance, has pushed back against the notion that the application of overwhelming force has always been the default option for decision-makers in confronting adversaries. He notes that 'from the Truman administration onward ... the typical model involved imposing economic or financial sanctions, followed by covert or clandestine operations carried out by the CIA, usually augmented by special forces and airpower; conventional forces were normally introduced only as a last resort.'[1] But, as this chapter will show, we can go even further back than this to trace the roots of such practices. Within the orthodox telling of the story of American force, vicarious warfare is conspicuous in its absence. But the precedents are, in fact, more apparent than dominant interpretations sometimes suggest – the clues were always hiding in plain sight.

There are a number of reasons for such amnesia, beyond the dominance of a certain interpretation of war in the American public imagination. In earlier periods, things that we might now recognize as constituting core practices associated with the vicarious tradition were perhaps understood, on the one hand, as independent capabilities or specialized functions that might be utilized in an ad hoc and stand-alone manner as circumstances required or, on the other, as ancillary approaches within the context of more traditional campaigns. Other features that would grow in importance were only apparent in immature forms due to the limitations imposed by existing conditions. What we can now understand as partial antecedents of vicarious warfare might have appeared as random episodes in the interludes between major wars or as stand-alone missions lacking any shared features beyond being lumped into some form of generic 'other' category for analytical or doctrinal purposes. This jumbled picture is nowhere more apparent than in the first century and a half of American history.

The military practices of the early republic reflected a confusion of ideals and realities. American warfare would be shaped by the tension between an instinctive mistrust of military institutions born of almost pacifistic anti-militarism and reinforced by a libertarian association of standing armies with tyranny and, contrary to this, a bellicose ruthlessness in satisfying an expansionist urge and defending the nation from emerging threats, both real and perceived. The picture that emerges is thus a mixed one of, on the one hand, strategic economization born of weakness and necessity, complemented by an ideological desire to distance war from government and society, and on the other, military institutions which pervaded society and a budding warlike spirit that helped ensure the nation's successful birth, early survival and subsequent rapid expansion. These tensions run through the whole history of American warfare until today, buffeted by internal politics, private commercial appetite, foreign intrigues and the lessons and legacies of the wars it has fought along the way.

Muddling through

From the outset, the United States has had an uneasy relationship with war. Born in the late 18th century through a brutal conflict sparked by the colonists' response to British monarchical excesses, its founders expressed a deep distrust of authority and an associated unease with war and military force.[2] The new nation was resolved to distance itself from the military confrontations of the Old World. Not only did many Americans believe this would negate the need for a large military, but standing armies were also associated with centralized governmental control and feared as enemies of individual liberty, enlightened civilized society and a cherished localism. In fact, many new immigrants were fleeing from military conscription in Europe.

Despite the near-fatal problems caused by inadequate central military administration under the Articles of Confederation throughout the Revolutionary War, the framers of the new Constitution restricted, at least in principle, the federal state's ability to significantly expand permanent military forces and the government's ability to resort to arms – other than in exceptional circumstances. As a result, military bureaucracy and supporting institutions such as military academies remained threadbare and underdeveloped until the Civil War.[3] Despite designating the president as commander-in-chief, important war powers were reserved for Congress on the assumption that this division would make it more difficult for the country to go to war. Similarly, although the militia system that emerged after independence was essentially a form of universal conscription,[4] it was primarily intended to fulfil its democratic function of increasing citizen commitment to the state. And, consistent with republican theory, it was designed precisely to limit the possibility of war because the people, knowing that they would bear the cost of war, would be reluctant to support bellicose policies, thus effectively rendering conscription a moot point.

Reflecting the wishes of an intensely individualistic citizenry, constitutional safeguards and arrangements ensured that raising the money or men to wage war would be a challenging prospect, at least as a large-scale centrally directed undertaking.[5] The nefarious threat posed to foundational liberal values by a large military establishment would reappear repeatedly as a tried and tested argument in public debate. At times it severely restricted both the strategic options available to leaders as well as the building of stronger defence capabilities. Thus, although easy to forget in a contemporary world dominated by an American military colossus, deeply rooted in the DNA of the American nation is a vicarious instinct – a profound concern, grounded in fundamental principles – to distance the practice of war from political society. This was inspired less by strategic than ideological rationales (ideas and practice regarding the former generally reflecting the conventional European inheritance), but it nevertheless predisposed the nation to seek ways of limiting military requirements, at least where major interests were not engaged.

Yet, however much Americans may have desired to turn their faces against the demands of war, in the republic's early years a number of military emergencies and security scares, both domestic and foreign, permitted the development of military institutions. The challenges involved mainly rebels (such as Shays' Rebellion over tax between 1786 and 1787 and the 1791–94 Whiskey Rebellion) and Indians (especially the British-backed Indians in the Old Northwest and Seminoles in the South).[6] Foreign threats mainly came from European imperial powers active on and around the continent. Promoted by nationalists such as President George Washington and Alexander Hamilton, these developments contributed to recognition (only grudgingly acknowledged by resistant Jeffersonian Republicans) of the need to maintain some form of national armed force 'for the common defence' that would complement the somewhat incompetent civilian militia while the nation remained vulnerable.[7]

Through fits and starts, a model ultimately emerged that would last for much of the 19th century, from the Northwest Campaign (culminating in General Wayne's victory at the Battle of Fallen Timbers in 1794), through the Quasi-War with France, the War of 1812 against Britain and the three Seminole Wars in Florida, to the Mexican War in the 1840s and beyond. A very small core peacetime professional army and navy began to crystallize as a 'cadre force' that would be supplemented by varieties of (typically poorly organized) citizen-soldier units made up of ordinary tradesmen and farmers. As late as the Spanish-American War at the close of the 19th century, volunteer units – essentially somewhere between regulars and militia, federally raised but only for short service – also remained an important component of military capacity.[8] Such motley forces of armed Americans were preoccupied principally with securing an expanding frontier against Indian attacks where the army was not available or sufficient: state militias and volunteers had to 'do the job that the federal army could not do.'[9]

As the Revolutionary War indicated, Americans when sufficiently roused would show little hesitation in taking up arms, and could fight with a tenacious ferocity. At the same time, its people were insatiable and violent in their appetite for territorial expansion, and its political leaders were confident beyond their current means that America was destined to become a great and powerful nation. Fulfilment of the young nation's 'manifest destiny' to expand across and settle the continent during the 19th century involved significant bloodshed, among soldiers and civilian communities on all sides caught up in the succession of skirmishes, reprisals and frontier clashes. These factors all but ensured that this restless nation would come into confrontation with others, thus testing proclaimed attitudes toward war and pushing constitutional limits to breaking point.[10]

As this violent dawn suggests, it is perhaps a myth that Americans were somehow inherently averse to war. In fact, the sole reference to the United States in Clausewitz's *On War* was a cursory nod to American fighting spirit despite the rudimentary nature of its military institutions.[11] The militia system certainly indicated a state that was prepared to call on its citizens to sacrifice themselves if required. Figures such as Jefferson 'were as quick as anyone to reach for the sword' when it suited them, and only eschewed war as a routine option because the nation's early weakness denied it them.[12] During the Quasi-War, Alexander Hamilton had even set about establishing and personally commanding a politicized 'New Army' of 50,000 troops to confront the French and Spanish.[13] Following in the Washingtonian tradition, prominent future political leaders, including most presidents, had fought and led men in battle. This only really changed with the entanglement in Vietnam: up to that point, 'military service was all but mandatory for anyone seeking the presidency'.[14]

Many early American military commanders displayed, and were celebrated for, their offensive-minded approach to operational art, in which they sought to fix the enemy and engage them in bold frontal assault. Washington himself had displayed this tendency when the opportunity arose. Subsequently, inspired by the Napoleonic ideal, men like Zachary Taylor in Mexico or Ulysses S. Grant and Robert E. Lee during the Civil War contributed their example to this unforgiving, no-nonsense way of war. When General Pershing considered how to employ the American Expeditionary Forces on the Western Front in 1917–18, he planned an all-out strategy 'of going for the annihilation of the adversaries' armed forces'[15] and showed little hesitation in throwing numbers at the German lines, 'accepting heavy losses in unsubtle attack and counterattack.'[16] During the inter-war years, sharpening the requirements for destroying enemy main forces through decisive battle remained the prime focus of doctrinal discussion,[17] and before long men of General Patton's ilk would have the opportunity to revive the tradition in practice.

Meanwhile, with respect to evolving socio-political norms and attitudes, rather than fearing the effects of war and militarism, American politicians and commentators over the years would repeatedly voice a contrary concern. They believed that as the nation's wealth and power grew, its commercial population would be made soft by luxury and become accustomed to material comforts; they would lose their patriotic martial spirit and masculine virtues, and so leave the nation exposed to foreign threats.[18] According to this view, only war was a reliable remedy. A common refrain in many other empires throughout history, such sentiments were voiced in support of war in 1812 and 1898, and would remain a persistent theme in America up to the present day, especially in this vicarious age of drones and proxy wars.

Vicarious stirrings

Even if it is true that a strain of belligerency ran through American blood, there is little doubt that war and military intervention remained controversial issues. The move toward a larger professional military was largely driven by strategic requirements, as we have noted, but it also reflected the beginning of a distancing of wider society from the demands of war, especially as the nation's territory expanded. Army units were typically stationed and served in remote frontier locations (rather than, as in Europe, being dispersed throughout the country), and thus most civilians had little interaction with soldiers.[19]

At the same time, the gradual diminution of the universalist pretensions of the early militia system, driven in part by a relaxation of immediate threats as the century progressed, reflected an increasingly popular desire to shift responsibility for war to smaller groups of willing warriors and professional soldiers. The militia system was almost always limited in important respects: required quotas were initially filled with volunteers, service was restricted to a few months (usually close to home), and various exemptions and substitutes were available. In time, the requirements would relax still further as the expansion of volunteer units replaced the increasingly obsolete and often ridiculed common 'cornstalk militia'.[20] The rapid demobilization of the mustered militias, combined with the swift contraction of the regular military in the aftermath of emergencies, suggested war was something to be 'contained', reflecting the central preoccupation of citizens to return to their private lives. In short, although the professional military expanded throughout the 19th century – suggestive of a growing appetite for war and a move away from Old Republican anti-militaristic ideals – this can, in fact, be interpreted as a move toward vicariousness insofar as this permitted the use of force but without implicating as many ordinary citizens, thus potentially rendering war politically less costly.

American citizens were certainly willing to take up arms to defend their homes and their political ideals when required but, unlike the all-embracing civic militarism of the classical Greek and Roman Republics, they generally did so somewhat warily. The US militia might train just a few days each year. Americans well understood that the polity's freedoms might be imperilled should its citizens become consumed by war or exalt their military leaders as gods, as had occurred in its ancient antecedents or, for that matter, more recently in Napoleonic France.[21]

In various contexts, America revealed a tendency to seek ambitious gains but without war or serious commitments of military power. Early efforts to pacify the Indian threat in the Old Northwest relied on piecemeal contingents, leading to an early instance of costly escalation when General St Clair blundered into an inglorious rout, suffering 900 casualties from the 1,400 strong force.[22] As tensions rose in the confrontation with the British during the Napoleonic Wars, Jefferson 'attempted to win concessions from Britain that only a war could gain, but without fighting a war.'[23] Later, the Monroe Doctrine of 1823, confidently asserting American hemispheric predominance and declaring the region off-limits to Old World imperialists, was only really possible with the behind-the-scenes backing of the British Navy. In any case, the doctrine failed to prevent subsequent European encroachments.[24] Regardless, this Latin America sphere of influence delineated by Monroe would ultimately provide US policymakers with a vast test-bed for attempts to produce outcomes favourable to national interests by staging small displays of force or by providing moral and material support to rebels and revolutionaries, approaches that would become perennial features of US foreign policy.

But an early episode much further afield is perhaps even more suggestive of later vicarious patterns: the 1805 Battle of Derna. It is doubly intriguing as it not only marks the tentative inception of the projection of American force abroad but also foreshadows events over two hundred years later when US forces would team up with local militias to fight Islamic State in the same area. This campaign against the Pasha of Tripoli in what is modern-day Libya was the culmination of the Tripolitan War designed to protect US merchant shipping from Barbary pirate raids in the Mediterranean. It was devised and led by Lieutenant William Eaton and secretly backed by the Jefferson administration, which 'saw no reason to buy from a weak state what he could achieve with less through a limited war'.[25]

Building on the success of earlier exploits (such as Stephen Decatur's daring raid into Tripoli harbour culminating in the burning of the USS *Philadelphia*), this operation involved just seven Marines as the core of a force made up of Arab and Greek mercenaries supported by three American warships offering shore-based protection. Designed to install the older brother of the Pasha as ruler, the minimalist and quasi-private nature of the raid has all the trappings of a modern CIA paramilitary operation. It was not the last time a policy of 'decapitation' would be attempted as a shortcut to objectives, nor the last in which erstwhile American allies would be abandoned in the process.[26] But this was not an operation that would be hidden or denied. Much like the 2011 raid by Seal Team 6 that killed Osama bin Laden, the mission's secrecy was swiftly abandoned on its successful execution, and Eaton's men were hailed as heroes and their exploits highly publicized. A society for the most part wary of militaristic display, sometimes chose, when it appeared politically convenient, to hype up and revel vicariously in the exploits of its secret warriors. The arch-Republican Jefferson was especially capable of displaying such contradictions, perhaps embodying the tensions common to the polity. In fact, he was an 'archetypal American idealist, intent on spreading the nation's principles even at costs it could not afford'.[27] Jefferson reflects that moralizing seam in the nation's behaviour which, as we will see, has been a major factor inspiring it to engage in foreign wars.

The Libya episode was consistent with an emerging pattern of force being used to support creeping expansionist pretensions driven by commercial appetite, but it also reflected other forms of security delegation and surrogacy adopted in the nation's early years. Americans frequently relied on non-citizen 'others' to take up some of the burden of fighting their battles: the survival of the Continental Army during the Revolutionary War had relied on impressed slaves – the First Rhode Island Regiment that performed an important action at Yorktown was 75 per cent black.[28] Indian tribes were recruited as auxiliaries and scouts. In some cases, these practices were suggestive of attempts to limit the loss of American blood. Yet in most cases, rather than being the policy of a strong state recruiting irregular proxies to fight on behalf of battle-shy Americans, such measures were adopted as expedients by weakly armed and isolated frontier communities requiring local knowledge while operating in unfamiliar territory.

Groups like the Rangers, as select forces composed of hardy mounted frontiersmen with the ability to conduct rapid surprise attacks and gather intelligence, have been viewed as prototypes of modern special forces. Along with the separate Texas Rangers, which were symptomatic of the high tide of Western mid-19th-century vigilantism in lawless borderlands, such forces were not, as today, the discrete or deniable instruments of an indefinite 'shadow war' designed to advance centrally determined agendas, but more improvised responses to emerging challenges. Similarly, and recalling Elizabeth I's policy against the Spanish, the actions of American privateers such as those operating against the British Navy during the War of 1812 were variously either tolerated, tentatively encouraged or actively sponsored by the federal government. Rather than being born of vicarious evasion, these were desperate measures adopted by a young state seeking any means of undermining a militarily powerful adversary. Nevertheless, basing operations on loosely affiliated irregular forces was not without its risks: such forces were consistently unreliable, and it was difficult to ensure they remained focused on centrally determined strategic objectives.

Continental expansion, which frequently involved the use of considerable force, was also essentially outsourced to acquisitive pioneers. This provided a measure of military and financial economization for the federal government before they ultimately sent regular forces, with faux reluctance, to uphold the 'natural rights' of American settlers and confirm the *fait accompli* of conquest prior to formal annexation.[29] Somewhat disingenuously, Jefferson had even viewed mass immigration as a way 'of delivering to us peaceably what may otherwise cost us a war.'[30] Even beyond the continent, the movement of 'merchants and missionaries' often ran ahead of official policy, as we will see later in relation to Hawaii.[31] Of course, much of America's empire was simply bought – most notably through the Louisiana Purchase – even if the threat or use of force established favourable conditions for exchange.[32] Many politicians resisted such privatized expansion as over time it inevitably induced the federal government to assert its authority and take up responsibility for newly acquired territory beyond its means, often with huge domestic political consequences.[33]

The expansion of American interests and influence did not always proceed smoothly. Where forces found themselves in situations of open battle, some of America's pre-eminent early strategic thinkers, while showing partial deference to the ideal of Napoleonic decisive battle, held, in fact, to a more cautious approach. Denis Hart Mahan, the influential West Point instructor, advocated doing 'the greatest damage to our enemy with the least exposure to ourselves.'[34] General Winfield Scott was capable of leading daring campaigns but nevertheless sought to prosecute them in a restrained manner. Unlike his more belligerent counterpart General Zachary Taylor commanding on the Rio Grande, Scott's Mexican campaign in the late 1840s was fought mainly according to a 'life-saving' strategy of deft manoeuvre designed to avoid bloody battles and limit the suffering of civilians.[35] This was in the context of President Polk's expansionist war of choice fought in an incrementalist coercive manner.[36] This is not dissimilar in its strategic rationale from some late 20th-century operations, many of which ended up costing more than planners had accounted for at the outset.[37]

Notwithstanding the strategic predispositions of some senior commanders, most such methods and approaches sprang in large part from weakness and necessity. They were also the outcome of conscious normative preferences: shortfalls in military capability could not be rectified by creating a large-scale regular force capable of responding to all threats and challenges, but rather by time-limited local expedients that could evade the political and constitutional cost of potential state militarization. Fortunately, most of America's early enemies were fairly weak themselves or suffered from logistical handicaps, as did the British during the War of 1812. Even the Civil War, which witnessed unprecedented levels of mobilization, was a temporary aberration in this respect: after it ended, 'in a twinkling the tents were struck and the Grand Army faded away.'[38]

Indeed, the Civil War is recalled specifically as a harbinger of 20th-century total war: a brutal slogging match with competing generals attempting to win decisive victories in uncompromising set-piece battles; this especially in the eastern theatre, such as at First and Second Bull Run, Fredericksburg, Chancellorsville, Gettysburg, Cold Harbour and Petersburg.[39] But any such account neglects the strong desire, especially on the Union side, to achieve a victory with as little bloodshed as possible.

In part this was politically motivated: Lincoln knew that if Southern communities were to be successfully integrated into a reconstructed union, bitter memories of wartime suffering at the hands of Northern troops would greatly complicate the task. Recognizing such concerns, the first crop of Union commanders set out to conduct the war in a restrained fashion. Many anticipated a short war (always something of a fantasy), while generals such as Scott and McClellan wished to fight a gentleman's war with the 'least possible destructiveness'[40] and according to the highest principles.[41] Scott's 'Anaconda Plan' aimed to strangle the South into submission through blockade, 'with less bloodshed than by any other plan'.[42] The unfolding bitter reality of relentless battles soon dissipated such hopes. But even as the war reached its dénouement, Sherman's march to the sea, laying waste to a large swathe of enemy territory, was partly conceived as a way of achieving a less costly victory through a form of psychological warfare. His aim was to crush Confederate spirits while also leaving the door open to peace.[43] Lincoln's emancipation proclamation, beyond simply outlining a new war aim, was deployed as a rhetorical weapon that he hoped would persuade Southerners to see that their cause was futile.

Much of the end of the 19th century after the Civil War was taken up with relentless engagements and skirmishes, around a thousand, according to some counts, against Plains Indians. This task was largely left to small bodies of undermanned professional forces – usually made up of poor immigrants, other minorities or unemployed Northern labourers – complemented by auxiliaries. Overall the strategic rationale underpinning these efforts was a harsh form of coercive ethnic cleansing, described as 'an amalgamation of attrition, exhaustion, terror, divide-and-conquer', designed to push the Indians off their lands without the requirement for costly large-scale campaigns.[44] Some serious confrontations, such as at Little Big Horn, did take place, but these events were disproportionately hyped in the popular telling relative to their actual significance.

Expansion on the cheap

Those leaders entertaining grander ambitions further afield spoke of achieving territorial expansion without resort to arms. Secretary Seward and others sought to achieve global influence 'not by force and conquest but through the erection of a system of mutual dependence' and, as president, even the great Civil War General Ulysses S. Grant could look to a future in which 'armies and navies will no longer be required.'[45] Late 19th-century strategic thought was dominated by conceptions of naval power projection, such as that championed by Alfred Thayer Mahan and his circle that offered 'a relatively anesthetic victory in war' as opposed to 'a repetition of Grant's costly battering campaign.'[46]

Furthermore, administrations were tempted with emerging opportunities for expansion on the cheap, either through the efforts of private American citizens providing military assistance to foreign belligerents fighting for causes their benefactors passionately supported, or, as in the extreme case of William Walker's 1854 'filibuster' mercenary campaign in Nicaragua, through the use of private force to take over a nation.[47] In some cases, the government would turn a blind eye or actively connive in these efforts, as was apparent during Cuba's Ten Year War between 1868 and 1878. This prefigures episodes during the Cold War, such as the Reagan administration's cultivation of private funding for the CIA-backed Contra rebellion.[48] In the earlier Cuba case, this behaviour almost instigated an unwanted war; in Nicaragua, it fuelled an illegal proxy conflict that mired the Reagan administration in scandal. Whether tentatively tolerated or actively assisted, the vicarious conduct of military efforts through private efforts has tended to end badly.

As America's imperial confidence grew, reinforced toward the end of the century by a dramatic expansion of the Navy manned by hot-blooded officers 'spoiling for a fight',[49] what would mature into Theodore Roosevelt's Corollary to the Monroe Doctrine entailed multiple small-scale interventions. These were often in 'backyard' countries around the Caribbean Basin but also further afield in places like Korea (1871), Hawaii (1893), Samoa (1899) and China (1900). The latter, involving desperate fighting in the midst of the Boxer Rebellion, demonstrated how the dispatch of small contingents designed to protect commercial interests (part of the Open Door Policy) could rapidly escalate into confrontations requiring significant reinforcements.[50] Hence, the initially limited Philippines engagement of 1898 (in the context of the Spanish–American War and closely linked to developments in China[51]) rapidly turned into a counterinsurgency war which lasted more than three years, involved over 126,000 soldiers, including National Guard units, and led to the deaths of over 4,000 Americans.[52] But unlike the Army-led Philippine War, most of these operations involved pocket-sized contingents of Marines, which became the ideal instruments of this early form of vicarious warfare – the regularity of their deployments generated less controversy and 'fewer international repercussions', whereas sending the Army might be interpreted as a serious declaration of war.[53]

These kinds of interventions in America's near-abroad became routine in the first quarter of the 20th century.[54] US forces were sent to Panama, Cuba, Honduras, Mexico, Nicaragua, Haiti and the Dominican Republic in order to ensure regimes were in place that were compatible with commercial American interests. Given the nation's professed peace-loving values, these operations might have generated significant opposition. That for the most part they did not – despite the best efforts of the perennially anti-imperialist camp, including large women's groups and influential voices such as Mark Twain – was due to their vicarious design.[55] Even with the growth of press sensationalism, the multitude of small-scale military missions that proliferated after the turn of the century during the periods of gunboat and dollar diplomacy rarely generated much domestic attention: their frequency and repetitive similarity bred apathy rather than anger.[56]

After the First World War, despite some investment in the Navy and Air Force, the Army had been greatly reduced to a level (around 130,000) just sufficient to defend American territories.[57] These cutbacks were reinforced by the economic depressions of the 1930s and defence expenditures were kept low until 1938.[58] Reflecting widespread public disillusion with foreign intervention, no major occupations took place between Haiti in 1915 and West Germany in 1945.[59] Yet the United States was by no means wholly militarily quiescent during this period – in fact, small-scale interventions, almost all fought by Marines, took place on a regular basis in the Caribbean, Central and South America.[60] As Westad has noted, 'the isolationism that America is often blamed for in the 1920s and 1930s was never a reality.'[61]

For instance, in Nicaragua during the 1920s and 1930s, having been repeatedly drawn back into fighting there and with administrations seeking to pull back from foreign entanglements after the costly Great War, there was increased emphasis on expanding the country's *Guardia Nacional* (National Guard), an early instance of what would come to be known as security force assistance. The commander of the Guard, Anastasio Somoza García, would go on to establish a political dynasty whose corrupt rule ultimately provoked the leftist Sandinista revolution, again entangling America in a messy war in the 1980s.[62] Training, advising or sometimes fighting alongside foreign forces were conceived as relatively low-cost measures to leverage developments abroad to promote US interests; these missions rarely went as smoothly as planned, foreshadowing problems that would become all too familiar to later 'light-footprint' operations.

Admittedly, naval power and small contingents of Marines allowed the United States to throw its weight around in its near-abroad, and these instruments might on occasion prove effective when used to 'teach Latin Americans to elect good men'.[63] But the United States lacked dependable means to support a programme of aggrandizement short of war, and it underestimated the difficult battles that might have to be fought when adversaries proved more committed than expected, as had been made clear in China and the Philippines. This underscores a wider observation, which we see repeatedly in the modern context, regarding the erroneous assumption among policymakers that just because a certain approach has worked in one context it will necessarily meet with the same success in others. This problem is reinforced by the tendency to focus on the immediate results of an operation (for instance, American commercial interests protected, unpalatable foreign leaders deposed, or American citizens saved) while ignoring the new liabilities or harmful unintended consequences generated by the action and which often only become apparent later.

Cycles of war and ... 'non-war'

Surveying America's early history we can thus observe an unceasing balancing act which involved keeping the demands of war as distanced from society as conditions allowed, without leaving the nation defenceless or threatening hard-won liberties. All of this did not preclude aggressiveness once battle was joined, but the rugged individualism that defined American culture bred a resistance to enforced military obedience or classical notions of heroic sacrifice.[64] These were values that would ultimately emerge, but only with growing American nationalism, predominantly forged through war and the associated cultivation of patriotic myths and heroes. Throughout the 19th century and first half of the 20th century there would be persistent lurches back toward a minimalist conception of the nation's military requirements. Yet, somewhat like a ratchet mechanism, the new normal would typically reset after each episode at a slightly higher position in terms of overall professional military capacity and underlying warlike patriotism.[65]

A pattern is apparent in all this, whereby wars, and especially very costly wars such as the Revolutionary War, the War of 1812, the Civil War and the First World War, are followed by periods of retrenchment or a general distancing from war, consciously sought. This typified the Jeffersonian perspective of the post-revolutionary period. And during the inward-looking Jacksonian era through the second quarter of the century it entailed maintaining a strong military with the intention of using it only in exceptional circumstances. In the aftermath of the Civil War, a pacifistic sentiment praising the 'ideal of a world without war' emerged among some Republican politicians.[66] Veterans of war who subsequently entered political office often attempted to steer clear of serious commitments of military force.[67] Later, and in a wider sense, much of the American public considered their involvement in the First World War a terrible mistake, thus prompting a turn to isolationism and military restraint.[68] During such periods, leaders once fired up for war often come to lament its evils and seek less burdensome means of securing the nation's interests, buttressed in their view by long-standing ideological concerns about the dangers associated with standing armies and the effects of war on the polity.

Yet, over time, as immediate memories of the costs of those earlier wars ebb and the battle-scarred veterans move off stage, voices reappear lamenting the decline of martial values and claiming the need to 'fight new forces', as Theodore Roosevelt put it. Before long, these hawkish strains provide the political conditions in which large-scale military engagement can once again come to be seriously entertained – and so the cycle repeats. There is, of course, more to events than such a brief summary can convey: the cycle is not deterministic, does not display any kind of clockwork regularity, and its precise form depends on the contingent course of events. However, shaped by the interaction of contradictory American attitudes to war, it reflects broad recurring patterns discernible into the present age. In more recent times, similar periods of retrenchment followed the end of the Second World War,[69] the Korean War, the Vietnam War and the 2003 Iraq War.

These latter two wars have been described as inducing their own societal 'syndromes' powerfully setting the nation against foreign wars. Put simply, such periods are the acute hangovers from costly wars. But far from presaging the complete rejection of military power as an instrument of policy, it is in these interregnums that vicarious methods become especially attractive: forceful alternatives that enable the pursuit of interests but that are conceived as 'non-war' and do not demand the sacrifice entailed by large-scale commitments. These 'inter-war' periods have witnessed some of the most vigorous and sustained applications of early forms of vicarious warfare. Moreover, these marginal demonstrations of force have not infrequently served to generate the conditions, scenarios and pretexts leading the country once again into large-scale wars.

Hawaii and the road to world war

During its first century or so, America was largely preoccupied with consolidating its institutions, managing continental expansion and confronting unresolved social and political issues, culminating in the Civil War of 1861–65. With its rapidly expanding commercial interests, America increasingly found itself drawn into a range of foreign entanglements, some of which called for marginal shows of force often executed by its steadily growing Navy.[70] An ideologically inspired 'concern' for the plight of peoples fighting for their freedom also encouraged encroachments abroad. Sometimes, the two motivations were entwined, as when Christian missionaries in China 'preached morality and profit at once by asking that saved souls wear North Carolina textiles.'[71]

Commercial and humanitarian factors were in play when at the end of the 19th century a reluctant McKinley was drawn into a war with Spain over Cuba and America emerged from it possessing a far-flung foreign empire, if indeed its earlier continental conquests had not already qualified it as a certain kind of imperial power. This was all suggestive of the kind of expansive global military interventionism that would later become the norm in the 20th century but that was only partially apparent at this time. Nevertheless, as we have seen, the same deep-seated tensions would persist as influences on behaviour, and increasingly encourage the adoption of vicarious methods of warfare.

We saw in Part I how empire, whether of a commercial or territorial nature, created expanding requirements to protect and police new interests and concerns. Where this entails the use of force, as it so often does, minimalist and indirect military methods present themselves as especially well suited to the task of securing the periphery – economical, effective, domestically uncontroversial and less liable to fuel anti-imperialist critique, at home or among international audiences. These military interventions, however small, generate yet additional rationales to protect and consolidate existing positions and create new political and strategic circumstances that serve as the context for future confrontations with potential adversaries. The creeping American expansion onto a far-flung archipelago in the middle of the Pacific Ocean, 2,000 miles from the mainland, highlights some of these processes.

US interest in Hawaii emerged haltingly over the course of the 19th century. The Monroe Doctrine's range was extended in the middle of the century to embrace the islands in response to European intrusions. This newly acquired Pacific coastline caused the nation to reconceptualize its manifest destiny as extending westward not only *up to* but *far out into* the shining sea. Preventing other powers from controlling Hawaii came to be seen as essential for protecting the American west coast from attack, while new commercial interests in Asia necessitated US naval control over the Pacific to secure the burgeoning trade.[72]

In this context, an 1887 treaty guaranteeing exclusive use of a coaling station there gave America, as President Cleveland put it, a convenient 'stepping stone' to Asia (this, despite the fact that the shortest route was in fact via the northern Alaskan coast).[73] But some of the most ardent annexationists were the influential American sugar companies in Hawaii seeking tariff-free trade with the main market back home. Men such as Lorrin Thurston won backing for their cause by arguing annexation would win the navalists influence over the seas and the missionaries influence over souls.

In this way, interests converged to transform a remote nondescript territory into a key strategic asset. From that point, any developments that threatened this status would prompt an American response. Such thinking lay behind US military involvement in the 1893 coup which, through the bloodless effect of its minimal yet resolute show of maritime force, deposed Queen Liliuokalani and installed a government sympathetic to US interests – an early instance of US-led regime change.[74] In 1898, amid the war with Spain – when, according to Mark Twain, the American eagle went 'screaming into the Pacific'[75] – Hawaii was officially annexed to the United States. Thus, small-scale vicarious military methods secured commercial interests and delivered a new imperial possession that was subsequently maintained through a light-footprint naval presence – all of this at little immediate cost.

But, as Secretary of State Walter Gresham had warned in the 1890s, such seemingly innocuous possessions – easy to acquire, relatively cheap to sustain – could lead to dangerous entanglements.[76] Almost half a century later, in 1941, due to new international circumstances, Cleveland's stepping stone would be turned into flint rock, fatefully igniting America's world war. Imperialist Japan, facing an oil embargo imposed by America, from which it had previously obtained over three-quarters of its all-important fuel, looked to expand into a Southern Resource Area and take control of the Dutch East Indies oilfields so that it could persist in its project of creating a Greater East Asia Co-Prosperity Sphere. The presence of US forces in the Philippines represented a relatively minor obstacle for this 'strike south' strategy.[77] But much more threatening was the US Pacific Fleet, which had been expanded under President Franklin D. Roosevelt and recently transferred from California to Hawaii.[78] Admiral Yamamoto believed, mistakenly perhaps, that 'we will have no hope of winning unless the US fleet in Hawaiian waters is destroyed.'[79] The inter-war theorist of airpower, Billy Mitchell, had warned in the 1920s that Japanese airpower, operating from carriers, might knock out the American fleet in a dawn raid against Pacific bases.[80] And this is precisely what the Japanese proceeded to do, calculating that an attack on Pearl Harbour might at least temporarily neutralize the US threat to its ambitions.[81] Short of abandoning their grandiose plans, Tokyo felt it had no other choice, and most American leaders were aware that depriving Japan of oil might force its hand.

America's participation in the Second World War was extremely likely, even if not inevitable, given the threat that fascist control of the European heartland and Japanese expansionism posed to long-term US strategic interests. President Roosevelt was struggling assiduously to persuade an overwhelmingly isolationist public that modern means of warfare, such as long-range airpower, rendered their sense of geographical invincibility void due to the purported 'annihilation of distance'.[82] He was seeking opportunities to enter into the war against Germany, against whom the United States was already fighting an undeclared naval war,[83] and ensuring the defeat of Hitler's Reich was the president's overriding preoccupation throughout the unfolding crisis.[84] A significant programme of rearmament was well underway and selective service conscription had been reintroduced in 1940.

Yet part of the stated rationale for Roosevelt's military build-up was a form of deterrence as he wished to avoid a war against Japan that would divert vital resources away from the central Atlantic theatre.[85] For Roosevelt, the Pacific Fleet at Pearl Harbour was performing precisely that function, dissuading further Japanese aggression while he gradually led a reluctant nation deeper into the war against Hitler. Tokyo unfortunately viewed the situation differently: the naval base was not only an intolerable threat to the eastern flank of its planned conquests but, more than that, an incredibly 'inviting target' for its newly modified long-range bombers and shallow-water torpedoes.[86]

Hawaii – that piece of 'the United States of America that was suddenly and deliberately attacked', as Roosevelt put it – was only American territory, and thus invested with hugely symbolic meaning, due to the consequences of earlier commercial appetite and absent-minded imperialism half a century before. That is why precious American men and materiel were situated on an isolated and vulnerable island outpost in the middle of the Pacific. When they were attacked, a resolute American response was inevitable. With hindsight, policymakers had come to define 'vital interests beyond American capabilities, thereby inviting a surprise attack on Pearl Harbour.'[87] The attack cost around 2,400 American lives and was a serious military setback. If US aircraft carriers – the backbone of the Pacific Fleet – had not fortuitously been absent from the base on manoeuvres, then the Japanese strike, even if perhaps not quite a knock-out blow, would have likely lengthened the war. That 'day of infamy', and the reckless German declaration of war four days later, propelled the United States into its most costly conflict.

In the shadows of global war

The Second World War was probably a struggle America had to fight anyway, but these events meant that the nation did not enter into the war on its own terms. The United States thus found itself in an unenviable state of strategic dislocation at the outset of the resulting 'involuntary' conflict, but from which it fairly rapidly recovered. The war, which lasted until 1945, represented a major reversal from the prevailing pre-war isolationism[88] and cast the United States into an expansive global role in the second half of the 20th century.

The way the war was fought did much to shape dominant warfighting doctrine through the Cold War and beyond, consolidating a 'big war' mindset among military planners. Much like the Civil War, to most Americans it is remembered for its total mobilization of society and the brutal fighting in defining campaigns – the Battle of Anzio, the D-Day landings, the Battle of the Bulge, the Battle of Leyte Gulf – led by hard-hitting commanders such as Generals Mark Clark, George Patton and Douglas MacArthur. Its major lessons were thus in a distinctly non-vicarious mould.

But in many other respects, it was an important incubator and catalyst for the subsequent development of vicarious methods. Led by a generation that received its education in modern warfare between 1917 and 1918, anxieties about casualties and other potential political costs shaped decision-making and modified wartime strategy.[89] There have been various arguments presented over the years, mainly by revisionist historians, that America sought to evade some of the cost of the Second World War at the expense of Stalin's Soviet Union by delaying the opening of a second front in the west,[90] and that they conspired with German Resistance groups to assassinate Hitler and cut a deal with the plotters.[91]

Most reputable scholars argue that there is little evidence to support these extreme claims. Nevertheless, vicarious experimentation was apparent in three main areas: surrogacy, secrecy and technology.

In the early years of the war, as China succumbed to Japanese expansion, continental Europe fell in the face of Hitler's onslaught, Britain held out alone and the Soviet Union produced a desperate resistance, Roosevelt promoted a policy that was essentially a form of surrogate warfare. Reflecting the prominence of anti-interventionist sentiment, by extending billions of dollars in lend-lease loans from 1941, the United States became the 'arsenal of democracy' and enabled its allies to survive and confront the twin threats of Germany and Japan by 'any other means than the use of US soldiers.'[92] As Hastings has phrased it, 'material aid saved American blood.'[93] After America entered the war, this assistance to its major state allies continued but was now accompanied by efforts to provide support to various irregular partisan and resistance forces. The main aim of this policy was to induce the Germans to spread their forces thinly – for instance, support for Yugoslav partisans kept many German divisions tied up in the Balkans, thus taking some of the pressure off Allied forces fighting their way up the Italian peninsula.

Much of this activity in support of irregular allies was overseen by the Office of Strategic Services (OSS) spearheaded by William 'Wild Bill' Donovan. Modelled on the British Special Operations Executive and working alongside them, the OSS constituted a proving ground for American institutional development of its secret warfare capabilities, even if covert deniability (versus clandestine secrecy for operational security or deception purposes) was not a prime concern during the war. Nevertheless, the techniques and fieldcraft developed during the war would be greatly expanded and heavily relied on in the future confrontation with the Eastern Bloc.

Aside from providing leadership, training and military support to anti-Axis resistance and partisan movements in Europe and Asia, this wartime forerunner of the Central Intelligence Agency (CIA) conducted a range of activities that included, among other things, commando missions of sabotage and assassination behind enemy lines. Jedburgh teams, which included within their ranks two future directors of the CIA, parachuted into Nazi-occupied Europe to link up with the Resistance before D-Day. In Burma, the famous Detachment 101 provided a powerful model for future paramilitary action through its creation of Kachin tribal forces. The OSS was also an important proving ground for the development of American special forces through the exploits of units such as Merrill's Marauders who fought alongside the Burmese guerrillas. While peripheral as a component of the overall war effort and never seen as a war-winning instrument, the partial experiments with clandestine commando-style operations during the war indicated the potential of such capabilities and provided an influential template when such forces were reimagined under President Kennedy.[94]

As we will see in the following chapter, one of the chief legacies of the OSS, aside from its operational inspiration, would be a CIA infused with a wartime spirit focused on paramilitary-style activity at the expense of the careful collection of secret intelligence – in theory, its primary role.[95] And the record of the OSS did not bode well in this respect: despite some successes, the organization was repeatedly exposed, heavily infiltrated and easily manipulated by its surrogate forces.[96] Mistrusted in the Pentagon and widely criticized as a failure, it was seen as being peopled by dangerous adventurers looking to expand paramilitary operations, commando raids and secret armies even beyond 1945, and to institutionalize these practices within the post-war security architecture.

Alongside the experimentation in secretive operational methods and capabilities, analogous developments were taking place in the political sphere. Building on earlier precedents, such as during the Mexican War and the Civil War, executive powers were greatly expanded and Congress largely sidelined from strategic planning processes.[97] Rationalized as a necessary expedient in extraordinary circumstances, important decisions in relation to the war were thus made by a small elite circle unencumbered by the usual checks and balances or democratic safeguards.[98] These supposedly exceptional wartime arrangements, largely dismantled in its immediate aftermath, would nevertheless exert a powerful legacy in terms of providing an intellectual justification for enhanced executive autonomy and secrecy in relation to military and security decision-making.[99]

Throughout the Cold War, many senior security officials understood the confrontation with the Soviet Union in decidedly hot war terms as if it was just a new phase in an ongoing drama. In their eyes, this provided a strong justification for the continuance of closed-door decision-making processes and the emasculation of oversight mechanisms, heralding a long era in which Congress would take a back seat in this sphere. The Second World War thus represented a major milestone on the road toward the imperial presidency and 'presidential war'.[100] Although the extent of executive prerogative would wax and wane through subsequent decades, the war was integral to the development of political and institutional conditions in which subsequent administrations could decide on and employ force through discrete interventions without the kind of scrutiny or public debate that had traditionally accompanied such actions.

Concurrently, impressive strides were made in the realm of weapons technologies and their associated doctrines of employment. Strategic bombing is typically remembered as a blunt instrument of terror, associated in the popular memory with the massive loss of life and huge devastation it caused in places such as Dresden, Hamburg and Tokyo. But it is easy to forget that strategic airpower was conceived by its inter-war proponents as a potentially revolutionary weapon that held out the promise of less costly war. In America, Billy Mitchell was the chief exponent of this new thinking, while across the Atlantic, men like Basil Liddell Hart, J.F.C. Fuller and Hugh Trenchard – who, like Mitchell, deplored the kind of wasteful bloodletting they had witnessed during the Great War – were working toward similar conclusions.[101]

Mitchell argued that an 'entirely new method of conducting war at a distance' was coming into being, and that the nascent air arm, by striking directly at an enemy's economic centres and populations, could rapidly induce collapse.[102] While inevitably entailing suffering, this represented, he argued, a more humane way of war because achieving decisive victory from the air meant that drawn-out and brutal land campaigns would no longer be required: 'a few men and comparatively few dollars can be used for bringing about the most terrific effect.'[103] As Howard has noted, to its early proponents 'air power opened a new world, free from the sterile slaughters of generals and the antiquated obsessions of admirals. It could be used with surgical precision in conflicts which, however painful, would be brief and effective.'[104] Ultimately, these theories were not borne out by the experience of the war – air superiority had to be achieved through terrible attrition and even then, relentless bombing, expected to break the will of the enemy, failed; indeed, it may even have promoted solidarity and a spirit of resistance.[105]

If a stark lesson of the Second World War had been that there was 'no shortcut to victory' through airpower, then the detonation of the world's first atomic bombs over Hiroshima and Nagasaki, causing Japan's swift surrender, resurrected those early hopes of economical war.[106] The decision by Truman to use the bomb was almost certainly intended to limit the huge costs that a land invasion of Japan would have entailed.[107] But as important, from the perspective of those in Strategic Air Command, was that they now believed they possessed the 'absolute weapon'. As Freedman notes, it appeared that the airpower enthusiasts 'had not been in error – merely premature.'[108] Gaddis similarly observes that 'all at once, the United States had obtained a military capability that did not depend on the deployment of armies on the battlefield.'[109] Only as the true destructive capability of the new weapons became clear, and recognizing the uncomfortable fact that the USSR after 1949 also possessed them, did they come to look less like the apotheosis of strategic airpower[110] and more like a severe threat to humanity that could only have utility – in a way that 'did not wholly offend common sense' – in non-use.[111]

Perhaps reflecting a vicarious mindset, strategists would for a number of years cling to the idea of the limited use of nuclear weapons.[112] This was seriously considered and subtly threatened during the Korean War,[113] amid the French debacle at Dien Bien Phu in 1954, and even within the context of the subsequent Geneva talks.[114] By the time experts like Henry Kissinger had come to reject such ideas, ballistic missiles had largely supplanted the bomber as the primary delivery vehicle in planning for nuclear war.[115] But emerging rocket technology opened up possibilities along rather different lines.

Rockets had a long but mostly inconsequential history until the Germans revealed some of the potential that technological developments had enabled through its use of V1 and V2 rockets as well as Fritz X guided bombs during the war.[116] These experiences prompted experiments with various projects in America. Although during the Cold War the focus of development was on ballistic missile technology as a major component of the nuclear deterrent, parallel progress in cruise missile development opened up new possibilities in conventional spheres. First, cruise missiles could be central to a more general reimagining of the original claims about the war-winning potential of airpower and centred around the potential inherent in so-called 'precision'. It is worth recalling that it was Americans who, during the Second World War, had initially attempted to achieve greater accuracy in their strategic bombing campaign, and at tremendous cost to their own forces, through the practice of daylight raids.[117] Advances in technologies that came of age during the war held out the prospect of progress toward weapons that might allow unprecedented precision and that would later inspire renewed enthusiasm among airpower specialists. Motivated by the failure of carpet bombing in Vietnam and the emerging technologies tentatively showcased toward the end of that war, theorists would emerge claiming that the capability to target assets of vital importance to an adversary would rapidly induce them to surrender.

Second, it is often forgotten that cruise missiles were initially conceived as a form of 'unmanned bomber' or remotely piloted vehicle.[118] However, the technologies associated with the former diverged in the 1950s from those of the latter (crude versions of which had been trialled during the war and indeed, even earlier during the First World War),[119] proceeding along different paths until the two separate lineages would be reunited in the 21st century to produce the most potent and pervasive weapons system of contemporary vicarious warfare: the sophisticated unmanned aerial vehicle (UAV), or drone, guided by advanced communications technologies and armed with precision-guided cruise missiles. The details of that story is for later chapters, and it would be some time until the associated technologies would mature sufficiently to turn such ideas into reality, but developments during the war set in train progress toward concepts and capabilities that later become major components of vicarious warfare. The following chapter continues the various threads of this story through to the end of the Cold War.

4

Cold Warfare

The Second World War confirmed America's ascent to great power status. The nation emerged out of the war with great wealth, unparalleled military capabilities and a series of bases spread around the world. This was not just a traditional territorial empire exercising significant and in some places direct control over foreign possessions; the United States also commanded huge indirect global influence, primarily through its role in shaping the post-war international architecture. It had vast commercial interests and its dominance was apparent, not only in traditional metrics of power but in cultural and ideological terms too. Of course, large swathes of the globe were firmly within the Soviet orbit or otherwise under the influence of regimes subscribing to forms of communist ideology, which American institutions, investments and ideas struggled to penetrate. But this applied mainly to the 'wasted landscapes of Europe's devastated east' – the USSR was in disarray in the years after the war, and other communist movements were fighting bitter struggles for survival.[1] American hegemony was the dominant fact of the post-war order, and this remained a constant of world politics up to the present day.[2]

Preoccupied with a convergence of intersecting geopolitical, economic and ideological concerns, the country was led by men who believed America required a preponderance of power to protect and promote its vital interests.[3] Porter usefully identifies four key factors that compelled policymakers to aggressively defend American primacy in the new geopolitical context: the nation's growing power after the Second World War encouraged it to 'pursue security through expansion'; various crises and strategic shocks – such as Pearl Harbour or the North's invasion of South Korea in 1950 – inspired a sense of growing vulnerability requiring preventive action beyond its shores; tempted by its growing power, America's universalizing liberal traditions encouraged it to shape the world in its own image, confident that greater security would come from a world community of like-minded democratic republics; and finally, a 'self-propelling dynamic of empire' meant its growing global purview created new frontiers and with it new insecurities, commitments and anxieties.[4] The practical measures this all entailed required America to overturn decades of foreign policy shibboleths warning about large military establishments, entangling alliances and going abroad seeking monsters to slay. Even if such principles had already begun to be honoured more in breach than observance, the sheer magnitude and scope of the commitments the United States was taking on represented a new departure with respect to the nation's conception of its place in the world.

This confluence of strategic imperatives set the scene for expanding interventionism as part of the global great game against the communist Eastern bloc, punctuated by only a brief period of relative respite in the 1970s before the onset of the so-called Second Cold War in the 1980s. The result was a profound militarization of US foreign policy and a new level of worldwide vicarious warfare unprecedented in its scope and magnitude. New actors entered the fray, new battlegrounds emerged, and new methods were developed. Operations were devised by officials who adopted a wartime mentality and saw threats, vulnerabilities and potential dominoes everywhere. The chief challenge was to combat the Soviet threat without sparking a major confrontation. Evolving approaches persuaded many strategists that this could be achieved without requiring significant political or material sacrifice; even better, its primary campaigns could be conducted out of public view, unconstrained by democratic scrutiny. Ultimate victory in this conflict seemed to confirm the wisdom of the cold warriors, thus inspiring future generations of policymakers to refine and expand on these approaches, only in quite different strategic contexts. Yet, as will be demonstrated, this was a misleading and dangerous conclusion to draw.

Arguing over origins

Fierce controversy surrounds the question of responsibility for the onset of the Cold War. While revisionist claims perhaps go too far in reversing the orthodox view pinning blame for the Cold War squarely on the Soviet Union, there is more than a little truth to the argument that certain American moves – some of a distinctly vicarious nature – contributed to the final collapse of the Grand Alliance and expedited descent into East–West confrontation, marked by the outbreak of the Korean War in 1950.[5] Was the decision to drop the atomic bombs less about a quick end to the Pacific war and more the first move of an already unfolding Cold War?[6] Craig and Logevall suggest that while the first bomb clearly had the Japanese audience in mind, there is good reason to believe that the second bomb was designed to reduce Soviet influence in shaping the future of post-war East Asia: its timing, only 72 hours after the first bomb, intended to induce a more rapid Japanese surrender, thereby removing any justification for further Soviet military moves into Asia.[7] But this is not the same as the probably misleading argument that the bomb was used to vicariously intimidate or blackmail Stalin into making major concessions during subsequent crises (such as in relation to the withdrawal of Soviet forces from Iran and the 'war scare' over Turkey in 1946).[8] Indeed, there is little indication that Stalin interpreted the bomb's use in this way, or felt directly threatened by the action. Developments in other areas would be more important in terms of contributing to mounting antagonism.

It became clear before the end of the war that the nature of governance in the Soviet-dominated sphere would not accord with American expectations, especially regarding the fate of Poland.[9] But how should America respond? Emerging from the war with 'unparalleled geopolitical preeminence', possessing a monopoly on the bomb, aware of the seriously debilitated state of the Soviet Union, and with the spectre of Wilson's earlier failures hanging over every move, President Truman gradually moved toward a policy of actively contesting Soviet influence at various points along its post-war frontiers, especially in East-Central Europe.[10]

He did so largely through limited vicarious means – after all, post-war demobilization was in full swing, and the American people felt strongly that 'their country had sacrificed enough in terms of blood and direct action to stem the rot in Europe and Asia.'[11] In short, as Leffler observes, Truman 'wanted to achieve US security objectives on the cheap ... he wanted others to bear the costs.'[12] Indeed, the strategy of containment itself, described by Kennan writing as 'X' in his famous 1947 *Foreign Affairs* article, that emerged was designed over time to bring about victory without significant bloodshed through the deft application of 'unalterable counterforce' at key points while the Soviet regime imploded from within due to its own internal contradictions.[13]

Soviet intelligence was well aware of US attempts to spy on its activities in Europe.[14] This was perhaps to be expected, but as the OSS and its successors (by 1947, the CIA) ramped up a serious campaign of pressure in its sphere of influence, about which the Kremlin were fully aware,[15] relations were almost bound to deteriorate. In Romania, the abortive 1946 attempt to build a resistance movement based on the National Peasant Party with American guns and money – one of the first post-war covert operations – was but a prelude to an expanding range of similar efforts to challenge communist-controlled territories.[16] These actions, combined with other provocative political, economic and military moves,[17] failed to take into account Stalin's mounting paranoia as well as the lengths to which he would go to protect national interests. After all, as Grose has argued, this was an American strategy of rollback in all but name, and long before it became open policy under Eisenhower.[18] Egged on by the warnings of Churchill, Kennan and others, Truman's March 1947 announcement of the explicitly anti-Soviet measure to provide military aid to the right-wing Greek government battling communist insurrectionists instigated an even more forceful campaign of military assistance and vicarious proxy intervention in support of other 'free peoples who are resisting attempted subjugation'.[19] In a somewhat spurious comparison, Truman reminded domestic critics, concerned about the US$400 million price tag, that this was just 1 per cent of that spent to win the war.[20]

Meanwhile, the CIA, accepting Kennan's logic that the USSR only understood the language of force, but adopting the ventriloquist's trick of speaking it through subservient surrogates, had, by the late 1940s, essentially taken upon itself the mission to free Europe from communist control by recruiting Russian, Albanian, Ukrainian, Hungarian, Polish, Czech and Romanian exiles into armed resistance groups designed to launch uprisings behind the Iron Curtain.[21] Almost all such efforts failed spectacularly.[22] Poorly conceived and heavily infiltrated by Soviet agents, these 'swashbuckling' missions throughout Central and Eastern Europe and East Asia sent hundreds of putative rebel fighters to their deaths.[23] Theoretically covert and deniable, this was 'pantomime secrecy' and the operations may, in fact, have been intended to signal US resolve.[24] Regardless, to the Soviet elite, these operations were a clear signal of a more aggressive intent recalling earlier American attempts to quash the Bolshevik revolution. Thus, even before the Korean War cemented the East–West conflict, this expanding vicarious campaign comprised of arms, advisors and acolytes in Soviet-controlled territory meant the die was already cast. There was little hope of resurrecting any semblance of American–Soviet comity.

A defensive Soviet attitude with respect to its western frontiers, seeking control and influence in the areas it had 'liberated', was perhaps to be expected given its severely enervated post-war condition and its strategic requirement for a buffer in the event of an Anglo-American offensive or the emergence of a strong revanchist German state: a reasonable concern given recent history.[25] Further, Stalin demonstrated restraint on a number of issues and made a number of conciliatory gestures between 1945 and 1947, suggesting he favoured cautious cooperation over conflict.[26] Truman perhaps could have adopted a more tolerant approach and done more to induce the Soviet Union to take the former course. But instead, the administration focused on 'the more portentous elements of Soviet behaviour and dismissed the more favourable signs.'[27]

Increasingly aggressive American behaviour – driven by an expansive conception of national security requirements and a crusading mission to fashion a US-led global liberal democratic and capitalist world order – seriously threatened core Soviet interests and contributed to Stalin's growing suspicions and anxieties regarding American intentions.[28] Such fears were hardly exaggerated given that by the late 1940s the United States was determined not only to rollback communist influence but to eliminate the Soviet Union from the great power chessboard altogether.

This is not to argue that the Soviet Union did not share some, or even most, of the blame for the slide into confrontation; its behaviour in East-Central Europe, Iran, Turkey and elsewhere did little to assuage US concerns about its intentions and fed the worst fears of hawkish officials. The Cold War emerged out of a process of interaction, and American vicarious methods were only one aspect of broader ideological and geopolitical dynamics that made rivalry and conflict quite likely.[29] But limited moves, which are conceived as shrewd means to achieve ambitious ends at little cost, that fail to take into account the adversary's position or what it perceives as its vital security requirements can backfire unless carefully calibrated within the wider strategic context. Ignoring local balances of power, America hubristically pursued hegemonic ambitions and idealistic ends of defending democracy, liberty and open markets, directly challenging Soviet influence in its periphery through, among other things, a series of bungled covert operations. But it soon became clear that American policymakers were unwilling to truly pay the price of such a policy.

The growing disproportion between ends and means was recognized by Kennan, who wanted the US to act 'only in those cases where the prospective results bear a satisfactory relationship to the expenditure of American resources and effort.'[30] Such calls for restraint were ignored. In the process, America not only pushed the Soviets to expedite the very suppression of the freedoms that covert operations were designed to prevent – a predictable defensive response to such moves in a totalitarian empire – but helped push the two newly designated 'superpowers' further into a hostile global contest.[31] Unlike earlier international heavy-weight stand-offs, the antagonists in this new struggle happened to be wielding the most destructive weapons known to humanity.

The sum of all fears

The Cold War was neither caused by nor was it ever really *about* nuclear weapons, but once the American monopoly was broken by the Soviet

Union's successful test of its own bomb in August 1949, the confrontation between the superpowers was henceforth significantly shaped by their possession of this awesomely powerful new capability. Thus, the ever-looming prospect of any military conflict escalating to an all-out nuclear exchange became a chief concern for American strategists. These would be cataclysmic wars which would be almost impossible to control and just as impossible to rationally justify according to traditional political objectives, beyond simply a forlorn hope to be 'the last man standing'.[32]

Such thinking did not emerge immediately, and, as noted, atomic weapons were initially conceived as only more powerful forms of conventional military force. This was before the emergence of thermonuclear weapons with an explosive power 1,000 times greater than those dropped on Japan at the end of the war. The development of such immensely devastating weapons gave new meaning to the prospective costs associated with war and became the inescapable backdrop to the era. Inhibitions concerning escalation did much to determine the shape of US military behaviour during this period. This meant force tended to be applied in peripheral zones well away from the American homeland, the strategically central Eurasian theatre, or other major centres of Western power, and often in the context of support for belligerents in civil wars in developing countries. For the most part, war was pushed to the margins, and fought through proxies and in the shadows.

Rather than representing a radical departure in terms of the drivers of vicarious warfare, the existence of nuclear weapons magnified long-standing cost concerns, only now those potential costs were of an order of magnitude greater than before. Fear of escalating conflict had long been a factor encouraging the resort to vicarious methods (earlier we saw how during the 19th century the deployment of small contingents of Marines to conduct foreign interventions was considered less provocative than sending the Army). Meanwhile, concerns about, for instance, economic or domestic political costs associated with the use of force did not disappear but took their place alongside this new imposing reality. While leaders now had to contemplate the fact that the end of humanity had been added to the list of the possible costs of war, they were not deterred from seeking to obtain their objectives through forceful means. In fact, as we will see, they did so on a ruthlessly persistent basis, surpassing anything seen in American history up to that point. Constrained by the imperative to avoid escalation yet desperate to combat communist influence around the globe, the Cold War nuclear stand-off, far from causing a complete rejection of war only intensified the quest for ways of employing force that might deliver results without generating unsustainable costs, including those that were now almost unthinkable.[33]

Strategic thinking in America and in other Western nations emerged to reflect the evolving practice of vicarious warfare. Theories of limited warfare (Robert Osgood), indirect strategies (André Beaufre and Basil Liddell Hart),[34] flexible response (Maxwell Taylor), coercive bargaining (Thomas Schelling) and precision airpower (John Warden) all reflected a preoccupation with finding ways to employ force in ways that might allow objectives to be attained without prompting nuclear war and possibly even 'without the shedding of blood'.[35] In fact, building on developments during the Second World War, the Cold War became a virtual workshop for refining the art of war 'on the cheap'.

New organizations and practices emerged. Specialized agencies were committed to the task of building surrogate armies, engineering covert regime change,[36] and carrying out assassinations and targeted killings, while dedicated units were trained to undertake cloak and dagger covert action, paramilitary operations and clandestine unconventional warfare. In some instances, mercenaries and even mobsters were hired for certain tasks.[37] Methods evolved for manipulating client states and secretly supplying irregular proxies with military hardware, money and advice so that they might fight to advance US interests. New weaponry was developed for projecting force from great distances, including advanced missile technologies. Various remote-control platforms – designed principally as instruments of superpower confrontation and intelligence-gathering but often repurposed – were built, used for a while and then abandoned in favour of different designs.[38] Finally, new political norms, executive prerogatives, institutional structures and legal loopholes emerged that could be exploited to evade political accountability and democratic oversight.

The following section will chart key developments in some of these areas during the course of the Cold War. This period, although appearing unique in character due to the stark reality of nuclear confrontation and the associated preoccupation regarding the prospect of escalation, was nevertheless a crucial chapter in the development toward contemporary dynamics.

Cold War contours

Despite the varying styles and foreign policy preoccupations of the different Cold War presidencies and the diverse contingencies they had to face, this period is notable for the consistency with which administrations resorted to vicarious approaches. Major conflicts were fought during the Cold War, but these larger wars provided contexts in which vicarious methods were further developed – much like had occurred during the Second World War – and that would be implemented elsewhere in a more independent fashion. Paramilitary partisan operations were run on the margins of the Korean War and important steps were taken at this time, under the direction of General Robert McClure, to revive and institutionalize special forces. In Vietnam, as we will see, policymakers searched for shortcuts to victory and ways for others to take on the major burden of fighting the war. But even as such wars unfolded, America was active in countless other theatres seeking to achieve its objectives in even more indirect ways.

Searching for the 'third way'

As the fraught post-war institutional turf wars between rival security agencies played themselves out, the passing of the National Security Act of 1947 led to the formation of the Central Intelligence Agency (CIA). It was followed swiftly by NSC (National Security Council) 10/2 of 1948, which charged the CIA to 'plan and conduct covert operations' and the CIA Act of 1949, which gave the agency legal cover and wide-ranging powers.[39] The burden for the new campaign of global vicarious activism thus fell mainly on this descendant of the OSS. Being staffed by many veterans of Donovan's wartime organization, this almost guaranteed that the organization would start out imbued with an offensive-minded temperament.[40] With influential backers like George Kennan desperate to take the fight to the Soviets,[41] the CIA interpreted the 1947 Act's brief mention of the 'other functions and duties' to be conducted by the agency in decidedly expansive terms.

The early architects of this emerging campaign of secret interventionism, men such as Frank Wisner and Allen Dulles, did not wait around. They set out with unbridled enthusiasm to fight the Cold War 'as if invasion were imminent.'[42] The adoption of NSC 68 in 1950 added the final seal of approval to this resolute investment in covert warfare. The CIA soon involved itself in a bewildering range of covert operations, guerrilla warfare and paramilitary activities: over 900 major covert actions would be conducted between 1951 and 1975.[43]

The heavy lifting for the paramilitary element of these efforts fell to the officers in the highly secretive forerunners of what would become the CIA's Special Activities Division of the Special Operations Group (SAD/SOG).[44] SAD's Latin motto – *Tertia Optio*, or Third Option – is perhaps indicative of its vicarious design, offering a forceful instrument somewhere between diplomacy and war. Its early focus, as noted above, was on building so-called 'secret armies' and embryonic resistance groups by providing them with arms, money and rudimentary training before launching them against Soviet-backed regimes. This concept, which had tentatively arisen during Truman's first term, was rapidly expanded during his second term after 1949 and continued into Eisenhower's presidency. Given its unquenchable appetite for action, the CIA was prone to manipulation by various groups in its quintessentially imperial, ultimately elusive search for 'third force' guerrillas that might fight communism on America's behalf.[45] The miserable record of these early efforts did not prevent such operations becoming a staple in the CIA's paramilitary tool kit, and which is still in evidence today.

The centrepiece of the incoming Eisenhower administration was its so-called 'New Look' policy, which focused US military planning on massive nuclear retaliation in response to any perceived Soviet aggression. Tellingly, Mandelbaum compares this to the modern armed drone programme, with its vicarious intent to 'protect American interest without putting tens of thousands of American troops in harm's way.'[46] While this posture might successfully deter Soviet attacks, Eisenhower, who was concerned that the growing cost of waging the Cold War might cripple the United States, felt that covert action offered the potential to not only contain but even 'rollback' Soviet expansion, inexpensively, without igniting a third world war.[47] He thought proxy campaigns represented 'the cheapest insurance in the world.'[48] Eisenhower's Project Solarium in 1953, a strategy planning exercise, resulted in NSC 162/62, which largely confirmed the strategy of assertive containment and committed the US to adopt measures short of war, including 'positive actions to eliminate Soviet-Communist control over any areas of the free world'.[49]

The president was very enthusiastic about covert action: he considered the CIA a 'silver bullet in the arsenal of democracy'.[50] Under his tenure 170 major operations, many using paramilitaries, would be launched across 48 nations.[51] The agency under Dulles at this time was 'as aggressive as it could be without actually becoming a military force.'[52] Eisenhower even wanted to take action in hugely sensitive East Germany by arming underground organizations capable of 'sustained warfare' and carrying out the 'elimination of key puppet officials'.[53] Some questioned the logic behind all this, fearing that the doctrine of massive retaliation when mixed with proxy brush-fire wars would lead inexorably to nuclear war. The linkage, however, was never so automatic in administration thinking.[54] Regardless, as the operational locus of the Cold War increasingly shifted to the developing world in the early 1950s, the CIA attempted to shape conflicts through vicarious means. This was increasingly supplemented by a policy of military assistance to allies involved in struggles against communist forces in the form of conventional weapons transfers, advisory missions and so forth:[55] the extensive American support for the French fight in Vietnam being an obvious example.

Two operations early in his presidency – the 1953 CIA-engineered coup *Operation Ajax* against Mohammad Mosaddegh in Iran and *Operation PBSUCCESS* in Guatemala the following year, which toppled the left-leaning democratically elected president, Jacobo Árbenz – 'fatally dazzled Eisenhower' and created the impression that the CIA could overthrow regimes it did not like with little difficulty.[56] Both had involved only small numbers of American agents, which was exactly what the administration required. An agency operative captured the thinking of the administration in the midst of the Guatemalan episode: 'is not our intervention now under these circumstances [operating through CIA-backed rebels] far more palatable than by Marines'.[57]

The seeming success of these operations, ably massaged in agency reporting, contributed greatly to the administration's embrace of similar approaches.[58] Guatemala was apparent proof that covert plausibly deniable action could work, although, as Echevarria notes, it was likely that knowledge of US involvement was in fact the critical factor causing Árbenz to give in.[59] Somewhat predictably, with policymakers overlooking such lessons, subsequent missions launched in the Middle East and Asia did not follow suit. The failed coup as part of *Operation Wakeful* in Syria in 1957 prompted the creation of an anti-American Syrian–Egyptian alliance with greater Soviet influence, and did irreparable damage to the American image in Syria, lasting until recent times.[60] The similarly bungled CIA attempt to overthrow the Indonesian government in 1958 through support to anti-Sukarno officers and the supply of military hardware to a rebel army on Sumatra and Sulawesi nearly dragged America into a civil war, and led to the rise of the world's largest communist party after Russia and China.

With a range of commitments spanning the globe and being reluctant to provoke serious Soviet retaliation, these actions were designed to shift the burden of the Cold War on to others and reduce the liabilities for America. The idea that covert operations could hit the USSR where it hurt while denying US involvement and evading domestic accountability was too tempting a prospect for the crusading cold warriors such as Allen Dulles and his army of cavalier operatives.

By the time Kennedy became president in 1961, the CIA had over a decade of mostly failed paramilitary operations under its belt. However, this fact did not discourage further operations. Although Kennedy's policy of 'flexible response' was a distinct change of course with regard to high-level military planning and nuclear strategy,[61] in most respects Kennedy continued and expanded Eisenhower's vicarious activities, ultimately overseeing 163 major covert operations in less than three years.[62] Advised by proponents of covert warfare such as Edward Lansdale and influenced by 'limited war' theories popular at the time, Kennedy was taken by the possibilities apparent in small-scale 'subterranean war'[63] and 'seemed to yearn for forms of conflict in which the intelligence and the bravery of special agents could make all the difference as an alternative to the bleak choices that he might face in the event of total war.'[64] To further support disavowable operations, the National Security Action Memorandum 162 in June 1962 promoted the use of 'third country volunteers' and 'foreign volunteers controlled and supported by the US': in other words, mercenaries. Such private military specialists were soon spearheading US actions in the Congo.[65]

Kennedy inherited not only his predecessor's appetite for covert action, but also fully prepared plans for a major intervention into Cuba. Although reckless and unrealistic in design, *Operation Zapata* seemed to offer the perfect test for the president's evolving thinking, and he hoped for 'the terrible swift sword [to be] delivered with righteous fervor against a contemptible foe.'[66] Hundreds of Cuban exiles trained and equipped by the US and organized as Brigade 2506 were dispatched with the intention to directly overthrow Fidel Castro or to survive the landings and launch a guerrilla war. As is well known, the Bay of Pigs operation was a disaster – deemed the 'most ludicrously sordid episode in US history', according to historian Michael Burleigh.[67] As a fierce anti-communist infused with an ideologically inspired, almost Wilsonian sense of mission to 'defend freedom' and win the Cold War, Kennedy promised to learn from the failure.[68] This did not stop his CIA from progressing with *Operation Mongoose*, overseen by Bobby Kennedy and the irrepressible Lansdale, which explored any and every means to harass Castro's regime and to excise the communist sore in America's backyard.

Thus, Kennedy was not to be dissuaded by the disaster on Cuba. In his address immediately after the debacle, he declared that,

> ... it is clearer than ever that we face a relentless struggle in every corner of the globe.... We dare not fail to grasp the new concepts, the new tools, the new sense of urgency we will need to combat it.... Too long we have fixed our eyes on traditional military needs, on armies prepared to cross borders, on missiles poised for flight. Now it should be clear that this is no longer enough.... We intend to reexamine and reorient our forces of all kinds – our tactics and our institutions.... We intend to intensify our efforts for a struggle in many ways more difficult than war.[69]

These efforts primarily involved tackling communist subversion by developing techniques of counterinsurgency. While much is made of Kennedy's interest in this area, his approach has less in common with the now commonplace understanding of the term as necessarily entailing large-scale resource-intensive campaigns. Kennedy's high-level inter-departmental Special Group (Counterinsurgency) developed an approach to tackling global irregular challenges, such as revolutionary infiltration, banditry and guerrilla activity, which closely prefigures elements of contemporary vicarious warfare developed in response to the Islamist terror threat.[70] Moreover, their ideas were similarly driven by the imperative to counter a range of global threats on a sustainable basis. These needed to be out of the public spotlight to offset a potential 'image problem' of engaging in numerous Vietnam-type campaigns while maintaining preparation for possible large-scale contingencies.[71]

The Special Group developed operational approaches of a distinctly minimalist and indirect nature, relying significantly on small unit operations and developing indigenous capacity for various policing, intelligence and paramilitary activities under the rubric of 'internal defence'. In the 1960s this saw application in locations as diverse as Thailand, Bolivia and the Dominican Republic.[72] Underlying these efforts was the assumption that the US would not take on the main burden of fighting insurgents, and that doing so would actually be counterproductive. While generally eschewing direct US military involvement (one document, for instance, warned against 'overly prominent participation of US personnel'), the Special Group did allow for a limited role for US troops in desperate circumstances.[73] These missions would be undertaken by expressly trained low-profile special forces. Kennedy had developed a 'schoolboy enthusiasm' for such elite soldiers.[74] In particular, he cherished the Army Special Forces, which had their signature 'Green Berets' bestowed on them by the president. He lauded the ability of specialized troops to assist partner militaries, raise partisan armies behind enemy lines and wage unconventional warfare against the Soviet bloc – ideas that would find practical expression in countless countries across the globe, not least in Indochina.

Economizing in Southeast Asia

One of the countries where the Green Berets had been deployed was Laos. Under Eisenhower the CIA had fought a secret war between 1954 and 1959 against the communist Pathet Lao. Kennedy now resolved to ramp up this effort. Cautious about committing American ground troops, the president believed he could achieve his objectives through the conduct of a paramilitary campaign led by the CIA.[75] Through *Operation Momentum* he wanted to double the Hmong tribal army that the CIA had begun to recruit to fight communist forces and help cut the Ho Chi Minh trail. Consistent with vicarious logic and 'third force' principles, Kennedy initially rationalized his intervention in Laos as 'threatening war in order to achieve peace'[76] – a gratifying calculation captured in the modern phrase, 'escalate to de-escalate'.[77] Far from bringing about de-escalation, and despite a 1962 agreement signed in Geneva, the irregular warfare and CIA's Air America bombings continued and expanded, killing communists and cutting supply lines well into the mid-1970s. It became one of the largest American paramilitary operations in the agency's history. By the mid-1960s, *Operation Momentum* involved 250 officers commanding a Hmong tribal army of 40,000.[78] A major driver of the expanding war in Laos was the deepening American commitment across the border, in Vietnam – in fact, the two commitments were closely intertwined.[79]

Before President Johnson deployed US combat forces into Vietnam in 1965, American involvement there was conducted firmly along vicarious lines. When Kennedy was assassinated in November 1963, approximately 15,000 advisors were already stationed in the country, and were increasingly being dragged into the fighting, with casualties beginning to mount. Still, the official line remained that this was not America's war to fight and that the aim was to enable South Vietnam to prevail without a major US commitment – 'JFK preferred to fight the war indirectly'.[80] This was all consistent with Kennedy's minimalist conception of counterinsurgency which 'assumed that the main work would be undertaken by local forces, assisted by American resources and advisors.'[81] Moreover, making use of the opaque institutional architecture of the security state erected after the war, Kennedy was able to craft and largely implement policy from behind closed doors. This meant that there was neither significant awareness among the American public about the growing commitment and nor was there serious democratic debate concerning the wisdom of US engagement in Vietnam.

Counterinsurgency efforts – such as the Strategic Hamlet Program, which sought, unsuccessfully, to separate the people from insurgents and to introduce social reform programmes – were indirect operations run in a manner similar to the anti-Huk Philippine 'limited intervention counterinsurgency' model from a decade earlier.[82] They were devised by small numbers of American experts and facilitated by special forces but implemented by the South Vietnamese. Army Special Forces, backed by the CIA, were leading other small-scale surrogate operations at this time, training tens of thousands of Montagnard tribesmen of the Central Highlands from 1961 as civilian irregular defence groups. Initially designed as village self-defence forces (in which capacity they proved quite effective), they were soon oriented for more offensive purposes as mobile strike groups after 1963.[83] Presaging recent similar developments in Afghanistan, employing irregular forces in such a manner proved operationally and politically problematic, especially when attempting to integrate tribal forces into state military structures; it also fuelled ethno–national separatist tendencies that undermined vital statebuilding efforts.[84]

The vicarious instincts that had, through a process of creeping incrementalism, pulled America deeper into the Vietnamese morass continued to influence strategic planning and political decision-making. Even as American involvement intensified under Johnson, for many critics at the time (and since), the problem was that the war continued to be fought in a notably limited fashion. Johnson desperately wanted to focus on his Great Society reform agenda at home rather than the 'bitch of a war' in that 'damn little pissant country.'[85] Battered by competing fears associated with escalation to a 'wider war' versus the domestic political and international strategic costs of capitulation, forceful vicarious measures seemed to provide Johnson with a workable middle option. This naïve faith was captured succinctly in the National Security Action Memorandum 288 of March 1964 in which Johnson demanded an approach of 'maximum results for minimal risks.'[86]

One way to achieve this, he hoped, might be through aggressive action in the shadows, an approach that had the added benefit of evading excessive public attention. No fan of the CIA's dirty tricks, Johnson nevertheless realized 'the only path between war and diplomacy was covert action.'[87] Clandestine activities against North Vietnam of assassination, sabotage and raising resistance forces had been run by CIA paramilitary officers intermittently ever since the 1954 Geneva Conference. Designed to evade the terms of the agreement and inspired by the almost identical model of maritime and ground operations conducted on the margins of the Korean War, American officers would train anti-communist Vietnamese commandos before infiltrating them into the North. Reflecting the clandestine service's eagerness to fight to the last surrogate rebel, most failed as spectacularly as those similar efforts attempted under Truman.[88] Johnson nevertheless authorized the revival of this paramilitary programme comprising airborne and maritime raids. It would evolve, as we will see, into the fateful *Operational Plan 34A (OPLAN 34A)*. These activities presaged the CIA's massive wartime expansion in the region, with the Saigon office becoming a huge paramilitary headquarters overseeing a mass surrogate army. The agency was being pulled yet further from its supposed primary role as a secret intelligence agency and toward becoming essentially a warfighting machine.

Aside from the allure of finding a paramilitary middle ground, also important in promoting vicarious rationales was the enthusiasm among the 'best and brightest' senior members of the administration for certain ideas associated with 'modish social science' and game theoretic principles of coercive bargaining and 'conflict management', most famously developed by Schelling.[89] These ideas focused on the way that carefully managed threats and discrete applications of force (intended to inflict pain as punishment for bad behaviour, signal US determination and exhibit capabilities held in reserve) would induce the adversary to submit while obviating the need for serious commitments of force: a classic vicarious mirage, especially attractive to an administration populated by managerialist minds such as Robert McNamara, Walt Rostow, McGeorge Bundy and John McNaughton. For the latter, simply sustaining the impression that America had acted resolutely was more important than the reality, even if South Vietnam was lost.[90]

This all contributed to the strategy of graduated escalation and coercive airpower that so infuriated those seeking more direct and uncompromising approaches. By late 1964, the 'tit for tat' strategic bombing laid out in *Operational Plan 37-64*, which ultimately found expression in *Rolling Thunder* in February 1965, was still carefully calibrated according to restrictive targeting criteria and punctuated by pauses, reflecting its communicative coercive intent. This persisted as the rationale behind a creeping campaign of pain and pressure.[91] An unprecedented tonnage of bombs was dropped on the North Vietnamese during the war. However, they never got the message, or at least it was lost in translation, likely because they read the halting campaign as irresolution on Johnson's part.[92]

As late as October 1964, Johnson was making the firm promise that 'we are not about to send American boys 9 or 10,000 miles away from home to do what Asian boys ought to be doing for themselves.'[93] However, an incident associated with a small-scale secret operation provided the basis for America's descent into the quagmire. As noted earlier, *OPLAN 34A* called for secret raids, beginning in early 1964, against the North Vietnamese coast in order to allow American destroyers to collect data on enemy radar installations as part of the *DESOTO* intelligence patrols. This was the setting for the probably apocryphal 'attack' on the USS *Maddox* which gave the administration the pretext it required to pass the fateful Gulf of Tonkin Resolution in Congress. It granted the administration the authority to take 'all necessary measures' to promote peace and security in the region, virtually locking the country onto a path leading to the full deployment of combat forces. This points to the way that apparently minor missions can draw leaders inexorably into more serious commitments – a major potential flaw in the design of vicarious approaches.

It is easy to see 1965 as a definitive break, marking the onset of a large-scale, American-led, big unit war of attrition.[94] Of course, many had advocated just such an approach since the early days of the Kennedy administration, such as when in 1961 Chairman of the Joint Chiefs, General Lyman Lemnitzer, channelling Theodore Roosevelt, encouraged Kennedy to 'grind up the Vietcong with 40,000 American troops … grab 'em by the balls and their hearts and minds will follow.'[95] The first Military Assistance Command, Vietnam (MACV) commander, General Harkins, was similarly conventionally minded and repeatedly called for the US to launch a large-scale conventional war.[96] Rostow and Bundy long advocated for large-scale bombing against the North, and the Army of the Republic of Vietnam (ARVN) had been built up as a miniature American force to contest an expected invasion from the north.[97] The infamous body count was already being employed as a grim measure of progress when after 1965 the conventional war tradition essentially won out and guided the military's prosecution of the war on the ground.[98]

Westmoreland's aggressive tactics, involving 'search and destroy' operations and 'free-fire zones', was firmly of a piece with the Taylor–Grant–Patton hard-hitting school of American generalship.[99] As Westmoreland's chief of operations put it, 'we are going to stomp them to death.'[100] The war undoubtedly became a brutal slogging match, leading to over 50,000 American fatal casualties. Meanwhile, from the air, *Operation Arc Light* entailed carpet bombing the South and, by 1968, 643,000 tons of bombs had been dropped on the North. Despite little evidence to suggest any of this was having a serious impact on the enemy's ability to resist, the military's default position was to call for yet more troops and yet more bombs.[101]

However, despite this conventional military mindset and the undoubted 'big war' approach that dominated impressions during the late 1960s, a lingering and increasingly meaningless vicarious mentality persisted. Johnson, for one, resisted mobilizing the Guard or Reserve in order to shield wider American society from its more obvious costs and to sustain the political fiction that he was not getting into a 'major war'.[102] But in terms of strategic rationale, especially within the political leadership, there was a forlorn hope that the next battle, the next bombing run, the next daring secret operation would be sufficient to convince the North to give up the ghost. Officials clung to the idea that they were still conducting operations within the realm of the 'third option'.

The war reverted more consciously and definitively to being prosecuted according to vicarious principles after President Nixon entered the White House. Nixon was determined to pursue his policy of disengagement but not at the cost of becoming the first president to lose a major war. His administration's efforts to this effect had three central planks, outlined below, all undertaken within the context of further congressional emasculation and the concentration of closed-door executive power.[103] Forty years later, policymakers would follow a similar course of vicarious transition in the context of the faltering war in Afghanistan.

First, there was a shift to 'counterinsurgency by proxy'[104] through his administration's policy of expediting the process of 'Vietnamization'. This entailed equipping South Vietnamese armed forces with modern firepower and handing over responsibility to them for combat operations as American forces were withdrawn. This had been central to American plans in the early 1960s and never completely disappeared as an objective, only it had taken a back seat as the generals assured civilian superiors that massed firepower was sufficient to deliver success.[105]

Second, alongside Vietnamization, a similar process was occurring within the irregular and covert sphere of operations. This involved the extensive employment of Vietnamese militia forces in the form of the Regional Forces, Popular Forces (or 'Ruff-Puffs') and People's Self-Defense Forces. Vietnamese were also recruited to serve in the Provincial Reconnaissance Units as the shock troops of the CIA's secretive Phoenix Program led by William Colby, which led to the killing and capture of tens of thousands of Viet Cong cadres. Tactically, this was impressive. However, the sheer extent of the assassination machine (in some ways foreshadowing General McChrystal's comparable 'industrial-scale' enterprise in Iraq) and the abuses it led to helped turn domestic opinion against the war as reports of the Program reached American audiences: in fact, the infamous My Lai massacre occurred in the context of a Phoenix mission.[106] All this represented a massive economy of force effort, in the hope that pressure against the enemy could be maintained but without the requirement for mass deployments of regular American troops. Having taken over from Westmoreland in 1968, General Creighton Abrams placed a renewed emphasis on population-centric pacification efforts, but in the context of an accelerating American drawdown.[107]

The third plank, 'escalate to de-escalate' thinking, re-emerged with Nixon's twin invasions of Cambodia in 1970 and Laos in 1971. Although representing a serious expansion of the war, both operations were carefully circumscribed and motivated in part by the misguided vicarious hope that they would be game-changers – in the former, knocking out the Viet Cong's floating command headquarters and in the latter, cutting enemy supply lines along the Ho Chi Minh trail, thus allowing America to reach the fabled 'crossover point' and turn the tide of the war.[108] Not unrelated to the Cambodia and Laos invasions, the huge *Operation Linebacker* bombing raids of 1972, along with the mining of Haiphong harbour, were a way to apply sustained pressure on the North without the requirement for costly ground operations in order to extract concessions as part of Kissinger's 'coercive diplomacy' (to facilitate a US withdrawal that did not look simply like an abandonment of the South) and strengthen his hand in the Paris talks.

This echoed earlier rationales, only the objective now appeared to be avoiding losing the war rather than winning it. The associated 'madman strategy' at this time even sought to suggest to the North Vietnamese that Nixon, with his visceral hatred of communism, might even be prepared to use nuclear weapons to prevent the fall of the South.[109] The *Operation Linebacker II* campaign in December 1972 – the 'Christmas bombings' – involved 11 days of fearsome strikes, with a small proportion of sorties employing state-of-the art laser-guided munitions (almost 10,000 were dropped). This action brought America's war in Vietnam to a close but also heralded a future, as we will see, in which similar weapons might be employed as a central element of a lower risk, more discriminating, even potentially bloodless form of war.[110]

As Michaels has observed, in broader perspective Nixon's shift of strategy in Vietnam, while stark compared to the Johnson era approach of large-scale direct military intervention, 'merely represented continuity with what the US had been doing for years anyway, which was playing a mostly small-scale indirect advisory and assistance role in dozens of countries faced with a "subversive insurgent" threat.'[111] Regardless, the hollow reality of Vietnamization and the illusory content of the concessions granted at Paris were revealed when North Vietnamese forces rolled into Saigon just two years later. If anything, Nixon's vicarious escalations had undermined the US negotiating position by pinning the final nail in the coffin of American support for the war: the geographical expansion of the war and the *Linebacker* bombings were widely denounced as monstrous and unnecessary.[112] Further, the Khmer Rouge, bolstered by the conditions created by America's invasion, came to power in Cambodia that same year.

Together, Nixon's actions reflected his preferred approach to achieve 'peace with honour'[113] on the cheap, and he certainly got what he paid for. Perhaps Nixon, and Johnson and Kennedy before him, should have heeded the closing words of the popular contemporary novel *The Ugly American*: 'If we are not prepared to pay the human price, we had better retreat to our shores … and learn to live with the loom of world Communism which would accompany such a move.'[114]

Vietnam presented successive American presidents with seemingly impossible dilemmas, making the costs of withdrawal or escalation appear equally unconscionable: the result was a reliance on a strategy in which a series of limited measures (which nevertheless reached massive levels) held out the magical promise of simultaneously achieving all it desired and preventing all it feared. Vicarious warfare would, on the one hand, prevent the fall of the South Vietnamese domino, preserve American prestige and credibility and justify the sacrifices already made. On the other hand, it would keep the war within manageable levels, preserve domestic support, limit the necessity of American sacrifices and prevent a larger possibly nuclear confrontation with the Soviet Union or China. In the end, this middle ground satisfied no one, delivering none of what was desired and, aside from the last, bringing all it sought to prevent.

The point here has not been to suggest that hawkish critics or later revisionist historians lamenting limitation proposed anything like realistic alternative 'theories of victory'[115] (and such questions will, of course, forever remain huge 'what ifs') or to somehow reclaim or re-describe Vietnam holistically as a vicarious war. Rather, it is simply to observe that at all stages – even, perhaps despite appearances, during its height between 1965 and 1968 – the means of the war were *consciously* limited in certain respects (even if in practice the result appeared almost total) according to a lingering vicarious intent or hope that the manner of the application of this force would suffice. As in other major wars in American history, many political and military officials sought shortcuts and economies that might evade the requirement for the bloody battles raging around them while simultaneously denying the prospect that America might curtail its aims by accepting concessions through negotiation. Some of this was simply the reasonable hope that new weapons or daring missions might save some lives or bring a swifter end to the war. But for others, the same hope that promised impressive results for minimal investments at the outset of the war continued to animate their behaviour throughout, while a misplaced faith in the efficacy of marginal applications of force precluded serious contemplation of other options.

Dénouement

While Vietnam dominated foreign policy through the middle of the Cold War, in other parts of the globe covert operations continued. The CIA was active throughout the events in the early 1960s that brought President Mobuto to power in the Congo and it helped defeat the Cuban-backed uprising in Bolivia led by Che Guevara, who was captured, interrogated and executed in 1967. As Westad explains, this approach of arming local leaders 'fitted an intervention-weary Vietnam War generation of US leaders', promising concrete results through 'US encouragement but little direct US support.'[116] Partly inspired by the Bolivian example, *Operation Condor*, beginning in the late 1960s, involved American support to right-wing dictatorships of the Latin American southern cone in their campaigns of repression and assassination against purportedly Soviet-influenced internal opponents. Thus, as détente took hold, and with the American people increasingly unwilling to support overly aggressive moves that might lead the country into any new quagmires, Nixon oversaw a contraction of the clandestine service and placed it under Kissinger's close control. Many activities, such as US support to rebel forces in Angola, were increasingly delegated to mercenaries, which, by the mid-1970s, 'had become the default option in the CIA's playbook for covert interventions.'[117]

After the shocking revelations in 1975 of abuses and 'dirty tricks' committed by the CIA, exposed during the 'Year of Intelligence',[118] President Carter, while not entirely eschewing covert operations, resisted returning the agency to the unruly ways of its first two decades, and professed his belief that military force had lost much of its utility in international affairs now that the Cold War was effectively in remission.[119] Official America, cautious about further military adventures, appeared to turn its face against war. The Pentagon reverted to preparing for big wars against conventional enemies.[120] And despite the growing chorus of criticism coming from a band of so-called 'neo-conservatives' demanding more forceful action, there existed little appetite for provocative moves of any kind, including those of a vicarious nature. Indeed, many in Carter's administration believed such actions, and the policy of containment that had inspired them, held much of the blame for Vietnam,[121] preferring to pursue instead an accommodationist foreign policy guided by human rights principles.[122]

However, as a series of worrying events in the late 1970s unfolded – communist adventurism in Africa,[123] the victory of the Sandinistas in Nicaragua, the revolution in Iran and the invasion of Afghanistan – Carter, supported by his National Security Adviser, Zbigniew Brzezinski, swiftly moved toward an 'unnaturally hawkish stance' more consistent with the earlier Cold War consensus.[124] While promising tough American responses to Soviet provocations, he also emphasized the need for patience, and set out to carefully ring-fence the types of interests that might necessitate the use of force (such as the security of Western oil supplies in the Persian Gulf). Nevertheless, vicarious methods were back on the table and communicated through public gestures, such as Brzezinski wielding an AK-47 alongside Mujahideen fighters on the Khyber Pass: the administration did, in fact, approve covert support for the Afghan insurgents, even before the Soviet invasion, but only in the form of fairly trivial financial assistance. And somehow symptomatic of Carter's restraint, the helicopters carrying Delta Force operators on the clandestine mission to rescue the hostages held in Tehran tragically never made it further than the *Desert One* rendezvous point.[125] But the world would not have to wait long before his successor transformed these largely symbolic moves into a sustained campaign of vicarious interventions across the globe.

President Ronald Reagan came to office in January 1981 as détente was giving way to a renewed Second Cold War and the Soviet Union under Brezhnev appeared to be on the march, expanding its influence throughout the developing world.[126] Reagan believed the administrations of the 1970s had gone soft on communism, presiding over the demise of American resolve in the face of communist aggression. Rejecting passive containment and reviving Eisenhower's notion of rollback, an offensively-oriented Reagan Doctrine gradually emerged determined to restore American self-confidence, communicate resolve and reverse Soviet influence.[127] Yet such a confrontational policy would not be easily implemented in a country still greatly affected by its supposed Vietnam syndrome. And despite tentative progress in arms control, fears of nuclear escalation still loomed over all moves.[128]

Vicarious approaches offered a way to square this circle and Reagan set about implementing aggressive policies that did not require great sacrifice by the nation[129] – or at least possibly only in relation to their pocketbooks. A massive programme of 'remilitarization', involving US$1.5 trillion defence spending between 1981 and 1985,[130] was designed to achieve 'peace through strength'.[131] But people's bank accounts didn't suffer too greatly – no thanks to the Gaffer's Laffer curve 'trickle-down' predictions but rather to the vicarious economics of financing through public debt. Meanwhile, by backing authoritarian governments in their struggles against leftist insurgents (US special forces played a small but important role in training the Salvadorian military, for example) and arming anti-communist rebellions in places like Afghanistan, Nicaragua, Cambodia and Angola, Reagan believed he could achieve his ambitious aims while avoiding another Vietnam or instigating large-scale Soviet retaliation.

The attractiveness of such policies lay in the fact that they 'demanded so little of the public while promising so much.'[132] These vicarious wars were mainly overseen by the CIA and supported operationally by SOF teams and other non-military private actors.[133] CIA Director William Casey, fired by intense anti-communist crusading zeal and frustrated by how tame the CIA had become, let the agency's clandestine service off the leash and returned it to its 'try-anything' roots complemented by the 'blowing something up' approach of the OSS Jedburgh teams in Nazi-occupied Europe, which he had helped run during the war.[134]

The main focus of Reagan's remote interventionism was in Central America, which rapidly became a chief foreign policy concern and a 'litmus test' for his Doctrine. In a revival of the domino theory, the administration believed that if communist regimes took power, the disease would spread throughout the whole of 'America's backyard' – its vulnerable 'soft underbelly' – and turn the Caribbean into a 'red lake'.[135] Thus, to paranoid officials, as the Sandinista regime developed closer ties with the Soviet bloc, Nicaragua began to look like 'another Cuba' that might export communism beyond its borders. In late 1981 the decision was taken to sponsor an anti-Sandinista guerrilla army, the Contras – a ragtag group effectively created by the CIA composed primarily of former Somozista guardsmen and trained by veterans of Argentina's dirty war from the infamous Batallón de Inteligencia 601.[136]

Aside from providing the rebels with the arms and equipment they required to conduct devastating raids into Nicaragua, the CIA taught them how to 'neutralize' Sandinista officials,[137] hired mercenaries to mine Nicaragua's harbours and launched clandestine bombing runs. There were even abortive ideas proposed to use a so-called developmental 'Predator' drone to launch kamikaze-style attacks against Nicaraguan gasoline infrastructure.[138] But the secret war only caused the Sandinistas to become increasingly dependent on the Soviet Union,[139] and led the administration to adopt measures that would almost lead to its fall in the form of the Iran-Contra scandal of 1986–87. Tellingly, the scandal only came to light following the capture of Eugene Hasenfus, a mercenary linked to the CIA, after his Contra supply plane was shot down in October 1986. This was part of a reckless plan, designed to evade a Congressional ban on Contra aid, overseen by Casey and implemented by his acolyte Colonel Oliver North assisted by various other shadowy private actors. It involved selling weapons to Iran in exchange for freeing hostages who were being held by Iranian Hezbollah proxies in Lebanon, which was the scene of another ominous vicarious intervention.

The US decision to send 800 Marines to police a cease-fire amidst the chaos unfolding in Lebanon in 1982 (supposedly Reagan's only regret while in office) underscored the more general problems associated with a tentative vicarious middle ground. Deployed into a politically complex and fluid situation and unclear about exactly what it was meant to achieve, the mission's objectives became more ambitions as events unfolded without serious consideration of the new vulnerabilities this created or a recalibration of required capabilities. Due to internal administration compromises this meant that, as the Pentagon feared, the force was kept 'too small to make a major impact on the local situation but large enough to attract attention and animosity.'[140] The US Embassy bombing in April 1983 and the huge bombing of the Marine barracks in October (conducted by Iranian-backed Shi'ite terrorists) revealed the untenable status of the US presence. Similar issues would wrack US interventions in the future, most notably in Somalia. With Lebanon still fresh in people's memory, in a speech a year later Defense Secretary Caspar Weinberger warned about the risks of believing that limited applications of American force could automatically solve difficult foreign problems and that military power should not be squandered on disparate risky missions.[141] It would be one of the starkest official condemnations of the kinds of military operations that are the subject of this book.

Tremors of terror

Although Reagan's rhetoric was forceful, in practice his administration generally proceeded with caution – Beinart claims that Reagan was, in fact, 'terrified of war'.[142] Not wanting to go beyond what American domestic opinion would allow or risk Soviet retaliation, Reagan was, for instance, initially somewhat hesitant in backing both the Contras in Nicaragua and the Mujahideen in Afghanistan. Lebanon had been allowed to get out of control, but coming just two days after the Barracks Bombing, the successful US invasion of Grenada in October 1983 was more indicative of Reagan's purported realism. Although fraught with mistakes that were not publicly apparent at the time, this was an important symbolic victory for Reagan and was conducted more along the lines that Weinberger would soon propose – popular, proportionate and politically prudent. The mission to put down a Marxist coup and rescue American students was over in days and involved a small force of around 7,000 mostly Marines and special forces.[143] In certain ways, this echoed the limited maritime interventions of the 19th century or the more recent 1965 *Operation Power Pack* in the Dominican Republic.[144]

The later 1986 attack against Libya, *Operation El Dorado Canyon*, in response to the bombing of a West Berlin nightclub, was a similarly isolated mission utilizing America's growing arsenal of stand-off precision-strike capabilities involving F-111 bombers armed with laser-guided bombs operating 2,800 miles from a base in England.[145] The risks, as in Grenada, were slight as the Soviet Union was unlikely to intervene in either case. Foreshadowed by events in Beirut, the Libya operation was arguably an early campaign in a growing war against Islamic terrorism. Moreover, the methods employed, which in addition to the airstrikes involved other covert activities on the ground, were, within the limitations of the time, an early indication of those that would dominate operations after 2001.[146]

Although not so apparent at the time, developments in another major theatre of Reagan's Cold War – Afghanistan – would also come to be seen in this light, as critical events in the emergence of the modern jihadist threat. Low-level covert assistance to the Afghan Mujahideen under *Operation Cyclone* was initially designed to 'harass' the Soviet occupation without causing a serious escalation of the war. US involvement was kept at arm's length by delivering foreign arms through Pakistan's military intelligence agency, the ISI. As the administration began to apply the Reagan Doctrine more vigorously during its second term, and spurred on by an impatient Congress, the decisions to seriously expand assistance in 1985 and to supply heat-seeking Stinger missiles in 1986 were now accompanied by the more ambitious aim of bringing about a humiliating Soviet withdrawal.[147] To the CIA this all represented an extremely cost-effective strategy to score a victory against their arch-enemy.[148] The main fear was that the advanced weapons, ideal for use by terrorists to bring down passenger jets, might fall into the hands of America's adversaries (indeed, Iran secured some), but the 'blowback' from this policy would be of a different, more ominous, kind.[149]

Despite the fact that by the mid-1980s the US covert effort was an open secret due to the introduction of the Stingers, widespread media reporting and Reagan's open hints, aid primarily continued to be channelled through Pakistani intermediaries to maintain deniability.[150] But this made it almost impossible for the small CIA team in the region to effectively monitor or control the distribution of these large infusions of aid to its end-users. This points to just one way that the vicarious design of secretive proxy wars, intended to distance US involvement, can undermine US control over its proxies and lead to harmful future consequences. While evidence of direct support to Osama bin Laden is slim, ultimately some of this assistance (including CIA training manuals)[151] found its way to 'Afghan Arab' volunteers within the resistance, contributed to an emergent 'terrorist infrastructure' in Pakistan, and strengthened fundamentalists like Gulbuddin Hekmatyar who would later direct attacks against their erstwhile sponsor.[152]

Islamist terrorism had become a growing concern since the 1960s, and a series of attacks through the early 1980s underscored the seriousness of the mounting threat to US interests. Events associated with the interventions in Lebanon and Libya, as discussed earlier, were part of this. And Iran-Contra was so shocking because, as Freedman explains, a 'war on terror' had begun to be a major theme of Reagan's presidency after the Beirut debacle, when Iran was seen as one of the states' responsible for the attack.[153] The covert operation in Afghanistan, underway throughout this time, thus represents an intriguing inflection point with respect to the focus of American vicarious warfare, insofar as some of the covert methods employed to support jihadists there would, before too long, be turned against just such groups, including many who had been part of that earlier fight. Indeed, planning to this effect was already under way.

Key aspects of this were special operations and precision weaponry. The growing terrorist threat was a major factor driving a renewed investment in special forces and unconventional warfare capabilities, which had been allowed to atrophy during the 1970s after the initial burst of enthusiasm under Kennedy and their extensive use in Vietnam.[154] Special forces were mistrusted and misunderstood within the wider military establishment, often viewed as somehow alien. Moreover, the failed *Desert One* rescue attempt had pointed to the urgent requirement for reform. Reagan set about doubling the special forces and a major Congressional-led process of reorganization began, culminating in the establishment of a unified Special Operations Command (SOCOM) in 1987, which put the special operations capabilities of the different branches under one roof.

Another area of progress was in relation to precision munitions. We saw earlier how, at the tail end of the Vietnam War, the first generation of such weapons were deployed. Bacevich recounts how strategists such as Albert Wohlstetter, greatly impressed by their promise, passionately campaigned for serious investment in this area, arguing throughout the 1980s that they would enable a new way of war.[155] Threats could be eliminated, even pre-emptively if necessary, through the bold, discriminating and efficient use of precisely modulated and limited military force. These weapons would not be used as mere coercive bargaining tools, but rather as instruments of decisive victory or leadership decapitation. It was not difficult to see how this idea could be applied to emerging terrorist targets, notwithstanding the potential legal barriers standing in the way (barriers that would soon be swept aside after 9/11). Thus, the development of both special forces and precision airpower were opening up new opportunities for employing military force as a scalpel rather than a bludgeon. But this was all still a matter of theory rather than proven practice.

It was at this time that Casey, North and Duane Clarridge – a leading CIA figure in the Nicaraguan war and indicted during Iran-Contra – were working up plans for 'super-secret attack teams' to capture or, in extreme circumstances, even eliminate terrorists.[156] Although not mentioning the planned teams, the top secret 1986 National Security Decision Directive 207 that resulted from their work advocated using 'all legal means available' to combat terrorism and that 'the entire range of diplomatic, economic legal, military, covert action, and informational assets at our disposal must be brought to bear.'[157] Foreshadowing the central features of contemporary vicarious warfare, Clarridge, as head of a new CIA Counterterrorism Center, advocated the targeted killing of terrorists and devised plans for pilotless drones fitted with weapons to hit terrorist targets.[158] These as yet fruitless plans would remain largely hypothetical through the 1990s, when an intelligence-led policing approach dominated counterterror efforts.[159] Thus, practices conceived in the twilight of the Cold War were already in the process, at least in theory, of being repurposed as the means for prosecuting a new global war after 2001. In the meantime, unmanned aerial technologies were rapidly maturing, and when the 9/11 attacks prompted a relaxation of the restraints around targeted killings, this provided the conditions for the first lethal strike by the still secret CIA weapon. In mid-November 2001, a Predator UAV, armed with Hellfire missiles, was used to eliminate Al-Qaeda's military commander, Mohammed Atef.[160] Casey and Clarridge's vision was effectively turned into reality, a decade or so later, over the agency's old battleground in the Hindu Kush against a veteran of the anti-Soviet jihad that they had once supported.

Through all this we can distinguish clear threads linking the wartime OSS, the secret wars of the Cold War and contemporary vicarious warfare. In 2011, Casey's protégé, Clarridge, was reported to be privately running a network of spies feeding information to his old covert conspirator-turned-conservative commentator, North, as well as to Pentagon officials in Afghanistan about possible militants to target. This seemed to somehow echo their recruitment of ex-CIA agents like Richard Secord and John Singlaub to help transfer arms to the Contras in the 1980s. But in a public statement, Clarridge remarked that the inspiration for his company was, in fact, the Second World War OSS, an organization that oversaw a raft of doomed missions, sending hundreds of agents to their deaths, which he described as 'a success of the past' and 'an effective model for the future.'[161] This reflected the wartime lens through which such officials continued to view global challenges, whether of a communist or jihadist nature. Appeals to the necessity for 'wartime prerogatives' would define official approaches in the renewed war against terror after 9/11.[162] But more importantly, this underscores the complex networks of inheritances and inter-connections linking the people, places and practices of vicarious interventionism across generations: policymaking true-believers, veteran operators and abandoned surrogates move on to seek new battlegrounds in which to apply their violent skills, and in ways that American society has consistently struggled to control.

Underwhelming oversight

We saw in the previous chapter how the American people have long maintained an ambiguous relationship with the wars of the nation. But the vicarious distancing between society and war that is a notable hallmark of the contemporary era truly starts to become apparent during the Cold War. This is primarily due to the huge disparity between the sheer magnitude of America's global (para)military activism and the relative level of disinterest displayed by the public in relation to these developments.

This was especially apparent before Vietnam, when a Cold War consensus around containment shielded administrations from serious dissent or public scrutiny.[163] The public was largely deferential in the face of a fairly homogenous foreign policy establishment confidently espousing an internationalist activist agenda and resolutely opposed to any form of appeasement. A democratic disconnect at some level was almost inevitable given the secrecy surrounding many decisions and the legacy of power amassed by the executive branch during the war. The situation was largely accepted without criticism, and Congress was not minded to seriously challenge it. The policy of plausible deniability adopted in NSC 10/2, primarily developed with foreign audiences in mind, afforded elites significant domestic latitude to launch operations with minimal scrutiny; moreover, some in the CIA were quite prepared to lie to the president in order to sustain their covert operations.

Congress and the American people were increasingly pushed to the margins in terms of decision-making in security affairs. There were few processes in place to investigate or hold to account those responsible even for the most disastrous of secret missions, thus contributing to a culture of impunity and reckless activism.[164] The Cold War consensus meant administrations did not have to be too concerned if missions were exposed or spectacular failures came to light: every effort had to be made to confront the Soviet Union, however risky, and whatever the sacrifice. The fact that Kennedy's approval rating *soared* in the aftermath of the Bay of Pigs is testament to such underlying attitudes.[165] Of course there were periodic exceptions that generated some public fervour, but in general this all meant that there was only superficial debate around the use of force, and Americans largely left the security establishment to carry on its work.

After the Vietnam War, the War Powers Act of 1973 and intelligence reforms such as the Intelligence Oversight Act of 1980 led to some tightening of procedures and shone some more light into executive activities, bolstered by growing Congressional assertiveness[166] and a melange of critical new voices. This went some way to curb the excesses of the post-war system but without completely constraining an increasingly imperial presidency or the continuing influence of a beltway 'blob' which, despite fierce debate over tactics, continued to champion a militarily activist grand strategy.[167] Meanwhile, the spectre of communism could still be employed by the executive to mobilize public support. But nor did the American people seriously demand a say in scrutinizing how the nation might project its power abroad. It is true that there were a number of highly vocal activist interest groups[168] at this time, spurred on by a much more sceptical attitude after Watergate and the disclosures about executive perfidy over Vietnam and CIA wrongdoing. Yet most Americans were tired of foreign or military affairs[169] and overwhelmingly preoccupied with economic issues such as inflation, unemployment and emerging challenges such as the drugs epidemic, crime and climate change. The Church Committee's findings were met with general indifference,[170] and Oliver North was viewed in some quarters as a patriotic hero. Congress itself was inclined to leave the dirty work of covert operations to a few specialist committees. The end of the draft and the resulting growing 'gap' between civilians and the military reinforced such trends.

In sum, reflecting our earlier consideration of the tensions inherent in the nation's attitude to war, it is possible to see how the American people were becoming increasingly distanced from the prosecution of its wars; it was far from absolute, but significant nonetheless. To some extent, society was a victim of the arrogation of executive power and elitist secrecy in prosecuting its wars in an underhand manner. Even Congress often dragged its feet in terms of responding to or restraining executive excesses, and in some cases actively connived in allowing this situation to arise.[171] Continuing popular apathy meant there was little pressure on representatives to claw back a meaningful voice for ordinary people. Elections remained, of course, one way to express disapproval or dissatisfaction. However, they can be a double-edged sword in terms of accountability – they may constrain up to an election, but then grant great powers for four years. This all helps to explain the somewhat schizophrenic situation in which the professedly peace-loving American people could find themselves citizens of a state engaged in an expansive campaign of global military interventionism. Such patterns would continue to be apparent into the contemporary era.

Emerging themes

To audiences today who know how things turned out or who have a clearer awareness of Soviet weaknesses, it is easy to forget that the communist threat appeared more fearsome to generations that had fought wars against other totalitarian powers and who had learned, perhaps too well, the lesson of appeasement. The broad intent and ambition behind the countless military missions of the period was clear – confront the Soviet threat wherever it was apparent in a largely indirect and, where necessary, deniable manner. This would not demand the sacrifice of American lives and would not escalate to nuclear war. The strategic promise was of local wins ultimately adding up to a total victory against communism. In certain circumstances vicarious approaches represented the 'least bad' option in terms of resisting communist provocations.

The balance sheet concerning the specific application of vicarious warfare approaches during the Cold War is undoubtedly mixed. There were indeed a number of 'quick wins' that removed troublesome leftist leaders, largely successful efforts to defend American allies in places like El Salvador, and even some significant victories such as the withdrawal of Soviet troops from Afghanistan. Certain limited military actions – in the Dominican Republic, Grenada and Libya – also appeared to be proportionate and decisive responses to discrete challenges. Efforts to assist Marxist rebels or prop up regimes that were being challenged as a result of American clandestine activities (in places such as Nicaragua, Angola and, most painfully, in Afghanistan) placed a severe strain on Soviet resources and political will. Thus, in some contexts a resolute American stand through measures short of all-out war looked to have paid real strategic dividends. However, it would be mistaken to conclude from this that it was the prosecution of vicarious warfare that won the Cold War. A number of considerations challenge that view, and on closer inspection the record looks rather less effective.

Although US actions, especially Reagan's support to the Afghan rebels, multiplied Soviet problems and influenced Gorbachev's 'immediate objective' to bring an end to superpower confrontation, we cannot overlook the Western diplomatic, economic and cultural efforts that slowly but surely chipped away at Soviet nerve and narratives. In fact, most challenges within the Soviet Union stemmed from deep-seated structural political, economic and technological weakness.[172]

We should also not forget that the Soviets were equally enthusiastic exponents of vicarious warfare, and a case can be made that this contributed to their ultimate demise. To take just one prominent example, initial moves in Afghanistan were designed not with the intent of occupation but rather to secure Soviet interests at little cost. Turning down repeated Afghan requests for the insertion of Soviet forces, Moscow sought to achieve this through the provision of military aid and advisors. Even as plans were developed to dispose of the unwanted leader, Hafizullah Amin, in late 1979, full military intervention had not been agreed; KGB efforts to assassinate him all failed. Finally, elite Spetsnaz (special) forces stormed the presidential palace and eliminated him while a 'Limited Contingent' of 30,000 troops invaded Afghanistan from the north.[173] Brezhnev had been promised by his advisors that this would be a short intervention; instead, it became a long and costly occupation.[174] In some respects, US and Soviet experiences mirrored one another during the Cold War as they became locked in an ugly wresting match, squandering resources, lives and goodwill fighting endless counterproductive proxy wars.

Some American operations simply failed at an immediate tactical level, often precisely due to the vicarious nature of the methods used and the perceived requirement for secrecy.[175] This was one of the main reasons for the Bay of Pigs failure. Kennedy, wanting a quiet coup, did not coordinate the landings with guerrillas already present on Cuba, provided obsolete bombers (because they could plausibly have been attained on the black market), and refused to countenance additional air support during the invasion[176] – facts all the more unfortunate as the original rationale had been rendered largely moot by the widespread reporting in mainstream newspapers of the CIA's preparations in Florida and Guatemala.[177] Similarly, the 1980 *Desert One* rescue mission was frustrated by the requirement for secrecy, which meant the operation was not subjected to sufficient critical scrutiny.[178]

Some successful operations led to significant 'blowback' over time. Covert operations of regime change provoked revolutionary sentiment or stored up problems for later: the hatred felt by Iranians toward the United States can, for instance, be traced back to the CIA-led 1953 coup,[179] and US-installed puppet regimes became lighting rods for Soviet and, from the 1960s, Cuban retaliation.[180] CIA-controlled mercenaries – as prominent symbols of Western capitalist imperialism – became central tropes of anti-American propaganda around the world.[181] In a more general sense, the support to the security forces of repressive regimes and unsavoury proxy armies exacerbated conditions such as regional instability, poverty and social injustice in which radical movements, not to mention emerging terror complexes, were able to grow.[182] Rarely was much thought devoted to what would come after tactical success:[183] few in the CIA stopped to question what would follow a successful elimination of Castro, and the assassination of President Diem in 1963 might have solved one problem but did not help create a stable South Vietnamese government capable of attracting widespread popular support.

Even where operations failed, rarely were the wider consequences as dire as proponents of intervention had suggested they would be. South Vietnam's defeat did not lead to the inexorable fall of countless dominoes that many had predicted. In many cases, communist client states that survived US attempts to topple them either became less-than-impressive poster boys for world communism or, as in Angola, costly drains on Soviet resources.[184] This suggested it was better in some cases to leave the USSR to make its own mistakes and waste its resources in trying to prop up its dysfunctional clients. Furthermore, the obsession with credibility and resolve that so animated US politicians was sometimes arguably only undermined by committing to a series of peripheral failing wars. Restraint might actually project a sense of confident strength while allowing America to husband its forces for use in defending truly vital interests.

Cold War vicarious interventions also revealed how small-scale missions can encourage 'mission creep' leading to unintended serious costly commitments through a process of incremental additions of US resources, as occurred in Vietnam and Lebanon. This even applied to covert operations, which were precisely designed to keep US involvement small and hidden. But small operations have sometimes begun with grand purposes, and when the goals could not be achieved, 'leaders were tempted to take the next step and the next.'[185] Where US involvement is denied but widely known to exist in practice, then reputational harm will be suffered regardless of the official position. Even those rare operations that manage to remain secret can cause policymakers, through institutional and personal attachments to the mission, to call for a doubling of effort rather than abandonment. These dynamics can place administrations in impossible binds, especially when covert operations are exposed. As an early Cold War CIA Deputy Director put it, 'a single misfortune that reveals CIA's connection makes it necessary to either abandon the cause completely or convert to a policy of overt military intervention.'[186]

Linked to this, the main selling point and rationale of vicarious warfare was that it provided the US with a means to strike forcefully at the Soviet Union without prompting escalation to nuclear war. Of course, nuclear war never ultimately occurred and, as Carson has argued, covert action may actually have contributed to preventing serious escalation in certain contexts.[187] Covertness can limit the influence of domestic hawks and can be used to simultaneously signal to the adversary both resolve and a desire to keep the conflict within bounds. In the midst of larger wars this argument makes good sense – significantly, most of Carson's cases are of this nature.[188] But it would be dangerous to extend this idea much further or to claim that the absence of escalation to nuclear war more generally during the Cold War was somehow thanks to the prosecution of multiple covert operations. Such a line of argument would come close to suggesting that forceful interventions were always and everywhere necessarily a good idea in the first place. We have argued that, for various reasons, this was not the case.

Moreover, there is ever a strong possibility of miscommunication. Proxy interventions may, in fact, be read as weakness rather than resolve, and they may foreclose more peaceful avenues for resolving differences. Likewise, what one side understands as a limited action might be understood in more existential terms by an adversary with the potential for generating incidents that spark a wider war. Indeed, the occasions on which the superpowers came closest to nuclear war were in contexts in which proxy interventions and covert operations had greatly heightened tensions. The Soviet decision to ship missiles to Cuba in the summer of 1962 was taken for a number of reasons, but scholars now understand that a major motivation was the Soviet desire to render Cuba invasion-proof after what Kennedy had attempted with the Bay of Pigs in 1961.[189] Moreover, it is unlikely they would have proceeded if the ground had not been laid by the failed invasion and had they not come to judge Kennedy as irresolute due to his pusillanimous behaviour during that debacle.[190] Crucially, as Craig and Gilbert conclude, although the great powers were able to avoid open war, 'their involvement in regional disputes on behalf of client states ... brought them dangerously close to it.'[191]

Conclusion to Part II

If ongoing contemporary military operations have been described as a 'forever war', between 1947 and 1991 America fought an everywhere war. Despite the sheer magnitude of the capabilities at its disposal, the requirement to sustain the fight across the globe spread those resources thin and created an inclination toward local economization and a search for strategic shortcuts, through delegation to proxy warriors or the swift sword of the special operator. This is consistent with how other imperial powers have sought to handle extensive commitments. Secrecy became ingrained as a default prerequisite for any forceful action, no matter how damaging to the mission or 'implausibly deniable'. Denial not only applied to the policy of not acknowledging America's hand in events, but also to the institutional psychology that allowed policymakers and operators to interpret any forceful activity as progress.

Working in the shadows had the added benefit of cloaking from the American public the unsavoury activities that cold warriors felt must be undertaken. People were ready to accept the need for a tough stance in the face of the Soviet menace, but not if implemented in a manner that offended the nation's perception of itself as the 'good guy', a point well illustrated by the reaction to Vietnam excesses or CIA wrongdoings. There is an argument to be made that the American people colluded in this arrangement, if we can call it that. All the killing, bombing, torture and repression – for that is what American policy often entailed, however noble the cause – could be performed by others and overseen by small numbers of discrete specialists in remote corners of the world. For the public, this was war at a remove: out of sight, out of mind.

The parallel secret espionage 'intelligence war', somewhat eclipsed by clandestine operations, is widely understood to have helped in keeping the Cold War from turning hot, but the obsession with reckless proxy wars, engineered rebellions and attempted coups and assassinations not only often damaged America's strategic position but on numerous occasions nearly brought about the very escalation that their secret operations were principally designed to prevent. Scattershot vicarious warfare arguably did more harm than good, both to US strategic interests in the Cold War and well beyond. Even those operations that were deemed successful at the time cast very long shadows that would continue to frustrate US foreign objectives up to the present day.

The afterglow of 'victory' in the Cold War, which many in the CIA believed they had helped win, would embolden policymakers to double-down on such approaches as they set out to confront a range of new threats in a very different strategic context. Through the massaging of outcomes in internal reporting and due to organizational cognitive dissonance, operations that appeared to be successful on the surface were uncritically accepted as such and subsequently drawn on to support similar approaches elsewhere without properly assessing their flaws, either in terms of tactical implementation or longer-term effects. As such, close-run wins and near-misses were heralded as definite successes, increasing the likelihood similar risky operations would be attempted in the future. Many of those overseeing the disastrous Bay of Pigs operation were afflicted by 'victory disease' picked up from the earlier apparently eponymous operation in Guatemala, *PBSUCCESS*. Such uncritically accepted and internalized lessons from earlier operations encouraged a veritable proliferation of vicarious operations that continue to inspire policymakers even today. In fact, the Cold War further encouraged the notion, at least for those who failed to look closely enough, that interests and objectives could be attained through force but at little cost.

Intra-elite tussles over strategic decision-making between proponents of the three traditions of American warfare outlined in the Introduction were apparent throughout the Cold War, and help account for the varying nature of the application of American power. The period was bookended by two major wars, in Korea and the Persian Gulf, and bisected by Vietnam; COIN had its time in the sun at points. Nevertheless, vicarious warfare dominated as the default approach. The Gulf War that was fought and won in 1991, toward the end of the Cold War, was conducted in anything but a vicarious manner, as if to justify the years of military doctrinal development devoted to just such a campaign and to bury the legacy of half a century of indecisive brush-fire wars. But the war was a false augur of future trends in American force. Although on occasion there would be attempts to replicate the Iraq model, not least again in Iraq, conditions were converging to further promote the vicarious model as the nation's dominant template for carrying out its policy of global interventionism.

PART III

Contemporary Dynamics

5

Drivers

Parts I and II surveyed the origins of vicarious warfare in both history and the American experience up to the end of the Cold War. This has allowed us to better understand both the practical and conceptual foundations of this form of war. The discussion revealed that although to an extent vicarious warfare might be understood as the offspring of a unique strategic context defined principally by the long war against terror, in fact it represents something more fundamental and enduring. That analysis also provided us with partial clues regarding the factors that might have contributed to its emergence. The remaining chapters in Part III take these ideas forward into the contemporary post–Cold War context.

Vicarious warfare has come to dominate American strategic practice over the last decade, but in its contemporary form it emerged out of developments apparent since at least the early 1990s, and in certain areas well before that. Therefore, in order to properly understand and explain the phenomenon as it confronts us today, we need to account (in this chapter) for the multiple factors driving its modern adoption. Chapter 6 then charts its gradual emergence over recent decades, in terms of both military practice and as an increasingly coherent and influential tradition of war vying for influence in decision-making circles. Finally, Chapter 7 considers some of the prominent strategic consequences arising from the prosecution of vicarious warfare over recent times.

★ ★ ★

As should be apparent from the foregoing chapters, no single factor can explain the emergence of vicarious warfare as a prominent mode of US warmaking. Some accounts present these developments simply as a direct reaction to the costs of the Iraq and Afghanistan Wars or as narrowly associated with the 'War on Terror'. We have already established the attractiveness of vicarious approaches during so-called inter-war periods.

But, while certainly important, that perspective overlooks important trends predating the 2000s and the use of vicarious approaches in missions beyond countering terrorist threats. This suggests deeper factors and forces are at work. In fact, the story is one that can only be told by accounting for multiple converging threads including underlying structural continuities, progressively evolving social, organizational and normative conditions, changing political and strategic contexts, and the impact of more immediate events and circumstances. Moreover, in seeking to explain why policymakers might turn to such approaches, the overall coherence and persuasiveness of the tradition in narrative terms is an important piece of the puzzle – in other words, the extent to which it is seen by officials as an effective approach in confronting contemporary strategic challenges. In this respect, the role of key decision-makers or influential strategic thinkers can be crucial in terms of promoting agendas.

These processes are too complex and conditional to be subject to a general causative theory of vicarious warfare. It would be mistaken to try to mechanistically identify fixed variables that explain its adoption in a predictable fashion. A more realistic approach, appreciative of historical contingency, is to present an analysis that seeks to capture some of the most important factors. It is a multifaceted and layered story that is still unfolding. It is also shaped by its own history – directly in terms of accumulated experience and more indirectly through the sedimentation of influential myths and narratives around dominant approaches. We have already detailed some of the relevant background developments in America's early history, some of which further matured and intensified throughout the Cold War. Contemporary vicarious warfare powerfully integrates, quantitatively and qualitatively, enhanced forms of earlier practice with entirely new aspects in various spheres that have emerged during the intervening years. These have all coalesced to an unprecedented degree in the second decade of the 21st century.

This chapter begins by considering some of the underlying factors that make proactive, forceful American intervention appear to policymakers as both essential and feasible. These should be understood as necessary but not sufficient factors because they do not necessarily preclude alternative military approaches more in line with the prescriptions of the other traditions of conventional battle or small wars. Why predominantly vicarious methods have come to the fore will become apparent as the chapter progresses to consider more specific and circumstantial factors associated with core sections of American society: namely, the military, the wider public and the media. The chapter concludes by bringing the analysis together to explain how, due to the confluence of developments in these various spheres, vicarious warfare emerges as an especially appealing solution for defence officials and political leaders facing multiple competing pressures and exigencies.

Deep continuities

In Part I it was suggested that vicarious warfare tends to be associated, if not exclusively or deterministically, with powerful states, especially those enjoying forms of imperial dominion. This does not mean it is the only form of war employed by them, or that some empires, due to the happy confluence of protective geography and benign external environments, have not experienced long periods of largely peaceful existence. Yet the converging requirements, incentives and opportunities that great power brings, somewhat counterintuitively, often leads such states to increasingly rely on vicarious approaches. The manifest reality of modern America's hegemonic status is therefore perhaps a good place to begin. A mixture of geostrategic, commercial and ideological ambitions and anxieties have driven the American eagle to spread its talons well beyond its shores, and to do so in a predominantly forceful manner.

Militant missionary: ideological underpinnings of interventionism

We have discussed how America emerged as the world's most powerful nation in the aftermath of the Second World War and how it subsequently sought to defend and expand its hegemonical position throughout the Cold War, undertaking a programme of preventive global interventions in defence of the liberal order it had created. Containing communism was central to this global activism, but expanding commercial interests in distant lands, supported by influential lobbies in Washington, have also compelled America to proactively protect its far-flung concerns, through force if necessary – a pattern evident since the nation's birth and especially from the late 19th century. But as Layne has argued (building on William Appleman Williams' notion of the American pursuit of an 'Open Door world'), action in defence of economic interests was not purely mercenary; it was also intimately linked to conceptions of ideology, security and national wellbeing.

Central to this was a belief that the American way of life, its prosperity and freedoms, was fundamentally dependent on an open system of global free trade. This, in turn, necessitated a world predominantly comprised of states that subscribed to US liberal values and remained open for

Americans to access their markets, resources and investment opportunities. Where this was not the case, the United States would have to act because a less open and less liberal world threatened not only the immediate interests of American companies and investors, but also core values at home: the rationale being that 'political and economic liberalism cannot flourish at home unless they are safe abroad.'[1] Furthermore, it was widely believed that an economically integrated and interdependent world of democratic trading nations would be more peaceful and safer.[2] These considerations converged to promote an expansive conception of American security, well beyond simple territorial defence or pragmatic realpolitik, especially when, after 1945, the US appeared to possess the means to put such an imperialistic strategy into practice, to convert its rhetoric into reality.[3] Underpinning and inspiring such rationales has been a deep and long-standing moralistic conviction pertaining to the essential righteousness of the American system and by extension, its foreign behaviour. In many respects, the idea of America as a force for good in the world has, in fact, served as a pre-eminent justification for its empire building since at least the late 19th century.

A missionary impulse to promote its republican values and institutions, fostered by a strongly held notion of American exceptionalism, has long animated the nation's foreign policy[4] – 'a conviction about [its] superior morality and social organisation ... and the destiny of the United States to spread its democratic revolution to the ends of the earth'.[5] As the self-appointed standard-bearer of 'progress' and champion of the free, this broad ideological project has persisted as a perennial factor colouring its engagement abroad. Of course, the United States is not alone in cultivating such grandiose ambition – in fact, the British Empire from which it broke free, and perhaps from which it inherited some of its haughty pretensions, was similarly moved to export the blessings of its civilization and enlightened institutions to the world.[6] In the US context, there have been two main schools of thought as to how this might be achieved: first, America as exemplar, the 'shining city on the hill', inspiring others to follow its lead and second, as activist, pushing other nations toward more liberal democratic futures, using force if necessary. The latter approach has appeared and reappeared in different forms, championed by proponents across the political spectrum, from hawkish liberal interventionists to assertive neo-conservative ideologues promoting a 'muscular Wilsonianism'. But regardless of the form it takes, the central reality of contemporary US foreign policy is an elite consensus advocating a forceful grand strategy of 'liberal hegemony'.[7]

Foreign policy agendas – whether about containment, commercialism or counterterror – are thus inescapably infused with intense ideological enthusiasm. The Soviet threat was not judged purely according to realist conceptions of state security but as an evil that must not be allowed to exist; securing economic interests was not simply about achieving GDP growth but part of a broader liberal agenda.[8] The imperative to defend and promote the liberal creed contributed to what has been described as a sense of 'perpetual moral crisis' during the Cold War, and which has not seriously subsided since.[9]

Such crusading liberalism continues to inspire US policymakers in reversing all manner of global evils – whether authoritarianism, oppression, ethnic cleansing or Islamist terror – and promoting ideals of neoliberal economics, republican democracy and freedom. It is an agenda that has manifested itself in military terms most prominently in modern times through what Freedman has termed 'offensive liberal wars', such as the humanitarian interventions of the 1990s or the neo-conservative attempts to forcibly impose democracy on Middle Eastern nations and elsewhere.[10] The influence of such essentially domestic ideological drivers of foreign behaviour are, according to Gray, more likely to be apparent when foreign threats are unclear – this perhaps explains why the moralistic element of US policy has risen in influence over recent decades, notwithstanding the fact that terrorism served to concentrate minds somewhat in the years following 9/11.[11] Even then, Islamist terror was framed not purely as a threat to security or interests, but as a malevolent force utterly opposed to American values and religious beliefs or even Western civilization as a whole.[12]

This potent normative ingredient strongly influences American strategic behaviour. For instance, imposing a Manichean lens on situations helps explain the demotion of diplomacy in favour of forceful alternatives when engaging with adversaries.[13] The cultivation of diabolical images of the enemy precludes reasoned engagement with them as independent rational actors: in short, moralism trumps politics.[14] For instance, the Taliban were consistently portrayed as 'less than human' savages, thus impeding negotiation or recognition of American behaviour that might be driving resistance.[15] Moreover, where force is deployed in the service of ideological or economic ambition, policymakers are likely to favour means that do not entail significant sacrifice from the nation – they are not animated by the kind of necessity accompanying wars fought for national survival (notwithstanding fiery elite rhetoric attempting to persuade otherwise). Ideology may be sufficient to compel intervention, but as the price in lives and money becomes apparent, the will sustaining the fight is likely to dissipate faster than if truly vital interests are engaged. In short, a foreign policy motivated by ideology points strongly, if not deterministically, toward the adoption of vicarious approaches.

The perils of passivity

While ideological ambition serves to fuel expansion and foreign entanglement, this tends to be simultaneously accompanied by progressively growing anxieties, due in part to the increasing scope and range of interests that accrue. Almost all projects of imperial enlargement get caught up in the 'self-propelling dynamic of empire': expanding frontiers entail new vulnerabilities and growing commitments.[16] These represent tempting targets that enemies could strike and that therefore need to be proactively defended. In the United States, and recalling our earlier discussion of Hawaii, the 'Pearl Harbour' mentality that is said to exist derives from a surprise attack against a remote and vulnerable American outpost.

Yet, in the contemporary context, policymakers harbour fears that even the homeland is directly at risk and that distant fortified frontiers no longer offer reliable protection. This perception has only grown with intensified globalization, WMD proliferation and the spread of transnational terrorist networks. 9/11 is often presented as proof in this respect. The old myth of an invulnerable 'fortress America', shielded from Old World malicious intent by two great oceans, has supposedly been rendered obsolete by the 'death of distance' in the modern context. From the 'bomber gap' of the 1950s to the modern 'zero-day' cyber security gap, security analysts have been preoccupied with a growing list of ways in which malign actors might unexpectedly and devastatingly strike at America or its vital interests around the globe.

These fears promote efforts to tackle threats before they arise. Betz highlights how 'policy-makers have become fixated by the apparent speed of events and convinced of the urgency of action to remediate or forestall threats.'[17] Porter has similarly observed that, in an 'age of anxiety', leaders are pressured to act, fearing the security and associated political consequences of failing to pre-empt global risks.[18] As a result, America's imperial footprint tends to be more dispersed, mobile and variable today, reflecting the location and nature of apparent threats as they emerge. In this sense, the US is not immune from classic imperial anxieties: the precise sources of and solutions to them might have changed, but the effect is familiar. Rather than wait for enemies to threaten the US homeland, policymakers prefer to adopt a 'forward defence' and engage threats overseas or 'take the battle to the enemy', as President George W. Bush put it in the aftermath of the 9/11 attacks.[19] Yet, whether or not global modernity has actually given rise to a proliferation of strategic dangers is not the focus here. The important point is that the *perception* among politicians is that they are assailed both internally and externally by all manner of inescapable risks. However apocryphal or overblown such risks may be, they have crucially served to shape warmaking behaviours and decision-making patterns.

Given contemporary media-driven political pressures and the existence, however overwrought, of global threats, often the most unthinkable option for decision-makers is disengagement – leaders 'may not have the luxury of noninvolvement'.[20] As a result, when contemplating the use of force abroad, the costs politicians fear are often primarily those associated with *inaction*. Betts observes that political leaders 'act because they focus on the danger of failing to do something rather than the danger of doing something and failing'.[21] Furthermore, foreign policy hawks, of both liberal and neo-conservative stripes, invoking the ghost of Munich, warn that failing to act will irreparably damage US credibility, signal weakness or encourage future aggression and atrocity; they promote a form of risk pre-emption through the proactive use of force. Thus 'positive' strategic and normative arguments, such as those associated with advancing interests and promoting freedom and democracy, are supplemented by powerful 'negative' imperatives associated with a range of ominous perils and vulnerabilities. As a consequence, the political calculus often points toward more, not less, intervention despite the strong evidence that the assumptions regarding expected political or security costs are largely illusory.[22]

Force of attraction

Whether action is designed to pre-empt threats or proactively promote US values, force is widely seen as a useable and uniquely effective instrument. At one level, there is a simple and mundane process operating here. Given its vast capabilities, regional commands and network of global bases, the option of launching military missions is always available to American leaders – a quick and tempting solution to deal with any emerging threat.[23] This recalls our observation in Part I that although empire brings significant challenges, it also appears to provide the means to solve them. In short, America often resorts to force simply because it can. It is in this way that, as Coker puts it, 'once a state has a capacity to do something it often fails to ask whether it should do it, only how it should.'[24] Reinforcing this habitual tendency of resorting to force, given its huge reserves of resources and power, America can generally absorb the fallout from costly or failing adventures. Walt observes that since the Second World War, 'the United States has had the luxury of being able to intervene wherever it chooses and then withdraw if things go badly ... leaving the local populations to their fates.'[25] Relatedly, wielding such awesome power simultaneously leads American policymakers to assume that they can forego the often difficult and messy task of engaging in processes of compromise or accommodation. To an unprecedented degree, war has become normalized in America. A nation once at least rhetorically committed to the cause of peace has embraced an intensive militarization of its foreign behaviour while the endless use of force generates only marginal Congressional pushback or public unease.[26]

This bellicose predisposition is supplemented and strengthened by a more general American faith in the efficacy of force. The military is widely seen as a uniquely effective and trusted tool in Washington, perfect for 'fixing anything that happens to be broken.'[27] Not only that, but there is a belief that military force can be used selectively and cheaply. It is a mindset also deriving from parallel streams in the American psyche, such as a 'presumption of unconquerable superiority',[28] an over-optimistic belief in the ability to control military developments and a problem-solving outlook favouring 'matériel over manpower', or technological quick-fixes over patient political process.[29] Furthermore, the sense of moral certainty accompanying the application of force encourages the conceit that America is only capable of wielding a righteous sword against those who must, by default, be evil. This sustains the faith among policymakers that force is not only necessary but will also prove effective. As a result, over-confidence and wishful thinking pervade strategic calculations – both critical ingredients driving vicarious assumptions that minimalist military action will prove sufficient.

Beyond the policy world, but intricately wound up with it, these patterns are all reflected in the popular and academic historiography of American war. For instance, fashionable 'stab in the back' myths, supported by sympathetic scholarly analyses, argue the military essentially 'won' in Vietnam and Iraq and that it was, in fact, the politicians who lost those wars through their misguided decisions.[30] In this way, even cases of apparent military failure can be rescued through such revisionist 'if only' arguments – a common technique used to justify persisting with counterproductive methods. In this telling, past failure was not due to the use of inappropriate methods but because of their incorrect application. Military voices in particular have been guilty of retrospectively arguing that poor outcomes resulted from excessive political interference. Such retrospective blame games are already underway in relation to the Afghanistan War, the results of which could have important effects on future strategic decision-making.[31]

★ ★ ★

Even if the application of knee-jerk minimalist force might assuage security anxieties, and however much militaristic moralism might favour shortcut approaches, these things alone are not sufficient to account for the contemporary dominance of vicarious warfare. In itself, a militarily activist foreign policy agenda does not prescribe any one particular mode of warfare: indeed, large-scale wars, complex counterinsurgency campaigns, discrete interventions, coercive bombing and covert paramilitary missions have all been put to work in preserving the *Pax Americana*. Yet the argument here is that a series of emerging and interconnected trends and developments – primarily in military, socio-cultural, political and strategic spheres – pertaining to the modern American polity have increasingly converged to make vicarious warfare an especially attractive proposition to contemporary US leaders pursuing primacy.

Wary warriors? Risk and the modern American military

The American military, while confident in its abilities, is often the least militaristic of all social actors insofar as it tends to display a cautious and conservative attitude toward decisions to go to war, mindful of the sacrifices it entails and the unpredictability of military events. All officers who have read their compulsory Clausewitz will be reminded of this even if it wasn't already obvious to them through experience.[32] Proverbially, generals favour resourcing operations with as many troops and as much equipment as possible. Assuming that the military will always overestimate necessary requirements, this in itself can push politicians to search for smaller-scale options or vicarious alternatives, thus evading lengthy and fraught negotiations that can attract unwelcome public controversy.

Once operations are launched, the military is famed for its warrior ethos and 'can do' spirit in ruthlessly pursuing objectives. At the tactical level, its ability to accept risk and sustain momentum in the face of mounting costs essentially defines its institutional identity, less thanks to a bloodthirsty appetite for heroic sacrifice but more a commendable professional and patriotic commitment to complete the mission and protect the nation.

Yet, over recent decades, some commentators have identified a growing culture of risk-aversion, especially within senior command echelons.[33] Barno and Bensahel, for instance, note 'a widespread culture of near-total risk aversion' in the Army, whereby 'leaders at all levels are held to impossible standards in a misguided, centralized attempt to limit every imaginable accident or error, whether on duty or off.'[34] This has fostered a growing enthusiasm for vicarious approaches in prosecuting war, in particular those centred around force protection and distance warfare.[35] Famously, the chief mission of American troops arriving in Kosovo after the 1999 war was to protect the force. Although less apparent later in Afghanistan and Iraq, such concerns continue to influence military behaviour (as we explore further in Chapter 7). Again, the causes of this are complex. Some refer primarily to external politically determined factors such as trends in military downsizing and professionalization, which means soldiers can no longer be treated as cannon fodder (as was purportedly the case with mass conscript armies), and are instead prized as expensive and rare skilled assets.[36] Others highlight widespread societal expectations of bloodless victory magnified by the intense media gaze accompanying modern war or political pressures to minimize casualties emanating from civilian superiors.[37] But developments within the military establishment itself also help to explain these patterns.

Commentators have pointed to emerging internal institutional processes that have resulted in a modern corporatized, bureaucratic and conformist organizational American military culture that values efficiency above all else.[38] Careerist officers and planners, looking out for their own interests, are incentivized to offer palatable advice to political leaders or conduct campaigns in ways that tick boxes in managerial terms but that have little relationship to strategic requirements. In Iraq, the unwritten expectation was that commanders should conduct at least one major offensive during their tour, ideally incurring minimal casualties. Brooks laments the military's 'zero-defect culture' which discourages risk-taking,[39] and Ricks has described an organization in which 'success goes unrewarded, and everything but the most extreme failure goes unpunished, creating a perverse incentive system that drives leaders toward a risk-averse middle where they are more likely to find stalemate than victory.'[40] To the bureaucrats and accountants in the Pentagon, soldiers represent millions of dollars of investment, and high-tech weapons systems are at once incredibly lethal but also fragile and vulnerable to low-cost offsetting tactics. In short, valuable personnel and equipment must be preserved, protected and employed selectively. Institutional or service biases may also argue against action in certain scenarios in order to preserve readiness for future large-scale conventional war that they view as their core mission – a form of hedging or delaying tactic that again might cause decision-makers to look for options beyond the military.

At the operational level, the so-called 'lawyering of war',[41] whereby command decisions are everywhere accompanied by legal opinion, has led to caution, hedging and avoidance of unnecessary hazards. This has also encouraged micromanagement by commanders concerned that they will be held liable for the actions of their troops that might later be judged unlawful.[42] Officers may come to believe that such dilemmas can be essentially bypassed if missions are delegated to other external actors. This way of thinking can trickle down to affect behaviour and decision-making within the rank and file. There is little evidence of any serious lack of 'warrior spirit' or bravery among ordinary troops, arguably apparent in a generalized resistance to technological automation and a disdain for the outsourcing of core combat roles. However, command reticence and legal concerns contribute to a general culture of risk-aversion that can spread throughout the force in a self-perpetuating manner. Moreover, some fear that the widespread adoption of vicarious methods over recent years – with many units being tasked with 'advise and assist' missions – may be diminishing the military's aptitude for combat missions and commanders' confidence in making tough decisions in the heat of battle.

Perhaps due to a confluence of these various factors, some point as evidence to the notion that bin Laden's escape in 2001 at Tora Bora may have resulted from General Franks' risk-aversion and desire to avoid taking casualties.[43] Others argue that a major reason for the deterioration of the security situation in post-war Iraq after 2003 resulted from the decision of military commanders to retreat into large bases while seeking to hurriedly hand over responsibility for security operations to unprepared Iraqi forces. All these developments in the military sphere are partial, and sometimes belied by events that suggest conclusions in the opposite direction. Some of the reporting is anecdotal in nature, and greater research into these issues is required. The evolution of these trends will no doubt also depend on how the strategic context evolves. But we should not overlook, perhaps contrary to expectations, the extent to which the shift toward vicarious warfare is being driven in part by developments internal to the modern American military and wider defence establishment. And all militaries reflect the society of which they are part; far-reaching changes in American society are an important part of the story that can help us further uncover the factors and conditions driving contemporary military dynamics.

Look, but don't touch: American society and war

Scholars have described fundamental shifts in social attitudes towards the practice of war. Indeed, in the 1990s it became axiomatic to claim that we live in a 'post-heroic' or 'post-military' era characterized by a decline of warrior culture in the West.[44] Many factors have been identified as contributing to these developments. Central to most accounts is the popular reaction to the huge death tolls in two world wars during the first half of the 20th century and the possibility of the end of humanity in a nuclear third. Modern war in many people's minds had simply become too costly to contemplate.

But wider societal changes were also said to have played a role. It was suggested that advances in medical science led to declining fatalism or that smaller families meant deaths in war had come to be viewed less as a virtuous sacrifice and more as an irreplaceable loss.[45] Scholars have argued that the rise of aggressive asocial individualism and transnational social movements have eroded state authority and with it the idea that governments can demand sacrifices from its citizens, especially in wars that are increasingly fought not for territorial nation-state defence but to tackle distant and amorphous risks.[46] Meanwhile, rising material prosperity meant war came to be seen as something that threatens citizens' enjoyment of the 'good life' or disrupts vital trade flows.[47] With the emergence of new forms of media, war could be a cause of unwelcome moral discomfort for armchair audiences.[48] Furthermore, an instinctive revulsion toward the immediate horrors of war conveyed through graphic news reports has, according to some, tended to obscure more than clarify, thus largely precluding comprehension of what political logic might exist: war is thus increasingly understood by many as a pointless, unconditional evil.[49]

These ideas have deep roots in liberal thought and are embodied in the many modern organizations and institutions explicitly dedicated to limiting the occurrence and human costs of war.[50] Widespread societal sentiments along these lines, or even simply the assumption that they exist, can place significant pressures on those responsible for directing the nation's wars to seek ways to limit their duration or the sacrifices required.

Politicians have developed a particular anxiety about casualties – a term that has increasingly expanded to embrace not only casualties within the armed forces, but also civilians and even enemy forces. In America this has been magnified by the widespread popular conception, reinforced by a noted academic study on the subject, that rising casualties – powerfully conveyed through images of 'body bags' displayed directly on American citizens' new televisions – was a major cause for the failure in Vietnam.[51] The determinants of public casualty sensitivity are contested, but research suggests that citizens are actually 'pretty prudent' regarding such matters, with opinion shaped not simply by absolute numbers but by other contextualizing factors such as the extent to which vital interests are engaged, the nature and clarity of principal objectives or the chances of success.[52]

Regardless, the strong perception among policymakers that the public *is* casualty-averse strongly influences decision-making.[53] Moreover, the apparent bloodless prosecution of some recent military campaigns, such as Kosovo in 1999 or Libya in 2011, has generated unrealistic expectations among the public that relatively surgical methods of applying force exist.[54] When events do not proceed according to this script, anger and opposition is likely to mount, especially given that, in general, evidence suggests Americans favour less risky military missions such as air strikes over deploying ground troops.[55] Thus, approaches that either minimize American casualties or keep operations out of the media limelight have become increasingly attractive to policymakers.

There is still a great deal of truth to these observations, but much of the literature on 'post-military society' appeared before the 9/11 attacks, and developments since then suggest the relationship of American society to war has become more ambivalent and problematic. Even if the public is unwilling to accept the need for personal sacrifice and is sensitive to any unnecessary or wasteful loss of life in futile adventures, few Americans are instinctively anti-war. The huge budgetary investments in the nation's defence, which in recent years reached around US$700 billion, is testament to a basic acceptance of the necessity for maintaining a powerful military, which remains one of the most trusted public institutions in the country.[56] This is not to deny the serious opposition that can arise in relation to certain episodes, but such protests rarely result in meaningful political effects – the large demonstrations prior to the 2003 Iraq War were given little attention in the media and essentially ignored by politicians.[57]

The changes go deeper than this, however. The nature of modern war, or at least its mediatized representation, has permitted a societal reconsideration of the prevailing assumption of war as necessarily evil. The fetishization and stage-managed presentation of 'smart bombs' and 'surgical strikes' – 'which ostentatiously foregrounds the weapons themselves while mystifying their more pernicious effects' – sustains the chimera of perfectly discriminate weapons, lends an aura of moral righteousness to American force and encourages popular triumphalism.[58] The appearance of high-tech and 'humane' campaigns, seen as forms of entertainment and spectacle rather than grave national undertakings, has meant war has 'regained an aesthetic respectability' within a public eager to consume tales of American military might or the audacious exploits of special forces.[59] This is far removed from the kind of generalized revulsion regarding war that had long characterized public attitudes since the early 20th century.

Furthermore, as Hanson has observed, there is huge popular enthusiasm in America for all things military: documentaries, blockbuster movies, re-enactment events, military history and video games. Part of this, he suggests, is driven by a desire to learn about largely lost notions of honour and sacrifice, but may also express 'an innate need to experience, violence, if only vicariously.'[60] There may be even more insidious aspects to the vicarious military entertainment industry. For instance, Mantello argues that the proliferation of special forces first-person shooter video games – often produced in close collaboration with the Pentagon and defence contractors – intentionally propagates sanitized images of modern battlefields and serves to 'validate covert military force as a legitimate tool of foreign policy.'[61] Tellingly, this 'new American militarism' rarely converts into sustained or serious interest in or critical engagement with ongoing wars.[62]

Compounding these developments, the end of the draft and creation of the professional All-Volunteer Force (AVF) in the 1970s means that only a tiny proportion – less than 1 per cent – of Americans serve. Few citizens have connections with the armed forces or have any meaningful military experience. This can exacerbate misunderstandings.[63] As a result it is often claimed that a large 'gap' has opened up between soldier and citizen, between 'war and the mall'.[64] The old citizen-soldier model has, according to Bacevich, given way to the division of society into two distinct camps: on the one hand, civilians with little understanding of military affairs and largely unaffected by war, and on the other, a small minority, the permanent warrior caste, who are sent to fight the nation's wars.[65] Perhaps in a form of collective guilt associated with this situation, the public has developed an almost unconscious, reflexive and uncritical adoration for the military, with those who serve universally seen as heroes and owed an immense debt of gratitude.[66] Golby and Feaver describe American citizens' relationship with the military as 'high regard at high remove ... an institution most Americans do not want to be a part of but hold in high esteem, from a distance.'[67] The righteousness of American military force is taken for granted by much of the public, and this contributes to an unquestioning attitude concerning the presumed necessity and effective conduct of most military operations. This, in turn, opens up the political space for politicians to use force as a ready instrument for projecting power, and for the country at large, it 'serves as a convenient device for dodging responsibility.'[68]

Yet, the causation increasingly works the other way around: the reliance on secretive and low-profile vicarious methods makes it even less likely that an already largely disinterested public will seek to seriously probe the specifics of military operations or compel their representatives to do so. Instead, to the extent that the public is even aware such operations are taking place, they have come to be seen as routine and expected aspects of US foreign activity. If anything, the most likely public response is enthusiastic applause when it is announced the next 'high-level terrorist' has been 'taken out' by a distant drone strike, ignoring the hundreds of other militants being slain beyond the daily news cycle. The sacrifices of American proxies might be faintly appreciated but barely lamented. Likewise, the deaths of military contractors receive little attention, and the AVF has the effect of insulating the political establishment from the more immediate consequences of its global military operations.[69] Many citizens are probably vaguely aware such fighting is taking place, but it is largely out of sight and thus out of mind.[70] This form of remote war 'engenders complacency and forgetfulness' and the low immediate cost in blood and taxes 'appeases an indifferent electorate'.[71]

Funded by debt, the costs, at least in the short term, appear negligible and the gains seem worthwhile.[72] Bacevich notes how Americans were willing to indulge the Obama administration's appetite for small-scale interventions, 'albeit more out of indifference or inattention than genuine enthusiasm.'[73] The furore produced over events such as the deaths of special forces soldiers during a 2017 raid in Niger only underscore these patterns. Congressional rage was more a function of surprise at learning that such military operations were taking place as opposed to concerns regarding the specifics of the case. Representatives understand that continuing military operations, especially those conducted against terrorists, have broad public support, and as a result feel little compulsion to probe the details or seriously educate themselves on national security issues. They are therefore, on the whole, not well placed to provide the crucial oversight role allotted to them. One former senator accused Congress of essentially abdicating its role in restraining executive adventurism, specifically referring to the dangers inherent in vicarious modes of warfare whereby average Americans are removed from 'the consequences and even the direct knowledge of military actions that a president might undertake at his or her sole discretion.'[74] This is a continuation of trends we witnessed in our earlier discussion of Cold War dynamics – modern means have only reinforced the democratic deficit associated with subtle and secretive low-level warfare.

In sum, not only are the American people largely unaffected by war in their day-to-day lives, but we can also observe a form of superficial and romanticized vicarious relish in the military operations prosecuted in their name. This exists alongside public political and moral disengagement characterized by widespread apathy and ignorance regarding the conduct or consequences of the nation's wars. This is all the more alarming given America's unceasing interventionism. The public continue to elect leaders who have overseen disastrous military adventures, and take immense pride in the military personnel overseeing the relentless elimination of countless militants in distant theatres, while cheering those impressive operations that politicians choose to let them know about. The prosecution of sustained, minimalist, low-exposure operations according to the vicarious warfare model allows the American people to place themselves at a remove from the difficult decisions that, in a democracy, should accompany the use of force. Indeed, the framers of the US constitution were insistent about the need to ensure democratic control over the decision to use force abroad. The distancing of society from war has the effect of diluting the people's responsibility for the effects of American military behaviour. This, in turn, degrades the quality and seriousness of democratic debate on American war, with potentially detrimental consequences for strategic practice.

Lost in translation: the role of the media

It might be thought that the modern 24/7 mass media, with its real-time reporting from contemporary battlefields, would act as a powerful force pushing back against such apathy and democratic disengagement. But the press has struggled to fulfil its fourth amendment function in this area, and media dynamics can actually be said to have exacerbated problems in certain respects.[75] To the extent that the media reflects public attitudes, this might be expected – consistent with the discussion earlier, there will likely be a strong demand for feel-good war stories and a general disregard for critical commentary. In fact, there is a serious dearth of high-quality commentary on foreign affairs and war in the mainstream American press. This is notwithstanding the impressive in-depth reporting conducted by journalists from organizations such as Public Broadcasting Service (PBS), *The New York Times* and *The Washington Post*, or more specialized organizations such as the Bureau of Investigative Journalism, Bellingcat, The Intercept and Airwars. But such reporting tends to be read or appreciated by small minorities who already care about such issues, while the mass of the public seem more preoccupied with sports and entertainment news, or Trump's latest tweet (admittedly sometimes related to the conduct of his vicarious wars).

And despite some journalists' brave efforts, drone wars or special forces operations are just incredibly difficult to report on, especially in a manner that might capture important broader issues.[76] These methods are not only secretive by design, but fleeting in their conduct: by default, unless granted exclusive (probably carefully managed) access, reporters are unlikely to be present 'in the moment'. Reports thus often have a second-hand, after-the-event feel, and this time lag has the almost inevitable effect of dampening the apparent importance or impact of the events reported. It is also difficult for the media to convey in a short dispatch how high-profile, discrete missile strikes or specific raids are, in fact, part of expansive ongoing global programmes. Coker observes how the rapidity of modern news broadcasts means 'fragments give way to fragments in no particular order and which do not lend themselves as a result to any overarching narrative.'[77]

Similarly, given the modern appetite for sound bites or spectacular stories, it is difficult to capture any sense of the amorphous nature of the often-harmful longer-term effects resulting from such practices. The allure of vicarious warfare for policymakers in terms of its direct 'positive' results (the death of a militant, the destruction of enemy bases) is likewise reflected in the ease with which those effects are captured in media representations. The immediate, seemingly effective outcome, is the news, while the longer-term consequences receive little to no consideration, at least beyond specialist outlets. Similarly, as Demmers and Gould explain, most military operations are largely hidden from public view, but when they do 'incidentally appear on our screens, the shadowy mix of alliances and actors involved makes it hard to trace lines of responsibility and underlying power constellations … larger audiences are (effectively) confused into indifference.'[78]

Even seemingly explosive exposés about ongoing wars, such as the release of the so-called 'Afghanistan Papers' in December 2019 by *The Washington Post*, barely registered on the media radar.[79] Despite controversial claims of 'massive institutional deceit'[80] – whereby officials had purportedly misled the public by making exaggerated claims of progress and had disingenuously suggested the war was winnable – the story revealed more about the lack of public engagement with the war as opposed to evidence of any grand cover-up. If anything, it showed that officials had been deceiving themselves as much as the American public, as analysts had been pointing out for some time.[81] In fact, much of the information had already informed publicly available reports,[82] and it was no great secret that the war in Afghanistan was a steadily failing enterprise. The muted public response was largely a function of the war's vicarious prosecution. Porter neatly explains the dynamics at play here:

> The state insulated its populace from [the war]: waging it with professional soldiers and private contractors rather than with citizen-soldiers or the draft, funding it not directly through taxation but through borrowing, and urging voters to keep shopping rather than engage. People could live with lies, in other words, because the impression grew that combat operations, however limited in their effectiveness, can affordably go on and on. Ultimately, most believed it didn't matter. They assumed they would be spared war's consequences.[83]

It is therefore of little surprise that the mainstream media gave such short shrift to the story. Unlike the scandalous Pentagon Papers from the Vietnam era, it was soon forgotten by most Americans and promptly eclipsed in the news cycle by a new case of executive adventurism. On 3 January 2020, Trump proudly announced the successful execution of a 'flawless precision strike that killed the number-one terrorist anywhere in the world, [Iranian General] Qasem Soleimani.'[84] Indeed, reflecting Trump's triumphalism, studies suggest that public views are strongly shaped by elite cues as transmitted through the media, thus the partial and distorted representations to which the American public has access only serve to exacerbate the problems of superficial engagement, apathy and unaccountability. Command of the 'bully pulpit' grants the executive significant power to shape public opinion while public militarism, rally effects, congressional lassitude and minimal citizen mobilization grants it a head start in sustaining popular support for military operations.[85]

But this power is not unlimited. Presidents may only have a limited window within which to maintain control over the framing of events.[86] This is even more likely in an age of real-time reporting, social media, cynical audiences and a security landscape characterized principally by wars of choice, or, as Dandeker puts it, *contested* choice'.[87] The uncertain nature of both threats and objectives combined with instant media responses can disproportionately magnify even marginal setbacks that might in other contexts be judged acceptable, and makes it difficult to justify the extra effort or sacrifice required. Wars are inherently unpredictable, and political leaders can see support rapidly drain away as casualties mount, campaigns begin to falter, elite consensus frays and critical voices in the mainstream media become more vocal. Beholden to electoral timetables and facing demands for the immediate satisfaction of citizens' expectations, politicians in advanced democracies are notably sensitive to the political implications of war.[88] Securing the legitimacy necessary to persist in high-profile, large and lengthy military commitments can be deeply problematic. These difficulties all played out at the height of the protracted conflicts in Iraq and Afghanistan. Policymakers struggled in vain to craft persuasive narratives that might sustain popular support.

In search of solutions

Capturing many of these contemporary concerns and dilemmas, in the mid-2000s General Sir Rupert Smith put forward the influential thesis that we had entered into an age of 'war amongst the people' fought increasingly within civil society, involving non-state actors as key belligerents, and crucially influenced by an ever-present mass media.[89] These wars rarely had clear end-states and as a result, tended to be 'timeless'. Such descriptions resonated with American soldiers tasked with eliminating countless bands of militants, and with politicians attemping to 'sell' never-ending missions to sceptical domestic audiences. Moreover, plentiful evidence to support Smith's contention that Western militaries were failing to sufficiently transform themselves to fight such wars was provided through subsequent experience. Some level of expedient adaptation did take place. However, with the benefit of hindsight the results look less positive, as suggested by the subsequent rise of Islamic State, significant Taliban gains in Afghanistan and metastasizing militancy elsewhere.

If there were already many in the American defence and security establishment who believed it was advisable to steer clear of such messy irregular conflicts, unfolding events only bolstered their cause. Yet irregular fighters, radical jihadists and other rogue actors continued to target American interests. So how might such threats be confronted without dragging America into more protracted wars among the people? Smith employed the metaphor of modern wars being fought as if taking place in a theatre, with key actors and audiences all mixed up, both on and off the stage. If this was the case, then perhaps the solution was to limit the intensity of the action, delegate the acting to less prominent understudies, restrict everyone else to 'the gods' and dim the lights so the audience can barely make out what is taking place. Evolving methods of vicarious warfare offered a way for American soldiers to avoid direct entanglement with the people while keeping the prosecution of campaigns at or just below the threshold of audience attention and scrutiny. This can be understood as an attempt to invert Smith's dictum and to fight what we might describe as war *without* the people.

In this light, advanced weapons systems, covert instruments and opportunities afforded by the expanding market in private military services all appear to provide ready-made means for handling a range of threats and challenges with minimal public exposure. Responsibility for fighting war is increasingly delegated to those explicitly designed to take considerable risks (special forces), those whom the public is relatively ambivalent about sending into harm's way (private contractors, surrogates) or those who seemingly have the capacity to sweep risk under the carpet (CIA). Indeed, the very existence of such instruments is itself a factor tempting policymakers to engage in vicarious warfare. The possibilities inherent in these operational methods, practices and approaches distort policymakers' perceptions concerning the expected costs of using force, and lowers the bar in terms of decisions on intervention.

Meanwhile, the cost of military operations for foreign populations in terms of civilian deaths and shattered livelihoods – which might generate public unease if the scale was known – is essentially bowdlerized and the 'humane' nature of interventions simultaneously hyped in the official telling. This can lead to harmful cycles whereby an inflated public expectation of bloodless warfare is managed politically by suppressing data or withholding relevant information, such as accurate civilian casualty figures.[90] This links to Levite and Shimshoni's argument regarding how policymakers 'endeavour to "de-societize", or detach, their own society from a conflict ... as a means either of enabling the state to pursue the conflict without engendering internal resistance.'[91] Walt details how these practices not only shield policymakers from unwelcome media attention, but also dangerously obscure the longer-term security costs resulting from their use: 'Americans will underestimate the costs of US foreign policy when they are unaware of what the government is doing. If Americans do not know the full extent of US drone strikes and Special Forces operations, for example, they will not understand why some victims of these attacks are angry and eager to retaliate.'[92]

★ ★ ★

In coping with the contemporary dilemmas of maintaining the *Pax Americana*, pursuing the nation's ideological mission and addressing global threats, US leaders inevitably look for ways to keep the necessary measures economically affordable, socially acceptable, legally permissible and politically viable. There is a balance to be struck between doing too much or too little. One extreme is deemed too costly, leading to excessive risk and unintended consequences; the other, inaction, as explained earlier, is politically risky. Policymakers have thus sought to walk the line between 'wanting to be seen by their voters to be doing something' while at the same time being 'unwilling to incur much cost.'[93]

The prospect of transcending many of the usual costs and risks of war becomes the modern philosopher's stone. It is a quest sustained by a messianic faith in the opportunities provided by new technologies, reinforced by the flattering lessons of earlier military operations that appear to fit the vicarious mould, and exacerbated by old-fashioned hubris and wishful thinking. Vicarious warfare thus encompasses a curious and dangerous mix whereby risk-aversion coexists, somewhat schizophrenically, with over-confidence regarding what force can achieve. This breeds intense military activism but with limited or inappropriate means and inadequate resolve in pursuit of uncertain objectives – a form of politically reckless yet operationally timid interventionism. Decision-makers come to believe that force can be applied economically, at arm's length, and in discrete, limited and controllable ways, evading various risks and restraints. Modern American vicarious warfare can be understood as the operational manifestation of seeking to fight war without the people, without major political, economic or legal consequence, and on an indefinite basis. As the following chapters demonstrate, it is also, in many respects, a dangerous mirage.

6

Emergence

The 1990s were supposed to usher in a new world order and more peaceful modes of transformation in international politics. Freed from the constraints of Cold War confrontation, many strategists predicted retrenchment in US global strategic commitments. However, these hopes ran headlong into the so-called 'new wars' of the 1990s, such as those in parts of Africa and the Balkans. This was not part of the script. To analysts who had for decades focused their attention on nuclear deterrence or the prospect of major war against the Soviet Union, these conflicts seemed to appear out of nowhere. That they were often continuations of Cold War proxy wars or sparked precisely due to the collapse of long-standing structures was largely irrelevant to a public increasingly exposed to images of human suffering in faraway places. Calls for policymakers to 'do something' gathered momentum.

Leaders at the Pentagon were generally opposed to involvement in low-intensity conflicts. After all, in 1991 the military had just demonstrated its prowess in high-end conventional war, thinking that all wars would have that particular shape. Meanwhile, the George H.W. Bush administration, lacking the guiding star of combating communism, steered a cautious path through this new and unfamiliar post-Cold War landscape. Colin Powell, as Chairman of the Joint Chiefs of Staff, was in the process of doubling-down on Weinberger's earlier restrictive doctrine, now adding the criteria of overwhelming force and clear exit strategies to the list of fundamental principles that would guide the use of military force. In 1991 and 1992, Powell and the Joint Chiefs were actively advising against military involvement in peripheral conflicts such as Somalia or Bosnia.[1]

Yet political elites did not necessarily see things this way. The sense of moral mission that had motivated America's confrontation with the Soviet Union was now, in victory, strengthened by a renewed confidence that its liberal republican system represented the world's future, if in fact the end of history had not already arrived.[2] This was joined by the kind of self-assurance that came with its status as the world's sole superpower, firmly underpinned by its conventional military dominance, as recently displayed during the Gulf War.[3] Some commentators urged policymakers to take advantage of this 'unipolar moment' given that the US could now more safely intervene where it wished with little serious risk of sparking a major inter-state war.[4] Great power politics seemed a thing of the past and the idea emerged among foreign policy elites of America as the 'indispensable nation' with a unique responsibility for tackling dangers around the world. Thus, not content to simply defend the new status quo, policymakers set out to right the world's wrongs. As democratic crusades go, this was a distinctly cautious and half-hearted one – in fact, Clinton's 1995 *National Security Strategy* explicitly asserted that it was *not* a crusade[5] – but there was no mistaking the enthusiasms animating it. And saving troubled nations from themselves necessarily implied forms of US intervention, even possibly involving military force.

Vicarious warfare appeared to provide strategists with the means to operationalize America's activist foreign policy. The marginal nature of the interests at stake more or less precluded taking great risks or committing large forces. Moreover, there was a strong desire to fight in a surgical and clean manner if possible, given the primarily humanitarian ends in view. The US had emerged from the Cold War with a suite of rapidly evolving stand-off precision weapons technologies and burgeoning special forces: in theory these constituted military scalpels that could be employed to excise foreign tumours with minimal mess. The likely targets were the ragtag rebels and undisciplined militants armed with outdated weapons and lacking serious training but capable of mass atrocity. The mere presence of advanced arms should, it was thought, be sufficient to discipline deviant warlords or promptly whip troublesome 'spoilers' into line.

Such expectations suffered major setbacks in practice. The 1990s would be a period of painful experimentation and hard lessons; unfortunately not always the right lessons. The experience in Somalia was an early especially grim chapter in this journey. But far from discouraging movement toward a vicarious future, the episode actually caused strategists to redouble efforts in this sphere. It is thus worth reflecting on this episode in detail.

Mogadishu blues

The faith policymakers had come to place in its special forces 'super-soldiers' was revealed in 1992 through America's first post-Cold War steps into Somalia.[6] In fact, many of the first operators swam in: Navy Seals were tasked with arduous underwater hydrographic reconnaissance missions around Mogadishu harbour, only to be greeted by the press as they emerged onto the beaches. This advanced guard prepared the ground for the now anti-climactic uncontested amphibious 'raid' by Marine contingents of the Unified Task Force coming ashore as part of the US-led *Operation Restore Hope*, a major humanitarian mission.[7]

Recent research suggests intervention in Somalia was actually motivated by quite pragmatic rationales, broadly in line with Powell's principles, envisioning a rapid forceful intervention of only a few weeks' length before handing over to the United Nations (UN).[8] Regardless, American forces remained in the country, and over the following months the operation was successful in protecting UN aid deliveries, paving the way for the UN Operation in Somalia (UNOSOM) II in May 1993.[9] This UN-led mission, operating under a more robust enforcement mandate, comprised thousands of heavily armoured international troops, supported by a sizeable US contingent including a special forces headquarters. Although earlier operations had managed to suppress much of the inter-clan fighting hindering the relief effort, recalcitrant Somali warlords, in particular General Aidid, persisted in attacks against the international mission.

As violent confrontations escalated through the summer of 1993, requiring at times the use of American AC-130 air support, pressure mounted on the US to assist in efforts to capture Aidid and his top lieutenants. Policymakers confidently believed they possessed the necessary instrument to achieve this. Secretary of Defense Les Aspin deployed Joint Special Operations Task Force Ranger to this end but, wanting to keep the mission low profile, he refused requests from the commander of US forces in Somalia for additional armour.[10] The first series of six raids as part of *Operation Gothic Serpent* were tactical successes, but they encouraged overconfidence and allowed Aidid's forces to learn American tactics. Launched on 3 October, the tragic seventh mission, immortalized as the 'Black Hawk Down' episode, turned into an all-night running battle after two helicopters were shot down by rocket-propelled grenade (RPG) fire. Eighteen Americans were killed, and one soldier's mutilated corpse was dragged through the streets of Mogadishu in front of rolling TV cameras.

Recalling Reagan's ill-fated operation in Lebanon, *Gothic Serpent* and the dramatic Battle of Mogadishu was a painful warning of the costly mission creep that can result from actions conceived as quick-fix interventions. It also indicated, as had the 1980 Iranian Eagle Claw disaster, that it can be dangerous to treat special operations as straightforward and independent silver bullet solutions: even minor mishaps can have disproportionate strategic consequences. This stands in contrast to their more effective use as a complement to larger operations, such as in the context of the initial

Restore Hope mission (or on the margins of *Desert Storm* two years earlier and *Operation Uphold Democracy* in Haiti a year later). As it happened, what should have been a routine raid became a defining event that would fundamentally shape US foreign policy during the Clinton years and beyond, while also apparently emboldening Osama bin Laden to confront a seemingly irresolute United States more directly.[11] The main effect of the debacle came at the political level, reflected in a general reluctance to cross the so-called 'Mogadishu line', which meant not allowing troops to be dragged into combat situations in the context of multinational peace enforcement operations.[12] This contributed to America's inaction as the genocide unfolded in Rwanda.[13] But it did not signal a complete rejection of military interventionism altogether, only the manner and terms of its conduct. In strategic and operational terms, the effect was to induce greater caution but also to push policymakers to demand and develop ever more vicarious solutions.

With respect to the development of special forces, far from discouraging further investment, the response was quite the reverse. *Gothic Serpent* was increasingly viewed as a tactical success: it had, in fact, achieved a number of its objectives, and the casualties from the battle had been kept low, given the circumstances.[14] Indeed, the main narrative to emerge related to the incredible heroism and professionalism of the troops.[15] Within the special operations community, Somalia was a major milestone, catalysing important tactical reforms. This meant that after 9/11 they would be better prepared to handle the ferocious tempo of missions asked of them, many of which were led by veterans of Task Force Ranger. Meanwhile, during the 1990s, special forces honed their skills conducting a dizzying range of tasks including special reconnaissance, security force assistance and non-combatant extraction.[16] But Mogadishu had highlighted the way that even minimalist combat operations could backfire if the public, often finding out about them for the first time, determine they are being used to pursue unclear objectives for interests perceived as being far from vital – in particular, those that did not pass Clinton's so-called 'mother test'. This hesitancy extended even to terrorism: within the Pentagon there was a 'reluctance to even discuss proactive measures associated with countering the terrorist threat through SOF [Special Operations Forces] operations.'[17]

Thus, despite a general operational uptick, special forces were not called on to undertake any missions of a similar scale or intensity similar to Mogadishu – policymakers were unwilling to seriously risk such precious assets. After Somalia there was a strong inclination to rely on airpower and long-range cruise missile strikes, sometimes complemented by local surrogate ground forces, thus avoiding large US troop deployments in messy peace operations. As Bacevich has observed, through the remainder of the 1990s, America 'waged war on the cheap and spared nothing in its efforts to avoid American casualties'.[18]

Keeping the activist flame alive

Since before the end of the Cold War, a new crop of airpower visionaries, centred around the Air Force's John Warden and John Boyd, had begun to develop far-reaching claims regarding the strategic potential of their speciality. The central message was that airpower was evolving to become the pre-eminent instrument of modern war, even to the extent that if employed correctly, it could win wars independently – a dream that had animated airpower thinkers since its inception, just as it had animated Mahanian navalists before them.[19]

However, this new generation offered approaches far more appealing than the indiscriminate strategic ('morale' or 'city') bombing from earlier periods. After rapidly achieving air superiority, American bombers equipped with precision-guided munitions would be able to target critical enemy nodes or 'centres of gravity' (what critics had earlier derisively termed 'panacea targets'),[20] conveniently organized into five concentric rings, from the most important central leadership ring, through industry, infrastructure, populace and finally, enemy forces. Conceiving the enemy as an interlocking system in this way meant that its parts could be disaggregated and struck simultaneously in a 'parallel' campaign, leading to overall 'paralysis'. Even better, a decapitation strike directly against the primary leadership ring may make further fighting unnecessary and limit civilian casualties: the ultimate shortcut solution.

Such ideas fed directly into planning for the Gulf War, and some even claimed afterwards that the air campaign had essentially been decided before the ground invasion began.[21] Studies soon revealed that this was a misleading conclusion to draw.[22] In fact, Clausewitz, almost two centuries earlier, and well before airpower was a realistic proposition, had expressed deep scepticism regarding 'the sophisticated theory that supposes it possible for a particularly ingenious method of inflicting minor direct damage on the enemy … [or through] limited but skilfully applied blows [to cause] such paralysis of the enemy's forces and control of his will-power as to constitute a significant shortcut to victory.'[23]

But the potent potential of low casualty 'airpower alone' wars was a beguiling prospect to politicians seeking ways to avoid protracted and costly ground commitments, especially in facing the new wars of the 1990s. These theories had not been geared toward scenarios involving civil war or humanitarian intervention, but airpower enthusiasts were quick to confirm their ready transferability. Thus, their ideas continued to influence practice, if not always in the way that Warden and his disciples had intended.[24] Pape suggested that after the Gulf War, 'increasingly the first question in debates over American intervention is becoming, Can air power alone do the job?'[25] Ever since, it has remained the primary component of vicarious warfare, especially given advances in unmanned platforms and missile technologies, and even when used in conjunction with special forces ground elements or indigenous allies.

American airpower was on display in the skies over Bosnia in 1995 during the *Deliberate Force* bombing campaign that helped bring the conflict there to an end. This outcome certainly boosted the pretensions of the air lobby, especially as Warden's ideas had influenced its prosecution.[26] This ignored the extent to which other vital factors had forced the Serbs to finally take their seats around the negotiating table at Dayton, but airpower certainly seemed to offer a vicarious antidote for addressing public discomfort over the use of force. The almost daily bombings conducted against Iraq in the late 1990s after Saddam's expulsion of UN weapons inspectors in 1998 barely registered among domestic audiences, prompting one observer to designate the campaign as 'Operation Desert Yawn.'[27]

But this enthusiasm for 'distance warfare', as some referred to it at the time, shrouded underlying issues.[28] While tactically compelling and generally effective in addressing symptoms, bombs could do little to solve underlying political problems or push the internal dynamics of target countries in more benign directions. Worse, they might also actually undermine developments on the ground or cause new complications. The Kosovo conflict of 1999 was a crucial test in this respect, and as such, a pivotal event in the evolving story of contemporary vicarious warfare. Although it reinforced lingering concerns with this mode of fighting (not to mention others associated with multinational operations), at the same time it pointed to possible future solutions.

The reversal of Milošević's brutal campaign of ethnic cleansing against Kosovar Albanians was motivated primarily by moral outrage and enabled politically by ensuring rough conformity with a set of tightly defined justifying criteria.[29] One of those, responding to earlier anxieties, was that intervention should engage important national interests in some way. In this case, policymakers claimed that condition was satisfied given the historic significance of the Balkans as a flashpoint for wider conflict, its strategic position on the doorstep of Europe, and the fact that the crisis came to be seen as a major test of the continuing viability of the NATO alliance. Regardless, of greater consequence for subsequent practice was the way the conflict seemingly demonstrated that a solution to the problem of military feasibility and fickle public support could be found by utilizing an emerging array of advanced weapons systems and munitions fitted with the new GPS-guided Joint Direct Attack Munition (JDAM) upgrade that made 'smart' weapons out of ordinary 'dumb' ones.[30]

The commander of the Kosovo campaign, General Wesley Clark, implemented a coercive campaign according to the rationale – not dissimilar to that which had guided American bombing against Vietnam – that marginal applications of force through demonstrative bombing would rapidly compel Milošević to yield. As he described it, the bombing was a 'low-cost, low-risk statement of intent' as opposed to the traditional brute application of overwhelming force.[31] The recent prosecution of *Deliberate Force* also fed gratifying assumptions based on the misleading conclusion that airpower had proved singularly effective in Bosnia. This was an especially ripe causal fallacy because key administration officials, such as Madeleine Albright, had been closely involved in the earlier operation and given the obvious but probably strategically meaningless fact that both theatres were located near one another in the Balkans.[32] This represents another example of how misleading models and analogies serve to encourage future ill-considered applications of vicarious methods.

Ultimately, the alliance had to wait an agonizing 78 days for the bombing to have its effect after more than 30,000 sorties has struck targets in Belgrade and Serb forces in Kosovo itself. Serious campaign weaknesses, such as a number of costly targeting mistakes (largely a function of NATO aircraft flying at high altitudes to avoid losses from anti-aircraft fire) and difficulties faced in accurately striking hidden and dispersed Serb ground forces were subject to some specialized commentary, but the big stories were the operation's ultimate success and the fact that it was apparently achieved through 'airpower alone', with precisely zero NATO combat deaths.

This conclusion ignored other possibly crucial factors that caused Milošević to submit, not least Russia's withdrawal of diplomatic support for Belgrade and the threat of a NATO ground invasion. It also overlooked the contribution of ground-based operations by America's irregular allies in the Kosovo Liberation Army (KLA), especially toward the latter stages of the war. Given the KLA's far from pure credentials – in fact, they were a distinctly undemocratic and unsavoury group – America sought to keep that particular relationship clandestine by working through CIA channels. Yet, Byman and Waxman quote a US Army General who admitted that 'what you had, in effect, was the KLA acting as a surrogate ground force.'[33] This echoed the 'unintended synergies' created by the more conventional offensives of Bosnian and Croat armies in 1995 that put significant additional, possibly decisive, pressure on Serb defences.[34]

In Kosovo, default alignment with and empowerment of the KLA would cause serious complications for years after the end of the conflict. Nevertheless, such lessons were largely overlooked by officials searching for means of exerting influence on the ground in wars where regular American soldiers were kept on the sidelines. Or at least it did not prevent them from embracing similarly dubious irregular surrogates in Afghanistan two years later.

Commentators and academics were starting to try to make sense of these developments through the 1990s, and concepts emerged which captured important themes that still pertain today. In a defining work of the period, Ignatieff described how the Kosovo conflict heralded an age of 'virtual war'.[35] The 'virtual mobilization' of society for war, requiring only their 'virtual consent', seemed to describe the way societies had moved to the other end of the spectrum away from the tribal warrior societies of prehistory in terms of societal organization for war. Ignatieff was concerned that a society that could wage riskless war might be encouraged to pursue reckless foreign adventures.[36] At this time, to outside observers the most likely contexts for the application of cost-free interventionism were failing and conflict-affected 'weak states' in the developing world, where force would likely be used in support of humanitarian objectives. As we have seen, American responses in such environments would inevitably be wrapped up in all manner of political and operational limitations.

What most worried scholars was that the new technologies would be put to work in forcefully promoting, as Der Derain put it, a 'new ethical imperative for global democratic reform' as a mode of not only virtual but *virtuous* war.[37] This was certainly true to the extent that, as noted earlier, moralistic enthusiasm was a major motivating factor driving American military interventions. With the actual bloodshed, mostly of others, almost always hidden from view, the misleading popular understanding of war as hygienic might lead to a 'shadowing of reality' and, Der Derian claimed, diminished responsibility for it insofar as society might 'sleepwalk through the manifold travesties of war'.[38] And this was even before the age of the armed drone.

Indeed, these works and others certainly pointed to crucial issues that did not disappear after 9/11 but would re-emerge in different ways. They captured many of the core elements that would coalesce to fuel contemporary vicarious warfare, as well as the many dangers inherent in such developments. Still, Ignatieff, Der Derian and others cannot be expected to have foreseen the way these methods, combined with new technologies, might be unleashed with unprecedented militaristic zeal when directed toward addressing a different kind of strategic challenge

– this despite brief but shocking glimpses of the ongoing lethal game of cat and mouse playing out at this time between Al-Qaeda and the CIA.[39]

For much of the 1990s, counterterror efforts, in particular operations to track Osama bin Laden, had 'largely dropped into the black world of covert plans and operations'[40] and were primarily conceived within a law enforcement framework. By the late 1990s events were hotting up. In response to Al-Qaeda's 1998 embassy attacks in Kenya and Tanzania, President Clinton launched long-range cruise missile attacks against Al-Qaeda training camps in Afghanistan and a chemical plant in Sudan. Although almost hopeless in their immediate effects – the former derisively condemned as simply 'rearranging the sand'[41] – the strikes nevertheless pointed to the way such weapons might be used in a counterterror capacity. Key to these developments was the suite of military capabilities being developed under the new rubric of the 'revolution in military terms' (RMA) and then 'transformation'. While primarily designed with major inter-state conventional battles in mind, the transformation of American armed forces would, however, supply much of the material foundation for future vicarious warfare, such as drones and stand-off precision-strike capability. Also, transformation was geared toward enabling more modular small-unit operations and information integration, which, as Niva has shown, would be essential elements of the networked counterterror methodologies that matured under Joint Special Operations Command (JSOC) in the 2000s.[42]

Indeed emergent trends, catalysed by transformation, pointed toward future modes of war, even if they would not unfold in the strategic contexts imagined by its architects. The evolving arsenal of bloodless war would, of course, be greatly supplemented in subsequent years with ever more advanced precision munitions fitted to unmanned platforms. In fact, the signature weapon of the 9/11 wars, the Predator drone, saw its first operational deployment in the Balkans, where it was used to help track Yugoslav war criminals. Within just a few years it would be hunting a new kind of prey, by which time it would have the capability not only to loiter and look, but also to strike and kill.[43]

The drone would also later constitute a key instrument allowing policymakers to use force well away from the prying eyes of an ever-more intrusive mass media. But in the meantime, more primitive forms of 'media management' were employed to limit serious public opposition or excessive scrutiny – pre-arranged scripted briefings allowed officials to frame the narrative and highlight the sanitized nature of its operations that American citizens were increasingly coming to expect. This raised the possibility that wars could be fought with blanket media coverage but without raising serious public indignation, especially if casualties could be minimized.[44] Even at this stage, such developments prompted General Smith to observe how wars had 'become media events far away from any ongoing social reality'.[45]

There were critical voices at this time concerned about where all this was leading. Kagan, for instance, held that millenarians promising 'cheap, bloodless, and fast' warfare were not just wrong but dangerous, potentially pulling America into wars leading 'to embarrassments, defeats, [and] high casualties.'[46] But here the important point is that set against the troubling interventions of the 1990s and associated 'compassion fatigue' that had reportedly set in among the public and politicians,[47] long-range airpower and the use of surrogate forces presented beguiling opportunities for those wishing to manage global risks, advance the liberal agenda and 'defend freedom'. According to Dueck, the conceit was that this permitted America to maintain hegemony on the cheap.[48] As Freedman notes, with the increasing convergence of these developments, it became possible to envisage 'war without tears, conducted over long distances with great precision and as few people as possible – preferably none at all – at risk.'[49] All these efforts still seemed partial and underdeveloped when the millennium came to a close. It would take the furnace of a new form of global war to forge a more advanced and complete mode of vicarious warfare, even if this process was masked by the demands of a long decade of large-scale encounters.

Navigating the 9/11 wars

The 9/11 attacks appeared to usher in a new era in strategic affairs. They recast the security calculus in Washington, prompting a new mood of national sacrifice and bringing more traditional concerns to the fore, even if the normative impulse remained a powerful motivating and legitimating force. America's response was swift and determined. Certainly, the strategic history of the subsequent period is defined primarily by large-scale operations in Iraq and Afghanistan, where the traditions of conventional battle and small wars determined the most prominent military efforts. The initial phases of these wars essentially constituted the 'dramatic strikes, visible on TV' that President Bush had promised in retaliation to 9/11 during a televised speech just days after the attacks. But he also spoke of 'covert operations' that would remain 'secret even in success.'[50] Indeed, a closer analysis, armed with the benefit of hindsight, reveals that many of the military approaches in evidence today were maturing as independent approaches on the margins of this new global struggle or otherwise as expedient adaptations to the experience of conducting demanding military operations during the bloody 2000s.

The initial phases of the 2001 war in Afghanistan reflected to some extent the continuing influence of the vicarious mentality that had characterized the interventions of the 1990s while simultaneously serving as an influential model and inspiration for future developments. The 'Afghan model' consisted of special forces working with indigenous allies on the ground combined with the application of coalition airpower according to an age-old 'hunter and hound' technique.[51] This combination of capabilities was perhaps more accidental than planned,[52] but in toppling the Taliban it seemed America had scored 'an unqualified triumph, and at very low cost'.[53] Bush thought it a 'bargain' victory.[54] Unsurprisingly, the cut-rate product he had bought turned out to be hopelessly defective – that just wasn't clear at the time. Recalling earlier problems in the Balkans, reliance on the Northern Alliance surrogate forces in 2001 had greatly complicated post-war politics by marginalizing majority Pashtun voices, and the newly empowered regional warlords would bedevil US efforts to build a functioning Afghan state. In the hubristic glow of victory, avenues for accommodations with the Taliban went unexplored and an early opportunity to forestall future conflict was missed.[55] These factors contributed to the subsequent resurgence of the movement over the coming years.[56]

The follow-on battle against hardcore militants holding out within the Tora Bora mountain cave complex (incidentally, financed by the CIA during the 1980s)[57] was fought in a similar manner. Given that Marine reinforcements had been refused, the special forces leading the fight had to rely heavily on tribal fighters. American overseers seriously misread the nature of the interests animating the surrogate militias, and failed to accommodate for their capricious fighting style, the combination of which enabled many Al-Qaeda militants to escape into Pakistan.[58] The early 2002 *Operation Anaconda* was larger in scale (as fears of an Afghan nationalist backlash to a large foreign presence subsided),[59] but it was crucially undermined by anxiety around possible casualties.[60] Overall, the reliance on air strikes, drones (some now armed), special forces and tribal allies meant that the best chance to destroy the otherwise elusive Al-Qaeda network had been missed, opening the way for the protracted battles that would follow.

Since even before the 2001 war, officials had been proclaiming the merits of maintaining a light footprint in Afghanistan.[61] Given the prominence the concept would attain later, it is sometimes forgotten that it emerged in this context; it also seems that the problems resulting from its early implementation were largely overlooked when revived in the 2010s. The light footprint involved a multinational International Security Assistance Force (ISAF) assuming responsibility for security in Kabul while a relatively small contingent of special forces carried on the hunt for militant remnants in the south of the country and small Provincial Reconstruction Teams (PRTs) were established in other parts of the country.[62] These operations were defined by two principal approaches: rapid direct action raids conducted out of fortified bases and the recruitment of irregular militias. PRTs became dependent on warlords for security, and the fact that SOF raids relied heavily on tribal allies for targeting intelligence meant that local groups were able to manipulate their American overseers, essentially using the resulting assaults to settle local scores. Despite – or as some have argued, partly *because of* this militarized policy – the Taliban made its dramatic comeback over the course of the early 2000s.

For America, a natural outgrowth of working closely with the tribes was an emerging policy of recruiting local militias to defend communities from Taliban attacks or, in some cases, to act as strike forces alongside special forces. If politicians were unwilling to provide serious resources, then an obvious solution, building on long-standing unconventional warfare concepts and earlier models such as the Vietnam-era Civilian Irregular Defense Group programme (see Chapter 4), was to induce ordinary Afghan civilians to join the fight. Through fits and starts and various iterations during the 2000s – notwithstanding worrying signs from these early efforts – the tribal policy was quietly expanded as a 'quick security fix' as Western forces struggled to contain the mounting insurgency.[63] Enthusiastic commentators promoted the policy in books and popular publications such as *Foreign Affairs*.[64] These efforts would eventually evolve by 2010 into the more permanent Afghan Local Police (ALP) programme. Known in the special operations community as Village Stability Operations, this unconventional warfare model involving US troops working closely with irregular forces was emerging as a central plank of America's wider counterterror policy.

Following the toppling of the Taliban regime in 2001, attention quickly shifted to Iraq, which, for many neo-conservatives in the Bush administration, was the real priority.[65] The 2003 Iraq War was large-scale and conventional. It is true that CIA and special forces conducted important clandestine missions inside Iraq preparing the ground for the invasion and directing Kurdish Peshmerga allies in the north, but these were ancillary supporting operations not intended to have an independent effect. The decision to keep troop numbers relatively low, at least compared to the recommendations of senior military figures, was arguably less about cost-evasion and more about assisting the administration's pre-war diplomatic manoeuvring. However, the small footprint did 'keep costs down and reduce the operation's vulnerability to scrutiny.'[66] It also helped sustain domestic support by signalling that there would be no messy nation-building mission after the war.[67] This was, in fact, something of an illusion: the administration was able to keep troop numbers artificially low – for the initial invasion and beyond – thanks to its heavy reliance on private contractors.[68] This was a political parlour trick that would continue to be used extensively over coming years.

Vicarious rationales were apparent in other respects. The minimalist force profile reflected Rumsfeld's faith, fortified by the theories of Warden's 'shock and awe' heirs, in the ability of America's nimbler transformed military to deliver a quick and decisive victory. Even better, the war might be decided by a swift knock-out blow: immediately before hostilities began, there were rumours of covert efforts to overthrow the Saddam regime from within,[69] and the major campaigns were preceded by a failed decapitation strike against Iraqi leadership targets at Dora Farms outside Baghdad.[70] Thus, notwithstanding the belligerent attitude of the war's instigators, some were enticed by the possibility of shortcuts to success: as Bush noted in his memoirs, 'by killing the dictator we might be able to end the war before it began, and spare lives. I felt a responsibility to seize this opportunity'.[71] Not only was this wishful thinking, but it also ignored the potentially problematic repercussions of a successful strike.[72] Regardless, it failed, and the campaign was won through a devastatingly rapid, if not entirely unproblematic, conventional offensive – although ironically, the speed with which it was conducted (motivated by vicarious imperatives) generated its own problems.[73]

As the post-war plundering evolved into a complex insurgency, large-scale conventional operations sought to crush opposition elements wherever they could be found; however, the overriding goal was to 'stand up' Iraqi security forces as quickly as possible so the Americans could 'stand down'.[74] Indeed, the vicarious mentality driving the war translated into the distinct lack of enthusiasm for assuming unnecessary risks or occupational responsibility in its aftermath. In fact, the way the war was fought and the decisions taken in the months following the end of combat operations clearly suggested that the kind of 'ownership' (of all the 'hopes, aspirations and problems' of the country's 25 million people) Powell had warned about before the war was exactly what America wanted to avoid.[75] In this sense, it not only wanted to distance itself from the costs of the war, but also from the consequences of its victory.

Prowling on the periphery

Although special operations were a sideshow in Iraq, by the mid-2000s they were nevertheless emerging as the instrument of choice for US policymakers and, in fact, SOCOM had been directed to become the lead combatant command for tackling terrorism. The pointy end of this stick would be JSOC – its elite sub-unified command comprising 'tier one' units from all military branches and specializing in direct action 'black operations', often working closely with the CIA. SOCOM's vision statement at this time clearly suggested special operations had moved beyond their traditional role conducting discrete missions such as hostage rescue or as an auxiliary force in larger conventional campaigns. They were now being primed to realize the nation's *strategic* objectives. The shadow war was also beginning its global expansion well beyond the major theatres of Iraq and Afghanistan – the CIA had been granted greater authority to conduct paramilitary covert operations on 17 September 2001,[76] and in 2004 an executive order enabled JSOC to undertake military action against targets in several countries with which America was not officially at war.[77] Meanwhile, SOF assisted the Filipino armed forces in their fight against Abu Sayyaf militants in the early 2000s,[78] and the CIA also took control of the gradually expanding armed drone programme, conducting targeted killings of terrorist adversaries in multiple theatres.

US activity in Somalia at this time reflected these developments. Concerned about indications of rising Islamic militancy in the region, JSOC, supported by CIA intelligence, had established a task force operating mainly out of a base in Djibouti that began covertly empowering a motley alliance of warlords and former Somali officials to hunt militants.[79] This was, as Gettleman observes, 'a strategy to stamp out the Islamists on the cheap'.[80] Some of its new allies-for-hire were from groups US forces had confronted in street battles during the early 1990s but who were now grandly styling themselves as the 'Alliance for the Restoration of Peace and Counter-Terrorism'.[81] In a roundabout way, this coalition did, in fact, bring a measure of peace, but only because its actions caused its own obsolescence – its US-sanctioned killings and abductions did bag some high-level targets, but also contributed to general lawlessness, undermined the fragile transitional administration and provoked such widespread opposition that Islamic militants were able to recruit widely among disaffected Somalis.[82] As a result, the Islamic Courts Union came to power in 2006 and managed to restore a measure of calm and stability. However, included in its largely moderate membership was a little-known extremist group, Harakat al-Shabaab. Such groups were precisely the kind American covert operations had been designed to crush, and their presence in power was deemed unacceptable: policymakers feared the establishment of a Taliban-style terrorist haven in the already volatile Horn of Africa.[83]

Rather than exploring ways to work with moderate elements in the new Somali administration, US officials instead calculated that the problems caused by one proxy war could be solved by another. A large-scale Ethiopian intervention was launched in 2007, backed by US airpower and clandestine ground assets. The Islamic Courts Union was promptly deposed, but the brutality of the new foreign occupiers brought predictable results. If Somalia was already a playground for Islamic militants, Scahill concludes that 'the Ethiopian invasion blew open the gates of Mogadishu for al Qaeda'[84] – as it grew in power, al-Shabaab fostered ties with the terrorist group, ultimately pledging allegiance in 2012. Aside from sporadic airstrikes and other limited covert actions over the next few years, according to its 'tailored engagement strategy', Washington largely delegated responsibility for security to the new African Mission in Somalia (AMISOM) peacekeeping force supported by US-funded DynCorp International military contractors.[85] America would increasingly be drawn back into the fight over the course of the following decade.

The light-footprint approach adopted in Afghanistan along with the various smaller-scale missions in places like Somalia and the Philippines provided some of the inspiration for studies that emerged in the 2000s, and which began to develop thinking around an approach to irregular challenges that was distinct from that of either population-centric COIN or major combat operations. For instance, Hoffman, in laying out the requirements to tackle what he termed 'complex irregular warfare', laid out the core principles of a model that would essentially be adopted in later years: he maintained that 'maximum influence should be sought from a minimum footprint … working with local militaries to solve the problems at hand … [in which] special operations forces will be especially useful.'[86] Ideas like this were an important step in developing the intellectual foundations of vicarious war. The extent to which this thinking was influencing official policy was revealed in the 2006 Quadrennial Defense Review, which promoted 'persistent but low visibility presence' in support of local allies.[87] Yet these ideas were, for the time being, overshadowed by the demands of escalating wars.

In light of the intensifying campaigns that emerged after 9/11, scholars began to rethink the existing notions of virtuality in American war. The concept of 'risk-transfer war' that Shaw developed to describe the emergent mode of US-led Western war identified common patterns connecting the first war in the Gulf with its 2003 sequel as well as the operations conducted during the intervening years. A defining characteristic, he suggested, was the way 'life-risks' are transferred from Western forces onto the enemy, local allies and civilians by relying on long-range bombardment.[88] Moreover, this was, he argued, an era of 'quick-fix' wars. These were precisely the kind of 'focused' interventions President Bush called for in a speech before 9/11, dismissing the folly of undertaking 'vague, aimless and endless deployments'.[89] But Shaw presciently raised, although did not pursue at length, the idea that the new war on terror had raised the prospect of just such 'long, messy, violent struggles', not unlike those fought within the framework of the Cold War, and that this might constitute a crisis for this new way of war. For policymakers responding to this predicament – preoccupied with the political imperatives Shaw had identified, but now facing the prospect of fighting 'permanent war' – vicarious methods would ultimately emerge as the answer.[90]

Such scenarios were only dimly apparent at that time. After all, politicians were desperately seeking rapid 'closure' in Afghanistan and Iraq, and consistent with Shaw's thesis, both wars in their invasion phases had resulted in minimal US casualties compared to thousands of Iraqis and Afghans, combatants and civilians alike.[91] This even encouraged scholars to pick up again the idea of 'bloodless war', at least for Western forces, that had emerged after Kosovo.[92] But this literature emerged before the most deadly phases of the Iraq and Afghanistan Wars. Despite an evident wish to disengage, America was being dragged deeper into the Middle Eastern morass.

Cautious counterinsurgency, industrial counterterror

As is well known, the security situation in both key theatres deteriorated rapidly in the mid-2000s as they were gripped by violent insurrection and rising sectarian and ethnic strife. These developments prompted major commitments of troops and civilian advisors in population-centric COIN campaigns. But the twin surges in Iraq and Afghanistan, far from indicating a renewed appetite for sizable 'boots on the ground' commitments or a readiness to accept serious sacrifices, were, in essence, futile efforts to rescue sunk costs in desperate contexts.

President Bush's decision in 2007 to send 30,000 additional troops to Iraq was courageous perhaps, but was taken not only against his own instincts but also in the face of considerable domestic political and military opposition. Moreover, the Awakening Councils, comprising thousands of local Sunni fighters – the 'Sons of Iraq' – that independently emerged before the surge between 2005–07,[93] essentially served as surrogate forces and provided the critical mass that contributed to the celebrated dampening of violence in the country as the decade neared its end.[94] Much was made of this aspect of the surge, and it would subsequently inspire accelerated efforts to recruit tribal militias in Afghanistan. Perceived lessons were transferred between these theatres arbitrarily despite the fact that this overlooked critical contextual factors unique to Iraq.[95] The policy was also implemented in a far more top-down manner in Afghanistan.[96] But even more worryingly, it was too early to discern the longer-term impact of the surge: in fact, the failure to integrate the militias into security structures or to provide Sunnis with a meaningful stake in Iraq's political system in the years following the surge was a major factor behind the rise of Islamic State.[97]

Like Bush in Iraq, President Obama was extremely reluctant to commit large numbers of additional troops to Afghanistan in 2009.[98] Ultimately, he sent 17,000 additional troops at the beginning of the year, and in December announced the deployment of 30,000 more. While COIN in Afghanistan involved large-scale deployments of troops into dangerous situations consistent with the small wars tradition, in broad terms the overall force posture was guided by risk-minimizing considerations. This was typified by bunkerization and reliance on massive firepower combined with the arming of local militias (directly building on Petraeus' Iraq model) and expedited 'transition' to local forces, or Afghanization, according to pre-determined exit timetables. The troop drawdown would begin as soon as mid–2011 and ultimately a date of December 2014 was set for the planned end of US-led combat operations. Moreover, in both Iraq and Afghanistan, extensive use was made of private security personnel: Obama's surge involved more contractors than regular forces.[99]

With the benefit of hindsight and considered in broader perspective, the Iraq and Afghanistan surges might be understood as short-term aberrations, and which, in the detail of their execution and through the effect of their desultory outcomes, ultimately only served to reinforce a trend toward vicarious warfare over the last decade.[100] Furthermore, these large-scale operations took place amid longer-term trends toward employing various forms of military outsourcing, force protection, stand-off weapons systems and clandestine operations. Regarding the latter, an important development was General McChrystal's massive campaign of targeted killing in Iraq. McChrystal refined JSOC's hunter-killer tactics by employing an intelligence fusion approach bringing together surveillance intelligence, targeting teams and strike forces to 'Find, Fix and Finish' ill-fated insurgents and then 'Exploit and Analyse' any captured intelligence.[101] The resulting 'F3EA' model has been described as an 'industrial counterterrorism' machine, and one that before long was being reassembled for use in Afghanistan where, by 2010, a JSOC Task

Force was killing 200 mid-level militant commanders every month.[102] But it would also soon be quietly rolled out in other 'non-war' theatres around the globe.

Linked to these developments, an important although initially abortive impetus for the shift toward vicarious warfare came in the context of the 2009 strategy debate over the way forward in Afghanistan. Setting themselves up against the COIN lobby, influential voices in Washington began to push the idea of a 'counterterrorism plus' model.[103] Of course, this could imply any number of approaches, from patient law enforcement to Iraq-style major warfare. But to this counterterror clique, the term essentially referred to updated variations on the 2001 Afghan model combined with emerging thinking on minimum-footprint operations, JSOC-led networked kill-capture campaigns and indigenous counterterror pursuit teams that had begun to gather steam in the mid-2000s. The most prominent proponent of this approach in the Obama administration was Vice President Joe Biden. Biden was drawn to the idea of radically drawing down US forces and focusing on discrete SOF-CIA missions and drone attacks, especially targeting Al-Qaeda in Pakistan.[104] Ultimately the COIN lobby won out in 2009, but only partially.

Even as the major campaigns of the Afghan surge were being fought during the early 2010s, such as *Operation Moshtarak* in Helmand province, the shadow war was intensifying. In some respects, this merely represented a continuation of existing activities, but it also reflected the dismal effect of the surge and its short-lived nature. Despite some evident progress in the areas where most of the surge troops had been deployed, it became increasingly clear that, in a wider sense and contrary to the perennially rosy declarations of senior commanders, it had failed to seriously turn the situation around. Some analysts even suggested that the Taliban had emerged even stronger.[105] Thus, while Biden's favoured approach had not been officially adopted at a policy level, on the ground its main elements were continued and expanded. The overarching mission thereafter essentially reverted to a strategy aimed at eliminating militant adversaries rather than winning hearts and minds. McChrystal's counterterror machine was increasingly brought to bear against militant networks through a ceaseless succession of air strikes and aggressive night raids.

Into the vicarious decade

It is difficult to designate a specific point in time when the contemporary vicarious age truly emerged; it did so in different places at different times. As we have stressed throughout this study, there is no singular or tightly defined model of vicarious warfare. As such, we can expect to see significant variation between different theatres with regard to its operational manifestation or the precise rationales driving its employment. Indeed, as we have seen, in some marginal theatres it essentially defined operations throughout the 2000s. However, as a more comprehensive if still ill-defined approach capturing important aspects of almost all American military commitments around the globe, it really began to emerge around 2011–12.

All US troops had been withdrawn from Iraq by December 2011, but thousands of defence contractors remained in the country along with a small 'residual force' of CIA counterterror personnel and Army Special Forces assisting Iraq's security institutions.[106] In Afghanistan, the withdrawal of American troops began in the middle of 2011 as efforts to transition responsibility for major combat operations to indigenous security forces were ramped up – the mission was shifting to an 'advise and assist' posture. The drone war was also radically expanded by President Obama – in Afghanistan, but mostly across the border into Pakistan, where it also included some covert ground operations. But South Asia was by no means the only theatre in which America was seeking to fight war on the cheap as the new decade began.

That same year, the Libya intervention suggested there was no serious decline in the activist appetite, but it also underscored America's strong reluctance to engage militarily on the ground. With the United States famously leading the multinational coalition 'from behind', the campaign was reliant on air and cruise missile strikes complemented by covert assistance to anti-Gaddafi rebels.[107] The Libya action also starkly revealed the way vicarious methods were rendering Congress almost irrelevant to crucial decisions around the use of force. The Obama administration essentially ignored Congress, seeking neither its approval nor consent, arguing that it was not a full-blown conflict because the 'operations do not involve sustained fighting or active exchanges of fire with hostile forces, nor do they involve US ground troops.'[108] Most members, perhaps recognizing public indifference, were conspicuous in their mute acceptance of this unprecedented executive justification.[109]

Of course, an obvious factor accounting for this shift in the early 2010s was the fall-out from the bloody wars in Iraq and Afghanistan. As many commentators have observed, there was a growing aversion among both the public and political elites for more large-scale 'boots on the ground' commitments, and so 'counterinsurgency' increasingly came to be seen as a dirty word. Moreover, the huge scale of public resources that needed to be diverted for those wars became especially intolerable following the 2008 global financial crisis and the onset of an era of economic austerity.[110] Large majorities opposed sending US troops to Libya, Syria and Ukraine, for instance.[111] As a result, President Obama placed significant emphasis on working with local 'partners' in order to spread the responsibility for security-related tasks. Indeed, as Malley and Finer point out, for a president 'who worried about straining the US military and causing counterproductive civilian casualties, the illusory notion that one could wage war with clean hands proved tantalizing.'[112] Libya had reflected this and after 2011, American warfare was more visibly oriented around a light-footprint approach that 'sought to combat foreign security threats with standoff strike capabilities and small contingents of SOF, often in support of indigenous ground troops, in lieu of major contingents of US ground troops.'[113] Niva has observed that the US military was 'being reconfigured away from mobilizing and sending large armies to fight or invade countries, towards using more efficient and agile networked forces.'[114]

The fall-out from the Arab Spring had prompted a swift military response by the US and its allies in Libya. But in Syria, where, after 2011, a brutal multisided civil war had developed, America struggled to determine an appropriate response. It was here that the light-footprint 'Obama Doctrine' became most apparent.[115] The ambitious objective that 'Assad must go' was not accompanied by anything like the kind of means that might realistically achieve that. Torn by the kinds of competing pressures outlined in the preceding chapter, the president was extremely reticent about sanctioning military intervention, but was equally not content to leave the situation alone.

Predictably, vicarious methods appeared to offer a third way between going to war, or doing nothing. In July 2012, Obama had drawn 'bright red lines' in relation to Assad's use of chemical weapons, but ultimately recoiled from authorizing a direct forceful response.[116] Instead, beginning in 2013, plans were hatched to infiltrate CIA-trained rebels into the country to help topple the Assad regime. And the CIA was primed for this mission: it had long had Assad in its sights, even before 2011.[117] Perhaps this was because such an objective called for the kind of focused and independent paramilitary operations designed to overthrow state adversaries that had been its specialization during the Cold War (as opposed to serving as adjuncts to the military in the midst of endless 'whack-a-mole' operations against non-state militants). Regardless, Obama signed a presidential finding authorizing the US$1 billion plan following enthusiastic advocacy by senior members of the administration and despite the findings of a CIA study detailing the desultory outcomes of earlier similar efforts.[118] The resulting rebel 'Knights of Righteousness', and other such impressively named groups, made few tactical gains, some were found to be complicit in war crimes, and US-supplied weapons, including TOW anti-tank missiles, found their way into the hands of America's enemies.[119] The programme was a costly failure and was ultimately cancelled by President Trump in 2017.

US hesitance in the aftermath of bloody campaigns in Iraq and Afghanistan was understandable, but still many commentators regretted the lack of forceful US intervention in Syria. But intervene it did, only in a manner that arguably only made matters worse: bungled efforts to back rebel proxies, careless arms supply programmes and pin-prick strikes in response to President Assad's use of chemical weapons. Torn by the potential political costs of action and inaction, resolute decision was absent and the result was a half-hearted effort that encouraged rebels in their futile resistance, while limited military and humanitarian responses sought to placate domestic audiences calling for a response to the unfolding atrocities. Unsurprisingly, this patent lack of US resolve was exploited by Assad and his regime's backers in Russia and Iran.

As the plan to unseat Assad by proxy fell apart, and not unconnected from this, a new threat arose in other parts of Syria and across the border in Iraq. Following the rapid advance of Islamic State during 2014, a US-led coalition formed to 'degrade and destroy' this unforeseen threat. *Operation Inherent Resolve* (ongoing at the time of writing) has been fought as an archetypal vicarious war – a gradualist stand-off campaign conducted primarily from the air combined with proxy forces receiving support from special forces units operating out of fortified forward bases supported by thousands of private contractors. A paramilitary programme similar in design to the one targeting Assad was also implemented by enthusiastic Pentagon officials. In line with emerging military concepts of working 'by, with and through' local allies, a US$500 million plan to have Army Special Forces train thousands of Syrian paramilitary fighters in Jordan and Turkey was launched in 2015. Echoing the fate of rebels sent into Europe early in the Cold War, the vast majority of the fighters, more intent on fighting Assad than Islamic State as American overseers intended, were immediately ambushed by the powerful Syrian Al-Qaeda affiliate, Jabhat al-Nusra, and a quarter of their US-supplied arms were seized.[120] Some fighters were even believed to have joined up with such extremist groups, prompting one Green Beret involved in the programme to describe his job as 'sitting in the back room, drinking chai while watching the Turks train future terrorists.'[121] The programme was quickly shuttered in late 2015, but special forces were nevertheless sent to assist other proxy forces in northern and eastern Syria over the following years.[122]

As of mid-2020, the campaign had largely succeeded in removing Islamic State from its major strongholds. Yet the evolving security situation remains fragile, with observers predicting vicious battles still to come.[123] Consistent with the argument of this book, the overwhelming emphasis in terms of resources and efforts has been on kinetic military action as opposed to patiently addressing the region's deep-seated social and political problems. Although the maps of territory retaken provide excellent 'visuals' in Pentagon press briefings, due to the vicarious methods adopted, the campaign may have generated more problems than it has solved. For instance, the way the operation to liberate Mosul was conducted means that, as Amnesty International has observed, 'there is a real risk that this battle will form one more chapter in a seemingly endless cycle of devastating conflict and atrocities'.[124] The cumulative effect of thousands of precision strikes has resulted in devastated cityscapes posing huge post-war challenges, and the concurrent sponsorship of proxy militia has empowered groups hardly conducive to fostering long-term stability. Tellingly, according to some estimates the militant group has more fighters in its ranks in 2020 than it did when the campaign began in 2014. It has been reported that Islamic State is regrouping in remote areas, and American special forces have recently been killed during operations conducted alongside Iraqi counterterrorism forces.[125] America maintains entangling commitments in the region but lacks the leverage to decisively shape developments or promote long-term solutions, while its minimalist ground force presence may provoke resistance and yet serve as a platform for future escalation.

Elsewhere, operations were launched to tackle Islamic State-affiliated groups across a wide swathe of North Africa, the Middle East and Asia. For instance, special forces were dispatched to help combat an Islamist uprising in Marawi in 2017, and Americans assisted in the fight against Islamic State ally Boko Haram in Nigeria. Islamic State militants also appeared in Libya, exploiting the messy fallout from the 2011 intervention thanks to the vicariously deficient commitment to post-war stabilization efforts. This prompted the insertion of US and UK special forces to link up with local militias, and culminated in a major effort, supported by US air strikes, to expel militants from the coastal town of Sirte in 2016.[126]

Even the ongoing war in Afghanistan began to increasingly look like these other smaller-scale peripheral operations. The large-scale combat commitment was gradually wound down and was finally replaced in 2015 by an ongoing NATO mission, *Resolute Support*. This had all the prominent features of vicarious warfare: transition of combat missions to Afghan forces and tribal militias; heavy reliance on airpower, drones and private contractors (reportedly over 8,000 in 2019);[127] as well as multiple covert operations and special forces missions under the rubric of *Freedom's Sentinel*.[128]

The contemporary global battlespace

The contemporary American strategic context – at least in terms of ongoing practice, as opposed to policy, planning and doctrine – is one still principally centred around the long war on terror that emerged following the terrorist attacks of 11 September 2001. However, the military missions that have been launched in subsequent years have greatly expanded beyond those associated with the immediate rationale for action mandated by the 2001 attacks. Indeed, this expansion has occurred not simply due to emerging political or strategic imperatives but in part due to the evolving opportunities provided by vicarious approaches. While it is true that most missions are still justified and sanctioned under the controversial 2001 Authorization for Use of Military Force (AUMF) passed by Congress in the wake of the 9/11 attacks, the scope of contemporary operations suggests only a loose and increasingly unsubstantiated correlation with the legal authorities contained in the 2001 law; it has been stretched almost to breaking point.[129] It is important for observers of modern American military interventionism to appreciate the multiple interests and motivations compelling military activism in different theatres.

Terrorism remains a core concern, but this is often joined by considerations relating to regional stability, humanitarianism, trade and energy security, geopolitical competition, alliance commitments, protection of foreign nationals, and a host of other interests that the United States continues to pursue around the globe. In some cases, the terror threat has been deployed as a convenient cover for the projection of US power for other reasons, some arguably more legitimate than others. In Africa, for instance, missions launched purportedly for counterterror reasons may simultaneously serve to promote wider US interests in an intensifying geopolitical competition with China across the continent. Similarly, in the Middle East, support to traditional strategic partners, weapons proliferation and energy security strongly influence US military decision-making, sometimes in ways that arguably undermine purported counterterror objectives.[130]

As the 2010s progressed and the large-scale wars of the previous decade faded from view, the now global scope of America's vicarious wars became increasingly apparent. Especially in Africa, there has been a notable militarization of US policy, building on a range of initiatives implemented during the 2000s.[131] Special forces – supported by private contractors such as Bancroft Global Development and Skybridge Tactical[132] – have been deployed to scores of countries on the continent, mostly across the Sahara-Sahel region, working with partner militaries to strengthen their counterterror capabilities through security assistance and training missions.[133] In some contexts, secretive missions have been launched under a little known authority, '127e', which permits local forces to be loaned to the US to be used for what are essentially remote-controlled direct action raids. According to officials, they are 'low cost in terms of resources and especially risk to our personnel'.[134] Working out of a constellation of 'enduring and non-enduring' bases and outposts across the continent, US forces (around 6,000 as of 2020) have engaged in combat in some 13 countries and troops have been killed or wounded in at least 6: Kenya, Libya, Niger, Somalia, South Sudan and Tunisia.[135] Drones and manned aircraft have been used for surveillance but also for lethal strikes, most notably in Somalia, Niger and Libya.

In 2017, Trump declared both Yemen and Somalia 'areas of active hostility', thus expanding the scope of US military efforts in those countries. The ongoing fight against al-Shabaab in Somalia became a major focus of effort. Trump loosened the rules of engagement as special forces spanned out across the country conducting clandestine kill-or-capture missions, and there was a major expansion of air strikes.[136] In just the first half of 2020 there were 40 strikes – one less than the total number between 2007 and 2016.[137]

On the other side of the Gulf of Aden, in Yemen, the bombing campaign against Al-Qaeda in the Arabian Peninsula was significantly ramped up, even as officials warned that 'this is not a place where we can have a glorious little war'.[138] This long-standing counterterror mission in the south was complicated by the 2015 intervention of Saudi Arabia and United Arab Emirates (UAE) to oust the Iran-backed Houthi rebels who had taken over the capital, Sanaa. The US would take a back seat in this war, but provided critical intelligence, aerial refuelling and munitions, effectively making it a proxy war in all but name: Byman quotes the Republican Senator Mike Lee who said 'it stretches the imagination, and it stretches the English language beyond its breaking point, to suggest the US military is not engaged in hostility in Yemen.'[139] Although distant and discrete, the American role was important nonetheless. Furthermore, this campaign underlined the acute contradictions that pervaded so many of its missions throughout the region: for instance, the Saudi coalition was recruiting Al-Qaeda militants into its anti-Houthi forces, and some weapons supplied by the US have found their way to hard-line Salafist militias.[140] In fact, Yemen emerged as one of the murkiest of America's proxy wars, its highly vicarious nature shrouding the nature and extent of US involvement let alone its share of the responsibility for the chaos engulfing the country and the mounting humanitarian disaster.[141]

Thus, vicarious warfare is being applied today in a wide variety of contingencies, encompassing both serious commitments and minor missions across large portions of the globe. In fact, it is the availability of vicarious methods that has partly facilitated this spatial proliferation 'across diverse geographies'.[142] Drawing off the work of the sociologist Zygmunt Bauman, Demmers and Gould employ the useful concept of 'liquid warfare' to suggest how the 'conventional ties between war, space and time have become undone' to be replaced by 'flexible, open-ended, "pop-up" military interventions, supported by remote technology and reliant on local partnerships and private contractors.'[143] Priority theatres change over time: for instance, US armed drone use was long centred on Pakistan's tribal areas but has since shifted to the Horn of Africa. American warfare is thus 'spatially dispersed and mobile' to the extent that the traditional battlefield has been replaced by a global 'multidimensional battlescape'.[144]

Futile persistence

Vicarious warfare traps America in strategically senseless and unending cycles of intervention. The much-reported 'withdrawals' that Trump has on occasion promised look less complete in reality than breathless accounts of wholesale abandonment and retreat suggest. Instead, the language of withdrawal is often a smokescreen directed at domestic audiences shrouding decidedly partial realities effected by rhetorical sleights of hand and qualified by subsequent 'conditions' that come to light after the brief media storm subsides. The 'boots on the ground' being pulled out typically apply only to conventional forces, not SOF. And even as regular forces are pulled out, thousands of US contractors remain – for instance, in 2019 there were some 53,000 present in the Middle East (compared to 35,000 American troops).[145]

These dynamics were all strikingly apparent with respect to the contortions accompanying Trump's highly publicized withdrawal from Syria in December 2018, which ended up being less final than his original tweets suggested. In Afghanistan, only time will tell if the US–Taliban agreement signed in February 2020 will lead to the kind of total withdrawal it promises. The continuing status of, for instance, CIA-backed paramilitary strike forces working alongside US special forces is unclear, but it is likely that precisely such covert surrogate forces, reportedly permitted in the agreement's secret annexes,[146] will allow America to sustain discrete counterterror operations against Al-Qaeda and Islamic State groups beyond pulling out 'all' US forces.[147]

Politicians, nagged by fear of domestic political punishment associated with premature disengagement (perhaps resulting from, for instance, future attacks against America judged as being linked to the decision) and wanting to avoid association with failed missions are, through vicarious means, able to maintain a hedging marginal toehold in operational theatres. Disengagement in practice tends to mean enduring US military influence maintained through 'over the horizon' long-range strike capabilities, proxy forces and secretive missions. Even where troop withdrawals are more complete, direct control of territory and populations is replaced by forms of more remote coercive management and ongoing virtual occupations.[148]

In 2008, reflecting deeply-help concerns regarding precisely these dynamics, a prominent defence expert and highly decorated soldier had asserted that American leaders should,

> ... abandon the belief that wars can be waged efficiently with a minimalist approach to the commitment of forces and other resources. The belief that progress toward achieving objectives ... could be achieved by doing just enough to establish security and help nascent governments and security forces assume responsibility for ongoing conflicts ... neglected the interaction with determined enemies ... and was based on a misunderstanding of the nature of those conflicts.[149]

These words were written by H.R. McMaster, who, for over a year between 2017 and 2018, was National Security Advisor of the United States. During his term in office, the exact approach he had criticized in his earlier article was continuing indefinitely in Afghanistan, and he was unable (perhaps forgivably given the temperament of his boss) to move American policy onto a different trajectory. Indeed, the situation in Afghanistan pointed to the way vicarious methods encourage lingering commitments, even in contexts where disengagement had supposedly been proclaimed.

Part of the explanation for the persistence of vicarious approaches is the growing consolidation of various lobbies associated with the tradition. At one level, hugely influential defence contractors as well as other organizations and politicians benefiting from continuing low-level global military operations were happy to lend their encouragement to interventionist agendas. Bacevich is frank in asserting that 'some individuals and some institutions actually benefit from an armed conflict that drags on and on. Those benefits are immediate and tangible. They come in the form of profits, jobs, and campaign contributions. For the military-industrial complex, and for its beneficiaries, perpetual war is not necessarily bad news'.[150]

But profit was not the only driving force. Many genuinely subscribed to the strategic concepts being generated within the tradition, although sometimes the distinction between sincere adherents and avaricious opportunists is difficult to determine. As the multiple vicarious interventions described earlier were taking place across the globe throughout the decade, various actors within the defence establishment, including military commanders, former special forces officers and Pentagon officials, sought to bring some intellectual order to the disparate approaches being adopted. Some drew off ideas that, as noted earlier, had been floating around for some time; others reached back to Cold War models or even turned to classic authors such as Sun Tzu and Liddell Hart for inspiration.[151] The concepts of 'by, with and through', 'light-footprint operations' and the 'indirect approach' all increasingly appeared in various military publications. But much of the output at this time seemed to be reflective more of post hoc rationalization, with officials seeking to confirm the sound strategic foundations of ongoing missions that were, in fact, impromptu responses to unpredictable developing situations.

Although there has been no equivalent 'FM 3-24 moment' for vicarious warfare – no single authoritative statement of doctrine embracing the idea in a holistic manner – the gradual sedimentation and consolidation of ideas concerning key methodologies could be interpreted as a growing body of unofficial emergent quasi-doctrine. This intellectual activity contributed to more developed understandings regarding operational forms that might enable the application of minimalist, remote and relatively risk-free force. Foreign policy and military elites were perhaps fearful that politicians were moving toward more total forms of disengagement, either generally or in specific theatres, and so developed intricate arguments that could persuade policymakers that there were indeed low-cost, low-profile options available to them. A number of sympathetic expert commentators contributed their own ideas broadly consistent with official thinking.[152]

The problem was that for almost two decades, if not longer, variants of middle-ground approaches – whether involving special forces, covert operations, proxies, drone strikes or military training missions – had been employed again and again, with overwhelmingly harmful results. Commentators might point to the notable absence of large-scale terror attacks on the US homeland, but it could be argued that this was the case *despite* rather than because of the endless vicarious interventions taking place. In the same way that it can be argued, as we saw in Chapter 4, that the aggressive campaign of covert paramilitary interventions during the Cold War were actually more part of the disease than the cure, this may well be the case today. In fact, Wertheim has argued that, for instance, the war on terror 'perpetuates itself by producing new enemies'.[153]

★ ★ ★

The fact that militant activity has tended to increase as US military operations have been expanded in various theatres – for instance, in Africa over the last decade[154] – must surely give decision-makers pause for thought. Instead, the typical reaction when faced by heightened militant activity is to call for yet more force. So, in 2020, given rising Islamist violence across the Sahel, Western forces are set to expand operations in support of local security forces, thus stalling and possibly reversing the drawdown of US Africa Command (AFRICOM) assets that in the late 2010s was reportedly due to take place.[155] It is in this way that vicarious warfare comes to be seen as the solution for the problems it has arguably helped create in the first place. The reasons behind these harmful effects are explored further in the following chapter.

7

Consequences

The preceding chapters have considered some of the prominent explanations for the emergence and persistence of vicarious warfare. Building on this foundation and drawing from a wide range of recent studies, this chapter will expose its principal operational manifestations to further scrutiny with the aim of uncovering its central dynamics and shedding greater light on the often counterproductive strategic consequences of this form of war, at least as it has been conducted by the United States over recent times.

The first section provides a foundation for the discussion by presenting core Clausewitzian insights that can aid appreciation of the political dynamics underlying the use of force, and specifically as they apply to vicarious warfare. This helps explain how apparent tactical gains can shroud serious deficiencies in strategic terms. The second section outlines how these dynamics play out in relation to three 'Ds' of delegation, danger-proofing and darkness, which are employed as short-hand descriptors for some of the central practices that have characterized contemporary American vicarious warfare.

Confused about Clausewitz

A number of studies advocating versions of vicarious approaches have deemed it necessary to set up their views against what they see as a dominating 'Clausewitzian' mentality in American strategic thinking. This, they argue, has compelled America to harmfully apply overwhelming force in pursuit of decisive victories, and has even promoted 'foolish beliefs about the necessity of slaughter'.[1] Instead, they suggest that America should play to its 'asymmetric' strengths in air and naval power, special forces and intelligence assets to target enemy vulnerabilities while simultaneously limiting America's exposure to risks, costs and casualties.[2]

From a slightly different direction, in a popular recent book McFate bluntly describes Clausewitz as the 'high priest of conventional war' who thought 'brute force and battlefield victory is everything'.[3] McFate's proposed solutions are more nuanced than a simple embrace of drones or proxy militias, which he largely rejects. Nevertheless, he proposes that America should adopt more indirect approaches, model the entire military along the lines of SOF, expand the use of mercenaries and establish an American foreign legion more suited to conducting extended foreign deployments.[4]

Putting aside for now the considerable evidence presented throughout this book that would seriously challenge the claim that American strategy has adhered to a singular battle-oriented approach, these thinkers nevertheless join a notable lineage of theorists of indirect or limited warfare who have felt it necessary to anchor their ideas in a rejection of Clausewitz.[5] Much like the 'new wars' theorists of the 1990s, the characterization, or rather the caricature of Clausewitz's ideas presented by these authors, appears to rely on long-standing popular but now widely discredited interpretations that have spread throughout large parts of the US military education system.[6] Their contributions will no doubt further entrench such misleading views.

Perhaps they missed the veritable renaissance in Clausewitzian studies that has occurred over the last two decades and that has done much to correct earlier misinterpretations, especially in terms of our understanding of Clausewitz's use of the term 'absolute war' (as an abstract philosophical 'ideal', *not* necessarily a real-world recommendation),[7] the politics of war and the meaning of his 'remarkable trinity'.[8] Or maybe they consciously *choose* to ignore this scholarship: setting up Clausewitz as a straw man in this way and seemingly rendering obsolete the greatest theorist of war is guaranteed to turn heads. They might also realize that a true Clausewitzian understanding would actually invalidate many of the grand claims they make for their versions of vicarious warfare. For good reasons, Clausewitz was profoundly sceptical of approaches that promised bloodless victory.

It is true that, notwithstanding the numerous qualifications he presents, there is a distinct orientation toward overwhelming force in the more prescriptive sections of *On War*, and, of course, he was writing in an era dominated by conventional wars (although not exclusively, as Clausewitz was well aware). However, his ideas were far more sophisticated than a simple preference for a singular way of war. Clausewitz, in fact, clearly stated that he believed that 'many roads lead to success ... the choice depends on circumstances'.[9] This recognition was based on his appreciation of the influence of ever-changing conditions on war and his insights regarding the political nature of war. In Book 8, Chapter 6A, he goes as far as to state that 'once the influence of the political objective on war is admitted, as it must be, there is no stopping it; consequently we must also be willing to wage such minimal wars, which consist in merely threatening the enemy, with negotiations held in reserve.'[10] This was not a proto-theory of vicarious warfare. Rather, Clausewitz was simply seeking to explain how the application of less than absolute force might be consistent with political imperatives.

Many modern critical accounts fail to move beyond their fascination with the tactical promise of emerging methods to consider wider political dynamics and effects: that failure represents a major flaw in their works (and with regard to the practice of vicarious warfare more generally). There is thus great danger in dismissing Clausewitz because he provided us with the conceptual tools required to understand core strategic dynamics.[11] Ironically, critical commentators were perhaps right to set themselves up against Clausewitz, but just not for the reasons they suggest. Clausewitz's insights on the politics of war can help us understand why vicarious approaches so often fail to deliver the benefits that its advocates promise. Thus, a brief consideration of these ideas is necessary.

The politics of force

Clausewitz's famous aphorism that 'war is merely the continuation of policy with other means' appears almost everywhere in the defence and strategic literatures, and often only in passing.[12] Its deeper meaning is often missed. However, a key aspect of recent Clausewitzian scholarship has centred around our understanding of that aphorism. First, it should be noted that the German word *politik* in the original can be translated as either 'policy' or 'politics'. With this in mind, there has been a move away from understanding the phrase as implying that war is or should be *subordinate to policy* and towards a perspective that better appreciates the implications of war as a *continuation of politics*. The former perspective was associated with the Cold War 'liberal reduction of Clausewitz to rationality' – in short, the notion that war could serve as an entirely rational instrument for the attainment of policy ends.[13] This was a convenient argument for civilian control over the military, especially apt in a nuclear age. The unilateral and rational policy perspective remains important. There is always an extent to which war derives from purposive behaviour, whereby actors employ military means in order to realize their objectives. And few would contest the notion that war *ought* to remain subject to the requirements of policy. However, the idea of 'continuation' takes us into the complex, multilateral, ever-shifting and emotion-laden realm of politics – a critical perspective in helping to understand why policy so often struggles to control or effectively utilize its instrument.[14]

To argue that war is a continuation of politics is to make a point beyond that of war's subordination to policy. Where subordination might imply the *substitution* of political behaviour by military force (that policy merely sets the goals and falls silent until military operations deliver a result), continuation powerfully conveys the 'indissoluble connection' between them: the idea that war is never an autonomous phenomenon, that the use of force is itself a form of political behaviour, and that it can never be 'divorced from political life'.[15] Crucially, as Clausewitz explains, 'war in itself does not suspend political intercourse *or change it into something entirely different....* The main lines along which military events progress ... are political lines that continue throughout the war into the subsequent peace.'[16] When force is employed – at whatever level, from the tactical to the strategic – the complex logic of politics does not cease; it simply continues in its most potent manifestation.[17] Thus, military events are essentially meaningless without being placed in political context and can only ultimately be judged according to the political effects they are intended to achieve.

A major implication of this is that military operations will *always* be inextricably embedded within what we can term a 'political web of war' – the panoply of relevant political actors that are affected by the (real and perceived) military and political consequences of war, and which, in turn, shape its course due to how those actors choose to respond to developments.[18] Such political actors include the major belligerents themselves but also other 'strategic audiences' that, in certain circumstances, can have a critical impact on outcomes. These other actors include internal organizations, domestic constituencies, allies, local civilians in a theatre of operations, regional states, international organizations or even global public opinion. So the use of force causes such actors to assess their situation and act accordingly, which, in turn, impacts on the course of events. In short, we must seek to understand how interests, relationships and political dynamics are being shaped by military moves.[19] And this can play out over extended periods beyond the immediate application of force. The problem is that politics is a ceaseless phenomenon – the achievement of military victory and policy aims in the short term can soon be overturned by evolving political dynamics, sometimes precisely due to the effects of military success. As Clausewitz observed, 'in war the result is never final'.[20] Politics has a disconcerting habit of delivering its own verdict on events.

But how is the use of force actually converted into political effect? At a simple level it is achieved through the death and destruction of the physical encounter. But beyond situations in which the enemy's complete destruction is the aim (very rare), objectives are usually limited in important respects. In such cases, the physical use of force alone is never entirely sufficient to generate the political outcomes desired, however much it may appear so. The immediate physical result is insufficient because its effect depends not only on the material outcome (soldiers killed, territory taken, infrastructure destroyed) but also the way it is processed, understood and given meaning by the adversary and other audiences.

Hence, from a strategic perspective – how war is supposed to achieve the political objectives in view – it is vital that those leading the war understand and judge not only the physical effects of force but also the impact it is having on the wider political situation, and whether actions are causing responses in key audiences that promote progress toward those objectives or that may actually be doing the opposite (leading, for instance, to greater enemy resistance, provoking opposition among key audiences, causing other actors to side with the adversary and so forth). Actors may think the use of force is doing *this* or having *that* effect but it may, in fact, be understood or interpreted in very different terms by the enemy and others.[21] In this sense, the message that certain forms of force communicates can be as important as the physical effects, and so the narratives that inescapably pervade and accompany war can have a disproportionate impact on political outcomes.

The importance of this 'cognitive domain' in war is now well established in contemporary strategic studies. Scholars, building on Clausewitz's foundational insights regarding passion, moral forces, psychological factors and the politics of war, have demonstrated that influencing the attitudes and behaviour of key audiences is a crucial consideration in securing objectives.[22] Managing the informational aspect of military campaigns – as recent revisions to US joint doctrine have emphasized – is increasingly central to strategic planning.[23] This is not to downplay or ignore physical effects. But the way the use of force is perceived by audiences has a major impact on vital political dynamics, and as such this should be accorded significant weight in determining the practicability of any particular strategy. Furthermore, the intense connectivity of the modern global mediascape means political leaders have to consider multiple strategic audiences, all drawing off a diverse range of information sources. The crucial point in strategic affairs is that the narrative – expressed and manifested both in terms of how physical force is employed and how it is rhetorically explained or justified – must be capable of actively shaping the behaviour of key audiences by providing a convincing rationale for action, whether the aim is to compel submission, precipitate dialogue or perhaps elicit popular support.[24] Freedman has noted that the aim is 'to convince others to act in such a way that the story will follow its desired course.'[25] The relevance of these ideas to assessments of the effectiveness of contemporary vicarious warfare will become apparent throughout the subsequent analysis.

The contemporary culminating point

A fundamental problem with the prosecution of vicarious warfare concerns the way tactical and operational wins are confused with strategic progress. Contrary to the Clausewitzian perspective, insufficient attention is devoted to political dynamics because almost all attention is focused on the material components of military activity and their immediate effects. A useful way of understanding this is to employ a modified version of Clausewitz's concept of the culminating point of victory.[26]

The idea essentially captures how one's own immediate superiority or seemingly positive military activity – such as advancing through enemy territory – can, despite appearances, be the simultaneous cause of impending strategic failure or at least the lessening of one's relative superiority vis-à-vis the enemy. Successful offensive action and victory itself brings certain obvious benefits, but over time these can also lead to rapidly diminishing marginal gains or even serious disadvantages, to the extent that the position of superiority might be lost or even reversed. This occurs through, *inter alia*, the operation of various military, logistical, psychological and political dynamics. In the classic conception, the attacker may stretch their supply lines too thin, exhaust their troops or enter into hostile enemy territory, while the danger to the defender's position might bring allies to its aid.[27]

For Clausewitz, this was principally an operational concept, but its essential dynamics can be understood to apply at a strategic level too. The concept allows us to appreciate how military 'successes' may simultaneously prove politically crippling. To put it simply, action generating immediate gains may, in fact, be sowing the seeds of future trouble.[28] It is a phenomenon that is captured in modern notions of 'victory disease', or the demotivating aphorism that 'nothing fails like success'.[29] In practical strategic terms it usually denotes a failure to tailor one's ambition to one's means. Vicarious methods cause the US to overstep the culminating point in a number of key respects, but principally in terms of generating political effects that largely negate whatever positive material or tactical progress they might bring. It is useful to outline some of the most prominent manifestations of this dynamic.

First, methods that appear useful and effective in the short term might produce harmful unintended consequences, often referred to as 'blowback'.[30] Negative effects may be more or less obvious and can appear almost immediately or over much longer periods as second- or third-order effects. For instance, some actions may prompt immediate opposition and resistance while others may contribute to the conditions that breed future problems. Such dynamics were apparent in relation to the Libya intervention – the immediately successful campaign of 2011 created an ungoverned space that became a cauldron of militant activity in the wider region and generated serious new problems for the United States, many of which remain unsolved.[31]

Second, some actions serve to frustrate important lines of political progress through counterproductive effects whereby they undermine the very thing they are trying to achieve, often precisely due to the vicarious nature of the methods used. This is apparent in relation to specific military actions and at a broader strategic level. Examples of the former might include the way security assistance breeds corruption in host nation security forces or how sponsorship of irregular proxies brands those groups as 'made in America', thus delegitimizing them in the eyes of local audiences.[32] Even larger conventional campaigns fought according to a vicarious mentality can be hamstrung by their own tactical prowess. This occurred with the 2003 invasion of Iraq: its minimalist form and intense speed – both designed to evade costs and maintain political support – created major strategic problems and created the conditions that would later demand much greater American sacrifices.[33] In strategic terms, Malley and Finer identify such an outcome when they explain that, 'one possible explanation for the resilience of the terrorist threat is that an overly militarized approach aggravates the very conditions on which terrorist recruitment thrives.'[34]

Third, vicarious methods can be seen to work at cross-purposes with other important efforts and agendas, applicable again to specific local issues or at a global level. So, heavily kinetic approaches can undermine sensitive diplomatic initiatives, while measures deemed critical for aggressive counterterror operations (such as arming militias) may run counter to objectives such as consolidating state institutions.[35] From an even wider grand strategic perspective, huge contradictions can emerge between, on the one hand, US foreign policy initiatives promoting peace, stability and human rights, and on the other, directly opposing consequences arising from America's hugely violent actions around the world. The ill effects of this hypocrisy can be aggravated by the apparent callousness associated with its actions, such as failing to provide honest reporting of casualties or to compensate victims caught in the crossfire of American force. Officials might retort that aggressive operations are required to create the conditions for peace, but to important audiences such imperialistic arrogance can breed deep cynicism and opposition that frustrates American efforts in both military and diplomatic spheres.

Fourth, vicarious warfare can work to the advantage of adversaries or otherwise encourage them to pursue escalatory actions. Indeed, the central political relationship in war is that between active belligerents – Clausewitz was adamant that war is an interactive phenomenon, a violent collision of wills and 'conflict of living forces'.[36] America's evident preoccupation with limiting costs through vicarious means represents a strategic vulnerability that opponents seek to exploit. Advocates of vicarious methods argue that in lieu of large-scale commitments, special operations and drone strikes are an effective means to coerce enemies and signal US resolve. But far from persuading enemies to lay down their arms, risk-averse approaches may be interpreted as American ambivalence or pusillanimity – a lack of appetite for the fight – thus emboldening them and inviting further aggression. As we saw earlier, in relation to the clash of vicarious European imperialists and their evidently non-vicarious antagonists, focusing attention on adversaries exposes very different attitudes toward the costs of war. Contemporary adversaries often display strategic patience and a willingness to suffer short-term setbacks and tactical sacrifices in exchange for long-term gain.

Certain American strategic approaches have inherent vulnerabilities that can be exploited by shrewd opponents. Coercive airpower has been a favoured tool of vicarious warriors, famously holding out the prospect of 'gratification without commitment'[37] and typically perceived as a 'quick and cheap solution to otherwise difficult and expensive international problems.'[38] But, as outlined by Byman and others, these methods can seriously backfire when they are evidently adopted to evade costs.[39] Enemies, recognizing this, and questioning the credibility of coercive threats, turn the associated lack of commitment against the coercer, adopting clever countercoercive moves.[40] The Kosovo campaign almost failed as a result of such dynamics.[41] Enemies also understand how violent campaigns of drone strikes, raids or abusive US-backed militias provoke popular resistance and grievances in ways that allow them to recruit from disaffected populations.[42] In seeking to sustain a counterproductive violent American presence, they might adopt 'strategies of provocation' involving high-profile attacks, especially against symbols of US power, provoking overreactions that play to their intentions.[43]

Fifth, beyond immediate adversaries, aspects of vicarious warfare can cause problems in relation to other key strategic audiences. Geostrategic rivals may well interpret increasing vicariousness as a sign of weakness or declining US commitment, and thus seek to raise the costs of continued engagement.[44] Evidence of limited will on the part of United States as the dominant coalition member in typically multinational modern operations can lead to forms of tokenism on behalf of allies: witness, for instance, the infamous 'national caveats' pertaining to the rules of engagement adopted by America's allies in Afghanistan. This can undermine operational coherence, jeopardize unity of effort and encourage premature disengagement as campaigns begin to falter.[45] Aligning with particular local factions or armed groups may send awkward messages to traditional allies (raising trust and commitment issues), and this can lead to significant tensions in diplomatic relations: consider the severe strains in US–Turkish relations and rising anti-Americanism in Turkey caused by American support to Kurdish militias in northern Syria.[46] Linked to this, relationships with proxy groups themselves can be stretched to breaking point as Americans seek to downplay the partnership to mollify state allies or regional actors.[47]

Sixth, initially minimalist deployments and seemingly low-risk missions can encourage the familiar phenomenon of gradual 'mission creep' leading to unwelcome and burdensome commitments. Missions that, on the face of it, represent cost-effective means of protecting interests or defending strategic positions repeatedly fail to factor in how other actors might react to the US presence or overlook the natural tendency among American operatives on the ground to recognize a host of new threats that need to be combated or opportunities that should be exploited. This almost mechanistically leads to expanded missions and requests for additional resources. Moreover, once engaged in a conflict, new concerns and liabilities inevitably emerge (such as reputational or credibility issues) that do not reflect the initial stake in the conflict or appetite for risk, but that nevertheless might cause policymakers to persist in otherwise futile or non-essential endeavours. In this way, contrary to Clausewitz's admonitions, military operations become untethered from the original political ends. We have seen how this occurred in some Cold War vicarious interventions: after the commitment of US-backed rebel armies to the fight, things often did not go to plan and presidents were then pressured to commit further, both to protect the mission and to signal continuing resolve.[48]

The seventh and final point relates to the tendency of planners to apply a blanket homogenizing 'war frame' to strategic challenges, viewing almost all issues as the outgrowth of a single monolithic incubus. Military action – eminently feasible thanks to the ready availability of vicarious methods – is thus deemed essential in the context of the 'wider war' even if ill suited to particular contexts. The war frame encourages officials to view all problems as military problems, and in this way offensive operations are rationalized and invested with a 'moral certainty' as if they are individual theatres within a Second World War-type global contest.[49] Military commitments launched in this context tend to be piecemeal and insufficient to adequately address the wider challenge, leading to subsequent mission creep.

Such thinking lay at the root of the relentless Cold War interventionism, as discussed in Chapter 4: any sign of leftist or radical nationalist inclinations among actors abroad was interpreted as part of a communist 'united global force' and an intolerable threat that needed to be excised.[50] This precluded serious interrogation of the wisdom of individual missions, while strategic planning for local contingencies was perverted by the demands of the 'overall Cold War framework'[51] – a major criticism of the Reagan doctrine. As Burleigh has noted, 'the passions aroused by the broader struggle were to distort perceptions of lesser conflicts whose origins were more local.'[52] The dominance of a Manichaeistic outlook, which led planners to simplistically view situations through a binary East–West lens of bad guys and good guys, overlooked regional complexities and local realities. This helps account for some of the frustrations encountered at the time as well as the failure to anticipate the longer-term negative consequences of US actions. It also allowed prospective proxies to more easily manipulate their superpower patron.[53] A dutiful 'good soldier' mentality among officials meant little thought was devoted to possible better ways to proceed or if restraint might have been a more sensible course. It became increasingly clear that deep-seated local crises could not easily be solved by simply providing American clients with American weapons, helpful advice and a push in the right direction.

This same homogenizing tendency, imposing a unitary terror framework on all putative threats in the strategic environment[54] – sometimes described as a form of 'global insurgency' – can help explain the difficulties vicarious warfare has recently encountered in numerous contexts.

★ ★ ★

Taking a broader view, Clausewitzian political logic is seriously subverted by the way vicarious warfare has essentially driven strategy and policy in America's wars.[55] Such 'tacticization of strategy' has been a persistent feature of recent wars.[56] Seeming tactical 'magic bullets' have convinced leaders that there are, in fact, bloodless, politically convenient routes to objectives. Indeed, the experience of recent years suggests that it has often been the tactical tail that has wagged the strategy dog.

Consider, for instance, the 2011 Libya intervention. Objectives rapidly escalated from protecting civilians to outright regime change (if, indeed, that had not been the intent from the outset). It is plausible to suggest that such far-reaching aims were only seriously entertained because earlier models (Kosovo 1999, Afghanistan 2001) suggested to policymakers that these missions could be carried out rapidly and successfully, without the need for ground forces, and at little cost. Transfixed by the apparent assurance of operational ease, insufficient thought was given to strategically harmful effects that might result. Ultimately, aside from likely worsening the humanitarian situation that the intervention was ostensibly designed to ameliorate,[57] it also left behind a deeply divided state, released thousands of weapons into regional markets, destabilized neighbouring countries such as Mali and exacerbated terrorist activity throughout North Africa.[58]

Sympathetic studies and emerging narratives, propagated by enthusiastic proponents of the vicarious tradition, reinforce these dynamics. Focusing on immediate positive results, they convey a powerful perception of ease and effectiveness while overlooking more troubling aspects. These ideas are catnip to policymakers seeking politically painless shortcuts to objectives. Clausewitz lived in a period when many vicarious methods were unimaginable or unavailable; however, he well understood the kind of dangerous thinking that motivates the quest for bloodless approaches. This prompted him to warn that 'a short jump is certainly easier than a long one. But no one wanting to get across a large ditch would begin by jumping half way'.[59] Unfortunately we have repeatedly witnessed the tendency for American decision-makers to do just that.

The next section presents a more fine-grained analysis that explains how this deficit of strategic sense applies to the three principle contemporary operational spheres of vicarious warfare: delegation, danger-proofing and darkness.

'3D' warfare

The three 'Ds' outlined in the remainder of this chapter represent shorthand means for categorizing a disparate range of contemporary practices for the purpose of analytical clarity; they should not be understood as entirely comprehensive. It is also important to note that there exists significant overlap between the categories. In operational terms, there are strong connections and dependencies between the three areas. So core special forces missions (darkness) include working with surrogate forces (delegation) and designating targets for long-range missile attack (danger-proofing). Many lethal drone strikes have been conducted as covert 'targeted killing' operations directed by the CIA. Offensive cyber operations are increasingly conducted by private corporations.[60] In this respect, the human or institutional agents of delegation, danger-proofing and darkness may be one and the same. Despite such blurred boundaries and mutual dependencies, the focus here is on their unique attributes as distinct modes of behaviour, allowing important consequences to be traced back to those particular attributes. Their collective harmful impact in terms of efforts to promote American security will be considered in the concluding section of this chapter.

It must be stressed that the aim here is not to cover every relevant issue in relation to these different areas. All have been subject to extensive in-depth research over many years, and there are now countless authoritative studies on topics such as drones, proxy warfare and covert action.[61] As there is insufficient space here to go into all the relevant issues, this chapter can only hope to scratch the surface. Its modest aim is to raise some of the most prominent issues as they pertain to the conduct of vicarious warfare and the wider argument of the book. With the Clausewitzian framework outlined above in mind, we can begin to understand why the strategic promise of vicarious warfare is rarely realized in practice.

Delegation

A central element of vicarious warfare involves shifting the burden of risk and responsibility on to others – as such, delegation refers to the contemporary pattern of increasingly externalizing the burden of war and contracting out security tasks to an assortment of proxy actors beyond the regular armed forces.[62] The risks of combat on the US side are essentially transferred to local allies such as private military and security companies, local security forces or irregular militias. This allows the true costs of war to be partially hidden.[63] Porch suggests the use of such proxies can 'lower the political and financial costs of intervention by desensitizing home populations to the human overheads of foreign adventures'.[64] Enthusiastic commentators have highlighted the benefits of training 'pro-Western – or at least anti-jihadist – locals to do the fighting and dying.'[65] In official doctrine and military publications, defence professionals have developed the conceptual underpinnings and operational requirements of 'by, with and through' indirect approaches, which are predicated on working with local regular and irregular forces.[66] Such groups are presented as loyal partners who will follow American orders and share American objectives in relation to specific threats or adversaries. For instance, remarking on the operation to retake Raqqa from Islamic State in 2017, the commander of US SOCOM, General Thomas, stated that 'we'll have that [city] back soon with our proxies, a surrogate force of 50,000 people that are working for us and doing our bidding.'[67]

Operationally, militias can provide the local knowledge, indigenous legitimacy,[68] and force density required to pacify peripheral areas of a country, especially where foreign presence is believed to drive resistance.[69] Others propose leveraging contingents of advisors to build up foreign security forces – Malkesian and Weston suggest that 'future challenges can be met, and even prevented, at a low cost by the aggressive use of military and civilian advisers.'[70] Private contractors, it is argued, act as operationally indispensable and valuable 'force multipliers.'[71] In short, officials claim all such armed auxiliaries can contribute meaningfully to victory, however defined.

These rationales all appear superficially persuasive. Impressive tactical victories have been achieved through delegatory approaches, especially where US forces have partnered with local forces, or where operations have been closely coordinated along the lines of the so-called compound warfare model.[72] However, the empirical record, especially when considered over the long term, presents a less positive picture. Most detached scholarship is profoundly sceptical. Tellingly, although military contractors and Western-aligned surrogate forces are increasingly familiar on the contemporary battlefield, often such outsourcing has been employed as a form of 'expedient cooptation' to rescue faltering missions as public support declines.[73] They are conceived as ideal instruments for quixotically salvaging sunk costs or forestalling imminent mission collapse.[74] Some cases are more positive than others. But problems stem from the inherent nature of delegated relationships, making it extremely difficult to craft effective narratives and coherent strategies.[75]

Buying power: modern mercenaries and private security

The exponential rise of the private security industry to the extent that, in some operational theatres, contractors have outnumbered American service personnel by three to one, is well documented. These developments have various causes, some associated with broader neoliberal economic trends and an increasing reliance on public–private security models.[76] But policymakers nevertheless understand how employing private military and security companies (PMSCs) can mitigate some of the costs and risks of conducting persistent military engagements. The kinds of active combat duties performed by companies such as Blackwater and DynCorp in Iraq have been quite rare. Typically, contractors have taken on supporting rear-echelon roles, such as logistics, technical maintenance, training and base security, although tasks such as loading missiles onto drones or conducting cyber operations have placed them very near to the front lines of vicarious warfare. Following controversial missions in Iraq and Afghanistan, and as the United States has moved away from large-scale COIN to focus on counterterrorism and threats from rival great powers, contracting has evolved over the last decade to embrace 'cyber-operations, intelligence analysis and drone piloting, and support for special forces in irregular conflicts.'[77]

The ready availability of PMSCs allows the scope of operations visible to domestic audiences to be kept small and casualties within these groups often escape public attention, thus shielding policymakers from unwelcome press.[78] Indeed, the Pentagon rarely provides clear data on contracted operations.[79] When major factors determining popular support for war centre around troop numbers and casualty figures, the lack of awareness regarding the true human cost of America's privatized wars seriously subverts informed democratic debate. The lack of transparency permits the executive to prosecute or expand contractor-run wars that the AVF would be incapable of conducting alone, and that the public might oppose if they knew the full scale of the commitment.[80]

Shifting the focus to actual operational theatres, the large presence of PMSCs has led to problems of coordination with regular military forces or proper alignment of their behaviour with strategic objectives.[81] Furthermore, high-profile incidents involving contractor abuses (such as the 2007 Nisour Square massacre of 17 Iraqi civilians by Blackwater guards), even if relatively rare, levy a disproportionate 'heavy soft-power cost' and undermine efforts to secure popular support in operational theatres.[82] Congress has held hearings and investigations into high-profile cases, but in general oversight has been marginal, especially of heavily privatized counterterror missions whereby military companies have worked with the CIA and JSOC on kill-or-capture missions.[83] While PMSCs appear to allow Western elites to buy political capital in exchange for large financial outlays, the return on their investment is questionable at best. Indeed, from a strategic perspective, experts claim that the benefits of outsourcing 'are either specious or fleeting, and its costs are massive and manifest.'[84]

While most major security contracts are awarded to large Western firms, the majority of the personnel are typically third country nationals or host nation citizens. Specific jobs are often subcontracted to local security companies through opaque outsourcing chains. In Afghanistan this led to Americans hiring warlords who had links with insurgents or who were implicated in 'murder, kidnapping, bribery as well as Taliban and other anti-Coalition activities.'[85] Reliance on private firms can frustrate efforts to forge a legitimate state monopoly of violence in host states, and, in the absence of reliable publicly provided security, citizens are increasingly compelled to rely on sectarian militias and protection rackets. Meanwhile, these firms draw qualified personnel away from local security forces, thus working at cross-purposes with US efforts (often also facilitated by contractors) to build national militaries.

State aid: national security forces

Building the indigenous military capacity of foreign state forces to defend themselves or confront threats in line with US interests and requirements appears to be an eminently straightforward and logical endeavour – simply train, arm and advise others to do the heavy lifting.[86] After all, Americans have the largesse, experience and specialized units required for the task. Most forms of this policy are captured within the overarching concept of security force assistance (SFA), encompassing those efforts during peacetime or in the midst of ongoing conflict that are small or large scale, short or long term, overt or covert, aimed at regular or irregular forces and either defensively or offensively oriented. In all cases, the attraction and rationale is clear and consistent: 'reduce the need for US troops to do the fighting by improving the ally's ability to do this themselves.'[87] But most comprehensive studies have demonstrated that SFA programmes are more difficult in practice than often assumed and have a distinctly poor record.[88] Karlin concludes that 'American efforts to build up local security forces are an oversold halfway measure that is rarely cheap and often falls short of the desired outcome.'[89]

Low-key, sometimes secret training missions have been overseen by SOF in scores of countries such as Pakistan, the Philippines, Somalia, Libya, Yemen, Kenya, Nigeria and Niger, to name but a few.[90] These small-scale training or 'advise and assist' missions are typically focused on counterterror objectives, and many involve training specialized elite units within foreign militaries, such as the Danab commando brigade in Somalia that is kept largely separate from the wider army.[91] Some have civic assistance 'hearts and minds' elements attached, but the emphasis has overwhelmingly been on preparing local forces for aggressive kinetic operations. Missions of this type in El Salvador during the 1980s and the Philippines in the early 2000s are often held up as models to be emulated.[92] But as with many other dimensions of vicarious warfare, studies boosting these apparent successes airbrush out important facts pertaining to the wider strategic picture or harmful longer-term political effects – future missions are thus confidently launched without a proper appreciation of the serious weaknesses associated with these approaches.[93]

Also troubling from a strategic perspective are a number of reports detailing how the activities of CIA-backed secretive Afghan paramilitary strike forces, in existence since the mid-2000s but expanded in recent years, have generated considerable local outrage.[94] As with the '127e' surrogate missions in Africa (see Chapter 6), such efforts appear to be less concerned with assistance than with cooption, utilizing indigenous forces for narrow US objectives. These kinds of forces, for instance the '02' unit operating out of Jalalabad, have been linked to extrajudicial executions and indiscriminate attacks against civilians through ramped-up strikes and raids, especially since 2017.[95] It is unsurprising, as experts claim, that such actions have aided terrorist recruitment and harmfully destabilized local power dynamics.

More concerted large-scale military reform efforts have only tended to follow mission deterioration, leading to rushed grandiose 'train-and-equip' programmes seen as the quickest route to the exit for Western forces, captured by the seemingly common-sense jargon of 'transition'.[96] Properly understood, transition is a process. However, the term has been misleadingly employed as denoting an objective in itself. Undertaken in the midst of punishing campaigns, the emphasis has been on rapidly fielding large conventional forces in pursuit of immediate security rather than ensuring quality or long-term sustainability. The result has been the creation of fragile, 'hollow' forces plagued by corruption, political divisions, enemy infiltration and operational deficiencies. Such problems arise when short-termist vicarious warfare rationales drive narrowly focused efforts as opposed to holistic security sector reform. Despite repeated rosy declarations about improving capability, local forces on the battlefield have remained heavily dependent on continuing operational support in order to just about hold the line, if that. Witness, for instance, the disintegration of the Iraqi Army facing Islamic State offensives in 2014,[97] or the way security forces in Afghanistan have struggled to hold back Taliban offensives: after Kunduz fell to the insurgent group in 2015, Western forces had to be deployed in combat roles alongside Afghan commandos to retake the city in two weeks of hard fighting.[98]

More seriously, if security handovers, implemented as desperate cost-minimizing or face-saving expedients, occur before necessary political conditions obtain or sufficiently robust governance arrangements are in place, then rapid military build-ups are a recipe for disaster.[99] Whatever the context, this is a problem faced in most SFA missions due to the often-corrupt nature of the governments receiving aid and the inability of Americans to ensure support reaches its intended recipients or is used appropriately. In fact, assistance often contributes to the militarization of political processes and the delegitimization of national security forces that are increasingly employed as the instruments of sectarian or tribal repression, thus contributing to deepening instability.[100] Host governments receiving US military aid have 'sought to focus on draconian internal security, or refused to accept international standards on the treatment of their own populations.'[101]

Concerns have been raised, for instance, regarding the way security assistance in Africa has served to prop up authoritarian regimes in the region while turning whole areas into active battlefields, with little by way of any overarching strategy directing such disparate missions. US support provides foreign leaders with the cover (and, by diverting resources, the means) to crack down on domestic opposition and allows them to avoid tackling fundamental societal problems; it can also disincentivize elites from negotiating political settlements with minority or separatist groups on their territory. Such dynamics help sustain the prominent causes of state fragility such as poor governance, corruption, societal inequality and conflict – bombs and bullets address only the symptoms while the conditions within which militancy thrives persist. Moreover, offensive operations launched by security forces under American tutelage only bolster terrorist propaganda and may be radicalizing new generations of militants.[102]

Re-emerging conflict vortexes, partly resulting from ineffective, abusive or politically controlled security forces, have a tendency to drag Western militaries back in to the fight – as witnessed repeatedly in Iraq and Afghanistan. In this way, advisory and assistance missions can serve as platforms for renewed escalation of commitments when indigenous forces falter in the face of inevitably heightened opposition accompanying US drawdown.[103] This is especially likely in the context of contemporary SOF-centric 'persistent engagement' advisory missions in which local forces are either led or accompanied by Americans in conducting direct action missions against high-value targets.[104] The line between assistance and combat can be blurry at best – for instance, the deadly Niger ambush of October 2017 came as such a shock to American observers because special forces thought to be involved in a standard training mission were, in fact, conducting kinetic combat raids.[105]

Proxy servers: unconventional warfare and irregular militias

Where security forces are overstretched, ineffective or simply not available, the US has often resorted to employing various forms of irregular surrogate forces. These might be utilized in a defensive community protection role (typically in a counterinsurgency context) or in a more offensive paramilitary role along the lines of the unconventional warfare model. Western support to rebels, militias, paramilitary groups and warlords displays extremely mixed results, typified by short-term gains balanced by serious long-term harm.[106] Despite inflated reports of irregular victories, most such actors have been associated with tactical deficiencies, widespread abuses and increasing radicalization: a problem associated with Western support to rebels in Syria.[107] Rebel forces, especially when managed remotely and often through intermediaries, can be incredibly difficult to control and, given information asymmetries, arms supplied to proxies can be difficult to monitor. We described earlier how US-supplied weapons have found their way to radical groups who have used those same weapons to attack Americans or their allies.[108] Having to work through intermediaries in Turkey and Jordan, the way anti-tank missiles provided to CIA-trained rebels in Syria ended up in the hands of Al-Qaeda affiliates echoes the agency's difficulty tracking the Stingers supplied via Pakistan to Afghan Mujahideen groups in the 1980s.[109]

Astonishing naivety has been displayed in assuming that the proxy's interests will remain aligned with US goals because they have been provided with patronage.[110] Such groups have their own agendas, their pursuit of which can undermine progress toward US strategic goals.[111] Proxies may also generate harmful liabilities: supporting one group makes enemies of others[112] or blinds sponsors to the opportunities of working with alternative actors.

The damaging and counterproductive effects of a reliance on militias have been apparent in various contexts such as Kosovo, Somalia, Libya and Afghanistan. So the promotion of *arbakai* militias within the ALP programme has generated fears among many Afghans of a return to the marauding groups during the devastating civil war of the 1990s, and it is a model with limited resonance beyond Pushtun regions.[113] In some cases, knowledge of US support can often serve to undermine the very groups they are seeking to empower: locals receiving support are branded as collaborators, stooges and puppets.[114] Similarly, militia actions can directly contribute to instability, providing opportunities for enemy exploitation. So Taliban gains in the north of Afghanistan, dramatically epitomized by the group's audacious seizure of Kunduz in September 2015, have been crucially enabled by US-sponsored militia infighting.[115] Even more damaging, at a strategic level and as noted in relation to PMSCs, policies that promote the creation and expansion of irregular armed groups contradict concurrent efforts toward building regular national security forces, leading to strategic disconnect and internal mission confusion.[116]

Reliance on militias can lead to forms of dependency whereby Western states are held hostage to the undisciplined behaviour of surrogates and inadvertently drawn into escalatory processes of over-commitment: 'the proxy, once embraced, must not be allowed to lose'.[117] The intensity of the interests animating the proxy may be such that when the sponsor wants to pragmatically wind down a conflict and enter into negotiations, the proxy can subvert its attempts and escalate the fighting. These groups can extract greater sponsor support or intervention by exploiting the typically ambiguous or unspecified nature of proxy alliance arrangements, the vested interests of bureaucrats managing the relationship or US concerns over credibility.[118] Empowering militias may help achieve certain immediate military objectives but create political problems over time, such as destabilizing rebel fragmentation (as witnessed in Libya after 2011),[119] proxies making unpalatable demands on attaining power or their pursuit of illiberal exclusionary agendas.

The requirement to protect and support proxies can also inadvertently pull the patron into conflictual situations that were not part of the original strategic intent. In mid-2017, US support to Kurdish and Arab militias on occasions brought it into direct confrontation with Iranian and Russian-backed Syrian forces, thus risking further escalation in a campaign intended to be restricted to defeating Islamic State.[120] Worse, these encounters may be designed by proxies precisely to elicit greater American involvement. In a broader sense, a perception that unconditional US sponsorship for local allies will be forthcoming where US interests are threatened may also encourage states or militia groups to launch risky or ill-considered military operations, confident in the belief that America will carry some of the risk or provide support if things go badly – a form of 'moral hazard' that can generate intensified conflict and instability.[121] On occasion surrogates may even turn on their US sponsors, a recurrent issue in Afghanistan with numerous 'green-on-blue' insider attacks and rogue militia incidents.[122]

A worrying pattern of abandonment (such as Trump's widely reported 'dropping' of the Kurds in 2019) can also undermine US efforts to effectively control its proxies. These groups, clear-eyed about the likelihood that they will be unceremoniously discarded once US objectives have been met or other priorities emerge, work to maximize their own gains while the spigot of arms and money remains open. Smart proxies – aware of the dismal record of providing long-term support to such groups – demonstrate sufficient deference before reasserting their own interests.[123] Abandonment from an ethical perspective is often less black and white than many commentators or the proxy's own propaganda might suggest: they often exploit and manipulate their sponsors as much as the other way around. But this doesn't invalidate the wider strategic point that such relationships, precisely because of these dynamics, are often fatally prone to disfunction.

Finally, among important audiences, America is frequently held responsible for atrocities and abuses committed by its proxies or for the wider instability generated by its policies.[124] Accusation of complicity and meddling can be hugely damaging for wider US strategic efforts, especially where widespread anti–Americanism already exists. It provides material for adversarial propagandists who claim that 'counterterrorism' is a rhetorical cover for a wider American crusade against Islam, or that empowering local groups is a divide-and-rule scheme to promote its imperial designs.[125] This is part of the reason why the US has historically often chosen to manage surrogate operations covertly, thus allowing a measure of deniability to limit the bad press and political fallout if exposed, however 'implausibly deniable' such operations might actually be.[126] There are few good options: attempts to achieve complete secrecy regarding the surrogate relationship risk future exposure (highly likely for such operations in the contemporary media environment), that will almost certainly prove damaging given the initial need for strict secrecy. In some cases, policymakers may calculate that there are narrative benefits to be gained through ambiguous 'openly secret' paramilitary operations – which may include demonstrating resolve, appearing tough, stoking nationalist sentiment or coercing adversaries – yet such methods are dangerously prone to misinterpretation, escalation or unintended consequences.[127] Where the relationship is overt, the other kinds of problems raised in this section will likely arise.

The available evidence from a variety of contexts suggests that the unthinking application of cost-evasive delegation consistently results in harmful blowback and counterproductive strategic consequences. Employing force to achieve political objectives is difficult enough even if the military instruments are one's own, subject to strict command and control; the challenge is multiplied when they are unwieldy and unpredictable proxies.[128]

Danger-proofing

If delegation relates to social-organizational forms of vicarious warfare, danger-proofing is more material in nature, referring to behaviour that allows for the application of force while minimizing physical harm to American personnel. It is typified by the American military's purported 'force protection fetish' but also the general resort to various forms of airpower and stand-off weapons systems, which offer safety through distance.

Conservation efforts: force protection and bunkerization

Record has detailed how a 'lack of loss' has become a primary imperative for militaries to the extent that self-protection can become the main mission.[129] It is a preoccupation apparent among political leaders, but also especially the higher echelons of military command – senior officers not only feel responsible for the safety of their men, but also worry that the public will automatically associate casualties with mission failure.[130] Protection is generally achieved by confining forces to heavily fortified bases, both large and small, combined with a general reliance on armour and overwhelming firepower. For instance, M777 Howitzers and M1–A1 tanks, better suited to large-scale conventional warfare, were employed in Afghanistan.[131] Even special forces operations – designed specifically to undertake high-risk missions – have not been immune from these developments.[132]

Heated debates surround this issue; however, there are strong arguments that casualty-minimizing approaches can actually contribute to the very problem they seek to solve. In peace enforcement or counterinsurgency contexts, tactical confidence, minimum use of force and non-aggressive 'soft' patrolling actually contribute to greater overall protection insofar as they facilitate the collection of human intelligence, enhance situational awareness and help build trust and rapport with locals. While such approaches are dependent on adequate strategic direction, proper resourcing and political resilience in the face of setbacks or provocations, Smith nevertheless notes how excessive protection 'jeopardizes mission success (and even increases the risk of casualties) by keeping troops holed up in barracks and bunkers' and prolonging the war.[133] As Mandel puts it, 'the best way to prevent the loss of life … is also the best way to achieve victory.'[134]

Protection may erode the overall deterrent effect of a force at the tactical level given the message of limited resolve it conveys: enemies may be emboldened or seek to challenge such measures.[135] Even counterterror missions have been hampered by the way excessive micromanagement stifles small-unit leader initiative – one former Reconnaissance Marine has referred to the 'immobilizing weight of protective requirements'.[136] Moreover, protective practices are enormously expensive, and huge fortified bases create additional vulnerabilities in supply that cause militaries to fight simply to sustain themselves: the so-called 'self-licking lollipop'.[137] Unedifying situations have arisen – comparable to parasites feeding off their hosts – in which Western militaries have been forced to indirectly pay adversaries protection money to prevent them attacking vital supply lines.[138]

The fact that professional soldiers cost millions of dollars to create and sustain in theatre is important here – indeed, it was estimated to cost US$1 million per year to sustain one American soldier in Afghanistan.[139] However, the politicization of decisions that have traditionally been the prerogative of military commanders, arguably best placed to determine appropriate force posture, has been a worrying trend: heightened protection is demanded to forestall negative reporting and associated political costs. Political interference tends to intensify as the prospect of mission success deteriorates and as public opinion increasingly equates casualties with failure. This can serve to hasten the downward spiral of counterproductive protective behaviour. Belated attempts to reverse the negative operational consequences of excessive protection – such as General McChrystal's notion of 'courageous restraint' in Afghanistan[140] – do little to undo the reservoirs of resentment generated through earlier aggressive operations or to develop trust and influence with locals.[141]

These dynamics pertain equally to the civilian components of stabilization missions. Progressive 'bunkerization' and restrictive risk-mitigation procedures, whereby security is prioritized ahead of mission effectiveness, has meant staff rarely venture out of fortified compounds, leading to operational blindness and situational ignorance.[142] Danger-proofing practices create harmful social 'distancing' dynamics; external actors tend to live in parallel worlds. Many only meet local citizens in the form of 'violent proximities', such as aggressive counterterror operations.[143] Distancing closes off communication channels and restricts opportunities for building meaningful relations, thus exacerbating existing forms of physical and cultural separation that adversaries only seek to widen.[144]

Moreover, in societies where rumours spread quickly, counterproductive behaviour fuels conspiracy theories. Locals assume interveners must have malign hidden agendas, reasoning that powerful states would not fail so egregiously unless they had other interests: strategic ineptitude is interpreted as willed action, with second-order corrosive effects in terms of trust and legitimacy. Through internal processes of denial, cognitive dissonance and institutional inertia, these practices persist, even as they simultaneously erode the foundations of the mission. Meanwhile, well-intentioned course corrections arrive too late to reverse deep-seated strategic deficiencies, and increasingly apparent failure has the effect of reinforcing these dynamics as frustration, distrust and mutual recriminations become commonplace. For many the solution is simply to eschew ground presence and interaction with locals altogether, and instead conduct wars safely from distant bases and platforms. But how effective are such alternatives?

Long-range projections: airpower, stand-off weapons and drones

An extreme form of danger-proofing, the use of airpower and stand-off long-range weapons systems such as cruise missiles or armed UAVs, or 'drones', allows war to be conducted at a safe distance from direct physical threat, at least in permissive environments. Ever since Douhet and Marshall, airpower has presented itself as a seductive shortcut to victory, and today remote control methods promise a form of 'proximity without risks'.[145] 'Indirect fire and air delivered munitions are', according to Betz, 'method[s] by which military commanders can buy out the perceived risks of committing more men to the fight.'[146] The difficulties American forces have faced conducting COIN operations prompted the air lobby to reaffirm these assumptions, even suggesting that airpower can play a central role in irregular warfare. Some enthusiasts proclaim the ability to effect 'air occupations', while others tout the special benefits of America's 'asymmetric advantage' in airpower that can 'present a truly show-stopping impediment to the nefarious schemes of her enemies' with 'impunity and little risk to Americans'.[147]

Such means of projecting force from a distance have certainly permitted the US to inflict immense attrition on enemies in multiple theatres and to coerce adversaries through relentless bombing. Yet, while potent in their destructive potential, it would be a mistake to overestimate their broader strategic utility, or to overlook unintended consequences in other spheres, both on the battlefield and far from it. Kane perceptively observes how airpower has often served effectively as a tool for opening wars but less so 'for resolving them satisfactorily.'[148]

In the first instance, prospective enemies are unlikely to willingly line up as the objects of target practice for American precision munitions – instead, they have adopted a variety of tactical countermeasures such as dispersal, deception, concealment amidst civilian populations or closely 'hugging' friendly forces to limit the ability of ground forces to call in air support. But more importantly, cruise missiles and airpower simply lack the capacity to shape political dynamics on the ground, beyond immediate coercion or killing.[149]

Part of the problem in this respect, when ground forces are absent, is the limited ownership of the situation once the bombardment ends, an issue that was clearly on display in the aftermath of the 2011 Libya intervention. The inevitable political vacuum that emerged following the ousting of Gaddafi was filled by multiple competing groups, and a viable political settlement was impossible to engineer without significant ground presence.[150] Linked to this, long-range strike and airpower-focused campaigns – whether of a 'shock-and-awe', leadership decapitation or attritional nature – can induce technological tunnel vision and political myopia given their singular preoccupation with delivering kinetic effects that may, in fact, actively harm or undermine critical political developments.[151] In the previous chapter we saw how this occurred in various contexts. It has been well documented how bombing can, for instance, cause enemy societies to cohere while consolidating public support around the nation's leadership.[152] The apparent solution of employing specialized units directing local allies on the ground – consistent with the Afghan model – may only exacerbate this problem by, for instance, legitimizing groups that complicate post-war dynamics or undermine diplomatic initiatives, as argued earlier.

Finding adversaries to eliminate or inducing enemies to submit can usually be achieved through airpower, despite whatever targeting hurdles are encountered along the way, and usually at very low risk. But this is what for McInnes represents its 'fatal attraction',[153] and is something that is exacerbated when consciously employed for its danger-proofing qualities – evasion of operational risk causes strategic 'risk rebound'.[154] The problem is often the lack of an integrated political strategy in the first place – a clear vision of how military actions are supposed to lead to long-term outcomes beneficial to American interests. The defence that this is a job for the politicians and diplomats is insufficient because it evades recognition of the fact that the war's conduct itself actively shapes, often negatively, the political context. In some cases, a more thorough examination of the situation could lead planners to the uncomfortable conclusion that military action might not be the best way forward, especially if there is an unwillingness to commit American forces on the ground from the outset.

Given the impressive capabilities of modern armed drones, some claim these limitations have been largely overcome; this, despite scepticism in some quarters with regard to their purely tactical effectiveness in light of high-profile intelligence failures leading to costly incidents.[155] Even when these weapons hit their targets, militant organizations 'exhibit a biological reconstitution capacity' precisely because the underlying causes of their regeneration have not been addressed and may even be exacerbated by unremitting punishment from the air. Despite bearing the brunt of drone campaigns, mid-level fighters are killed, but new recruits endlessly appear.[156] The prospect of euphemistic militant 'network overmatch' is chimerical, especially when placed in a holistic strategic context: as McChrystal remarks, 'just the strike part of it can never do more than keep an enemy at bay'.[157] Worse, aggressive drone use in the midst of counterinsurgency campaigns can generate 'strategic disconnect', undermining concurrent lines of operation and serving to reinforce 'negative distancing dynamics', further alienating critical populations.[158]

Enemy suicide bombings and 'symbolic revenge attacks' can be understood as retaliations against a mode of war difficult to counteract directly – a brutal attempt to achieve 'escalation dominance' which, although often immediately self-defeating, can pay strategic dividends.[159]

Regardless, the obvious enemy response is to either evade strikes through deceptive practices or to raise the political costs of their use for Western operators by, for instance, using human shields and moving among civilian populations.[160]

Although the precise numbers of civilians killed in drone campaigns remains contested, assessments by independent investigative bodies put the numbers at orders of magnitude above those of official estimates. Innocent casualties are not only unspeakable human tragedies, but also cause mounting strategic liabilities for the US, something that renders the killings all the more senseless. Experts have emphasized a pattern of strikes leading to increasing levels of radicalization – the 'accidental guerrilla' phenomenon – thus perpetuating the overall threat their use seeks to prevent.[161] For instance, recent reporting has detailed how an uptick in US strikes in Somalia has driven recruitment into militant organizations such as al-Shabaab.[162] The chain of causation – from drone strike to new militant – is often viscerally direct, but may also constitute more ambiguous processes. Generalized grievance, alienation and despair bred of menacing overhead surveillance and perpetual mortal threat, inflamed by shrewd terrorist propaganda, provoke opposition.[163]

The weight of evidence suggests that the political costs of drone strikes may well outweigh whatever purported tactical gains they deliver.[164] With Congress providing little meaningful oversight and the public paying scant attention, as drone warfare retreats again into unaccountable secrecy and obscurity under Trump, rigorous reappraisal of the costs and consequences of the policy has not been forthcoming.[165]

Darkness

The final prominent dimension of contemporary vicarious warfare considered here is that of darkness, employed as a broad term to encompass the use of covert action and special forces operations, but that can also usefully be expanded to include rapidly developing offensive cyber warfare. These kinds of operations take place in the shadows, beyond the media glare and subject to only minimal oversight.[166] The particular attraction of these instruments is that they are seen by decision-makers as offering 'a third option between doing nothing and having a war'.[167] Prior to the contemporary period it might have made more sense to consider these spheres of activity as stand-alone subjects; however, one of the most notable features of vicarious warfare today is the extent of the cross-over between them in terms of organizational competencies and operational integration.

Special effects: black ops, CIA paramilitarism and SOF expansion

Given their shared origins in the wartime OSS, there has always been overlap between the CIA and SOF, especially in relation to the practice of unconventional warfare where, for instance, the Secret War in Laos was CIA-led but involved significant special forces involvement. And there is a long history of the CIA's clandestine service, today known as the Special Activities Center (SAC), assuming operational control over elite members of the special forces (in recent times, usually from within JSOC) to make up the numbers in paramilitary operations. Such 'sheep-dipping' and close integration of CIA-SOF teams through the Defense Sensitive Support System has become a hallmark of modern counterterror and (para)military operations.[168] The raid that led to the assassination of Osama bin Laden in 2011 is an example of this: CIA Director Panetta was in nominal charge of the mission, but its operational implementation was almost entirely handled by JSOC Commander Admiral McRaven.

These arrangements enable the larger JSOC to be used more widely in a covert manner under the cover of the CIA's Title 50 legal authorities while at the same time, not unintentionally, allowing senior officials to circumvent certain Congressional restrictions and reporting requirements.[169] Linked to this, commentators have long observed the progressive militarization of the agency due to its disproportionate focus on covert action. Nonetheless it is striking to observe the extent to which in the modern era the CIA has been tasked to support military missions and conduct military-style operations.[170] Meanwhile, the military has increasingly ventured into domains previously considered the exclusive preserve of the CIA. Thus, while important legal and operational distinctions remain, it nevertheless makes sense to discuss covert action, special forces and, to some extent, cyber operations together here. This applies especially in relation to the often-similar strategic consequences these instruments cause.

This blurring of boundaries and partial merging manifests itself in operational terms in what has been described as the 'global shadow war'. CIA teams, increasingly supported by special forces, have been at the forefront of conducting lethal drone strikes as part of an ongoing campaign of targeted killings, mainly beyond officially designated active war zones. SOF have come to play a central role in US warfare, well beyond their marginal use in the second half of the 20th century. They have doubled in size to around 70,000 and are present in some 70 per cent of the world's nations.[171] And with countries like Yemen and Somalia declared areas of active hostilities since 2017, the scope for joint JSOC-CIA offensive missions has expanded even further. Together these specialized forces have, alongside other remarkable achievements, cleared the way for follow-on conventional forces, won impressive battlefield victories, produced made-to-order surrogate forces, rescued proxies facing defeat and spearheaded the unrelenting attrition of enemy fighters through countless surgical strikes and direct action raids.

Not only do these shadow warriors constitute flexible, rapidly deployable and supremely capable military instruments, but they also hold out the promise that 'major results can be obtained for minimal outlay':[172] a tempting 'easy button' for intervention.[173] Such expectations have been reinforced by the wider cultural glamorization of SOF and covert operators in films, books and even expert analysis, which, in turn, has influenced the views of senior political leaders. Commentators have observed a bipartisan 'infatuation' with special forces,[174] which has been exploited to advance their bureaucratic and political influence.[175] Furthermore, 'black' covert (unacknowledged) and clandestine (tactically secret) operations conducted beyond the media gaze seemingly allow elites to attain important objectives while evading difficult political questions. Covert action can allow policymakers to act in cases where either 'mere remonstrance or diplomatic protest and sending the marines' are not attractive options.[176] Although it is misleading to assume operations can be launched arbitrarily or with impunity, officials have been able to exploit various legal loopholes to evade serious scrutiny and, given its contemporary prestige and prominence, SOCOM itself has been subject to little civilian oversight.[177] The low-key nature of SOF missions means it is difficult for even well-informed experts let alone the wider public to keep track of their activities. And given that these forces are not publicly defined as 'boots on the ground', this allows officials to either hide intervention or play down the extent of US commitments.[178]

This has all contributed to extremely high demand for these operatives, resulting in a punishing tempo of operations. Some SOCOM commanders and security experts, for instance, believe this is unsustainable and may break the force.[179] Despite some worrying signs, the operational integrity of covert and SOF capabilities is not seriously in doubt. But the strategic effectiveness of their persistent global *use*, characterized by an almost unthinking approach devoid of overarching policy direction, certainly is. In particular, counterterrorism efforts have essentially been put on autopilot with default secretive, aggressive and heavily kinetic direct action missions substituting for a comprehensive strategy.[180] This has meant little thought has been devoted to achieving integration with broader regional priorities or possible counterproductive effects that might result within specific areas of operation – theatre-level commanders are left to 'tease out how to advance American policy as they gauge it from their own professional experience and judgment.'[181] Part of the problem is that it has been assumed that covert or clandestine military operations can achieve independent strategic effect when, in fact, this is rarely the case.[182]

Meanwhile, failed operations can cause considerable domestic and international embarrassment, disproportionate to whatever tactical advantages they might have achieved. Indeed, as our earlier discussion of Cold War covert operations made clear, the record of such strategies is not auspicious, and they have not infrequently contributed to serious blowback for America, even setting aside the harmful consequences of recurrent, purely tactical, mishaps.[183] We have seen how such outcomes have resulted from poorly conceived covert security assistance missions, with loosely controlled paramilitary proxies committing serious abuses against civilians. In a similar manner, an over-reliance on military force in various theatres can drive resistance and feed into damaging local political dynamics. For instance, in Afghanistan, the harmful consequences of aggressive night raids has been well documented – studies have detailed the way in which such missions create a backlash among Afghan communities, drive previously peaceful civilians to join the Taliban and undermine diplomatic efforts.[184] The creation of cookie-cutter local hunter-killer forces – such as counterterror pursuit teams in Afghanistan or Somalia's Alpha Group – in effect multiplies and sustains these violent, often abusive, practices. As a corollary to this, the emphasis on enemy attrition distracts officials from addressing critical underlying issues. In Libya, commentators have noted how piecemeal SOF offensives only address the symptoms of a broader national malaise.[185]

Initially intended as discrete usually time-limited missions, knee-jerk covert and clandestine direct action deployments have not infrequently pulled America into ill-considered and undesired lingering commitments that are prone to escalation. These missions can be difficult to wind down and thus end up binding the US, in a form of 'strategic stickiness', to regions where the precise interests being defended are vague or ill defined.[186] And given that oversight is minimal and decisions are often taken by a few officials with the necessary clearance, the presence of small numbers of operatives on the ground in volatile environments risks expanding wars along new lines or into new areas without proper debate or due strategic consideration.[187] Sometimes the core interest becomes simply preserving the presence: hardly a sound Clausewitzian politically focused rationale for maintaining these rare assets in combustible situations.[188]

Some argue that the criticism of shadow operations being utilized as shortcuts to victory is unfair because they are, in fact, designed as holding actions or simply to raise adversary costs. But history reveals how limited aims can soon encourage more ambitious ends, especially where early tactical successes breed arrogance, as occurred in Afghanistan and Nicaragua in the 1980s.[189] Objectives often run ahead of available means or lead officials to take dangerous, sometimes legally dubious, steps. Furthermore, given that such goal inflation results more from developments on the ground, little attention is devoted to how success will actually advance wider US interests.[190] US backing for the Ethiopian invasion of Somalia in 2007 failed to consider the political fallout that might result, and it is unclear if the CIA's *Timber Sycamore* paramilitary operation in Syria seriously thought much beyond the immediate toppling of the Assad regime, had it been successful. Similarly, the strong desire to do something, often simply because it can, causes America to align itself with dubious causes, rushing in without consideration of the broader context. America's support of Savimbi's South African-linked UNITA rebel group in Angola during the Cold War appeared to many as tacit legitimation of apartheid; today, US training of various African security forces has aligned the US with unsavoury and authoritarian regimes in the region. Moreover, US meddling can prove useful to enemy polemicists, something the Taliban, Assad and Venezuela exploit in their public pronouncements just as effectively as Castro, Khomeini and the Sandinistas had done before them.[191]

Headhunters: enemy leadership decapitation

Partly as a method to avoid becoming entangled in such contradictory commitments in the first place, a central focus of contemporary shadow warfare has been the attempted 'decapitation' of enemy leadership cadres (beyond the more generalized targeted killings of mid-level militants). Brooks suggests this is indicative of a growing 'individualization of warfare' and that is certainly preferable to the various forms of indiscriminate bombing of the past; intriguingly, she suggests it may even have the positive effect of allowing due process protections to be applied in the midst of conflict.[192] Regardless, the strategic rationale here is tempting and simple, as Kiras explains: 'destroying the leadership, or "carving out the brains" ... severs the link between the brain and the body.... Removing the most senior leaders, while inflicting overwhelming shock in key areas throughout rest of the system, will cause paralysis and collapse at the strategic level.'[193]

While arguably representing the ultimate strategic shortcut, decapitation has a poor record in practice, and has not infrequently led to damaging unintended consequences.[194] Some quantitative studies suggest decapitation can be effective when employed against armed non-state groups, increasing the chances of their 'mortality' over time.[195] Johnson and Sarbahi argue that drone strikes have reduced terrorist activity in Pakistan. However, they focus only on short-term effects in their study.[196] Building on findings that many groups survive beyond decapitation,[197] Long has convincingly concluded that targeted killings can, at best, disrupt well-institutionalized groups but 'cannot defeat the organisation'.[198]

Recent attempts to take out top insurgent and terrorist leaders have on occasion prevented attacks that may have occurred otherwise but have nevertheless failed to defeat targeted groups, and may even have contributed to their metastization and longer-term lethality. Following the killing of Osama bin Laden in 2011, Al-Qaeda remains a palpable long-term threat. The Taliban remains a menace to the Afghan state despite losing many top leaders to American drone strikes: experts believe the May 2016 decapitation strike against Taliban leader Mullah Mansour had little militarily value, and may have undermined progress toward negotiations.[199] Islamic State continues to recruit significant numbers into its ranks despite the fact that its long-time leader, al-Baghdadi, blew himself up during an American raid in 2019.

Dark web: offensive operations in cyberspace

Similar in many respects to special forces, covert operations and drone warfare, weaponized malware seemingly provides policymakers with discrete, surgical weapons that can project national power with a small footprint combined with unrivalled levels of secrecy and deniability.[200] Indeed, it has been suggested that many of the authorities and missions associated with cyber operations can draw from the special operations playbook.[201]

The Snowden documents revealed that as early as 2011, the US intelligence services had conducted over 200 offensive cyber operations that year.[202] Around that time, the Pentagon was still operating in a fairly constrained fashion. However, over recent years, its Cyber Command (elevated in 2018 to unified combatant command status) has increasingly pushed for an aggressive and offensive-minded approach to cyber strategy – dubbed 'persistent engagement'[203] – that reflects 'an instinct born of more than a decade of counterterrorism operations' whereby cyber operations come to resemble SOF raids.[204] Reflecting this, the commander of US Cyber Command recently underscored the importance of 'taking this fight to the enemy', and President Trump has loosened the constraints on the conduct of offensive cyber operations.[205] America has a growing arsenal of offensive cyber weapons that it has (reportedly) deployed against terrorist websites, North Korea's Musudan ballistic missile systems and famously, against the Iranian nuclear centrifuges in the form of the Stuxnet virus, which has been described as a 'fully automated covert operation'.[206]

The secretive nature of cyber attacks and the lack of official disclosure around cyber policy has meant that the efficacy of such instruments has largely evaded robust democratic debate. At one level, and reflecting our earlier discussion about drones, contrary to the claims of their proponents, US cyber operations have struggled to inflict significant damage on adversaries beyond causing them short-term tactical setbacks. For instance, targeted Islamic State online content resurfaced fairly swiftly using different servers and networks, and North Korea successfully resumed its ballistic missile tests in 2017 using different engine designs. Experts have argued that it is a myth that cyber offense is 'an effective and easy way to stop rival states from hacking America' and, more to the point, that there is a serious potential for counterproductive blowback.[207] There have been worrying cases of American cyber weapons being repurposed by hostile hackers. So, North Korea's WannaCry ransomware attack in 2017 propagated using a US-designed 'EternalBlue' exploit that had been stolen by a hacker group known as the Shadow Brokers.[208] Other cyber weapons, like Stuxnet itself, can lead to unintended collateral effects when they spread to affect friendly systems.

However, blowback will likely manifest more in terms of patterns of deepening mistrust between antagonists, disruption to sensitive diplomatic processes and unpredictable escalation.[209] It is not inconceivable that cyber crises could spiral out of control or cause America to stumble into full-blown military confrontations. Sanger highlights the significant risk of miscalculation and escalation in pursuing an offensive strategy when America cyber defences remain weak and networks highly vulnerable to adversary retaliation.[210] It is thus far from clear that cyber weapons – seemingly the 'perfect weapon' with which to conduct vicarious warfare – are any more immune from the kinds of drawbacks that apply to all such methods that seek to confront adversaries in the dark. Coker concludes that 'cyber-attacks do not really offer a quick fix, any more than they offer an escape from the risk trap: doing too little, or doing too much.'[211]

★ ★ ★

At a broader level, pervasive covert interventions – whether through direct force, by proxy or in cyberspace – undermine fundamental international laws and norms pertaining to non-interference in the affairs of sovereign states and thus the foundations of the liberal order that the US claims to uphold. Moreover, subverting internal political processes also demeans America's purported status as standard bearer for global democracy. At home, operational darkness often translates into political darkness over time as it restricts important decisions to ever-narrowing privileged groups and subverts democratic processes of scrutiny, oversight and accountability, increasing the chances of future missteps. In this light, Treverton's conclusion over 30 years ago still applies today: 'even the "successes" of covert action seem ambiguous or transient in retrospect, accomplished at significant cost to … America's image in the world' and its own core values.[212]

Conclusion to Part III

Delegation, danger-proofing and darkness – as the prominent contemporary operational manifestations of vicarious warfare – are all adopted for their apparent attraction as low-cost, risk-minimizing and tactically effective approaches to defeat adversaries and deal with an array of security challenges. Superficially, at least, these benefits and strengths are real. Yet such approaches have the potential to cause harmful strategic effects.

They provide American leaders with the impression of positive momentum. Immediate operational successes have the effect of convincing policymakers that they are practically feasible and effective in confronting adversaries. Few would doubt the lethality of drone strikes in military terms. Similarly, territory taken by US-aligned militias provides sponsors with comforting perceptions of activity and control. In this way, they breed a form of dependence or even addiction. This is perhaps captured in the notion of 'Predator crack' among commanders who become reliant on drones,[213] but the idea can apply to all the approaches discussed earlier.

The illusion of 'progress' distracts decision-makers from contemplating the wider strategic picture or potential second- and third-order negative effects. In fact, vicarious methods often actually contribute to restricting the ability of Western forces to shape crucial political dynamics on the ground, while inadvertently leading to unforeseen liabilities, unintended confrontations and escalating commitments. Vicarious warfare encourages excessively kinetic military approaches that serve to exacerbate complex problems, prevent progress toward more realistic negotiated solutions or, through forms of operational tunnel vision, cause planners to miss potentially mission-fatal blind spots. Beyond that, the overarching policy itself, which may be wrong or misguided, is often insufficiently questioned or reassessed. Meanwhile, the mounting costs borne by civilians – directly through bombings, raids and abuses, or indirectly through protracted conflict and psychological trauma – cumulatively foster discontent and continued resistance.

This is all not necessarily to argue that the approaches outlined in this chapter are entirely without merit, or that they should not be employed in certain circumstances. Rather, it is the excessive prominence given to them and the extent to which they have come to drive policy and strategy that leads cumulatively to counterproductive outcomes.

Conclusions

Vicarious warfare is descriptive of an approach to waging war that seeks to distance its means from its ends. In simple terms, it refers to the prospect of war on the cheap, fought at a reduced price in blood, treasure or political capital relative to ambition. This can manifest itself in behaviour at all levels and in all spheres of war, from the tactical to the strategic, from individual soldier to the wider populace. It is willed to varying extents by all major societal actors, whether political and military leaders or ordinary citizens. It is not synonymous with attempts to banish war from the human experience, as pacifists might desire; rather, the defining characteristic of vicariousness is the attempt by societies, however consciously or unconsciously, to loosen or untether the cords that bound the practice of war to its manifold costs and requirements while still seeking to reap its potential rewards.

In early human history, the conduct of war tightly tethered group members to one another and to its inescapable consequences. The fighting was immediate and bloody, usually close to home, and implicated almost everyone in a community whether directly or indirectly. Sacrifice was an expected and necessary thing. Given that the outcome of battle might determine a group's chances of survival, it would not be entered into lightly, and decisions would typically be arrived at collectively. Accountability for leadership in war, entailing command in battle and sometimes lasting only for the duration of the immediate crisis, would be similarly direct, sometimes essentially decided by war itself. Of course, this is an idealized image. Ritual, stratagem or crude forms of distancing and protection might serve to shield individuals or groups from some of war's risks and costs, but in most important physical, social and political respects, there were few opportunities for vicarious distancing.

If it is possible to argue that human society has travelled a long road to reach the present American apotheosis of vicarious warfare, it has certainly not been a straight one leading to any form of teleologically predetermined destination. Instead, it has been meandering and circuitous, with much backtracking and many dead ends, quite literally in some cases. During the 19th and early 20th century, it seemed the world was moving toward an almost opposite, distinctly non-vicarious future driven by prominent ideologies, heroic ideals, norms of patriotic sacrifice, total societal mobilization and the apparent lack of military options beyond attritional battle. Yet widespread revulsion at the huge cost of modern total war has provided the pervasive backdrop to more recent developments. Meanwhile, new opportunities presented themselves that promised to limit the sacrifices required. This might be in the form of new technologies and weapons or new ways of employing existing capabilities. Every so often bold strategic thinkers claimed to have discovered less costly shortcuts to objectives. Some vicarious options have always been available in theory, such as less societally invasive forms of military mobilization or outsourcing to irregular proxies and mercenaries. Whether societies chose to avail themselves of these things has always depended on various prevailing conditions and circumstantial factors.

It is hardly surprising that groups might look for ways to evade war's bloody realities. Indeed, many advocates of vicarious approaches have been motivated by commendable, well-meaning, even noble intentions. Ideas along these lines – such as various kinds of indirect strategies – have often emerged in 'inter-war' periods following especially costly episodes that prompted thinkers to devise ways of avoiding future repetitions of senseless slaughter, at least as perceived by them. As noted, the immense carnage of the two world wars still influences contemporary thinking, reinforced by subsequent blood-spattered episodes and the looming spectre of apocalyptic nuclear war. This is all entirely human. Unfortunately, sometimes more cynical calculations have been at play: elites have designed operations in such a way as to reap maximum personal, political or institutional benefits while others pay the financial or blood price; no less shamefully, the wider population has been content to look the other way as its leaders prosecute brutal shadowy wars in foreign lands. This is equally human, perhaps, but either way this behaviour tends to be harmful. Both the strategic saints and cynics typically end up failing to realize their ambitions.

Just as the conventional and small wars traditions of American force can manifest in a variety of forms, so too does vicarious warfare. It can be said to rhyme, not repeat, across different periods or contexts. Its appearance will be shaped principally by the broader geo-political strategic context, the state of existing technology and military methods available, existing strategic theories and doctrines, and domestic political currents. So, a common vicarious mirage throughout history has entailed adopting approaches that might achieve a decisive short war. According to some commentators, today this has seemingly been replaced by an expectation of near-continuous military campaigns but fought within acceptable thresholds of price, pain or public concern (an approach that perhaps explains President Obama's curious idea of 'sustainable victory').[1] As such, it would be mistaken to ascribe any fixed framework concerning the implementation of vicarious warfare in practice. Rather it is really about the rationales and mentalities driving and directing the use of force.[2]

The point is that we should not confuse prominent instruments or approaches with the phenomenon itself. The narrow conflation of vicarious warfare with small-scale operations or forms of military outsourcing can lead to it easily being confused with the strategies adopted by weaker actors. But where weak states have, for instance, utilized mercenaries, this was driven not so much by cost-evasive rationales as pragmatic necessity.[3] We saw how America in its formative years sometimes relied on privateers, Indian auxiliaries, slaves and foreign surrogates. While such measures allowed the nation to evade difficult constitutional questions associated with maintaining a large standing army, usually these were reasonable expediencies in desperate circumstances. As the United States rapidly grew to become an imperial power, the rationales changed. Empire, as broader history would suggest, typically induces a search for strategic shortcuts. The pursuit of primacy – sustaining and expanding American liberal hegemony – is the critical underlying political condition driving the contemporary prosecution of vicarious warfare.

Building on important developments during the 19th and 20th centuries, and especially during the Cold War, we have charted the way vicarious thinking has influenced most major American military operations over recent decades, even when, on the surface, large-scale campaigns dominated impressions. In particular, the 2010s can be described as the quintessential vicarious decade. The long war on terror continues to provide the most obvious strategic context within which vicarious warfare is implemented, but, as this book has sought to show, it would be mistaken to associate the broader phenomenon narrowly or simplistically with that particular scenario.

Beyond purely coalescence in terms of practice, we have also argued that vicarious warfare – although not referred to as such by its proponents – has come to constitute an increasingly coherent and distinctive tradition of American warfare. A growing body of policymakers, practitioners and pundits have formulated the essential outlines and operational methodologies for fighting war on the cheap. In terms of policy, Clinton and Bush laid important foundations, but Obama embraced its core elements outright and embedded them more firmly in official plans. Meanwhile, for all the differences in tone, rhetoric and political orientation, Trump has essentially taken this inheritance forward in the form of what Lynch describes as a form of 'belligerent minimalism'.[4]

There have been changes in direction in particular theatres and shifts in emphasis regarding certain operational elements, but overall we have witnessed a consolidation of the tradition in both theory and practice. This all underscores the extent to which vicarious warfare is a phenomenon driven by deeper conditions and factors beyond any particular administration. It may also apply beyond America itself.

While the contemporary manifestation of vicarious warfare is most clearly apparent in relation to the United States – the specific focus of this book – there is no theoretical reason why it cannot apply to other actors. Its practice generally assumes large states with extensive foreign regional or global interests possessing the requisite power, wealth and influence to: acquire weapons capable of effectively projecting force from a distance; recruit and manage proxies and private forces; and create specialized armed units capable of operating in a clandestine manner. But beyond such material requirements, the social and normative context must be such that vicarious warfare is deemed both necessary and in some respects a welcome thing. Researchers have partially detected these attributes in other Western states such as the United Kingdom,[5] France[6] and even Germany,[7] or in the behaviour of regional powers such as Iran, Russia and China.[8] The relevance of the phenomenon to other actors is beyond the scope of this book, as is the question of what the future might hold for vicarious warfare: a few general reflections must suffice in that respect.

Given the centrality of, for instance, armed drones to popular related concepts such as 'remote warfare', it is tempting to focus on the possibilities inherent in technological advances, especially given far-reaching developments in this sphere – for instance, in missile technologies, cyber warfare, robotics and artificial intelligence[9] – potentially enabling vicarious methods unimaginable to earlier generations. This might not simply apply in terms of radically expanding the distance from which force can be projected using new lethal autonomous weapons systems, but also the way advanced means of exploiting information might enable new forms of networked, self-organizing and decentralized 'chaoplexic' organization.[10] This might, for instance, greatly increase the speed, lethality and perhaps even the invisibility, both tactically and politically, of special operations while also reducing risk. Cutting-edge information technologies, such as deep fakes, may enable leaders to find new ways of shielding key audiences from the ongoing reality of military operations through media manipulation or disinformation. Perhaps technology will also take vicarious warfare into new geographies and domains such as the Arctic, underwater or space. But consistent with the main arguments presented in this book and its Clausewitzian foundations, it is likely that more consequential factors will relate to developments in society and politics.

Wars always reflect the nature of the societies that wage them. Technology can be one factor causing societies to change, but political ideologies, influential strategic myths and narratives, cultural norms, values and beliefs or socioeconomic structures can ultimately prove more influential, crucially determining how emerging technologies will be developed and put to use: as Coker notes, 'every technology is a function of social life and every weapon has a social history'.[11] It is change in this respect that will likely do most to determine the future shape of vicarious warfare. Especially significant will be evolving social attitudes toward the state, war and the idea of sacrifice. But the future of vicarious warfare might be determined more by the extent to which it is judged to be an effective instrument for achieving security – in other words, the extent to which it is judged to offer strategically sound approaches for solving pressing problems and threats. The conclusions of the book in this respect are stark.

Military promise, strategic peril

Vicarious warfare is a strategically neutral concept. Simply because actors attempt to minimize costs and requirements relative to ambitions in the way they fight does not automatically determine whether they will be successful or not – sometimes good fortune can suffice. The analysis in this book has sought to provide a balanced appraisal of this form of war grounded in a realistic consideration of the pressures and constraints faced by decision-makers, neither ignoring its real potential advantages nor overstating its adverse effects. The aim has not been to simply criticize or condemn policy, but also to *understand* the powerful factors encouraging and driving existing approaches, recognizing the political, strategic, bureaucratic and ethical dilemmas decision-makers have to contend with in determining courses of action in uncertain, complex and demanding situations (see Chapter 5).

In adopting a broad catch-all concept such as vicarious warfare, we must be mindful not to throw the baby out with the bath water. It would be short-sighted to pronounce a blanket condemnation. As noted, some of the means, methods and approaches that have been utilized as vicarious instruments in recent years may constitute entirely reasonable and effective means for addressing issues and threats in particular scenarios. They represent genuine attempts to square difficult circles in terms of efforts to provide security or protect national interests when the perception, and possibly the reality, is that citizens will not accept serious sacrifice. Vicarious warfare offers undoubted military operational advantages while permitting successive American administrations to maintain a persistent tempo of operations that evades rigorous democratic scrutiny. Affording the prospect of 'maximum payoff with minimal investment', these are enormously appealing qualities, especially to embattled democratic leaders confronted with intensive internal scrutiny and multiple external challenges.[12] It may indeed be the least bad course where decision-makers have few serious alternatives. Some operations have succeeded, but this was usually where the goals, expectations and operational parameters were carefully circumscribed.[13] One benefit might be that, as Clausewitz observed, wars fought in this way will be 'less costly if they succeed and less damaging if they fail'.[14]

However, a core argument of the book is that the typical rationales and justifications underpinning the prosecution of vicarious warfare are generally misplaced. The analysis demonstrated that its advantages are typically outweighed by longer-term harmful, self-defeating and counterproductive strategic effects. Too often decision-makers have uncritically reached for vicarious military responses, in part simply because they are available to hand. As much as it might appear a natural choice for confronting the global threats American faces, it is not synonymous with 'easy war' – like any strategic approach, it comes with costs and consequences that might well outweigh the real advantages it offers. This generally results because a vicarious mentality encourages behaviour disrespectful of the nature of war itself.

In the form of his famous trinity, Clausewitz taught us that war is always composed of three fundamental elements: politics, chance and passion.[15] It is action directed toward and shaped by the purposes of those who wage it, and cannot be disentangled from the wider political environment of which it is part; the existence of an intelligent foe sets up a complex interactive process tending toward escalation and which is defined by uncertainty; and as an intensely human social phenomenon, it always engages the emotions, which will greatly determine the way adversaries react or the extent to which any war has support among key constituencies and is deemed necessary, politically legitimate or ethically justifiable.[16] Vicarious approaches can subvert coherent strategic behaviour in all these areas.

First, where military instruments essentially come to drive strategic behaviour, then force will almost by default be detached from the policy objectives it is supposed to serve. This is all the more likely when war is put at the service of an imperial project driven by ideological enthusiasms and commercial avarice (as we have argued has often been the case for America) rather than vital interests or strict necessity. In these circumstances, the required means are likely to be misjudged and costs underestimated as promoting moralistic ideals or defending economic investments provide little concrete basis for military planning. The typically discretionary nature of such missions largely precludes robust commitment and they are likely to be unsettled by even minor setbacks. Meanwhile, the focus on securing immediate military outcomes distracts attention away from consideration of critical wider and longer-term political dynamics: positive tactical action may, in fact, be generating significant political problems and, because the costs of persisting with force appear low, potentially fruitful diplomatic engagement or compromise solutions will likely be squandered, even if decision-makers understand final military success is unattainable. Likewise, the militarization of policy means that insufficient resources are devoted to addressing the deeper underlying factors driving continued resistance or conflict, and which are often only exacerbated through the relentless application of force.

Second, vicarious warfare fails to appreciate the uncertain and contingent nature of military operations or how small steps almost inevitably lead to larger commitments: even a minimal presence or marginal actions can generate new requirements and liabilities or pull forces into unexpected confrontations, not least due to enemy reactions. Indeed, those adopting vicarious approaches tend to be hubristically disrespectful of the strategic acumen of adversaries or heedless of the options available to them. Enemies can seek to escalate the war in surprising ways, often inspired by the lack of resolve that the use of vicarious methods conveys. Indeed, we have discussed how some approaches can be self-defeating precisely due to their minimalist rationales and design, such as an often unnecessary requirement for covert plausible deniability or coercive force lacking credibility. The immediate tactical potency of vicarious instruments, and the existence of cases that misleadingly appear to confirm their efficacy, also encourages over-confidence, wishful thinking and complacency. There is thus little incentive for strategists to devise more innovative or effective approaches. Furthermore, where military approaches dominate, the enemy is almost always vilified in order to justify the requirement for continued aggressive operations, thus further entrenching counterproductive approaches and blocking off avenues for timely negotiation or disengagement.[17]

This is in part due to the powerful emotions that are inevitably sparked by war – the third element of Clausewitz's trinity. But alongside adversary demonization, the use of vicarious methods causes vital emotional and psychological responses (that usually accompany war) to be suppressed through processes of dissociation, denial and cognitive dissonance. Vicarious force is presented as surgical and even humane, wrapped up in comforting verbalizations, such as 'disposition matrix' or 'signature strike', which hide the reality of the death and destruction that they inevitably produce, and which dwarf the scale of the limited inputs required. But, as Brodie recognized half a century ago, 'like any other kind of deliberate insensitization or self-deception, it has a price.'[18]

The dehumanization of war brought about by drone warfare and remote killing can remove compunctions about violence and undermine the sense of shared humanity that historically promoted restraint on the battlefield.[19] This is not only bad news for foreign populations, but a strategic outlook untroubled by moral scruples can cause American planners to perilously overlook the intense emotional reactions that its interventions generate within those communities. And from a domestic perspective, the collective denial resulting from the illusion of sanitized war allows the public to continue supporting military campaigns, oblivious to their harmful human and strategic effects. Moreover, the distancing of the people from decisions and the diminution of accountability processes largely precludes the kind of societal engagement and investment that is necessary to sustain military operations. Secrecy, surrogacy and riskless force might appear to allow policymakers to bypass the often-fraught processes involved in justifying the wars they wish to prosecute. But given the potential for commitments to escalate, for secret operations to be harmfully exposed and for various costs to mount over time, there is likely to be an eventual reckoning in these respects. And if the necessary popular will behind intervention is ultimately lacking, events can rapidly spiral toward outright failure.

Building on this latter observation, a good measure of the wisdom of any use of force is the extent to which it can command broad support within the electorate and their chosen representatives. The only way to ensure this is to expose decisions to as wide a circle of opinion as operational security permits. Policymakers often disingenuously appeal to this latter requirement to justify their evasion of scrutiny, but this is difficult to sustain in an age when few serious military operations can remain secret for long and when they are usually open secrets anyway. Moreover, the often-harmful effects resulting from such operations would cast considerable doubt on the validity of such arguments. The various political and legal frameworks that evolved to subject American leaders to such democratic scrutiny, especially since the 1970s, were designed precisely with this purpose in mind: to expose strategic decisions to multiple perspectives and to invest operations with an imprimatur of democratic support and legitimacy. According to Mead, the jostling tumult of democratic decision-making can have a beneficial effect on foreign policy as it ensures actions broadly reflect the wishes of wider American society.[20] Furthermore, if there is truth to the political science contention that democracies are more likely to be successful in war, then the extent to which vicarious methods dilutes the efficacy of oversight structures or allows policymakers to evade or subvert democratic processes can be hugely damaging for American security.[21]

Contrasted with the direct and palpably 'positive' results that vicarious warfare delivers in terms of immediate operational effects, the costs and consequences are hidden insofar as they tend not to be clearly correlated with specific military actions but rather emerge and accrue over longer time frames and in spheres beyond those associated with the initial application of force. The causal chains at work here are often diffuse, opaque and complex – an issue that not only complicates analysis but also undermines accountability for military-strategic failings.

Narrative traps

Diminished accountability itself perpetuates the problem through the perverse incentives and culture of impunity that it generates, and also militates against genuine lesson learning: subsequent critical accounts based on more sober assessments struggle to displace powerful narratives of presumed success, often massaged and promoted by supporters. Conceptualizing vicarious warfare as a broader phenomenon and emergent 'tradition' of American war, we are able to better appreciate why, despite lacklustre results, it continues to exert a powerful hold over security elites and the wider public.

Policymakers must be alert to the danger of being too easily persuaded by partisan narratives and misleading simplistic shibboleths that can distort understanding of the true effectiveness of such operational methods, especially those promising low-cost, high pay-out solutions to security challenges. Strategic choices should not be held hostage to any one agenda proffering blueprint approaches based on its favoured prescriptions. Really the issue is not one of choosing between the models presented by the different traditions – which inevitably leads to *templated* rather than necessary *tailored* approaches – but rather designing operations so that they offer the best chance of producing political outcomes that are conducive to American interests. This requires a deft hand and an open mind.

Although by no means exclusive to this particular tradition, part of the problem here is the way advocates of the vicarious tradition distort the lessons of earlier episodes to suit their agenda. Far from meeting the ideal Clausewitz outlined in terms of in-depth critical historical analysis,[22] more common has been the selective corralling of history for nakedly partisan purposes. Spurious myths around earlier interventions serve to rationalize new interventions or ongoing practice.[23] Michaels and Ford describe a form of 'rhetorical re-description' of past events that often takes place, utilized in order to justify a proposed course of action or to 'persuade someone that an action that had previously been "condemned may seem worthy of praise"', or vice versa.[24] Deploying historical analogies in this way is a common technique of influence given their potential powerful resonance and persuasive effect – a uniquely effective and effortless 'political device to sell a particular policy or discredit an opponent's alternative.'[25] What we have seen repeatedly throughout this study is the enthusiastic adoption of vicarious approaches justified by appeals to earlier seemingly successful models without sufficient interrogation or critical evaluation of their true effectiveness or long-term strategic benefits. Sometimes this was because certain adverse consequences had not yet become apparent or were not subsequently integrated when they did. But more often it was due to analysts' myopic focus on the tactical efficacy of past cases or, more cynically, a conscious decision to leave such negative aspects out of accounts in order to propagate a narrative of success.

Such airbrushed models can become powerful rhetorical weapons for those seeking to promote vicarious approaches. This was especially apparent in relation to the 'Afghan model' based on the 2001 intervention. The integration of special forces, supporting stand-off airpower and surrogate irregular forces, was proclaimed as a uniquely effective mode of war, greatly influencing military approaches through the 2000s and beyond. Yet, with hindsight, it is clear that the model was deceptive and in fact sowed the seeds of many future problems. Indeed, some more perceptive analysts at the time feared that it would be too uncritically adopted as a model for fighting future wars quickly, easily and cheaply.[26]

Deeper costs

Perhaps most concerning here is the deeper self-harm being inflicted on the nation through its ongoing prosecution of vicarious warfare. Commentators fear that the burden of fighting a low-level 'forever war' of questionable legal, moral or strategic justification will have a corrosive impact on the integrity and proper functioning of the American political system as a whole. Anxiety has been expressed in relation to the societal price of under-scrutinized and habitual warfare manifested in the steady erosion of foundational values. Brooks has explained how persistent warfare, in an age when war and peace are increasingly blurred, permits the curtailment of privacy, rights and liberties due to the exceptional authorities 'wartime' allows.[27] Traditional checks on the executive's warmaking powers – as captured in the Constitution, War Powers Act and other statutory laws – have been significantly weakened due to how force can be applied in ways that do not appear to meet traditional thresholds for triggering Congressional interventions, legal challenges or wider public contestation. The US role in the Yemeni civil war, for instance, has gone almost unnoticed, while the killing of tens of thousands of adversaries in numerous theatres around the globe has elicited an ambivalent domestic response. Essential features of the democratic process, such as transparency and public contestation, are being eroded by a reliance on contractors, proxies, drones and covert teams as well as the progressive normalization of the low-level use of force. Looking to the future, there may be serious unanswered questions associated with the expansion of executive power afforded by new generations of autonomous weapons.[28] These developments are all the more ironic, not to mention hypocritical, given the values America claims to be upholding through its interventions.

Vicarious warfare can also be seen to sustain the societal militarism that provides the cultural context in which these corrosive practices can thrive. If most citizens do not experience war's costs directly and, as argued earlier in the book, are generally only cognisant of its immediate short-term benefits, it can become something they begin to romanticize and even actively come to desire through ignorance of its real consequences. In the late Roman Republic, the growing popularity of gladiatorial contests was arguably reflective of a population less and less exposed to the reality of fighting due to growing military professionalization but that nevertheless wanted to experience the battles and triumphs of the state vicariously. Elites exploited this public appetite for militaristic spectacle to advance their own political careers and agendas. Ominously, these developments accompanied creeping authoritarianism and the growing power of military-political leaders, prefiguring the ultimate collapse of the republican system itself. In this light, vicarious warfare is ideal for a modern demagogue like President Trump. He can claim that he is fulfilling his popular campaign promise of ending large-scale costly wars while nevertheless simultaneously overseeing never-ending battles around the globe. When it suits, he can exploit the popular appetite among his nationalist base for triumphal displays of American military muscle, publicly glorying in actions such as the targeted assassination of an Iranian general or air strikes against Syrian chemical weapons facilities.

Beyond America, vicarious warfare makes a mockery of core international principles pertaining to state sovereignty and non-intervention, thus corroding the basis of the world order that America purports to defend. This is not even to mention the huge toll that America's wars have taken on foreign societies – indeed, such profound ethical questions are too vast in order to be able to do them justice here, but it is at least reasonable to suggest that, beyond its strategic rationales, vicarious warfare has evolved as a way for Americans to distance themselves from the troubling moral consequences of the military actions taken in their name. The euphemistic contortions and evasions accompanying modern modes of war leads Coker to ask whether this 'spares us from having to ask the really embarrassing question – do we have such clarity of moral vision that we can kill with a good conscience?'[29]

It is unlikely that decades of unremitting global warfare – even when conducted in the shadows – will not begin to take its toll on cherished American values, as the founders clearly warned over two centuries ago. Arguably such domestic self-harm has yet to be fully revealed or properly understood, although the rise of xenophobic intolerant populism, bitter partisan division and creeping authoritarianism are perhaps an ominous portent of things to come.[30] But this harm will likely not stop at the water's edge. Given the indissoluble connection between domestic and foreign affairs that has been a central feature of its history from the nation's birth, it would be surprising if the erosion of democracy at home does not adversely redound on wider US interests.[31] This at a time when there are global challenges requiring urgent attention and rival challengers knocking at the door. America is in serious need of an open and honest public conversation about its use of force abroad so that it might more safely and confidently navigate the emerging strategic landscape. This will only be possible if there is greater clarity, coherence and consistency regarding the kind of nation America both publicly professes and actually intends to be.

★ ★ ★

This book has aimed to catalyse further debate around modern American military practice. The core arguments should cause policymakers to seriously re-evaluate the often-presumed advantages that vicarious methods offer. Cool-headed discretion is required in determining which situations are truly deserving of responses involving the use of force. Restraint is required to resist the temptation of instinctively reaching for quick and easy solutions to immediate challenges as well as the resilience to accept the short-term costs associated with compromise. Forethought is required to ensure adequate consideration is devoted to the likely wider and longer-term consequences of military actions. Empathy is required to better account for the way key strategic audiences might interpret and react to the application of American force. Humility is required to understand that the liberal values that the nation holds so dear are not so easily exportable and that force is usually a poor, possibly even counterproductive, instrument for accomplishing that. Integrity is required to ensure choices are geared toward producing outcomes that serve collective national interests as opposed to narrow short-termist personal or organizational agendas. And knowledge of the fundamental nature of war and strategy is required so that decision-makers are not too easily swayed by those presenting appealing arguments promising low-cost shortcuts to success. At a broader level, American citizens must accept greater responsibility for the military force employed in their name.

While the political incentives, technological temptations and social dynamics that drive the prosecution of vicarious warfare are powerful, growing awareness of the likely costs and consequences pregnant in its use may lead to a more cautious and circumspect attitude toward its casual or excessive employment. A central conclusion here must be that if leaders and the societies they represent are not ready to pay the full price of war for the objectives they desire, seeking cut-rate solutions can be a dangerous path to take. While some actors are on occasion able to evade an ultimate reckoning, it is generally advisable to ensure that one is willing and able to cash the cheque should the god of war catch you unawares demanding payment of debts accrued.[32] Those failing to heed such advice often end up paying more than they originally bargained for, and with interest. Proportionality in aligning means and ends is essential. As Edmund Burke once put it, 'in all fair dealings the thing bought must bear some proportion to the purchase paid.'[33]

Epilogue:
Implications for American
Grand Strategy

Scholars of American grand strategy assess the broad contours of US foreign policy and offer prescriptions regarding the best way forward. Their focus is on the overarching purpose or 'vision' of US global engagement, identifying vital interests and suggesting how they can best be secured by employing the resources available to the nation in ways that accord with foundational values. Some analyses closely parallel the argument here, but at the level of the nation's overarching foreign policy behaviour. For instance, Dueck has described the way America's 'limited liability' grand strategy – whereby it pursues ideologically inspired ambitious ends with limited means to avoid costs – has resulted in suboptimal outcomes in terms of influence, prosperity and security.[1] The perspective here has been narrower than this, focused on the application of one specific element of US power: military force. Nevertheless, this book informs those debates insofar as the chief conclusions add weight to realist perspectives that counsel a measure of restraint in US foreign policy, and they raise serious questions for those who would seek to wield force in a habitual fashion, as if it was an unexceptional tool on a par with diplomacy or economic measures.

The application of military force is often seen as unproblematic in some sweeping grand strategic articulations, especially those associated with the pursuit of continued US primacy and liberal interventionism. War, however small-scale or remotely conducted, is a distinctly unpredictable and unwieldy instrument that can easily escape the control of its users and lead them down unintended and perilous paths.[2] Circumspection is vital in this respect. Any decision to employ force is a serious matter, deserving of careful consideration, democratic deliberation and measured strategic assessment. As Clausewitz reminded us, 'war is no place for irresponsible enthusiasts. It is a serious means to a serious end.'[3]

Given the harmful consequences associated with the practices of delegation, danger-proofing and darkness surveyed in Chapter 7, in some extreme situations, where it is judged that vital American interests are engaged, more robust direct responses may be preferable to the kind of minimalist or outsourced approaches we have discussed. Some analysts lean toward the apparent logical solution of consistently employing overwhelming force, as in essence the earlier Weinberger doctrine recommended.[4]

Yet the argument here does not necessarily exclusively entail a 'go big or go home' approach. While there may be a good case for material preponderance, size is not everything. Decision-makers must be mindful of the trap of prioritizing cost-avoidance as a first-order concern, as opposed to a sober assessment of necessary means and likely costs judged according to strategic requirements.[5] In fact, sometimes there is obvious sense in tailoring means to fit the mission, but it is equally essential to appreciate that rarely can significant objectives be achieved without serious investment of resources or sacrifices in some areas. Naturally, leaders wish to limit casualties, expenditure and adverse political side-effects, but an exclusive or obsessive predisposition in this respect – simultaneously marginalizing considerations as to why force is being used in the first place and to what end – typically results in counterproductive behaviour that generates the very costs they sought to avoid. In short, the problem is one of attitude over arithmetic.

Even then, debating the relative effectiveness of different forms or degrees of force is often the wrong discussion to be having. Many of the threats to American security are not solvable through bombs and bullets, proxies or Predators. America must also move beyond automatically designating as a battlefield any region associated in some way with terror, radicalization or other sources of insecurity. The nation has many other tools at its disposal, and addressing challenges will likely require the skills of accomplished diplomats and development specialists rather than generals or paramilitary officers. Crucially, as Kennedy puts it, 'US power in the world needs to be exercised with care and with appropriate respect for other regional and local traditions and customs.'[6]

More effective approaches may require politicians to absorb short-term costs and setbacks in some spheres, make compromises with adversaries, oversee difficult processes of disengagement, and show resilience and restraint in the face of provocations. This may be the only way to escape the never-ending spirals of war, resistance and radicalization that characterizes current approaches, which, in the long run, will likely prove cumulatively more costly in blood, treasure and insecurity. The application of ill-considered military force generally exacerbates problems.

★ ★ ★

There is no certainty that the strategic patterns identified here will persist indefinitely as more traditional scenarios of great power conflict loom on the horizon. The issues covered in this book are thus inevitably coloured by such concerns. Expert commentary is preoccupied with the growing power of China and its projection of influence abroad, both in the Asia-Pacific region, but also further afield. The perceived threat posed by Russia has attracted significant attention, especially following its annexation of Crimea in 2014 and its assertive moves in Eastern Europe and the Middle East. The tense situation concerning Iranian and North Korean nuclear programmes has also engaged American strategists. The developing consensus is that we are entering into a new era in which US power will be increasingly constrained by the (re-)emergence of new poles of power in the international system. The importance of these issues, or sets of issues, has emerged as an uncritically accepted reality: indeed, 'great power competition' is the new buzzword in Washington. But there remains significant contention regarding the precise nature or seriousness of these concerns, or what the implications might be in terms of US foreign policy or military strategy. As such, this book was written at a time that could well be understood as an inflection point in US foreign policy and global politics more generally.

In fact, the existence of potential large-scale conventional threats may be one factor driving vicarious methods in the long ongoing war against terror as the US defence establishment licks its wounds from the visceral wars of the 2000s and prepares for the kinds of battles it has long viewed as its *raison d'être*. The extent to which in the future the requirements of large-scale conventional conflict displaces the prosecution of more limited and disparate commitments along the lines of vicarious warfare is an open question. A great power war – for instance, between China and the United States – would likely relegate vicarious warfare to a second-order concern. But short of major war, a more confrontational situation than exists at present, perhaps resembling in certain respects the Cold War, may cause the present era of vicarious warfare to be amplified – only in new forms, new places and new strategic contexts.[7] Some commentators believe China is unlikely to contest America through conventional warfare, preferring instead to sponsor insurgents and proxies that threaten US allies and interests around the globe in a series of low-intensity conflicts.[8] This scenario is no less concerning, especially if the record of vicarious approaches during the Cold War is anything to go by.[9]

So, whether or not a 'Thucydides trap' inevitably locks the United States and China on a path to war – to paraphrase Thucydides, the growth of the power of China and the concern this generated in America made war inevitable – evolving great power confrontation could play out according to any number of scripts, not all necessarily large-scale or narrowly conventional.[10] In one form or another, vicarious warfare is likely to persist.

★ ★ ★

Africa could be important to watch in this respect. As we have described, the region remains a major hub of military activity for America and its allies who are conducting an array of vicarious missions ostensibly focused on the terror threat. A rapidly growing and transforming continent – with burgeoning markets to corner and large reserves of precious resources to tap – may emerge as the setting, if indeed it is not already, of a modern-day 'scramble for Africa'.[11] Russia is active in North Africa but, more importantly, China is investing heavily and expanding its influence in various countries as part of its Belt and Road Initiative, many of which are traditional US partners and host multiple ongoing operations.

As Chinese economic and military power grows, and so too its confidence in asserting its interests abroad, it may see advantages in bringing governments under its influence or even more forcefully challenging US-backed surrogates and allies. African nations may soon be placed in a position of having to choose a side, shaped by competing considerations of interest and ideology (liberal free markets or authoritarian state capitalism; the rule of law or rule through law), thus raising tensions where US and Chinese outposts and operations rub up against one another.

To support its rapidly expanding presence in the area, in 2017 China took the bold decision of establishing a People's Liberation Army Support Base in Djibouti, strategically located at the entrance to the Red Sea and not far from America's large Camp Lemonnier. Reports have already emerged of brewing tensions.[12] This comes at a time when America has significantly escalated its campaign of air strikes in neighbouring Somalia. The situation is largely benign at present, but there is no certainty this will last. Especially concerning is the way that America has, over the last three decades, become increasingly habituated to employing force in a routine and knee-jerk manner, largely untroubled by legal constraints, domestic opinion or fears of wider geopolitical shockwaves. This may lead officials to believe that the vicarious instruments they have come to rely on – such as covert operations, proxies, drones and private companies – can be repurposed or redirected to confront emerging challenges. Equally, China may read vicarious behaviour as evidence that the US is not seriously invested in the region, thus encouraging more assertive moves. In this light, and echoing the discussion in Chapter 3, perhaps the Horn of Africa will become the new Hawaii.[13]

There are, of course, similar areas of friction beyond Africa: at various points along the extent of the Belt and Road, high in the Himalayan borderlands, across an unfreezing Arctic and throughout the Pacific. Commentators increasingly point to the internet and space as emerging zones of heightened contestation. And this is not to mention more obvious potential flashpoints such as Taiwan or the South China Sea. A serious crisis could promptly bring an end to the vicarious era, to be replaced by a renewed American appetite for sacrifice, service and more traditional forms of war. As we have shown, there are strong factors working against this. Yet history reveals how suddenly things can change, especially when the pain associated with earlier costly wars is forgotten, ideological passions fuel aggression, new ominous threats appear to demand action, and war comes to be seen as easy.

Notes

Acknowledgements

1   In this book, America, US and United States of America are used interchangeably.
2   Kennedy and Waldman, 'Ways of war in the 21st century', 104.
3   Waldman, 'Vicarious warfare'; Waldman, 'Buy now, pay later'; Waldman, 'Strategic narratives'.

Introduction

1   Kennedy, 'Inaugural Address'. Or, as Handel notes, 'a war that involves the nation's vital interests' must be won 'often *regardless of the costs involved*': Handel, *Masters of War*, 138; original emphasis.
2   Gray, *Strategy and Politics*, 41, 70.
3   Mayer, 'Trigger happy', 262.
4   In this light, Gaddis asks whether any of the participants in the First World War would have entered it had they been able to foresee its costs: see Gaddis, *On Grand Strategy*, 273. All calculations regarding the likely costs of different strategic decisions are inescapably pervaded by chronic uncertainty and unavoidable, likely mistaken, assumptions. As such, it would be unrealistic to expect strategists to foresee all the future costs or second- and third-order effects associated with the use of force, and the analyst must be mindful of unfairly exploiting the benefit of hindsight: see Hammes, 'Assumptions', 2010; Betts, *American Force*, 16.
5   Such denial often affects strategists whose main anxieties centre around probable sacrifices, but it is also apparent in those whose ends are unlimited because, when for them 'the world is not enough', how else can they overcome a reality that resolutely stands in their path? The potential costs have to be ignored. *Non sufficit orbis* – 'the world is not enough' – was struck in a commemorative medal for Phillip II. 'Because ends only exist in the imagination, they can be infinite.... Means though are stubbornly finite: they are boots on the ground, ships in the sea, and the bodies required to fill them': Gaddis, *On Grand Strategy*, 12, 125. Allison terms this strategic flaw 'vision blindness, when an actor is mesmerized by an ideal but unachievable end': Allison, 'The new spheres of influence', 40.
6   The nature of the interests at stake or the threats faced are important too, but as Clausewitz astutely observed, 'the same political object can elicit differing reactions from different peoples, and even from the same people at different times': Clausewitz, *On War*, 81. Whether the aim is the total destruction of the enemy or something more limited, this same attitude can apply.
7   Clausewitz, *On War*, 585.

8   Handel makes a similar point: 'the line between economy and false economy in war is difficult to define': Handel, *Masters of War*, 138.

9   Demmers and Gould, 'An assemblage approach to liquid warfare', 365.

10 Kiras, *Special Operations and Strategy*, 12.

11 Levite and Shimshoni, 'The strategic challenge of society-centric warfare', 104.

12 In his classic work, *The American Way of War*, Weigley posited that strategies of annihilation – as opposed to those of attrition – were dominant, especially after the Civil War. Concerned principally with military thought rather than actual practice, according to Weigley annihilation was something implemented through overwhelming firepower, decisive battle, maximum effort and directly closing with the enemy. Linn later presented a correction to this view, and one which Weigley largely accepted. Linn's critique rested on the notion that recurrent features of US military practice also included defensive, deterrent and continental strategies as well as a capacity for opportunistic, impromptu adaptation as circumstances required. Nevertheless, the debate over annihilation and attrition is, when considered in light of the broader tradition, really a matter of detail, if indeed the distinction is conceptually coherent at all: Linn, '"The American way of war" revisited', 529–30.

13 It should be noted that the boundaries between the traditions are often more blurred than the ideal-types might suggest. Nevertheless, at the core they represent distinct ways of employing force that are sufficiently unique to aid analysis.

14 Cassidy, *Counterinsurgency and the Global War on Terror*, 99–126. Tierney offers a related distinction between 'crusade' and 'quagmire' traditions, broadly reflecting the distinction here, but focused more on public views about war: Tierney, *How We Fight*, 7–11.

15 Gentile, 'Progress, dissent and counter-insurgency', 190; Hoffman, 'Complex irregular war'.

16 Gray quotes Huntington: 'the United States is a big country, and we should fight wars in a big way': Gray, 'Strategy in the Nuclear Age', 596. See also Mead, *Special Providence*, 221–2.

17 Mead, *Special Providence*, 254. Once generals commit to fighting war along the lines of this tradition, politics tends to fall out of view. In contrast to the well-known Clausewitzian adage, in the American experience these wars tend not to be viewed as the continuation of politics but rather the failure of it. In practice, this has prompted calls, at least from generals subscribing to this notion, for clear military autonomy during war and minimal civilian interference.

18 Cassidy, *Counterinsurgency and the Global War on Terror*, 105–6.

19 Bellamy, *Knights in White Armour*, 225.

20 Strachan, *Carl von Clausewitz's On War: A Biography*, 3–4.

21 Franks, quoted by Strachan, *Carl von Clausewitz's On War: A Biography*, 4.

22 After the South's act of secession in America, the Civil War essentially became a conflict between two rival sovereign states. Other smaller-scale yet conventional campaigns, such as Grenada in 1983 and Panama in 1989, are sometimes invoked as examples of the tradition. See Linn, '"The American way of war" revisited', 527. Also, precisely due to its disproportionate influence, this tradition can be seen to have guided warfighting approaches even in situations of insurgency and civil conflict. Of course, the prominent example in this respect is Vietnam. Between 1965 and 1968, General Westmoreland oversaw a largely conventional attritional campaign. Critics such as John Nagl and Andrew Krepinevich have suggested that it was the US military's preoccupation with fighting big battles that prevented it from adapting to effectively confront the Viet Cong insurgency. Alternatively,

revisionist historians have argued that the war should have been fought in a *more* stridently conventional manner, ideally involving an invasion of North Vietnam itself. See Nagl, *Learning to Eat Soup with a Knife*; Krepinevich, *The Army and Vietnam*.

23 Finlan, *Contemporary Military Strategy*, 10–11; Mazarr, 'The folly of asymmetric war', 46.

24 Ulysses S. Grant and William Tecumseh Sherman of the American Civil War are presented as true fighting generals. John J. Pershing who commanded American forces in the First World War was prototypically offensively minded. George S. Patton, Omar Bradley and George S. Marshall in the Second World War are popular exemplars of this tradition, as is Douglas MacArthur, who led forces in both that war and the Korean War. More recent additions would include Norman Schwarzkopf, who commanded US forces during the Persian Gulf War, and Tommy Franks, who led the invasion of Iraq in 2003.

25 At the risk of causing confusion, small wars are not necessarily small in size, scope or ambition. The term is taken from the title of a popular early 20th-century text on imperial warfare by Colonel Charles. E. Callwell, which then stuck and is now widely used to describe wars sharing a broad family resemblance. Callwell defined small wars as those that don't involve regular troops on the opposing side. The 'smallness' of the wars he wrote about was more indicative of their somewhat marginal political importance and the way that they were small-scale relative to the major inter-state wars of the age. Callwell's original meaning and the measures he advocated are not all applicable to the way the term is utilized here: Callwell, *Small Wars*; Kane, *Strategy*, 8. Small wars as defined here in fact often involve very large commitments in various respects – perhaps not the most apt label, but hopefully one enjoying sufficient common understanding as to warrant its use.

26 Including, *inter alia*: pacification, peace enforcement operations, large-scale counterinsurgency campaigns, some forms of armed humanitarian intervention, post-war occupations experiencing continuing violence or 'hot stabilization' missions in countries transitioning out of conflict.

27 Dandeker, 'From Victory to Success', 25.

28 Marine General Victor Krulak developed the concept of the 'three-block war' to capture the way troops could find themselves conducting offensive, peacekeeping and humanitarian tasks in the same operational theatre: Krulak, 'The strategic corporal'.

29 Tierney argues that American strategic culture is largely disdainful of unconventional war: Tierney, *Chasing Ghosts*, xiii.

30 Lansdale is the subject of a major recent hagiographical book-length treatment by Max Boot, *The Road Not Taken*.

31 Shy and Collier, 'Revolutionary War', 854.

32 They suggest that conventional war, while arguably culturally dominant within the military, has, in actual practice, been outnumbered by the sheer number of wars fought in the small wars tradition.

33 Michaels and Ford, 'Bandwagonistas', 353.

34 Bacevich, 'The Petraeus Doctrine'.

35 Michaels and Ford, 'Bandwagonistas', 352.

36 Mazarr, 'The folly of asymmetric war', 40, 48.

37 Freedman, 'The counterrevolution in strategic affairs'.

38 Obama, 'President Obama outlines a new global military strategy'.

39 Liptak, 'Photos highlight start differences in Trump and Obama approaches'.

40 Even soldiers in combat have admitted to a strange sense of vicariousness. Writing about his experience as a Marine during the Vietnam War, Philip Caputo recounted the strange 'sensation of watching myself in a movie … one part of course was doing something, while the other part watched from a distance.' Quoted in Coker, *Rebooting Clausewitz*, 188.

41 Krieg and Rickli, 'Surrogate warfare'; Heng, 'The continuing resonance of the war as risk management perspective'; Rasmussen, *The Risk Society at War*.

42 In a similar respect, vicarious warfare is not necessarily synonymous with the idea of 'limited war'. This concept, which has Clausewitzian origins but was rediscovered and developed during the early Cold War, is concerned primarily with wars fought for limited political objectives. But whether ends are limited or unlimited, the central idea of vicarious warfare is to keep the means (and all the manifold associated costs and requirements) low relative to the ends sought. Limited war is preoccupied more with ends, vicarious warfare with means (although most definitions of limited war assume a corresponding restriction of means). The limited war theories of the 1950s were associated strongly with and indeed importantly motivated by the non-use of nuclear weapons (means) and centred around the implications of restraint in terms of not seeking the adversary's complete destruction (ends): the concern was with how to use 'measured' force in such a way as to attain less than 'total' objectives vis-à-vis the enemy – subtly different to the logic driving vicarious methods: see Osgood, *Limited War Revisited*, 2–3.

43 Clausewitz, *On War*, 605.

44 Coker, *Rebooting Clausewitz*, 43.

45 Similarly, it does not claim to describe a particular form or type of war, such as 'conventional war' or 'irregular war'. Such categorization, aside from being potentially misleading in itself, seeks to capture something about the defining character of particular wars in a holistic sense. Milevski, 'Respecting strategic agency'. It spans categories such as irregular or conventional war because it can plausibly be applied in the context of either.

46 In particular, see Freedman, *The Transformation of Strategic Affairs*; Strachan, *The Direction of War*; Simpson, *War from the Ground Up*; Betz, *Carnage and Connectivity*; Betts, *American Force*.

47 Chief among these are: Ignatieff, *Virtual War*; Mandel, *Security, Strategy and the Quest for Bloodless War*; Shaw, *The New Western Way of War*; McInnes, *Spectator-Sport Warfare*.

Chapter 1

1 So, in Homer's *Iliad* – the defining epic of Western war – we find that as much as it glorifies the exploits of heroic warriors, everywhere 'war is mentioned, it is joined by epithets such as "bloody," "full of tears," … "full of suffering," "terrible," and "destructive"': van Creveld, *The Culture of War*, 254. And not for nothing did Homer depict Ares as 'the most hateful' God of all: van Creveld, *More on War*, 16.

2 Howard, *The Invention of Peace and the Reinvention of War*.

3 Heuser, *The Evolution of Strategy*, 39, 98.

4 Hanson, 'Land Warfare in Thucydides', 606.

5 Goldsworthy, 'War', 85-98.

6 Heuser, *The Evolution of Strategy*, 51.

[7] Keegan, *A History of Warfare*, 362. Similarly, an insurgent strategy of exhaustion – of hit and run guerrilla tactics – might misleadingly appear vicarious, but such groups are typically willing to accept significant costs over time and take many risks when necessary.

[8] Howard, *The Lessons of History*, 167.

[9] Van Creveld, *More on War*, 20.

[10] Coker, *Barbarous Philosophers*, 24.

[11] Dyer, *War*, 90.

[12] Gat, *War in Human Civilisation*, 183–7, 298.

[13] Dyer, *War*, 94.

[14] Nolan, *The Allure of Battle*; van Creveld, *The Art of War*.

[15] Holland, 'America is not Rome'.

[16] A typical preceding stage before the emergence of more democratic forms of governance was rule by individual tyrants who exploited the emergence of hoplite infantry power to challenge aristocratic dominance: see Fox, *The Classical World*, 58–61, 88–92.

[17] Famously associated with Greek hoplite battle but utilized in the warfare of many historical city-based states, such as Lagash or the Muslim armies of Mecca and Medina. Massing ordinary citizens into large formations was made possible by the ease of communication associated with city life, provided battles were fought close to home and swiftly, so as not to disrupt the livelihoods of these farmer-soldiers.

[18] At age 18 Athenian men (*epheboi*) were enlisted in a mandatory two-year military training period: see Coker, *Barbarous Philosophers*, 19. Following the radical reforms of Cleisthenes in the late 6th century BC, political rights were even extended to poorer inhabitants of the city in return for their military service as rowers in the Navy: see Ryan, *On Politics*, 10.

[19] Fox, *The Classical World*, 97.

[20] Van Wees even suggests that, despite the regularity of war and its prominence in politics and art, if anything it was social, political and economic life that shaped Greek warfare more than the other way round: see van Wees, 'War and Society', 273, 298–9.

[21] Coker, *Barbarous Philosophers*, 15.

[22] Ryan, *On Politics*, 11.

[23] Gat, *War in Human Civilisation*, 309.

[24] Gaddis, *On Grand Strategy*, 33.

[25] 'The army was their wall and "every man a brick"': Ryan, *On Politics*, 8.

[26] Hanson, *The Western Way of War*, 15.

[27] Scholars have presented nuanced descriptions of Greek warfare, noting how mercenaries, poor citizens and slaves sometimes fought alongside middle-class hoplites in campaigns that often involved raiding, ravaging and deception. Spartan helots fought in battles at Plataea and Thermopylae, and Thucydides relates how women were involved in the communal conflict in Corfu.

[28] This was not the only factor which caused the Periclean strategy to be dropped, although adherence to traditional 'strategic culture' was something that Cleon could readily draw on in seeking to sway the assembly to his faction's view: see Kagan, 'Athenian Strategy in the Peloponnesian War', 33–8.

[29] Kagan, 'Athenian Strategy in the Peloponnesian War', 54.

[30] Kagan, 'Athenian Strategy in the Peloponnesian War', 54.

[31] As in Greece, ordinary soldiers had to furnish their own armour and weapons – this was the main criterion of their eligibility for service and determined their

position in the army. Roman senators were drawn from the knightly class, and in order to stand for office a man must have served: see Ryan, *On Politics*, 133–4.

32 Bernstein, 'The strategy of a warrior-state', 61.
33 Consuls commanded armies and appointed senators from the highest social classes. Senators, who held the magistracies, shaped military and foreign policy. The people held the magistrates and consuls to account through elections. All had a role to play in ensuring continued effectiveness in war: see Ryan, *On Politics*, 131–2.
34 Between 327 and 241 BC the Romans enjoyed only five years of peace: see Bernstein, 'The strategy of a warrior-state', 57.
35 Bernstein, 'The strategy of a warrior state', 69.
36 Kane, *Strategy*, 71–2.
37 Clausewitz, *On War*, 593.
38 Heuser, *The Evolution of Strategy*, 119.
39 Coker, *Rebooting Clausewitz*, 15.
40 Kagan, 'Athenian Strategy in the Peloponnesian War', 28.
41 Strassler, *The Landmark Herodotus*, 801.
42 Gaddis, *On Grand Strategy*, 35.
43 Ryan, *On Politics*, 27.
44 Van Creveld, *Command in War*, 48–9.
45 Howard, *The Invention of Peace*, 15.
46 War 'was what the ruling elites were for. Their capacity to conduct it legitimated their authority': see Howard, *The Lessons of History*, 167. Van Creveld notes that the change whereby commanders no longer fought with weapon in hand came surprisingly late in history: van Creveld, *Command in War*, 17.
47 Gray, *Strategy and Politics*, 114–15.
48 Howard, *The Invention of Peace and the Reinvention of War*, 8.
49 McNeill, *The Pursuit of Power*, viii.
50 For the latter, the idea of constant racial struggle was central to its philosophy and entailed preparing the entire Germanic *Volksgemeinschaft* for that purpose.
51 Coker, *Barbarous Philosophers*, 43.
52 In Greek warfare, typically understood as the side holding the field at the end of a day's fighting. This reflects the way that the agonal mode of war – while pitiless, direct and demanding broad citizen mobilisation – might nevertheless serve to limit the overall suffering by producing a relatively quick and 'final' decision.
53 As Howard taught, it was 'peace' that truly had to be invented, and only over recent centuries through the concerted efforts of philosophers, political activists and lawyers: see Howard, *The Invention of Peace*.
54 Gat, *War in Human Civilisation*, 407.
55 Dyer, *War*, 81.
56 Single combat persisted into classical times, and examples are mentioned in Herodotus, such as the Battle of the Champions between Sparta and Argos in 546 BC. The practice also re-emerged later in medieval chivalric warfare.
57 Bernstein, 'The strategy of a warrior-state', 64.
58 Roth, 'War', 368.
59 Dyer, *War*, 92.
60 Shaw, *The New Western Way of War*, 73.
61 Dyer, *War*, 196.
62 Keegan, *A History of Warfare*, 294.
63 Dyer, *War*, 145–6.

[64] Uprisings by ordinary people resisting heavy taxes, excessive conscription or extended service in distant campaigns might occur periodically, but the general pattern of mute acceptance to various forms of autocratic rule predominated. Chiefs, lords and monarchs were generally able to impose their will on their subjects, who, being scattered across the rural landscape and lacking reliable means of communication, were unable to organize effectively. Moreover, such downtrodden and poor rural masses were militarily ineffective, thus further undermining any possible claim to political influence they might entertain: see Gat, *War in Human Civilisation*, 298, 329–30.

[65] Marwick, quoted in McInnes, *Spectator-Sport Warfare*, 19.

[66] Kane, *Strategy*, 64. We see the remnants of this kind of aristocratic rear-guard action in Clausewitz's time, when, after Napoleon's defeat in 1815, conservative officials were desperate to return war to its aristocratic basis despite the best efforts of reformers such as Gneisenau and Scharnhorst; Paret, *Clausewitz and the State*, 255–71. Even as late as the First World War, senior commanders, still often drawn from the nobility, were reluctant to accept the irrelevance of their beloved cavalry in the face of modern firepower.

[67] Howard, *War in European History*, 54, 69; Heuser, *The Evolution of Strategy*, 60–1.

[68] Kennedy notes that in the late 16th century, up to *three-quarters* of government expenditure could be devoted to war or dept repayments on war debt: see Kennedy, *The Rise and Fall of the Great Powers*, 91. With the military revolution of the early modern period, 'keeping up with the arms race in standardized men and cannons was staggeringly expensive. Even in the richest states, there was never enough money, and matching means and ends soon became the greatest challenge for governments. The crudest solution was to cook the books. Governments blithely defaulted on debts, let inflation run riot, and, when all else failed, simply stopped paying their troops': Morris, *What Is War Good For?*, 3557.

[69] Conklin, 'The theory of sovereign debt', 489.

[70] Gaddis, *On Grand Strategy*, 121–50; Maltby, 'The Origins of a Global Strategy', 154; Kennedy, *The Rise and Fall of the Great Powers*, 79.

[71] Kennedy, *The Rise and Fall of the Great Powers*, 92.

[72] Kennedy, *The Rise and Fall of the Great Powers*, 92.

[73] Clausewitz, quoted in Handel, *Masters of War*, 150.

[74] This was hardly surprising. Peasants and merchants were unlikely to be persuaded by royal rationales, especially when the revenues were used to fund distant wars completely disconnected from their own security.

[75] Parker, 'The Making of Strategy in Habsburg Spain', 131–2.

[76] Phillip's Genoese lenders issued an embargo on specie delivery to his army in Flanders when he failed to pay his loans, with serious military consequences for his campaigns against the Dutch: see Conklin, 'The theory of sovereign debt', 484. See also Kennedy, *The Rise and Fall of the Great Powers*, 59.

[77] In England, when Charles I 'launched a fleet by extending the payment of ship monies to inland counties, the uproar contributed to his ultimate downfall': see Maltby, 'The Origins of a Global Strategy', 155. The French revenues had been exhausted through incessant royal warmaking, and yet further expenditure to support the American colonists was the final straw for Louis' subjects: see Keegan, *A History of Warfare*, 348.

[78] Explaining his decision to go to war against the Dutch in 1672, he stated that 'Ambition and [the pursuit of] glory are always pardonable in a prince ... a king need never be ashamed of seeking fame, for it is a good that must be ceaselessly

and avidly desired.... All conquerors have gained more by reputation than the sword.' Unfortunately, reputation in Louis' case was unable to compensate for his dire lack of resources: see Lynn, 'A Quest for Glory', 184–7.

79 Lynn, 'A Quest for Glory', 189.
80 Lynn, 'A Quest for Glory', 183.
81 Blanning, *The Pursuit of Glory*, 534–35.
82 Lynn, 'A Quest for Glory', 203.
83 Lynn, 'States in Conflict', 178.
84 Bond, *The Pursuit of Victory*, 14.
85 Clausewitz, *On War*, 259.
86 Lynn, 'States in Conflict', 178. With sovereign wealth so closely associated with military effectiveness and given the typically precarious financial basis of the monarchies, rarely has war been so circumscribed for fear of its potential economic ramifications.
87 Quoted in Heuser, *The Evolution of Strategy*, 55.
88 Black, 'The Military Revolution II', 49.
89 Dyer, *War*, 221–2.
90 Howard, *War in European History*, 73.
91 'The fate of North America was settled, French hegemony in Europe was resisted, the Turks pushed back from much of Europe': see Black, 'The Military Revolution II', 54.
92 Howard, *War in European History*, 66.
93 Strachan, *European Armies and the Conduct of War*, 15.
94 Marshal de Saxe, quoted in Weigley, *The American Way of War*, 220.
95 Black, 'The Military Revolution II', 50.
96 Some of the later monarchs to die in battle were the Swedish Gustavus Adolphus in 1632 and Charles XII in 1718; George II was present at the Battle of Dettingen during the War of the Austrian Succession in 1743.
97 In Sweden especially: see Black, 'The Military Revolution II', 53.

Chapter 2

1 Restrictions which were extensive in a constitutional monarchy such as England, limited in an absolute monarchy like France, and more or less non-existent in the despotism of Tsarist Russia.
2 Kennedy, *The Rise and Fall of the Great Powers*, 78. These were never expected to 'defeat' Spain, but in line with mercantilist zero-sum thinking, any loss for Spain would be a gain for England in the overall strategic accounting. As Gaddis notes, she let her mercenaries risk their ships and settlers, but not her Navy or Treasury: see Gaddis, *On Grand Strategy*, 153. Still, this proxy sponsorship soon led to escalation and costly further direct commitments. In Elizabeth's case, these policies contributed to a formal alliance with the Dutch, the dispatch of English troops to the continent in 1585 and the naval confrontation with the Spanish Navy in the late 1580s, including the famous Armada.
3 The latter would primarily be utilized as auxiliary forces supplemental to native forces. They were widely seen as more effective than untrained peasants, especially if, as tended to be the case, mercenaries were recruited among warlike pastoralists on the periphery or other groups known for their fighting prowess: see Gat, *War in Human Civilisation*, 198, 247, 266, 368–9. Into the early modern era, mercenaries would continue to make up part of the royal standing armies but were

increasingly integrated, sometimes into specialized foreign units, or were recruited on an individualized basis, often as officers.

4   Van Creveld, *Command in War*, 51.
5   Gat, *War in Human Civilisation*, 268, 306–7.
6   Seventeenth-century Sweden was one of the earliest states in this period to move toward a military based on conscript quotas and rising taxation. Mercenaries nevertheless made up the bulk of the army and did most of the fighting abroad: see Howard, *War in European History*, 57–8.
7   Roberts and Westad, *The Penguin History of the World*, 633.
8   This was Louis XIV's basic strategy in his foreign campaigns of aggrandizement.
9   Porter, *The Lion's Share*, 104.
10 Porter, *The Lion's Share*, 49, 62, 104, 110.
11 Ignatieff, *Empire Lite*; Kaplan, 'The trap of empire and authoritarianism'.
12 Keegan, *A History of Warfare*, 262.
13 Gaddis, *On Grand Strategy*, 215.
14 Kennedy, *The Rise and Fall of the Great Powers*, 61.
15 Hence why the Portuguese and Dutch Empires remained primarily of a trading nature, aside from their small colonies in East Africa and South Africa respectively. The English, with a somewhat larger population, similarly began in this fashion, but slowly moved to a more colonial basis.
16 Bismarck, for instance, had to camouflage his budget for foreign campaigns: see Porch, 'Imperial wars', 110.
17 Roberts and Westad, *The Penguin History of the World*, 268–9.
18 Such as Rome's disastrous defeats at the Teutoburg Forest (AD 9), Abritus (AD 251), Edessa (AD 260) and Adrianople (AD 378).
19 Reynolds, *America, Empire of Liberty*.
20 Keegan, *A History of Warfare*, 357.
21 Roberts and Westad, *The Penguin History of the World*, 643.
22 Roberts and Westad, *The Penguin History of the World*, 635–6.
23 Porter, *The Lion's Share*, 167.
24 Porter, *The Lion's Share*, 56.
25 Looking further back, we see similar patterns. The world's first empire ruled by Sargon of Akkad in Mesopotamia was composed of professional forces and heavily reliant on mercenaries: see Dyer, *War*, 140. Darius the Great's ancient Persian empire was sustained by a mixed force comprising a courtly elite, regular troops, foreign mercenaries and temporary levies: see Gat, *War in Human Civilisation*, 347.
26 Beard, *SPQR*, 266–8. This would, of course, have significant blowback for the Republic, as it was these armies that Caesar, Pompey and others would use to fight each other during the Civil War, leading ultimately to the rise of the Roman Empire.
27 Until conscription, of mainly peasants rather than townspeople, was reintroduced by Diocletian as a desperate measure following the chaotic 3rd century AD and difficulties faced in recruiting sufficient numbers to defend against growing barbarian incursions.
28 Goldich, 'American military culture from colony to empire', 58–9, 64.
29 The distinction between native Romans and *foederati* became less distinct after Caracalla's momentous decree granting citizenship to all free inhabitants of the Empire in 212.
30 Kane, *Strategy*, 67; Roberts and Westad, *The Penguin History of the World*, 227.
31 Heuser, *The Evolution of Strategy*, 42, 90.

32 Quoted in Porter, *The Lion's Share*, 13.
33 Millett et al, *For the Common Defense*, 2604–16.
34 Ferguson, *Empire*, 256.
35 Porch, 'Imperial wars', 97; Black, *Introduction to Global Military History*, 71. Examples include the French Zouaves and Foreign Legion or the sepoy infantry and Gurkha units in the British Indian Army. In the middle of the 19th century Britain held India with 277,746 troops, of which only 45,522 were European – the Indian Army functioned like a 'self-replenishing cup': see Porter, *The Lion's Share*, 15, 30. More than two-thirds of Clive's troops at the key battle of Plassey in 1757 were Indian: see Ferguson, *Empire*, 36.
36 Millett et al, *For the Common Defense*, 4411.
37 Rivalry in India between France and Britain largely played out as a form of proxy war in which the powers provided support for rival Indian princes: see Roberts and Westad, *The Penguin History of the World*, 642.
38 Caesar adopted this approach in Gaul, and it was common practice in the British and French Empires.
39 Similar processes can be perceived in other continental empires (for instance, Assyrian, Persian, Macedonian, Roman and Byzantine) and maritime empires (for instance, Athenian, Carthaginian, Venetian and British).
40 Gat, *War in Human Civilisation*, 306.
41 Keegan, *A History of Warfare*, 357.
42 Ferguson notes how the British home population in Victorian times had 'an insatiable appetite for tales of military derring-do': see Ferguson, *Empire*, 256.
43 These were an inheritance from the Etruscans but were radically expanded by the Romans, especially under Commodus in the 2nd century AD: see Kyle, *Spectacles of Death in Ancient Rome*, 8.
44 Porter, *The Absent Minded Imperialists*.
45 Porter, *The Lion's Share*, 290.
46 Porter, *The Lion's Share*, 115.
47 As one Liberal Chancellor in 1892 noted: 'even Jingoism is tolerable when it is done "on the cheap"': see Porter, *The Lion's Share*, 105.
48 The demise of the Roman Republic came about largely due to powerful consul generals (most famously Julius Caesar) accumulating great power and serving well beyond the traditional term of office due to their command of armies in protracted imperial campaigns abroad.
49 The term itself comes from the Roman practice of glorifying its imperial military victories with lavish parades through the capital. In Britain, armies of propagandists in the late 19th century fed the public with empire-boosting entertainment.
50 Morefield and Porter, 'Revenge of the forever wars'.
51 Keegan, *A History of Warfare*, 364.
52 Strachan, *European Armies and the Conduct of War*, 5.
53 Machiavelli, *The Prince*, 39–47.
54 Coker, *Rebooting Clausewitz*, 136.
55 Heuser, *The Evolution of Strategy*, 42–3, 90.
56 Van Creveld, *The Art of War*.

Chapter 3

1 Echevarria, 'Strategic anarchy and the American way of war', 10.
2 Bacevich, *The New American Militarism*, 225.

³ West Point was established in 1817 but remained a 'neglected foundling': see Weigley, *The American Way of War*, 55.

⁴ Estimated to have affected about one-tenth of the population, which is a large proportion in historical terms.

⁵ Maslowski, 'To the Edge of Greatness', 207.

⁶ Over time, especially with the establishment of the reservations, the Indian threat would come to be conceived as a *foreign* threat.

⁷ The afterglow of the militia's reputation gained during the Revolutionary War was a strong factor promoting continued reliance on them and a source of propagandistic material for their supporters. The suboptimal nature of the Uniform Militia Act of 1792 did little to promote its military effectiveness.

⁸ Battles close to home were fought largely through the common militia, while military ventures further afield often involved ad hoc expeditionary volunteer units assembled to augment diminutive regular forces: see Maslowski, 'To the Edge of Greatness', 227.

⁹ Kagan, *Dangerous Nation*, 66.

¹⁰ As Mead notes, during America's first 140 years, virtually every administration sent forces abroad: see Mead, *Special Providence*, 17.

¹¹ Clausewitz, *On War*, 220.

¹² Kagan, *Dangerous Nation*, 62–3.

¹³ Maslowski, 'To the Edge of Greatness', 221.

¹⁴ Mandelbaum, *Mission Failure*, 136.

¹⁵ Heuser, *The Evolution of Strategy*, 184.

¹⁶ Weigley, *The American Way of War*, 202.

¹⁷ Weigley, *The American Way of War*, 220–2.

¹⁸ Kagan, *Dangerous Nation*, 72, 144–5, 283, 297.

¹⁹ Goldich, 'American military culture from colony to empire', 60.

²⁰ Hummel, 'The American militia and the origin of conscription', 61.

²¹ Holland, 'America is not Rome'. America's closest 'Rubicon moment' would come much later when General Douglas MacArthur – who considered himself, if not quite a god, then at least 'God's right-hand man' – returned from Korea to a hero's welcome in 1951 obsessed with expanding the war into China and employing atomic bombs if need be: see Ferguson, *Colossus*, 89; Hastings, *The Korean War*, Chapter 10.

²² Millett et al, *For the Common Defense*, 1836–49.

²³ Kagan, *Dangerous Nation*, 142.

²⁴ Mead, *Special Providence*, 200.

²⁵ Jefferson, quoted in Kagan, *Dangerous Nation*, 98; Boot, *The Savage Wars of Peace*, 23.

²⁶ Boot, *The Savage Wars of Peace*, 23, 26.

²⁷ Herring, *From Colony to Superpower*, 64, 97.

²⁸ Kagan, *Dangerous Nation*, 44.

²⁹ Kagan, *Dangerous Nation*, 136–8.

³⁰ Quoted in Kagan, *Dangerous Nation*, 81.

³¹ Mead, *Special Providence*, 53.

³² Ferguson, *Colossus*, 35–41. Jefferson saw the Louisiana Purchase as a form of 'immaculate conquest' obtained without force: see Kagan, *Dangerous Nation*, 134.

³³ Until the Civil War, this primarily involved the question of the extension of slavery into newly formed states.

³⁴ Quoted in Weigley, *The American Way of War*, 88.

[35] Weigley, *The American Way of War*, 65–76.

[36] Polk had wanted to acquire an 'enormous empire at small cost': see Millett et al, *For the Common Defense*, 2793.

[37] Echevarria, *Reconsidering the American Way of War*, 77–9.

[38] Weigley, *The American Way of War*, 167.

[39] Maslowski, 'To the Edge of Greatness', 237.

[40] Weigley, *The American Way of War*, 134.

[41] Kagan, *Dangerous Nation*, 266, 268.

[42] Maslowski, 'To the Edge of Greatness', 237.

[43] Echevarria, *Reconsidering the American Way of War*, 85–6. Sherman typically permitted Southern civilians to leave their homes before they were burned down.

[44] Echevarria, *Reconsidering the American Way of War*, 93.

[45] Kagan, *Dangerous Nation*, 280–1.

[46] Weigley, *The American Way of War*, 192.

[47] LeoGrande, *Our Own Backyard*, 12.

[48] Incidentally, a rebellion seriously hobbled due to deep anti-Americanism generated by earlier 'Yanqui' imperialist meddling.

[49] Boot, *The Savage Wars of Peace*, 40.

[50] Boot, *The Savage Wars of Peace*, 69–98.

[51] McKinley believed that a US presence in the Philippines would grant it greater capacity to influence developments in China. Various imperialist nations were competing to carve up China to exploit the country for trade, thus threatening US commercial interests that were reliant on maintaining the 'Open Door': see LaFeber, *The American Age*, 200–1.

[52] Polk, *Violent Politics*, 40–5.

[53] Boot, *The Savage Wars of Peace*, 145.

[54] Burleigh describes a 'cascade of US military interventions' during this period: see Burleigh, *Small Wars, Faraway Places*, 421–2.

[55] A more typical response was surprise and bewilderment on hearing about US operations in these countries. For instance, exasperated contemporaries asked, 'Why are we in Nicaragua and what the hell are we doing there?': see Ferguson, *Colossus*, 58. Almost identical protestations greeted the deaths of US special forces in Niger about a century later, in 2017.

[56] LeoGrande, *Our Own Backyard*, 12–13.

[57] Cohen, 'The strategy of innocence?', 429, 440, 453.

[58] Kennedy, *The Rise and Fall of the Great Powers*, 425.

[59] Ferguson, *Colossus*, 303.

[60] Cohen, 'The strategy of innocence?', 453–4.

[61] Westad, *The Cold War*, 29.

[62] LeoGrande, *Our Own Backyard*, 13–16.

[63] Desch, 'America's liberal illiberalism', 19.

[64] Maslowski, 'To the Edge of Greatness', 210. As Dennis Hart Mahan had observed, the American people were perhaps warlike, but unmilitary.

[65] For instance, the peacetime size of the Army after the First World War was about one-third larger than the pre-war strength, despite the dramatic reductions from 1918 levels: see Cohen, 'The strategy of innocence?', 429.

[66] Weigley remarks on the general post-Civil War 'indifference to military affairs': see Weigley, *The American Way of War*, 169. Boot notes 'the pacifist mood that so often takes hold after a big war gripped the country again': Boot, *The Savage Wars of Peace*, 56.

67 Such as Walter Q. Gresham, Grover Cleveland and William McKinley: see Kagan, *Dangerous Nation*, 280, 363–4, 371, 387.

68 Cohen, 'The strategy of innocence?', 429.

69 At least initially, in the first years after the war, in terms of the rapid and far-reaching demobilization of armed forces: see Hogan, *A Cross of Iron*, 23.

70 In describing his long years of military service during much of the first quarter of the 20th century, the highly decorated Marine Major General Smedley Butler explained how he was essentially 'a high class thug for Big Business, for Wall Street and the bankers … a racketeer, a gangster for capitalism': see Burleigh, *Small Wars, Faraway Places*, 422.

71 LaFeber, *The American Age*, 219.

72 Mead, *Special Providence*, 149.

73 LaFeber, *The American Age*, 205.

74 Kinzer, *Overthrow*, 9–30.

75 Twain, 'Mark Twain home, an anti-imperialist', 5.

76 Kagan, *Dangerous Nation*, 364.

77 Another ill-considered imperial acquisition, somewhat reluctantly and inadvertently falling into American hands after a series of events sparked by the vicarious victory of Commodore Dewey's small Asiatic squadron over the Spanish in Manila Bay on 1 May 1898: see Zelikow, 'Why did America cross the Pacific?'. A Japanese attack on US forces in the Philippines or even its loss would have been painful to accept but might not have been sufficient to turn stubbornly anti-war opinion and nullify the opposition of a virulently isolationist 'America First' lobby, or trigger the kind of nationalist reaction that Pearl Harbour ultimately did.

78 Hastings, *All Hell Let Loose*, 185; Kennedy, *The Rise and Fall of the Great Powers*, 428. The Philippines and Hawaii were indissolubly linked in this respect as Japan's decision to attack Pearl Harbour was a consequence of its logic that in order to strike south it would have to subdue American bases in the Philippines – hence, war with the United States was inevitable, and they decided on a pre-emptive attack against the hub of US naval power: see Zelikow, 'Why did America cross the Pacific?', 37.

79 Quoted in Brogan, *The Penguin History of the USA*, 564. As Brogan notes, the Pacific fleet posed no immediate threat to Japanese moves in East Asia: see Brogan, *The Penguin History of the USA*, 566.

80 Weigley, *The American Way of War*, 229–33.

81 Roberts, *Storm of War*, 186–9.

82 Hasting, *All Hell Let Loose*, 183; Dallek, *Franklin D. Roosevelt*, 341, 377, 420.

83 Westad, *The Cold War*, 40; Hastings, *All Hell Let Loose*, 189.

84 Roosevelt had to walk an agonizing personal and political tightrope for many months. He was torn by, on the one hand, his deep commitment to defeating Nazism, and on the other, his clear appreciation that public opinion was not prepared to tolerate entering the war unprovoked (not to mention his belief that American forces were not yet adequately prepared for war). For all his fierce rhetoric, he was unwilling to actively pull a reluctant American people into war, even refraining from exploiting a number of German U-boat attacks on American shipping through 1941 as a pretext to declare war. He thus directed American efforts to comprehensively support the anti-fascist struggle without the shedding of American blood while also preparing for war. But this had to be done in ways that would not be seen by the public or his isolationist opponents as engineered to trigger US entry into the war. The fact that by at least mid-1941 Roosevelt

saw US involvement as more or less inevitable does not necessarily mean he was entirely insincere in publicly asserting that he would keep America out of the fight, if possible: see Dallek, *Franklin D. Roosevelt*, 364–5, 399, 421–3; Brogan, *The Penguin History of the USA*, 564.

85 Reiter, 'FDR, US entry into World War II', 179–80. This, despite the fact that public opinion, warped by racist attitudes, was more supportive of a tough stance against Japan than Germany: see Hastings, *All Hell Let Loose*, 189. See also Dallek, *Franklin D. Roosevelt*, 437–9; Beevor, *The Second World War*, 248.

86 Dallek, *Franklin D. Roosevelt*, 441.

87 Leffler, *A Preponderance of Power*, 3439.

88 Westad, *The Cold War*, 47.

89 Indeed, the US public had come to see the First World War as a 'failed crusade': see Westad, *The Cold War*, 40.

90 Gaddis, *The Cold War*, 19

91 The Office of Strategic Services (OSS), especially through Allen Dulles, had maintained extensive contacts with the plotters, and some agents suggested such an agreement could end the war 'in the West at one stroke, and save perhaps many hundred thousand lives….' However, the Allied leadership consistently rejected all such opportunities out of hand: see Powers, *Intelligence Wars*, 33.

92 Westad, *The Cold War*, 46.

93 Hastings, *All Hell Let Loose*, 189.

94 Prados, *Safe for Democracy*, 28–30.

95 Powers, *Intelligence Wars*, 18; Prados, *Safe for Democracy*, 30.

96 Weiner, *Legacy of Ashes*, 6–7.

97 This was the culmination of a more gradual pre-war process beginning in the late 1930s and culminating in the War Powers Resolution after Pearl Harbour. Mead notes how the powers of the federal government almost always grow greater in the midst of war: see Mead, *Special Providence*, 52.

98 Maslowski, 'To the Edge of Greatness', 231, 240.

99 Cohen, 'The strategy of innocence?', 455.

100 Mead, *Special Providence*, 69–70.

101 Heuser, *Evolution of Strategy*, 320–1, 330.

102 Heuser, *Evolution of Strategy*, 306.

103 Weigley, *The American Way of War*, 235.

104 Howard, *Studies in War and Peace*, 143–4.

105 Pape, *Bombing to Win*. Even if the bombing campaigns failed in this respect, they nevertheless did play a critical role in bringing about Allied victory: see Overy, *Why the Allies Won*, 132–3.

106 Howard, *Studies in War and Peace*, 145. Many airpower advocates felt vindicated in their claims that airpower, now fitted with the new ordnance, could decide wars alone: see Heuser, *Evolution of Strategy*, 311. Although the lesson of Japan's surrender was flattering, it was already close to collapse before the bombs were dropped, and the Soviet entry into the Pacific War was an important factor affecting Japanese calculations: see Freedman, 'The First Two Generations of Nuclear Strategists', 736–7.

107 Estimated by planners to lead to the loss of half a million lives: see Nichols, 'No other choice'.

108 Freedman, 'The First Two Generations of Nuclear Strategists', 736.

109 Gaddis, *The Cold War*, 25.

[110] As late as 1955, the Chairman of the Joint Chiefs of Staff could 'see no reason why they shouldn't be used just exactly as you would a bullet or anything else': see Freedman, 'The First Two Generations of Nuclear Strategists', 747.

[111] This realization was further underscored by the development of the awesomely powerful hydrogen bomb and reliable missile technologies. This did not stop theorists such as Herman Kahn suggesting that nuclear war could be controlled by policymakers on a 44-rung ladder of escalation: see Freedman, 'The First Two Generations of Nuclear Strategists', 762. The political inutility of nuclear weapons and the acceptance of deterrence through mutually assured destruction was largely accepted by the 1960s, although how to sustain that status continued to preoccupy nuclear strategists, and some later even advocated 'theories of victory' for nuclear war.

[112] In the dark days of the Vietnam War in early 1968, during the Tet Offensive and with the American base at Khe Sanh close to collapse, Johnson toyed with the idea of using nuclear weapons: see Hastings, *Vietnam*, 406. Controlled limited use of nuclear weapons is perhaps an American trait, reflecting vicariousness even in relation to the most extreme of weapons: see Gray, 'Strategy in the Nuclear Age', 597.

[113] MacArthur was dismissed not for suggesting nuclear weapons should be used against China but for pressing such a course of action publicly and above the heads of his civilian superiors. Even Truman was contemplating using nuclear weapons later in the war: see Hastings, *The Korean War*.

[114] Hastings, *Vietnam*, 57–8, 65, 71–81; Carver, 'Conventional Warfare in the Nuclear Age', 783.

[115] Freedman, *The Evolution of Nuclear Strategy*, 23–6, 158–60.

[116] Mahnken, 'The growth and spread of the precision-strike regime', 48. The Congreve rocket – which resembled a larger version of the modern firework – was used during the Napoleonic Wars and the War of 1812 in both naval and land engagements. Coker notes how they were used spectacularly at the 1813 Battle of Leipzig: see Coker, *Rebooting Clausewitz*, 137.

[117] A turning point away from daytime 'precision bombing' came after the disastrous late-1943 Schweinfurt raids during which around a quarter of bombers were lost: see Heuser, *Evolution of Strategy*, 322.

[118] Heuser, *Evolution of Strategy*, 311.

[119] In 1918, towards the end of the war, the inventor Charles Kettering developed an airborne contraption for the US Army dubbed the 'Bug', designed to deliver bombs onto enemy formations; it was never deployed in combat. In the Second World War, two similar projects, *Operation Aphrodite* and *Anvil*, involved repurposing old bombers laden with massive amounts of explosive in largely futile attempts to attack V1 launch sites. After pilots had brought the planes to the required altitude, they would parachute out and the planes (now essentially guided missiles) were directed toward their target via remote control from an accompanying manned 'mothership' bomber. JFK's older brother Joseph died in one of these operations: see Blom, *Unmanned Aerial Systems*, 45–8.

Chapter 4

[1] Mead, *Special Providence*, 10.

[2] Bessner and Logevall, 'Recentering the United States in the historiography of American foreign relations'.

3   Leffler, *A Preponderance of Power*.

4   Porter, *The Global Village Myth*, 59–61.

5   Some have argued that it didn't have to be this way. Layne notes that 'postwar relations between Washington and Moscow might have evolved in a more traditional mold of great power relations, in which competition is dampened by mutual restraint, legitimate security interests are accommodated, and spheres of influence are recognized': see Layne, *Peace of Illusions*, 52.

6   This is the famous Alperovitz revisionist argument.

7   Craig and Logevall, *America's Cold War*, 562–618.

8   Truman officials had considered this but had no strategy to back it up. Secretary of State Byrnes believed the American bomb might serve as an 'implied threat' in negotiations with the Soviets after the war, although he was not sure exactly how: see Leffler, *A Preponderance of Power*, 1646. This reflects the way officials at the time believed that atomic weaponry might serve as the ultimate vicarious weapon, the mere threat of which would be sufficient to induce the bloodless submission of adversaries. On the war scare, see Mark, 'The war scare of 1946 and its consequences'.

9   Before the war was over, Roosevelt already felt Stalin had broken his promises made at Yalta: see Gaddis, *The Cold War*, 22. Regarding Poland, the war had effectively begun over its fate and was where, in 1944, the Soviets had declined to assist the uprising in Warsaw despite being camped outside the city: see Westad, *The Cold War*, 60.

10   Layne, *Peace of Illusions*, 51.

11   Westad, *The Cold War*, 65. See also Leffler, *A Preponderance of Power*, 1667, 1882, 2117, 3725.

12   Leffler, *A Preponderance of Power*, 3439.

13   Kennan, 'Sources of Soviet conduct', 581.

14   Mark, 'The OSS in Romania 1944–45'.

15   Grose, *Operation Rollback*, 80.

16   Corke, *US Covert Operations and Cold War Strategy*, 25; Weiner, *Legacy of Ashes*, 18–19; Powers, *Intelligence Wars*, 15–17.

17   Especially American plans for the future governance and political rehabilitation of Germany, the economic rebuilding of Europe through the Marshall Plan, and the establishment of a globe-spanning network of military bases effectively surrounding the Soviet Union. On the latter, see Leffler, *A Preponderance of Power*, 2192–274. Subsequently, the provision of aid to Tito and the establishment of the North Atlantic Treaty Organization (NATO) in 1949 were further provocations.

18   Grose, *Operation Rollback*.

19   Truman, 'Address before a Joint Session of Congress'. As Leffler notes, by mid-1947, US policymakers were 'showing a growing disposition to consider covert operations and military force should economic aid and even military assistance prove inadequate': see Leffler, *A Preponderance of Power*, 6534. As with most instances of proxy support, the application of the policy in Greece very nearly led to direct US military intervention when the situation appeared desperate in late 1947.

20   Burleigh, *Small Wars, Faraway Places*, 59–60.

21   Weiner, *Legacy of Ashes*, 33. Often built on the foundation of relations with the partisan underground during the war, some of these armies were comprised of as many as 40,000 men. See Cormac and Aldrich, 'Grey is the new black', 487.

22 Andrew, *The Secret World*, 679. Weiner describes them as 'quixotic paramilitary missions to support imaginary resistance movements': see Weiner, *Legacy of Ashes*, 68.

23 Weiner, *Legacy of Ashes*, 44–7, 56. This disregard for the lives of its surrogate allies would be a recurring theme throughout the Cold War and beyond: see Powers, *Intelligence Wars*, xvi.

24 Cormac and Aldrich, 'Grey is the new black', 487.

25 'Within their lifetimes most Russians had experienced two German invasions, and Stalin expected Russia's traditional foe to rise again': see Leffler, *A Preponderance of Power*, 1987, 3789.

26 Layne, *Peace of Illusions*, 53. Kennedy-Pipe emphasizes the Soviet Union's post-war vulnerability, Stalin's expectations of continued Grand Alliance cooperation after the war, the understandable realpolitik considerations behind Soviet moves in Europe, and a series of concessionary moves and withdrawals elsewhere. Conversely, descriptions of the USSR as a dangerous 'superpower' and the image of Stalin as a villain suited Truman who faced significant domestic obstacles in legitimizing America's new global role and the abandonment of isolationism: see Kennedy-Pipe, 'Revisioning Stalin's Cold War', 119–22. Powers similarly notes that it is possible that the Soviets 'had more modest ambitions [than the Americans feared] when they determined to hold on to the countries of Eastern Europe': Powers, *Intelligence Wars*, 46. Leffler also states that 'most scholars now agree that [Stalin's] aim was to consolidate Soviet power within his orbit rather than to seek new gains in the West': Leffler, *A Preponderance of Power*, 6326.

27 Leffler, *A Preponderance of Power*, 2066.

28 Layne, *Peace of Illusions*, 57.

29 Westad, *The Cold War*, 68.

30 Burleigh, *Small Wars, Faraway Places*, 53.

31 Layne, *Peace of Illusions*, 51–70.

32 Although this did not stop nuclear strategists from trying: 'the quest for a nuclear strategy that can serve definite political objectives without triggering a holocaust has occupied some of the best minds of our time': Freedman, 'The First Two Generations of Nuclear Strategists', 735.

33 O'Rourke, 'The strategic logic of covert regime change', 120–3.

34 Carver, 'Conventional Warfare', 788–9.

35 Heuser, *The Evolution of Strategy*, 461.

36 O'Rourke notes that the US conducted 64 covert regime change operations (at least 3 per administration) during the Cold War, 39 of which failed: O'Rourke, 'The strategic logic of covert regime change', 93.

37 As Vos notes, 'mercenaries resolved a profound dilemma between a perceived geostrategic necessity to intervene in remote brush-fire wars and the much-dreaded domestic repercussions that could result': Vos, 'Plausibly deniable, 38–9.

38 Blom, *Unmanned Aerial Systems*.

39 Weiner, *Legacy of Ashes*, 40.

40 Corke, *US Covert Operations and Cold War Strategy*, 6.

41 Leffler, *A Preponderance of Power*, 7960. At least initially in Kennan's case; he later modified his views.

42 Powers, *Intelligence Wars*, 19.

43 Andrew, *The Secret World*, 679; Burleigh, *Small Wars, Faraway Places*, 141–2.

44 In 2016, SAD was renamed the Special Activities Center (SAC). These were specialized operational units within what is colloquially known as the Clandestine

Service but which has gone by various official titles (presently the National Clandestine Service).

[45] Ferguson, *Colossus*, 95.

[46] Mandelbaum, *Mission Failure*, 152.

[47] Weiner, *Legacy of Ashes*, 74.

[48] Quoted in Mumford, *Proxy Warfare*, 100.

[49] United States Government, 'NSC 162/2', 25.

[50] Weiner, *Legacy of Ashes*, 80.

[51] Andrew, *The Secret World*, 679.

[52] Powers, *Intelligence Wars*, 18.

[53] Weiner, *Legacy of Ashes*, 76.

[54] Freedman, 'The First Two Generations of Nuclear Strategists', 741–2.

[55] Much of this activity was carried out under the authority of NSC Action 120d 1954, which was later formalized as the Overseas Internal Security Program in 1957: see Rempe, 'An American Trojan horse?'.

[56] Powers, *Intelligence Wars*, 153.

[57] Weiner, *Legacy of Ashes*, 101.

[58] Andrew, *The Secret World*, 679.

[59] Echevarria, *Reconsidering the American Way of War*, 136.

[60] Powers, *Intelligence Wars*, 153; Weiner, *Legacy of Ashes*, 139.

[61] Kennedy's military adviser, Maxwell Taylor, had developed these ideas in his popular book, *The Uncertain Trumpet*, championing a versatile US military that was capable of responding to limited communist aggression: see Olson and Roberts, *Where the Domino Fell*, 77.

[62] Weiner, *Legacy of Ashes*, 180.

[63] Freedman, *Strategy*, 188.

[64] Freedman, *Kennedy's Wars*, 8.

[65] Vos, 'Plausibly deniable', 42–4.

[66] Sidey, 'The lessons John Kennedy learned from the Bay of Pigs'.

[67] Burleigh, *Small Wars, Faraway Places*, 441.

[68] Westad, *The Cold War*, 289–90.

[69] Kennedy, 'Address before the American Society of Newspaper Editors'.

[70] The experience also pointed to some of the counterproductive effects of the approach (explored further later) with respect to the way 'US assistance would also be used to enhance a state's repressive capabilities': see Michaels, 'Managing global counterinsurgency', 59.

[71] Michaels, 'Managing global counterinsurgency', 59.

[72] Yates, *Power Pack*.

[73] Michaels, 'Managing global counterinsurgency', 36, 45–6, 51.

[74] Burleigh, *Small Wars, Faraway Places*, 496.

[75] Westad, *The Cold War*, 291; Blaufarb, *Organizing and Managing Unconventional War in Laos*; Lloyd-George, 'The CIA's secret war'.

[76] Westad, *The Cold War*, 292.

[77] Ross, 'Time to terminate escalate to de-escalate'. This rationale recently reappeared as President Trump's post hoc rationale for a drone strike that killed the high-profile Iranian General, Qasem Soleimani – as Trump perhaps naively explained, 'We took action last night to stop a war. We did not take action to start a war.'

[78] Weiner, *Legacy of Ashes*, 256.

79 As Westad notes, the Geneva Conference that resulted from the Laotian Secret War contributed to Kennedy's deepening involvement in Vietnam: see Westad, *The Cold War*, 292.

80 Burleigh, *Small Wars, Faraway Places*, 475.

81 Freedman, *Strategy*, 190. Some have suggested that Kennedy planned to withdraw from Vietnam completely after winning the 1964 election: see Olson and Roberts, *Where the Domino Fell*, 90. Revisionist historians claim that this is not true: Moyar, *Triumph Forsaken*.

82 Lembke, *Lansdale, Magsaysay, America, and the Philippines*, 37.

83 *Operation Switchback* transferred the programme over to central US military command and integrated the tribal forces into South Vietnamese military structures: see Nagl, *Learning to Eat Soup with a Knife*, 128–9.

84 Henriksen, *Afghanistan, Counterinsurgency and the Indirect Approach*, 17–22.

85 Lawrence, *The Vietnam War*, 98.

86 Karnow, *Vietnam*, 411–13.

87 Weiner, *Legacy of Ashes*, 237.

88 Karnow, *Vietnam*, 377–9.

89 Burleigh, *Small Wars, Faraway Places*, 474; Heuser, *The Evolution of Strategy*, 346–7.

90 Freedman, *Strategy*, 190–1.

91 In 1968 Johnson stated that 'our objective in South Vietnam has never been the annihilation of the enemy. It has been to bring about a recognition in Hanoi that its objective – taking over the South by force – could not be achieved': Johnson, 'Withdrawal speech'.

92 Boot, *The Savage Wars of Peace*, 291.

93 Johnson, 'Speech at Akron University'.

94 Although at this point, this precise intention for the *employment* of American combat troops was still uncertain and may have been more limited and defensive in nature than ultimately transpired.

95 Maslowski and Winslow, *Looking for a Hero*, 80.

96 Burleigh, *Small Wars, Faraway Places*, 480.

97 Boot, *The Savage Wars of Peace*, 288.

98 Burleigh, *Small Wars, Faraway Places*, 483.

99 As Boot notes, 'his way was the army way, the American way, the World War II way: Find the enemy, fix him in place, and annihilate him with withering firepower': Boot, *The Savage Wars of Peace*, 293.

100 Olson and Roberts, *Where the Domino Fell*, 108.

101 Maslowski and Winslow, *Looking for a Hero*, 81.

102 Correll, 'Origins of the total force', 95.

103 Mead, *Special Providence*, 73.

104 Mack, 'Counterinsurgency in the third world', 245, 246.

105 Olson and Roberts, *Where the Domino Fell*, 204.

106 St Clair and Cockburn, 'Armies, addicts and spooks'; Marshall et al, *The Iran Contra Connection*, 191.

107 Quite successful pacification efforts, such as those organized under the Civil Operations and Rural Development Support (CORDS) office, continued throughout the war but were always a sideshow to the main effort, with the heavy lifting done by South Vietnamese troops or local militia. Meanwhile, the Marine Combined Action Program (CAP) involved just 2,500 Marines at its height working alongside the indigenous Popular Forces militia.

108 Hastings, *Vietnam*, 483–4. As Nixon stated in a public address on 30 April 1970, 'we take this action not for the purpose of expanding the war … but for the purpose of ending the war in Vietnam, and winning a just peace.' Quoted in Olson and Roberts, *Where the Domino Fell*, 219.

109 Hastings, *Vietnam*, 72.

110 Sixteen B-52 bombers were lost in the raids but, compared to the huge losses incurred during the Second World War, this represented a significant step forward. Less than 30 years later during the Kosovo conflict only two aircraft would be downed.

111 Michaels, 'Managing global counterinsurgency', 58.

112 Hastings, *Vietnam*, 572–3.

113 Nixon, 'Address to the nation announcing an agreement on ending the war in Vietnam'.

114 Quoted in Olson and Roberts, *Where the Domino Fell*, 72.

115 According to hardliners in the Kennedy and Johnson administrations, the war should have been taken to the North and the restrictive rules of engagement removed, thus allowing the war to be fought in a more ruthless manner, even utilizing nuclear weapons according to some. For a historical 'revisionist' work making similar arguments, see Moyar, *Triumph Forsaken*.

116 Westad, *The Cold War*, 354.

117 Vos, 'Plausibly deniable', 46.

118 Andrew, *The Secret World*, 687.

119 Retrospectively, Carter was proud of his achievements in this respect: 'We kept our country at peace. We never went to war. We never dropped a bomb. We never fired a bullet. But still we achieved our international goals': see Cadwalladr, 'Interview: Jimmy Carter'.

120 Freedman, *A Choice of Enemies*, 39.

121 Melanson, *American Foreign Policy since the Vietnam War*, 94–100.

122 As such, most covert operations were put to this end, and were principally of a political or propagandistic nature.

123 In Angola and Ethiopia especially. Brzezinski 'suggested that détente had been lost in 1978, in the "sands of the Ogaden," where Soviet advisers had supported Ethiopia in its dispute with Somalia': Freedman, *A Choice of Enemies*, 97.

124 Freedman, *A Choice of Enemies*, 87. Suggestive of his ultimate intent to adopt vicarious warfare measures, Carter promised to 'do the maximum, short of a world war, to make the Soviets see that [the invasion of Afghanistan] was a major mistake': Freedman, *A Choice of Enemies*, 103.

125 Colonel 'Charlie' Beckwith, the creator of Delta Force and fellow Georgian, had persuaded Carter that the mission would succeed using his magnificent new counterterror force: see Bowden, 'The Desert One debacle'.

126 Tucker, 'Reagan's foreign policy', 234.

127 Halliday, *The Making of the Second Cold War*, 245.

128 Reagan harboured a genuine terror of nuclear war: Beinart, 'Ronald Reagan'.

129 Tucker, 'Reagan's foreign policy', 12. Beinart describes Reagan's political genius was in understanding that 'what Americans wanted was a president who exorcised the ghost of the Vietnam War without fighting another Vietnam': Beinart, 'Think again: Ronald Reagan'.

130 McCormick, *America's Half-Century*, 217.

131 Jentleson, *American Foreign Policy*, 165; McCormick, *America's Half-Century*, 216.

132 Tucker, 'Reagan's foreign policy', 27.

[133] Conservative security analysts enthusiastically supported the use of mercenary forces as a means of shaking off the Vietnam syndrome and securing public support for low-risk campaigns in support of anti-communist allies: see Vos, 'Plausibly deniable', 48.

[134] Coll, *Ghost Wars*, 94–5; Powers, *Intelligence Wars*, 270–1.

[135] Levering, *The Cold War, 1945–87*, 175.

[136] The US had previously provided backing to Argentina's dirty war between 1976 and 1983.

[137] This was in the form of a manual circulated to the Contra rebels that the CIA adapted from an earlier Vietnam-era Green Beret manual on special operations, and which advocated selective assassination as an effective tool.

[138] Woods, 'The story of America's first drone strike in Afghanistan'.

[139] Pastor, *Exiting the Whirlpool*, 79. Aid to the Sandinista regime from Cuba and Moscow was believed to have reached some US$500 million by 1986.

[140] Freedman, *A Choice of Enemies*, 132.

[141] Weinberger, 'The uses of military power'; Freedman, *A Choice of Enemies*, 149.

[142] Reagan launched only one direct land war (Grenada) and one air war (Libya). In this light, Tucker has distinguished between Reagan the 'ideologue' and Reagan the 'realist': see Tucker, 'Reagan's foreign policy', 12–13.

[143] Pastor, *Exiting the Whirlpool*, 71.

[144] The US had been providing support to 'loyalist' rebels who were contesting the recent overthrow of Dominican President Donald Reid Cabral by supporters of the left-leaning 'constitutionalist' Juan Bosch. What began as a mission to rescue American citizens amid mounting violence escalated into a significant but limited American military intervention involving over 40,000 troops.

[145] Hickey, *Precision-guided Munitions and Human Suffering in War*, 200.

[146] Stanik, *El Dorado Canyon*.

[147] The decision to expand aid was set out in National Security Directive 166, and US assistance was ultimately estimated to have been worth around US$2 billion up to the time of the Soviet withdrawal: see Maley, *The Afghanistan Wars*, 66.

[148] Coll, *Ghost Wars*, 88, 127.

[149] Coll, *Ghost Wars*, 150; Freedman, *A Choice of Enemies*, 118–20.

[150] Jones, *In the Graveyard of Empires*, 39; Coll, *Ghost Wars*, 130; Cormac and Aldrich, 'Grey is the new black', 483.

[151] Burke, *The 9/11 Wars*, footnote 51, 514.

[152] Coll, *Ghost Wars*, 145.

[153] Freedman, *A Choice of Enemies*, 169. In fact, Oliver North had been involved in counterterrorism operations around the Palestine Liberation Front hijacking of the MS *Achille Lauro* and *Operation El Dorado Canyon* strikes.

[154] Marshall et al, *The Iran Contra Connection*, 189, 224; United States Special Operations Command, *Command History*, 5.

[155] Bacevich, *The New American Militarism*, 159–65.

[156] Coll, *Ghost Wars*, 137; Marshall et al, *The Iran Contra Connection*, 221–2.

[157] United States Government, 'National Security Decision Directive Number 207', 3.

[158] The Pentagon was also experimenting with drone capabilities at this time with the intention of tracking terrorists in places like Lebanon, but there was resistance to arming them: see Woods, 'The story of America's first drone strike in Afghanistan'.

[159] Coll, *Ghost Wars*, 141–4.

[160] An earlier attempted strike had failed to kill the Taliban leader, Mullah Omar.

[161] Mazzetti, 'Former spy with agenda operates a private CIA'.

162 Bacevich, *The New American Militarism*, 175.

163 Melanson, *American Foreign Policy since the Vietnam War*, 5–16.

164 Powers, *Intelligence Wars*, 55.

165 Cormac and Aldrich, 'Grey is the new black', 479.

166 Gray, 'Strategy in the Nuclear Age', 584.

167 Porter, 'Why America's grand strategy has not changed'.

168 In general, but also some that arose in relation to specific controversial events, such as those that combined to fiercely condemn and protest Reagan's Contra war in Nicaragua.

169 'It has long been axiomatic the general public neither cares nor knows much about military affairs': Gray, 'Strategy in the Nuclear Age', 589.

170 Marshall et al, *The Iran Contra Connection*, 206.

171 Marshall et al, *The Iran Contra Connection*, 208.

172 'The key developments hastening the demise of the Soviet empire came from within … the Helsinki accords probably made a greater contribution to undermining Soviet Union than did the reconstitution of US military power in the 1980s. In short, the most persuasive explanation for the final outcome of the Cold War is to be found in Soviet ineptitude, in the internal contradictions of the Soviet system, and in the courage of the dissidents who dared to challenge Soviet authority': Bacevich, *The New American Militarism*, 179. Mead supports this view: see Mead, *Special Providence*, 66.

173 Braithwaite, *Afgantsy*, 37–102; Freedman, *A Choice of Enemies*, 87–94.

174 Westad, *The Cold War*, 498.

175 Some CIA covert operations (such as in Ukraine, Syria, Indonesia and Cuba) failed due to simple issues of poor planning and tactical incompetence and a lack of situational awareness – ironically what the agency should have been best at if they had focused on the primary intelligence-gathering mission instead of paramilitary missions.

176 Poznansky, 'Revisiting plausible deniability', 8; Burleigh, *Small Wars, Faraway Places*, 447; Echevarria, *Reconsidering the American Way of War*, 137; Weiner, *Legacy of Ashes*, 174–5.

177 Cormac and Aldrich, 'Grey is the new black', 483.

178 Freedman, *A Choice of Enemies*, 81.

179 Powers, *Intelligence Wars*, 154; Weiner, *Legacy of Ashes*, 92. Burleigh notes that the way the Shia clerics were marginalized during the coup later allowed them to appear as patriots compared to the Shah (seen as an American-installed puppet) and his hated CIA-trained Savak secret police: see Burleigh, *Small Wars, Faraway Places*, 283.

180 Westad, *The Cold War*, 347.

181 Vos, 'Plausibly deniable', 51–2.

182 Krieg, 'Externalizing the burden of war', 110; Westad, *The Cold War*, 339–63. For instance, as Kinzer notes, 'Most "regime change" operations have achieved their short-term goals…. From the vantage point of history, however, it is clear that most of these operations actually weakened American security. They cast whole regions of the world into upheaval, creating whirlpools of instability from which undreamed-of threats arose years later': Kinzer, *Overthrow*, 5.

183 Weiner, *Legacy of Ashes*, 156–7.

184 Gray, *War, Peace and International Relations*, 195.

185 Treverton, 'Covert action and open society', 1011.

186 Andrew, *The Secret War*, 680.

187   Carson, *Secret Wars*.
188   The main cases are the Spanish Civil War, Korean War, Vietnam War and the War in Afghanistan: see Carson, *Secret Wars*, 99–282.
189   Gaddis, *The Cold War*, 75–7.
190   Burleigh, *Small Wars, Faraway Places*, 457.
191   Craig and Gilbert, 'Reflections on Strategy in the Present and Future', 863.

Chapter 5

1   Layne, *Peace of Illusions*, 32.
2   Desch, 'America's liberal illiberalism', 17, 22.
3   Layne, *Peace of Illusions*, 29–36. Desch suggests this impulse for promoting 'benign hegemony' became even more pronounced after the end of the Cold War: see Desch, 'America's liberal illiberalism'.
4   Herring, *From Colony to Superpower*, 4; Walt, *The Hell of Good Intentions*, 57–8.
5   Mead, *Special Providence*, 172.
6   Porter, *The Lion's Share*, 18–20, 136–7.
7   Walt, *The Hell of Good Intentions*, 53.
8   Kennedy-Pipe, 'Nick Rengger and two wars'.
9   Lears, 'Imperial exceptionalism'.
10   Freedman, *The Transformation of Strategic Affairs*, 39–44.
11   Gray, *Strategy and Politics*, 56.
12   Kennedy, 'The Manichean temptation', 629–30.
13   Kennedy, 'The Manichean temptation'.
14   Fettweis, 'Misreading the enemy'.
15   Waldman, 'System failure', 836–7.
16   Porter, *The Global Village Myth*, 61.
17   Betz, *Carnage and Connectivity*, 27, 39.
18   Porter, *The Global Village Myth*, 1–10.
19   Quoted by Betz, *Carnage and Connectivity*, 34.
20   Byman and Seybolt, 'Humanitarian intervention and communal civil wars', 34.
21   Betts, 'Pick your battles', 20. Echevarria has noted how this tendency has been apparent through US military history: 'leaders frequently accepted the risk of employing limited or even insufficient force, either because they felt doing nothing was worse or because they did not fully understand the potential consequences of failure': Echevarria, *Reconsidering the American Way of War*, 168.
22   So, Porter demonstrates that belief in the existence of global threats is a myth encouraging endless war, Walt dismisses the claim that failing to respond to humanitarian crises will encourage further atrocity, signal American decline or damage its reputation, and Press argues that, far from enhancing one's credibility, 'fighting unnecessary wars reveals one's weakness and reduces one's power for dealing with future crises over more important stakes'. Byman and McCants similarly argue that, contrary to appearances, the contemporary terrorist threat is significantly exaggerated: Porter, *The Global Village Myth*, 1–14; Walt, 'The great myth about US intervention in Syria'; Press, *Calculating Credibility*, 159; Byman and McCants, 'Fight or flight'.
23   Mayer, 'Trigger happy', 273.
24   Coker, *War in an Age of Risk*, 123.
25   Walt, *The Hell of Good Intentions*, 90.
26   Moyn and Wertheim, 'The infinity war'.

27 Brooks, 'Civil-Military Paradoxes', 50.

28 Greider, quoted in Fallows, 'The tragedy of the American military'.

29 Byman and Waxman, 'Defeating US coercion', 109–10.

30 Daddis, 'Iraq and longing for Vietnam'.

31 Golby and Feaver, 'It matters if Americans call Afghanistan a defeat'.

32 Waldman, '"Shadows of uncertainty"'.

33 Lythgoe, 'Our risk-averse army'.

34 Barno and Bensahel, 'Six ways to fix the army's culture'.

35 Erdmann, 'The US presumption of quick, costless wars', 366.

36 Shaw, *The New Western Way of War*, 36–7.

37 This latter point has contributed to a reported sense among generals that the real enemies are perhaps in Washington rather than on the battlefield.

38 Heltberg points to 'the mushrooming of management technologies such as Key Performance Indicators, Balanced Scorecard, risk management systems, performance reviews, time-tracking templates, and assessment systems that permeate many organizations today. While each of these technologies might be helpful in their specific purpose, it seems in their totality that instead of helping leaders to manage, they are often managing the leaders': Heltberg, 'Art, craft, or science'.

39 Brooks, 'Civil-Military Paradoxes', 60.

40 Ricks, 'General failure'.

41 'The real problem with the entry of lawyers into the prosecution of warfare is that it encourages the illusion that war is "clean" if the lawyers say so and breeds a culture in the military in which commanders can avoid hard decisions and risk with the shield of "my lawyer told me not to"': Rizer, 'Lawyering wars', 944.

42 For instance, orders to subordinates might be unrealistically crafted to countenance lethal force only as a last resort. This can seriously jeopardize soldiers' lives, undermining their basic right to use force in self-defence in war, due to the hesitation induced for fear of prosecution.

43 Ricks, 'General failure'.

44 Shaw, *Post-Military Society*; Luttwak, 'Toward post-heroic warfare'.

45 Luttwak, 'Where are the Great Powers?', 25–6.

46 Coker, *War in an Age of Risk*, 79–80, 149.

47 Even during the widely supported Second World War, policymakers sought to minimize domestic disruption and shield citizens from its costs through debt financing, wage and price controls and tax deferrals: see Echevarria, *Reconsidering the American Way of War*, 41.

48 McInnes, *Spectator-Sport Warfare*; Porter, 'Soldiers fighting alone', 11.

49 Brooks, 'There's no such thing as peacetime'.

50 Howard, *War and the Liberal Conscience*.

51 Mueller, 'Trends in popular support for the wars in Korea and Vietnam'.

52 See, for instance, Gelpi et al, *Paying the Human Costs of War*; Jentleson and Britton, 'Still pretty prudent'; Larson, *Casualties and Consensus*.

53 Payne, 'Presidents, politics, and military strategy', 168; Byman and Waxman, 'Defeating US coercion', 109.

54 Ward, 'Fewer civilian casualties'.

55 Eichenberg, 'Victory has many friends', 174.

56 Brooks, 'Civil-Military Paradoxes', 38.

57 Significant minorities have come out in numbers in recent decades to protest against American wars, organized around a core of pacifist activists, who consistently

express their opposition to force, whatever the cause or context. Yet these events occurred in response to major applications of American war, and temporary outpourings of rage are usually followed by low-level, lingering resentment.

58 Beier, 'Outsmarting technologies', 269–71.

59 Bacevich, *The New American Militarism*, 22. See also McInnes, *Spectator-Sport Warfare*.

60 Hanson, *Father of Us All*, 11.

61 Mantello, 'Playing discreet war in the US', 270.

62 Bacevich, *The New American Militarism*.

63 Brooks, 'Civil-Military Paradoxes', 21–3.

64 Porter, 'Soldiers fighting alone', 5–6; Garamone, 'DOD official cites widening military–civilian gap'.

65 Sacrifice in the nation's wars, as a result, is only really vicarious in form: see Bacevich, *The New American Militarism*, 236.

66 Fallows, 'The tragedy of the American military'.

67 Golby and Feaver, 'Thank you for your lip service?'

68 Bacevich, *The New American Militarism*, 237–8.

69 Goldich, 'American military culture from colony to empire', 64. As Walt notes, 'because members of the armed services have joined voluntarily, they cannot easily complain about being sent in harm's way and are less likely to question the merits of using US power abroad': Walt, *The Hell of Good Intentions*, 173.

70 As Bacevich observes, 'that even apart from fighting wars and pursuing terrorists, US forces are constantly prowling around the globe … elicits no more notice (and in some cases less) from the average American than the presence of a cop on a city street corner': Bacevich, *The New American Militarism*, 17.

71 Holmes, 'Warmaking by remote control is a false choice'.

72 *The Economist*, 'The wars in Iraq and Afghanistan have cost most Americans nothing'.

73 Bacevich, *The New American Militarism*, 232.

74 Webb, 'Congressional abdication'.

75 Aday, 'The US Media, Foreign Policy, and Public Support for War'.

76 McKelvey, 'Covering Obama's secret war'.

77 Coker, *Rebooting Clausewitz*, 106.

78 Demmers and Gould, 'An assemblage approach to liquid warfare', 365.

79 See www.washingtonpost.com/graphics/2019/investigations/afghanistan-papers/afghanistan-war-confidential-documents

80 Carroll, 'Lessons to be learned from the Afghanistan Papers'.

81 Waldman, 'System failure', 839–40; Waldman, 'Buy Now', 95–6.

82 Schroden, 'There was no "secret war on the truth" in Afghanistan'.

83 Porter, 'Afghanistan and the lies we tell ourselves'.

84 Trump, 'Remarks by President Trump on the killing of Qasem Soleimani'.

85 Payne, 'Presidents, politics, and military strategy', 167.

86 Aday, 'Leading the charge', 445; Aday, 'The US Media, Foreign Policy, and Public Support for War'.

87 Dandeker, 'From Victory to Success', 29.

88 Payne, 'Presidents, politics, and military strategy', 168.

89 Smith, *The Utility of Force*.

90 Malley and Pomper, 'An accounting for the uncounted'.

91 Levite and Shimshoni, 'The strategic challenge of society-centric warfare', 92–3.

92 Walt, *The Hell of Good Intentions*, 175.

93 Betz, *Carnage and Connectivity*, 92.

Chapter 6

1 Western, 'Sources of humanitarian intervention', 112–13, 116–17, 121–2.
2 Fukuyama, *The End of History and the Last Man.*
3 Lissner, 'The long shadow of the Gulf War'.
4 Krauthammer, 'The unipolar moment'; Mayer, 'Trigger happy', 265–6.
5 'This is not a democratic crusade; it is a pragmatic commitment to see freedom take hold': White House, 'A National Security Strategy of Engagement and Enlargement', 23.
6 The Horn of Africa had been a pivotal locus of East–West proxy competition during the 1970s and early 1980s, but with the relaxation of Cold War tensions in the late 1980s, both superpowers significantly disengaged from the region: see Gasbarri, 'From the sands of the Ogaden to Black Hawk Down', 77–86.
7 The Marines were joined by tens of thousands of other American forces as well as contingents from other nations.
8 Recchia, 'Pragmatism over principle'. The decision may also have been seen as a way to pre-emptively forestall the prospect of intervention in Bosnia, which officials such as Powell adamantly wished to avoid but that was looking ever more likely given mounting popular pressure and Clinton's election victory: see Western, 'Sources of humanitarian intervention'.
9 Hirsch, 'The Black Hawk Down effect'.
10 Montgomery, 'Ambush in Mogadishu'.
11 In his 1996 fatwa he claimed that the episode had proven American 'impotence and weakness': see PBS, 'Bin Laden's fatwa'.
12 An arguably valid decision given the host of issues afflicting UN peacekeeping operations at the time. US troops were, however, sent in large numbers as part of peacekeeping operations in Haiti, Bosnia and Kosovo during Clinton's term in office.
13 Carroll, 'US chose to ignore Rwandan genocide'.
14 Karcher, *Understanding the "Victory Disease"*; Runkle, 'The lost lessons of "Black Hawk Down"'.
15 South, 'The Battle of Mogadishu 25 years later'. This narrative was further reinforced through the popular account by Mark Bowden and film of the book: see Bowden, *Black Hawk Down*; Scott, *Black Hawk Down.*
16 Foreign special forces deployments more than doubled during the 1990s.
17 Runkle, 'The lost lessons of "Black Hawk Down"'.
18 Bacevich, *The New American Militarism*, 57–8.
19 Heuser, *The Evolution of Strategy*, 305.
20 Heuser, *The Evolution of Strategy*, 333–5.
21 Kagan, *Finding the Target*, 103–43, 160–6.
22 Press, 'The myth of air power in the Persian Gulf War and the future of warfare'.
23 Clausewitz, *On War*, 228. Thucydides described an even earlier indication of the problems associated with such strategies. Complementing a strict territorial defence, Pericles' strategy of punishment through intensifying coercive naval attacks on Spartan assets failed to persuade the enemy that continued aggression would be futile and costly: see Kagan, 'Athenian Strategy in the Peloponnesian War', 40.
24 Kagan, *Finding the Target*, 191–2.
25 Pape, quoted in Heuser, *The Evolution of Strategy*, 311.
26 Heuser, *The Evolution of Strategy*, 186–7.
27 Quoted in Bacevich, *The New American Militarism*, 196.
28 Bernstein and Libicki, 'High-tech'.

29 Clinton had outlined these earlier, and they closely reflected those promulgated later by the UK Prime Minister in his 'Doctrine of International Community' speech in Chicago in April 1999.
30 Beier, 'Outsmarting technologies', 266–7.
31 Clark, *Winning Modern Wars*.
32 Furthermore, Ambassador Richard Holbrooke, the main architect of the Dayton accords, had only recently published his account of events in Bosnia in which he reiterated the conventional wisdom regarding the key role of airpower. This further bolstered the confidence of officials believing that similar methods would work decisively in Kosovo. Blankshain and Stigler, 'Applying method to madness'.
33 Byman and Waxman, 'Kosovo and the great airpower debate', 29.
34 Kagan, *Finding the Target*, 188–9.
35 Ignatieff, *Virtual War*.
36 Ignatieff, *Virtual War*.
37 Der Derian, 'Virtuous war/virtual theory'.
38 Der Derian, 'Virtuous war/virtual theory', 773–4.
39 Such as the 1993 World Trade Center bombing, the 1998 Embassy bombings and the attack against the USS *Cole* in 2000.
40 Clark, *Winning Modern Wars*, 115–16.
41 Freedman, *The Transformation of Strategic Affairs*, 65.
42 Niva, 'Disappearing violence', 190.
43 In the late 1990s, drones were used for reconnaissance missions against Al-Qaeda and also to laser designate targets for missile strikes: see Woods, 'The story of America's first drone strike in Afghanistan'; Coll, *Ghost Wars*, 527–34.
44 Shaw, *The New Western Way of War*, 16, 37.
45 Smith, *The Utility of Force*, 9.
46 Kagan, 'High-tech'.
47 Ignatieff, *The Warrior's Honor*, 97.
48 Dueck, *Reluctant Crusaders*, 114.
49 Freedman, *Strategy*, 218.
50 Bush, 'President Bush addresses the nation'.
51 Echevarria, *Reconsidering the American Way of War*, 150; Biddle, 'Allies, airpower, and modern warfare'.
52 Finlan, *Contemporary Military Strategy and the Global War on Terror*, 75–97; Kagan, *Finding the Target*, 290–3.
53 Mandelbaum, *Mission Failure*, 164.
54 Burke, *The 9/11 Wars*, 71.
55 Waldman, 'Reconciliation and research in Afghanistan', 1050–2.
56 Shaw, *The New Western Way of War*, 27; Kagan, *Finding the Target*, 298–9.
57 Weaver, 'Lost at Tora Bora'.
58 Burke, *The 9/11 Wars*, 68–70.
59 In fact, there was overwhelming support for the foreign presence in Afghanistan immediately after the intervention.
60 Smith, *Killer Elite*, 226.
61 Burke, *The 9/11 Wars*, 48.
62 Rashid, *Descent*, 198–201.
63 Reid and Muhammedally, 'Just Don't Call It a Militia', 3; Henriksen, *Afghanistan, Counterinsurgency and the Indirect Approach*, 68.
64 Mann, *Game Changers*; Jones, 'It takes the villages'.

65 Its decision to do so was a major reason for the subsequent deterioration of the situation in Afghanistan.

66 Echevarria, *Reconsidering the American Way of War*, 153.

67 To some extent it was also simply a function of the military's failure to plan for 'Phase IV' contingencies.

68 Avant and Sigelman, 'Private security and democracy', 255.

69 Clark, *Winning Modern Wars*, 147.

70 Kagan, *Finding the Target*, 324.

71 Bush, *Decision Points*, 254.

72 Echevarria, *Reconsidering the American Way of War*, 154.

73 Coker, *War in an Age of Risk*, 111–14.

74 Burke, *The 9/11 Wars*, 241.

75 Coker, *War in an Age of Risk*, 123.

76 On this date, 'the President signed a covert action Memorandum of Notification (MON) granting the CIA unprecedented counterterrorism authorities': see Senate Select Committee on Intelligence, 'Committee Study of the Central Intelligence Agency's Detention and Interrogation Program'.

77 Schmitt and Mazzetti, 'Secret order lets US raid Al Qaeda'; Ryan, '"War in countries we are not at war with"', 366.

78 Clark, *Winning Modern Wars*, 152.

79 Amnesty International, *The US Hidden War in Somalia*; Scahill, 'Blowback in Somalia'. These developments reflected broader concerns that North Africa would become a sanctuary for terrorists pushed out of Afghanistan and the Middle East. As earlier as the end of 2002, US Special Forces were present in countries right across the north of the continent: see Ryan, '"War in countries we are not at war with"', 371.

80 Gettleman, 'The most dangerous place in the world'.

81 Wax and DeYoung, 'US secretly backing warlords in Somalia'.

82 Henriksen, *Afghanistan, Counterinsurgency and the Indirect Approach*, 30.

83 Henriksen, *Afghanistan, Counterinsurgency and the Indirect Approach*, 34–5.

84 Scahill, 'Blowback in Somalia'. Henriksen arrives at a similar conclusion: 'The Ethiopian invasion and occupation rekindled Somali revulsion against their foreign overlords and enhanced the spread of an even more virulent extremism as manifested by the al-Shabaab militias': Henriksen, *Afghanistan, Counterinsurgency and the Indirect Approach*, 69.

85 Williams, 'Subduing al-Shabaab', 95.

86 Hoffman, 'Complex irregular war', 399.

87 Burton, 'The promise and peril of the indirect approach', 47.

88 Shaw, *The New Western Way of War*, 86, 94–5.

89 Bush, 'A period of consequences'.

90 Shaw, *The New Western Way of War*, 24–5, 130.

91 No US soldiers were killed in the invasion phase of the 2001 Afghanistan war. There were less than 200 combat deaths in the invasion phase of Iraqi Freedom, an historically low number given the scale of the campaign.

92 Mandel, *Security, Strategy and the Quest for Bloodless War*.

93 Lynch, 'Explaining the awakening'.

94 Some analysts suggested that much of the decline in violence occurred because the sectarian cleansing had essentially burned itself out, although this view has been challenged: see Biddle et al, 'Testing the surge', 13–18; Desch, 'Correspondence', 185.

95 Waldman, 'System failure', 835.
96 Penney, 'The Anbar awakening in context', 114.
97 Kilcullen, *Blood Year*, 83–4, 89.
98 Sanger, *Confront and Conceal*, 15–34.
99 Perry, 'Blackwater vs bin Laden', 44–5. Defense Department contractors alone reached as high as 190,000 in Iraq and over 100,000 in Afghanistan in the late 2000s.
100 As Finlan notes: 'Afghanistan and Iraq are not the future of warfare. In time, they will be seen in their proper historical context as aberrations': Finlan, *Contemporary Military Strategy and the Global War on Terror*, 197.
101 McChrystal, 'It takes a network'.
102 Burke, *The 9/11 Wars*, 476.
103 Woodward, *Obama's Wars*, 102.
104 Woodward, *Obama's Wars*, 159–60.
105 Waldman, 'System failure', 828.
106 Denselow, 'The US departure from Iraq is an illusion'.
107 Tierney, 'The legacy of Obama's "worst mistake"'. In many respects, the intervention had much in common with the Kosovo air war of 1999 given the humanitarian motives, reliance on airpower, coordination with rebels and centrality of coalition warfare: see Stapleton, 'The problem with the light footprint', 3.
108 Savage and Landler, 'White House defends continuing US role in Libya operation'.
109 Webb, 'Congressional abdication'.
110 Bunker, 'Defeating violent non-state actors', 57–8.
111 Lears, 'Imperial exceptionalism'.
112 Malley and Finer, 'The long shadow of 9/11', 60.
113 Stapleton, 'The problem with the light footprint'.
114 Niva, 'Disappearing violence', 198.
115 Goldberg, 'The Obama Doctrine'.
116 Goldberg, 'The Obama Doctrine'.
117 Murphy, 'US Special Forces sabotage White House policy gone disastrously wrong with covert ops in Syria'.
118 Mazzetti et al, 'Behind the sudden death of a $1 billion secret CIA war in Syria'.
119 Bulos et al, 'In Syria, militias armed by the Pentagon fight those armed by the CIA'.
120 Stapleton, 'The problem with the light footprint', 6.
121 Murphy, 'US Special Forces sabotage White House policy gone disastrously wrong with covert ops in Syria'.
122 By April 2018, there were over 2,000 US troops in Syria stationed in about 20 bases, most of them in northern Syria close to the border to Turkey and on territory controlled by the Kurds: see Krishnan, 'Controlling partners and proxies in pro-insurgency paramilitary operations', 5. Moreover, problems with arms transfers continued – in early 2020 it was reported that the Pentagon could not account for over US$700 million in weapons and equipment provided to partner forces: see Keller, 'The Pentagon lost track of $715 million in weapons and gear funneled to anti-ISIS allies in Syria'.
123 Hiltermann, 'Iraq'.
124 Amnesty International, *At Any Cost*, 45.
125 Gilsinan, 'The inconvenient truth about ISIS'.
126 Ryan and Raghavan, 'Special Operations troops aiding Libyan forces in major battle against Islamic State'.

127 Editors, 'End the war in Afghanistan'.

128 Schreer and Waldman, 'Strategy on Autopilot', 58–71.

129 Goldsmith and Waxman, 'Legal legacy of light-footprint warfare', 14–15; Zenko, 'The true forever war'.

130 Observers have linked the almost unconditional American alliance with Saudi Arabia as central to patterns of radicalization in the wider region: see Cockburn, *The Rise of Islamic State*.

131 Ryan, '"War in countries we are not at war with"', 370–3.

132 Mahoney, 'US defense contractors and the future of military operations"', 189–90.

133 Burkina Faso, Cameroon, Central African Republic, Chad, Democratic Republic of Congo, Kenya, Libya, Mali, Mauritania, Niger, Somalia, South Sudan and Tunisia.

134 Rempfer, 'Special operations launches "secret surrogate" missions in new counter-terrorism strategy'; Morgan, 'Behind the US secret war in Africa'.

135 Turse and Naylor, 'Revealed'. The death of Operator Karl Milliken, killed in Somalia in May 2017, was the first US combat death there since the Black Hawk Down incident in 1993: see Cooper et al, 'Navy SEAL killed in Somalia in first combat death there since 1993'.

136 Sperber, 'Inside the secretive US air campaign in Somalia'.

137 Atherton, 'Trump inherited the drone war but ditched accountability'.

138 De Luce and McLeary, 'Trump's ramped-up bombing in Yemen signals more aggressive use of military'.

139 Byman, 'Yemen's disastrous war', 147–53.

140 Elbagir et al, 'Sold to an ally, lost to an enemy'.

141 Elbagir et al, 'Sold to an ally, lost to an enemy', 147–53.

142 Niva, 'Disappearing violence', 199.

143 Demmers and Gould, 'An assemblage approach to liquid warfare', 366.

144 Demmers and Gould, 'An assemblage approach to liquid warfare', 366.

145 Gregg, 'Use of military contractors shrouds true costs of war'.

146 Dozier, 'Secret annexes, backroom deals'. For the full text of the agreement, see *The Washington Post*, 'The US–Taliban peace deal'.

147 This issue is raised in Human Rights Watch, *Abusive Night Raids by CIA-Backed Afghan Strike Forces*.

148 Demmers and Gould, 'An assemblage approach to liquid warfare', 367; Levite and Shimshoni, 'The strategic challenge of society-centric warfare'.

149 McMaster, 'On war', 27.

150 Bacevich, 'Endless war in the Middle East', 5.

151 Henriksen, *Afghanistan, Counterinsurgency and the Indirect Approach*; Meilinger, *Limiting Risk in America's Wars*.

152 Byman and McCants, for instance, outlined an intricately calibrated scheme for *avoiding* a persistent 'forever war' but which would in practice likely entail just that: see Byman and McCants, 'Fight or flight', 69–74. Similarly, Brands and Feaver ran through a spectrum of options open to policymakers in the fight against Islamic State. The seemingly inescapable logic of their argument meant rejecting large-scale campaigns or disengagement, and instead opting for a middle ground 'counter-ISIS plus' approach, going beyond light-footprint commitments and utilizing more aggressive air strikes, SOF and security force assistance (SFA) programmes while incentivizing local governments to adopt necessary reforms: see Brands and Feaver, 'Trump and terrorism', 32–4.

153 Wertheim, 'The price of primacy'.

154 *The Economist*, 'Jihadists in the Sahel threaten west Africa's coastal states'; Turse, 'Pentagon's own map of US bases in Africa contradicts its claim of "light" footprint'.

155 Cooper et al, 'Pentagon eyes Africa drawdown as first step in global troop shift'.

Chapter 7

1 Meilinger, 'Busting the icon', 139.

2 See, for instance, Meilinger, *Limiting Risk in America's Wars*; Corn, 'From Mars to Minerva'; Melton, *The Clausewitz Delusion*; Dunlap, 'America's asymmetric advantage'; Deptula, 'Air and space power, lead turning, the future'. Many of these authors, although not all, tend to be airmen, or at least closely associated with the airpower community.

3 McFate, *Goliath*, 29, 205.

4 McFate, *Goliath*, 38, 98–102, 113–40, 203–5.

5 Indeed, many modern authors tend to blindly adopt Liddell Hart's earlier misleading claim in his *The Ghost of Napoleon* (1914) that Clausewitz developed the idea that 'the destruction of the enemy's armed forces was the only true object of strategy', even if he himself later nuanced that argument. Heuser usefully explains that the idea that there is one such Clausewitzian model of war results from a failure to discriminate between Clausewitz the Idealist and Clausewitz the Realist: see Heuser, *Reading Clausewitz*, 43, 114. For a useful recent corrective, see Leonard, 'That Clausewitz-is-irrelevant "hot take" isn't blasphemous'.

6 John Keegan presented a wholly misleading and narrow representation of Clausewitzian ideas in his popular, *A History of Warfare*. As Bassford observed, Keegan painted Clausewitz as 'the brutal philosopher of pitiless, aggressive total war': see Bassford, 'John Keegan and the grand tradition of trashing Clausewitz', 320. This echoed Hart's earlier similar rendering. At least André Beaufre – influenced by Hart and a prominent advocate of indirect approaches – recognized that the focus on decisive victory was a 'pseudo-Clausewitzian aberration' based on distorted understandings of his 'analysis of Napoleon's recipe for success': see Heuser, *The Evolution of Strategy*, 452, 461. In all this ironies abound insofar as Clausewitz was one of the first true theorists of limited war, he thought defence the stronger form of war, and his writings actually underscore the dangers of pursuing the kind of 'Clausewitzian victory' – in narrow military terms – that Keegan and others erroneously imputed to him: see Bassford, 'John Keegan and the grand tradition of trashing Clausewitz', 330. Other widely read works that reinforced mistaken interpretations include Weigley, *The American Way of War* and Summers, *On Strategy*.

7 Bassford, 'John Keegan and the grand tradition of trashing Clausewitz', 331.

8 For instance, see Echevarria, *Clausewitz and Contemporary War*; Strachan and Herberg-Rothe, *Clausewitz in the Twenty-First Century*; Waldman, *War, Clausewitz and the Trinity*.

9 Clausewitz, *On War*, 94.

10 Clausewitz, *On War*, 604.

11 Strangely McFate asserts that 'war is armed politics, nothing more', yet conveniently omits to acknowledge our debt to the Prussian as the first thinker to seriously articulate this vital truth, perhaps because it does not fit his neat, simplistic and misleading dismissal of Clausewitz the 'lion' in favour of Sun Tzu the 'fox': see McFate, *Goliath*, 184.

[12] Clausewitz, *On War*, 87.

[13] Strachan and Herberg-Rothe, 'Introduction', 11.

[14] Waldman, *War, Clausewitz and the Trinity*, 100–1.

[15] Clausewitz, *On War*, 609.

[16] Clausewitz, *On War*, 605; emphasis added.

[17] Clausewitz explains that while war might have its own distinctive 'grammar' – the character and dynamics of fighting – its basic underlying logic is always political, in the sense that both war and politics are social forces that determine the distribution of power among groups. This reveals why those who believe policy should make way for purely military solutions once war begins are mistaken and short-sighted. Such assertions are merely subjective points of view: but these actors cannot escape the fact that war will have political consequences however much they believe or desire otherwise.

[18] Waldman, 'Politics and war', 8–9.

[19] 'All operations have political consequences. They can increase or diminish a nation's ability to achieve its goals; they can commit it unwisely to new and unforeseen objectives; they can, by failure of calculation or execution, discourage its allies or bring new support to the side of the enemy': Craig, 'The Political Leader as Strategist', 482.

[20] Clausewitz, *On War*, 80. Elsewhere he states that, 'war does not contain in itself the elements for a complete and final settlement.'

[21] Short of imposing a 'Carthaginian peace', force has political effect through how it is perceived by the enemy as much as through the physical reality itself.

[22] Waldman, 'Strategic narratives and US surrogate warfare', 162–4. See also, for instance, Freedman, *The Transformation of Strategic Affairs*; Betz, *Carnage and Connectivity*; Simpson, *War from the Ground Up*.

[23] Grynkewich, 'Introducing information as a joint function', 6–7.

[24] Betz, 'Searching for El Dorado', 38.

[25] Freedman, 'The Possibilities and Limits of Strategic Narratives', 24.

[26] Clausewitz, *On War*, 566–574. He also employed the concept of the 'culminating point of attack' referring to a similar dynamic at the tactical level: see Clausewitz, *On War*, 528.

[27] Handel, *Masters of War*, 182.

[28] As Elliott has observed, 'short term judgements invariably contain the asp of longer-term consequences within them': Elliott, *High Command*, 21.

[29] Gray, *Modern Strategy*, 52.

[30] Johnson, *Blowback*.

[31] Bell, 'Libya crisis'.

[32] Treverton, 'Covert action and open society', 1000; Salehyan, 'The delegation of war to rebel organisations', 507.

[33] Coker, *War in an Age of Risk*, 111–14.

[34] Malley and Finer, 'The long shadow of 9/11', 67.

[35] The strategic disconnect between counterterror and counterinsurgency approaches has been starkly apparent throughout the war in Afghanistan, for instance, fatally undermining the entire basis of the mission there in a self-defeating downward spiral.

[36] Clausewitz, *On War*, 174.

[37] Cohen, 'The mystique of US airpower', 109.

[38] Pape, *Bombing to Win*, 2.

[39] Pape, *Bombing to Win*; Byman et al, *Air Power as a Coercive Instrument*, 75–84.

[40] Byman and Waxman, 'Defeating US coercion'.

[41] Byman and Waxman, 'Kosovo and the great airpower debate', 31–5.

[42] Some argue that vicarious methods negate the requirement for large-scale occupations, thus minimizing the possibility of nationalist opposition. But this ignores the way America's supposedly hidden but usually plainly apparent hand can fuel similar forms of resistance: while the American public might be entirely ignorant about activities US forces are undertaking, local actors usually understand when militias are CIA creations, security forces are operating at the behest of US SOF, airstrikes are enabled by US weapons and intelligence or mercenaries are paid from US coffers. Enemy actors exploit these local perceptions in their propaganda, and even where the US hand is not necessarily active, their false claims and misinformation will reach receptive audiences.

[43] Kidd and Walter, 'The strategies of terrorism', 69–72.

[44] Tehran's provision of support to the Taliban can partly be explained by Iran's reading of Trump's Afghanistan strategy – characterized primarily by risk-evasive approaches centred on airpower, security assistance and sponsorship of militias – as indicative of faltering US political will and thus susceptible to coercive manipulation: see Constable, 'After Taliban assault in Western Afghanistan, allegations of an Iranian role'. Recently, Iran has adopted a similar strategy in Somalia by providing support to al-Shabaab, and likely for similar reasons: Fraser-Rahim and Fatah, 'In Somalia, Iran is replicating Russia's Afghan strategy'.

[45] Raitasalo, 'Moving beyond the "western expeditionary frenzy"', 378–9.

[46] Cunningham, 'In Turkey, soaring support for Syrian offensive and rising anti-Americanism'; Pamuk and Bektas, 'Turkey fires on US-backed Kurdish militia in Syria offensive'.

[47] Proxies may be driven to engage in damaging activities intended to sustain US support (such as perpetuating the conflict) or adopt hedging strategies by aligning with other actors in ways that run counter to US interests.

[48] There was, for instance, immense pressure on Kennedy to send troops to save the Bay of Pigs operation, underscoring the difficulty of withdrawal or cutting losses even in the context of minimalist American commitments, and even if only conducted through proxies: see Powers, *Intelligence Wars*, xi.

[49] Eyre and Littleton, 'Shaping the Zeitgeist', 180.

[50] Mead, *Special Providence*, 61.

[51] Westad, *The Cold War*, 496.

[52] Burleigh, *Small Wars, Faraway Places*, 107.

[53] Gaddis, *The Cold War*, 134.

[54] Shaw, *The New Western Way of War*, 24–5.

[55] Coker, *War in an Age of Risk*, 128.

[56] Handel, *Masters of War*, 353–60.

[57] There is also good reason to believe that NATO's intervention encouraged the militarization of the Syrian uprising: see Kuperman, 'A model humanitarian intervention?', 123, 131–2.

[58] Kuperman, 'A model humanitarian intervention?', 129–33.

[59] Clausewitz, *On War*, 598.

[60] Mahoney, 'US defense contractors and the future of military operations', 186–8.

[61] Respectively, for key contributions, see Rogers and Kennedy-Pipe, *Drone Warfare*; Mumford, *Proxy Warfare*; and Prados, *Safe for Democracy*.

[62] Krieg, 'Externalizing the burden of war'; Mumford, *Proxy Warfare*, 45. Delegation can be complete, entailing total substitution of the sponsor by a proxy force, or

partial, involving simultaneous direct American troop presence or concurrent operations, such as advisory missions or 'compound warfare'. At an extreme, it might even be understood to include active toleration of the activities of certain groups that America otherwise would have the power to prevent – for instance, US toleration of the actions of Iranian-backed Shia Popular Mobilization Forces in Iraq. For an interesting discussion around various contemporary conceptual and empirical issues associated with surrogate and proxy warfare, see Rauta et al, 'A symposium'.

63 Avant and Sigelman, 'Private security and democracy', 262–3.

64 Porch, 'Expendable soldiers', 700.

65 Hennigan, 'US special operations'.

66 Votel and Keravuori, 'The by-with-through operational approach', 40–7; United States Army and Marine Corps, *FM 3-24*, 122, 153, 193. A Counterterrorism Partnership Fund was specifically established to finance such programmes.

67 Thomas, 'SOCOM'.

68 Linked to this, within the context of the war on terror, delegation to Muslim proxies allows America to avoid perceptions of the fighting as being about 'America versus Islam': see Scheipers, 'Auxilliaries at war in the Middle East', 126.

69 Byman, 'Friends like these', 87–8.

70 Malkesian and Weston, 'War downsized', 114.

71 Schooner, 'Why contractor fatalities matter', 79.

72 Compound warfare might take the form of US air strikes coterminous with proxy operations on the ground (for example, Bosnia 1995, Kosovo 1999, Afghanistan 2001, Syria 2014–present). This is distinct from advisory missions in which US forces work directly alongside the proxy in a purely supporting role, although sometimes the distinctions are blurred where advisors find themselves engaged in firefights.

73 Vlahos, 'Fighting identity', 7.

74 Krieg, 'Externalizing the burden of war', 102.

75 Inherent problems are captured especially well in studies that apply a principal-agent lens. See, for instance, Byman, 'Friends like these'; Biddle et al, 'Small footprint, small payoff'; Salehyan, 'The delegation of war to rebel organisations'.

76 Perry, 'Blackwater vs bin Laden', 42–3; Stanger, *One Nation under Contract*.

77 Mahoney, 'US defense contractors and the future of military operations', 181.

78 Gregg, 'Use of military contractors shrouds true costs of war'; Avant and Sigelman, 'Private security and democracy', 246–9; Schooner, 'Why contractor fatalities matter', 78–91.

79 Stanger and Williams, 'Private military corporations'.

80 Privatization allows policymakers to 'circumvent the domestic political constraints over the mobilization of military personnel: see Cusomano, 'Bridging the gap', 97; Avant and Sigelman, 'Private security and democracy'; Perry, 'Blackwater vs bin Laden', 41–55.

81 Avant and de Nevers, 'Military contractors and the American way of war', 93.

82 For instance, the US reaction to the Blackwater contractor killings in March 2004 was a major factor prompting the ill-fated first battle of Fallujah: see Ricks, *Fiasco*, 332. The same company was also involved in the massacre of 17 civilians in 2007. The majority of interrogators at Abu Ghraib were employees of CACI International.

83 Rissen and Mazzetti, 'Blackwater guards tied to secret CIA raids'. Experts have also expressed concern regarding the increased outsourcing of what were traditionally strictly in-house functions, such as intelligence collection and interrogation.

84 Friedrichs and Friesendorf, 'Privatized security cripples statebuilding', 43–8.

85 United States Senate Armed Forces Committee, 'Report of the Inquiry into the Role and Oversight of Private Security Contractors in Afghanistan', i.

86 As Lujan puts it: 'Partner nation security forces become more proficient and their leaders more professional': Lujan, *Light Footprints*, 13.

87 Biddle et al, 'Small footprint, small payoff', 91–2.

88 Biddle et al, 'Small footprint, small payoff', 94.

89 Karlin, 'Why military assistance programs disappoint', 112.

90 'In Pakistan, American advisors are training Islamabad's troops to fight Taliban insurgents in that country's northwestern areas. In the Horn and in the Philippines, SOF are playing a well-executed indirect role to preempt a full-blown insurgency by transferring COIN techniques to local African forces and the Filipino army': Henriksen, *Afghanistan, Counterinsurgency and the Indirect Approach*, 66–7.

91 Williams, 'Building the Somali National Army', 367.

92 Henriksen, *Afghanistan, Counterinsurgency and the Indirect Approach*, 51–2; Biddle et al, 'Small footprint, small payoff', 107–12, 126–7.

93 As Ucko states, 'where the approach is said to have worked – in Colombia, El Salvador, or the Philippines – outcomes have been less impressive than commonly recognized and/or were conditional on key factors that are not easily reproduced': Ucko, 'Systems failure', 238. Indeed, in El Salvador, the war was not won by the Salvadorian armed forces but through a negotiated settlement; the actions of the military had led to thousands of civilian deaths and contributed to cycles of poverty and social breakdown that continue to frustrate the country's development. In the Philippines, Islamist militancy remains a potent threat, largely because underlying issues have not been sufficiently addressed.

94 Human Rights Watch, *Abusive Night Raids by CIA-Backed Afghan Strike Forces*, 13–14; Purkiss et al, 'CIA-backed Afghan unit accused of atrocities is able to call in air strikes'; Ferguson, 'In Afghanistan, fighting the Taliban increasingly involves covert operations'; Ghazi and Mashal, 'US bombs Afghan militia behind insider attack, officials say'; Kibbe, 'Conducting shadow wars', 374.

95 Human Rights Watch, *Abusive Night Raids by CIA-Backed Afghan Strike Forces*, 15.

96 Porch, 'Expendable soldiers'.

97 Intensively trained indigenous special forces units have proven more militarily effective – such as Iraq's elite Golden Division, Afghan Commandos and the Somali Donab – but they do not enjoy sufficient numbers to offer lasting security, plus they have sustained heavy losses by virtue of shouldering the burden of the fighting.

98 Farrell and Semple, 'Making peace with the Taliban', 83–7.

99 Deni, 'Security Assistance', 12973–88. Furthermore, creating powerful centralized national security forces may generate resistance among populations where state institutions have long been absent, leading local actors to rely on alternative arrangements, or where expanding state presence has historically been associated with brutal repression among local powerholders where there are strong traditions of regional autonomy, or among minorities where armed forces are dominated by different ethnic or sectarian groups. On this, in relation to Somalia, see Williams, 'Building the Somali National Army', 380–2.

100 Byman, 'Friends like these', 102–4.

[101] Johnson, 'Upstream engagement and downstream entanglements', 651. Support has also disincentivized governments from making wider social and political reforms insofar as they come to rely on force to address their problems (arguably mirroring the American problem at the global level).

[102] Guido, 'American way of war in Africa'.

[103] Small-footprint aid that fails to solve the military problem creates powerful incentives for American presidents to escalate lest they admit failure under domestic partisan criticism. Policy failure can encourage mission creep and mounting commitment, even when the policy is initially limited to SFA: see Biddle et al, 'Small footprint, small payoff', 131.

[104] Burgos, 'Pushing the easy button', 123; Byman and Merritt, 'Special Operations Forces', 86.

[105] Savage et al, 'US kept silent about its role in another firefight in Niger'.

[106] Felbab-Brown, 'Hurray for militias?', 274.

[107] Scheipers, 'Auxilliaries at war in the Middle East', 127–32.

[108] Even a CIA internal study concluded that providing arms to rebels rarely works: see Mazzetti, 'CIA study of covert aid fueled skepticism about helping Syrian rebels'.

[109] Reuters, 'Arms supplied by US, Saudi end up with Islamic State, researchers say'.

[110] Felbab-Brown, 'Hurray for militias?', 255.

[111] Rauta, 'A structural-relational analysis', 458–59. For instance, the Syrian Democratic Forces (SDF), working with US special forces on the ground and backed by coalition airpower, displayed remarkable adherence to American commands in confronting Islamic State. However, as that threat receded, narrower interests rose to the surface, resulting in behaviour antithetical to American wishes and intentions. Some Kurdish fighters provocatively unfurled banners of their imprisoned leader Abdullah Öcalan in liberated Raqqa (thus further angering America's NATO ally, Turkey), and SDF cadres prematurely abandoned the battle against Islamic State to assist People's Protection Unit (YPG) efforts to resist the Turkish incursion into the Afrin enclave and reinforce the Manbij area: see Schmitt and Norland, 'Amid Turkish assault Kurdish forces are drawn away from US fight with ISIS'.

[112] US-backed proxies have often used their new-found strength to settle local scores. As Johnson notes, 'military alliances with local groups risk stirring rivalries and internal power struggles in areas outside government control': Johnson, 'Upstream engagement and downstream entanglements', 663. This occurred frequently in Afghanistan whereby US-aligned tribes would designate other tribes as Taliban, thus causing them to be targeted and thereby turning those groups into new American enemies, an example of how proxies can manipulate sponsors due to information asymmetries: see Gopal, *No Good Men Among the Living*, 135–48.

[113] For a detailed discussion of such issues, see Jones and Munoz, *Afghanistan's Local War*.

[114] Salehyan, 'The delegation of war to rebel organisations', 507; Betz and Phillips, 'Putting the strategy back into strategic communications', 57.

[115] Haymon and Kugelman, 'What's behind the Taliban's major gains in Northern Afghanistan?'

[116] Boyle, 'Do counterterrorism and counterinsurgency go together?', 333–53.

[117] Brown, 'Purposes and pitfalls of war by proxy', 247.

[118] Borghard, 'Arms and influence in Syria', 4–7.

[119] Mezran and Miller, 'Libya'.

[120] Stein, 'The trouble with Tanf'.

121 Byman, 'Friends like these', 81; Kuperman, 'A model humanitarian intervention?', 106, 134–5.

122 Long, '"Green on blue"', 167–82; Ghazi and Mashal, 'US bombs Afghan militia behind insider attack, officials say'.

123 Prados, 'The continuing quandary of covert operations', 364.

124 There is also a high likelihood of damaging accusations of US complicity when proxy abuses come to light – the US is implicated in the abuses, human rights violations and illicit activities of those groups it empowers.

125 Zalman and Clarke, 'The global war on terror', 101–13.

126 Cormac and Aldrich, 'Grey is the new black', 478.

127 Cormac and Aldrich, 'Grey is the new black', 493–4.

128 Hughes, 'Syria and the perils of proxy war', 532.

129 Record, 'Force protection fetish', 5.

130 Feaver and Gelpi, 'A look at … casualty aversion'.

131 Greentree, 'A war examined', 333.

132 Long, 'The limits of Special Operations Forces', 38–9.

133 Smith, 'What costs will democracies bear?', 488. Walt makes a similar related point: 'Military objectives may be jeopardized if commanders are overly reluctant to put troops at risk. The desire to protect US troops also encourages overreliance on airpower, leading to greater civilian casualties and undermining efforts to "win hearts and minds." The result is another paradox: the Pentagon has to keep US casualties low in order to preserve public support back home, but doing so makes it harder to win these wars, and public support for them eventually evaporates anyway': Walt, *The Hell of Good Intentions*, 174.

134 Mandel, *Security, Strategy and the Quest for Bloodless War*, 53. Similarly, Betz notes 'the problem is that our tactics exacerbate the problem. The thinking has now pervaded the collective DNA of western forces, and a risk averse deployment posture is now the accepted norm. Overly restrictive force protection measures and insufficiently permissive rules of engagement at the start of an operation create this paradigm': Betz and Stanford-Tuck, 'Teaching your enemy to win', 19.

135 Cornish, 'Myth and reality', 123.

136 Nealen, 'The decline of American warmaking Part 2'; Sperber, 'Inside the secretive US air campaign in Somalia'.

137 Ledwidge, *Losing Small Wars*, 28.

138 De Young, 'US indirectly paying Afghan warlord as part of security contract'.

139 Greentree, 'A war examined', 330.

140 Hall and McChrystal, *ISAF Commander's Counterinsurgency Guidance*.

141 Lujan, *Light Footprints*, 29.

142 Duffield, 'Risk management and the fortified aid compound', 453–74; Waldman, 'System failure', 829–30.

143 Andersson and Weigand, 'Intervention at risk', 537.

144 Malkesian and Weston, 'War downsized', 120.

145 Andersson and Weigand, 'Intervention at risk', 529.

146 Betz and Stanford-Tuck, 'Teaching your enemy to win', 18. Coker has similarly noted how drones 'are the perfect weapons for an age of austerity, far cheaper than landing troops in the desert, and often far more precise. They are the keys to a "light-footprint strategy"': Coker, 'Confront and conceal', 107.

147 Dunlap, 'America's asymmetric advantage'.

148 Kane, *Strategy*, 122.

149 Kagan, *Finding the Target*, 10–14, 27; Walt, *The Hell of Good Intentions*, 84.

[150] Ucko and Egnell, 'Options for avoiding counterinsurgencies', 16.

[151] Scales notes that 'without a reliable ground force to exploit the advantages of air strikes and to quell the chaos that too often follows aerial assault, a campaign conducted exclusively by air might cause harm in the long term': Scales, *Scales on War*, 170.

[152] Pape, *Bombing to Win*, 10.

[153] McInnes, 'Fatal Attraction?', 30.

[154] Shaw, *The New Western Way of War*, 2.

[155] Long, 'Whack-a-mole or coup de grace', 511.

[156] Bunker, 'Defeating violent non-state actors', 63; Bergen and Tiedemann, 'Washington's phantom war', 13.

[157] As cited in Rose, 'Generation Kill', 7.

[158] Hudson et al, 'Drone warfare', 127. As Boyle concludes, drone strikes 'corrode the stability and legitimacy of local governments, deepen anti-American sentiment and create new recruits for Islamist networks aiming to overthrow these governments': Boyle, 'The costs and consequences of drone warfare', 3.

[159] Pape, 'The strategic logic of suicide terrorism'.

[160] Hawramy and Graham-Harrison, 'Islamic State using hostages as human shields in Mosul – UN'.

[161] Kilcullen, *The Accidental Guerrilla*, 33–5.

[162] Sperber, 'The "collateral damage" of the US's unofficial war in Somalia'.

[163] Kilcullen and Exum, 'Death from above, outrage from below'; Cronin, 'Why drones fail', 46. The failed 2010 Times Square bomber, Faizal Shahzad, declared that the effects of drone strikes had driven him to undertake his attack.

[164] Kennedy, 'The Manichean temptation', 634; Boyle, 'The costs and consequences of drone warfare'; Cronin, 'Why drones fail', 53; Maass, 'From U-2s to drones', 219.

[165] Atherton, 'Trump inherited the drone war but ditched accountability'.

[166] Moran, 'Time to move out of the shadows', 1240, 1247–8.

[167] Prados, 'The continuing quandary of covert operations'.

[168] Murphy, 'US Special Forces sabotage White House policy gone disastrously wrong with covert ops in Syria'.

[169] Kibbe, 'Conducting shadow wars', 386.

[170] Oakley, 'The problems of a militarized foreign policy for America's premier intelligence agency'.

[171] Byman and Merritt, 'Special Forces Operations', 83.

[172] Prados, 'The continuing quandary of covert operations', 367.

[173] Burgos, 'Pushing the easy button', 110; Thomas and Dougherty, *Beyond the Ramparts*; Kiras, *Special Operations and Strategy*, 2.

[174] Johnson, 'The growing relevance of special operations forces in US military strategy', 287.

[175] Kiras, 'A theory of special operations', 85.

[176] Colby, 'Public policy, secret action', 65.

[177] Lyckman describes this as the 'legal fuzziness' surrounding these operations: see Lyckman and Weissmann, 'Global shadow war', 256; Kibbe, 'Conducting shadow wars', 379–82; Mitchell et al, 'America's Special Operators will be adrift without better civilian oversight'.

[178] In many instances, special forces working within the CIA SAD have operated under covert Title 22 and Title 50 (as opposed to usual military Title 10), authorities thus further sidestepping scrutiny.

[179] Barno and Bensahel, 'How to fix US Special Operations Forces'.

[180] Byman and Merritt, 'Special Operations Forces', 80, 84; Mitchell et al, 'America's Special Operators will be adrift without better civilian oversight'; Johnson, 'The growing relevance of special operations forces in US military strategy', 290.

[181] Haynes, 'The hidden costs of strategy by special operations'.

[182] Kiras, *Special Operations and Strategy*, 21. Even the assassination of Osama bin Laden did not lead to the defeat of Al-Qaeda and caused serious issues in American relations with Pakistan, with harmful consequences in other spheres: see Robinson, 'The future of Special Operations', 11.

[183] Gallagher, 'Welcome to the age of the commando'.

[184] Open Society Foundations and The Liaison Office, *The Cost of Kill/Capture*.

[185] Megerisi, 'Libya's hollow victory over the Islamic State'.

[186] Burgos, 'Pushing the easy button', 116.

[187] Byman and Merritt, 'Special Operations Forces', 90.

[188] Haynes, 'The hidden costs of strategy by special operations'.

[189] In the former, the goal of increasing the cost of occupation became bringing about Soviet defeat. In the latter case, the interdiction of arms to El Salvador became the attempted overthrow of the Sandinista regime.

[190] So, it was unclear how a Mujahideen victory in Afghanistan, bringing undemocratic and Islamic fundamentalist factions to power, might benefit American foreign policy beyond expediting the Soviet exit.

[191] This can apply even where the US is not necessarily involved: given the sheer ubiquity of real CIA interventions, adversaries can credibly blame US actions for the nation's problems, thus deflecting criticism and strengthening their hold on power.

[192] Brooks, *How Everything Became the War and the Military Became Everything*, 131–4.

[193] Kiras, *Special Operations and Strategy*, 14.

[194] Hosmer, *Operations Against Enemy Leaders*, 31–44.

[195] Price, 'Targeting top terrorists', 9–46; Johnston, 'Does leadership decapitation work?'.

[196] Johnston and Sarbahi, 'The impact of US drone strikes on terrorism in Pakistan', 204.

[197] Jordan, 'Heads will roll'.

[198] Long, 'Whack-a-mole or coup de grace', 511.

[199] Felbab-Brown, 'The hits and misses of targeting the Taliban'.

[200] Burgos, 'Pushing the easy button', 119; Sanger, *The Perfect Weapon*, 4850.

[201] Paul et al, *The Other Quiet Professionals*.

[202] Zenko, 'The true forever war'.

[203] Schneider, 'Persistent engagement'.

[204] Sanger, *The Perfect Weapon*, 4918.

[205] Nakasone, 'A cyber force for persistent operations', 11.

[206] Elkus, 'Covert operations and policy', 14.

[207] Valeriano and Jensen, 'The myth of the cyber offense'.

[208] Sanger, *The Perfect Weapon*, 4718.

[209] Libicki, 'Tangled web'; Lindsay, 'Stuxnet and the limits of cyber warfare'; Slayton, 'What is the cyber offense–defense balance?'.

[210] He also warns of the dangers of keeping US offensive cyber policy wrapped in layers of secrecy because 'until America discusses publicly … what we *will not* do in cyberspace, we have no hope of getting other countries to limit themselves as well': Sanger, *The Perfect Weapon*, 4966.

[211] Coker, 'Confront and conceal', 107.

[212] Treverton, 'Covert action and open society', 1006.

[213] Call, *Danger Close*, 71.

Conclusions

[1] Obama, 'Address to the nation by the President'.

[2] Even large-scale deployments can be motivated by such thinking, for instance, the idea that a massive display of force can induce the enemy to submit before the fighting even begins. This has been less common in the contemporary context and thus not a major part of the story here. It is likely less common today because the massive mobilization of force is hugely politically costly and controversial in itself, and would likely require extensive societal mobilization, simultaneously generating public unease and fears about casualties. This effectively renders such options off-limits in most scenarios.

[3] Similarly, the asymmetric methods and strategies adopted by irregular groups, such as insurgents or terrorists, are generally a function of necessity driven by the weakness relative to state adversaries rather than any ingrained predisposition toward minimizing costs or requirements.

[4] Lynch, 'Belligerent minimalism'. In line with the argument here, Zenko observes that although Trump 'definitively declared that "great nations do not fight endless wars" … the wars he inherited will not end. Rather, their composition and objectives will shift from a large acknowledged troop presence … to smaller covert forces focused on gathering intelligence for partner-led raids and US airstrikes': Zenko, 'Trump is America's first contradiction-in-chief'. Should Joe Biden win the 2020 presidential election, there is little reason – especially given his record as part of the Obama administration – to expect any major departure from current practice, excepting, of course, significant change in the strategic context.

[5] Knowles and Watson, *Remote Warfare*.

[6] Recchia and Tardy, 'French military operations in Africa'.

[7] Noetzel and Schreer, 'All the way?'.

[8] Vrolyk, 'Insurgency, not war, is China's most likely course of action'. Arduino has also described how China may increasingly come to rely on private forces, drones and other forms of remote power projection to secure its Belt and Road Initiative: see Arduino, *China's Private Army*.

[9] For instance, in March 2018, the US Army announced plans to develop small UAVs capable of lethal force without human oversight: see Renic, 'A gardener's vision', 66. Levite and Shimshoni note how, 'a massive effort has recently been launched to leverage breakthroughs in artificial intelligence and telecommunications, with the aim of fielding autonomous fighting capabilities designed to enable Western forces to engage in messy societal conflicts without the use of ground troops': Levite and Shimshoni, 'The strategic challenge of society-centric warfare', 102.

[10] Bousquet, 'Chaoplexic warfare'.

[11] Coker, *Rebooting Clausewitz*, 137.

[12] McMaster, 'Learning from contemporary conflicts to prepare for future war', 578.

[13] Echevarria, *Reconsidering the American Way of War*, 144, 169.

[14] Clausewitz, *On War*, 97.

[15] Clausewitz, *On War*, 89.

[16] For a detailed analysis of Clausewitz's trinity, see Waldman, *War, Clausewitz and the Trinity*.

17 Payne, 'Fighting on'.
18 Brodie, *War and Politics*, 7.
19 Renic, 'A gardener's vision', 57, 60.
20 Mead, *Special Providence*, 84–6.
21 Because, it is argued, they are more careful about choosing which wars to fight and, once engaged, certain attributes of democracy enhance military effectiveness, such as popular support, committed soldiers, effective decision-making and economic strength. See, for instance, Reiter and Stam, *Democracies at War*.
22 See Book II, Chapter 5 of Clausewitz, *On War*.
23 Referring to interventions in the Balkans, Carpenter outlines how 'success … creates the irresistible temptation for officials and policy lobbies to try the same techniques during future international crises'. He also discusses how crimes of 'our' proxy ethnic cleansers are downplayed: see Carpenter, 'Cynical myths and US military crusades in the Balkans'.
24 Michaels and Ford, 'Bandwagonistas', 354.
25 Brands and Suri, 'Introduction', 268.
26 The reliance on local forces created huge problems for post-war political stability through the way it armed and empowered a range of unsavoury actors. The limited number of US ground forces and the less than total loyalty of allied surrogate forces was a major factor allowing Al-Qaeda and Taliban forces to escape into Pakistan where they were able to regroup and launch a major insurgency, which Western forces have been struggling to address ever since.
27 See, in particular: Brooks, *How Everything Became the War and the Military Became Everything*. As Brooks puts it in a separate related article, persistent warfare 'is the central challenge to hard-won global gains in human rights and the rule of law: Most of the institutions and laws designed to protect rights and prevent the arbitrary or abusive exercise of state power rest on the assumption that we can readily distinguish between war and peace, yet there is no longer any principled way to do so': Brooks, 'There's no such thing as peacetime'.
28 Mayer, 'The new killer drones'.
29 Coker, *Rebooting Clausewitz*, 141.
30 Löfflman, 'America first and the populist impact on US foreign policy'.
31 Mead, *Special Providence*, 26; Shapiro, 'Ask not what your country can do for foreign policy'.
32 Clausewitz expressed a similar sentiment when he observed that, 'the decision by arms is for all major and minor operations in war what cash payment is in commerce … regardless how rarely settlements actually occur, they can never be entirely absent': Clausewitz, *On War*, 96–7, 99.
33 Quoted in Gaddis, *On Grand Strategy*, 161.

Epilogue

1 Dueck, *Reluctant Crusaders*, 26–30.
2 Walt reminds us that 'using military force … cannot be turned on and off like a light switch or simply dialed up or down as circumstances require': Walt, *The Hell of Good Intentions*, 76.
3 Clausewitz, *On War*, 86.
4 Porter, 'The Weinberger doctrine'; Betts, 'Pick your battles', 16–17; Hooker, 'A short précis on strategy', 62.

[5] As former Secretary of Defense Robert Gates recently put it, 'The objective of any military intervention must be clear, and the strategy and resources committed must be adequate to fulfill the objective': Gates, 'The overmilitarization of American foreign policy', 122.

[6] Kennedy, 'The Manichean temptation', 635–6.

[7] Scales, 'The great duality and the future of the army'. Even if the deeply interconnected global economy is insufficient to encourage restraint, commentators sometimes overlook the extent to which the mutual possession of nuclear weapons continues to exert a major disciplining effect on modern strategic dynamics, thus making major war somewhat less likely.

[8] Xuetong, 'The age of uneasy peace'; Vrolyk, 'Insurgency, not war, is China's most likely course of action'.

[9] Zakaria, 'New China scare'.

[10] Allison, 'The Thucydides trap'; Walt, 'Everyone Misunderstands the Reason for the US–China Cold War'.

[11] Herman, 'The coming scramble for Africa'.

[12] Damon and Swails, 'China and the United States face off in Djibouti as the world powers fight for influence in Africa'; Headley, 'China's Djibouti base'.

[13] There are, of course, similar areas of friction beyond Africa, high in the Himalayan borderlands, across an unfreezing Arctic and throughout the Pacific. And this is not to mention more obvious potential flashpoints such as Taiwan, the South China Sea and the East China Sea.

References

Aday, Sean, 'Leading the charge: Media, elite cues, and emotion in public support for war', *Journal of Communication*, 60/3, 2010, 440–65.

Aday, Sean, 'The US Media, Foreign Policy, and Public Support for War', *Oxford Handbooks Online*, 11 January 2018, www.oxfordhandbooks. com/view/10.1093/oxfordhb/9780199793471.001.0001/oxfordhb-9780199793471-e-025

Allison, Graham, 'The Thucydides trap: Are the US and China headed for war?', *The Atlantic*, 24 September 2015, www.theatlantic.com/international/archive/2015/09/united-states-china-war-thucydides-trap/406756/

Allison, Graham, 'The new spheres of influence: Sharing the globe with other great powers', *Foreign Affairs*, 99/2, 2020, 30–40.

Amnesty International, *At Any Cost: The Civilian Catastrophe in West Mosul* (London: Amnesty International, 2017).

Amnesty International, *The Hidden US War in Somalia: Civilian Casualties from Air Strikes in Lower Shabelle* (London: Amnesty International, 2019).

Andersson, Ruben and Florian Weigand, 'Intervention at risk: The vicious cycle of distance and danger in Mali and Afghanistan', *Journal of Intervention and Statebuilding*, 9/4, 2015, 519–41.

Andrew, Christopher, *The Secret World: A History of Intelligence* (London: Penguin, 2019).

Arduino, Alessandro, *China's Private Army: Protecting the New Silk Road* (Singapore: Springer Nature, 2018).

Atherton, Kelsey, 'Trump inherited the drone war but ditched accountability', *Foreign Policy*, 22 May 2020, https://foreignpolicy.com/2020/05/22/obama-drones-trump-killings-count/

Avant, Deborah and Renée de Nevers, 'Military contractors and the American way of war', *Daedalus*, 140/3, 2011, 88–99.

Avant, Deborah and Lee Sigelman, 'Private security and democracy: Lessons from the US in Iraq', *Security Studies*, 19/2, 2010, 230–65.

Bacevich, Andrew J., 'The Petraeus Doctrine', *The Atlantic*, October 2008, www.theatlantic.com/magazine/archive/2008/10/the-petraeus-doctrine/306964/

Bacevich, Andrew J., *The New American Militarism: How Americans Are Seduced by War* (New York: Oxford University Press, 2013).

Bacevich, Andrew J., 'Endless war in the Middle East', *Cato's Letter*, 14/3, 2016, 1–8.

Barno, David and Nora Bensahel, 'Six ways to fix the army's culture', *War on the Rocks*, 6 September 2016, https://warontherocks.com/2016/09/six-ways-to-fix-the-armys-culture/

Barno, David and Nora Bensahel, 'How to fix US Special Operations Forces', *War on the Rocks*, 25 February 2020, https://warontherocks.com/2020/02/how-to-fix-u-s-special-operations-forces/

Bassford, Christopher, 'John Keegan and the grand tradition of trashing Clausewitz: A polemic', *War in History*, 1/3, 1994, 319–36.

Beard, Mary, *SPQR: A History of Ancient Rome* (London: Profile Books, 2016).

Beevor, Antony, *The Second World War* (London: Weidenfeld & Nicolson, 2012).

Beier, J. Marshall, 'Outsmarting technologies: Rhetoric, revolutions in military affairs, and the social depth of warfare', *International Politics*, 43/2, 2006, 266–80.

Beinart, Peter, 'Think again: Ronald Reagan', *Foreign Policy*, 7 June 2010, https://foreignpolicy.com/2010/06/07/think-again-ronald-reagan/

Bell, John R., 'Libya crisis: Wishful thinking still isn't a viable strategy', *Comparative Strategy*, 35/2, 2016, 139–53.

Bellamy, Christopher, *Knights in White Armour: The New Art of War and Peace* (London: Pimlico, 1998).

Bergen, Peter and Katherine Tiedemann, 'Washington's phantom war: The effects of the US drone program in Pakistan', *Foreign Affairs*, 90/4, 2011, 12–18.

Bernstein, Alvin H., 'The strategy of a warrior-state: Rome and the wars against Carthage.' In *The Making of Strategy: Rulers, States, and War*, edited by Williamson Murray, MacGregor Knox and Alvin Bernstein, 56–84 (Cambridge: Cambridge University Press, 2007).

Bernstein, Alvin H. and Martin Libicki, 'High-tech: The future face of war? A debate', *Commentary*, January 1998, www.commentarymagazine.com/articles/high-tech-the-future-face-of-war-a-debate/

Bessner, Daniel and Fredrik Logevall, 'Recentering the United States in the historiography of American foreign relations', *Texas National Security Review*, 3/2, 2020, https://tnsr.org/2020/04/recentering-the-united-states-in-the-historiography-of-american-foreign-relations/

Betts, Richard K., *American Force: Dangers, Delusions and Dilemmas in National Security* (New York: Columbia University Press, 2013).

Betts, Richard K., 'Pick your battles', *Foreign Affairs*, 93/6, 2014, 15–24.

Betz, David, *Carnage and Connectivity: Landmarks in the Decline of Conventional Military Power* (London: C. Hurst & Co, 2015).

Betz, David, 'Searching for El Dorado: The legendary golden narrative of the Afghanistan War.' In *Strategic Narratives, Public Opinion, and War: Winning Domestic Support for the Afghan War*, edited by Beatrice de Graaf, George Dimitriu and Jens Ringsmose, 36–55 (Abingdon: Routledge, 2015; Kindle edition).

Betz, David, 'Carnage and connectivity: How our pursuit of fun war brought the wars home', *War on the Rocks*, 2 February 2016, http://warontherocks.com/2016/02/carnage-and-connectivity-how-our-pursuit-of-fun-wars-brought-the-wars-home/

Betz, David and Vaughan Phillips, 'Putting the strategy back into strategic communications', *Defence Strategic Communications*, 3, 2017, 41–69.

Betz, David and Hugo Stanford-Tuck, 'Teaching your enemy to win', *Infinity Journal*, 6/3, 2019, 16–22.

Biddle, Stephen D., 'Allies, airpower, and modern warfare: The Afghan model in Afghanistan and Iraq', *International Security*, 30/3, 2005/06, 161–76.

Biddle, Stephen D., Jeffrey A. Friedman and Jacob N. Shapiro, 'Testing the surge: Why did violence decline in Iraq in 2007?', *International Security*, 37/1, 2012, 7–40.

Biddle, Stephen, Julia Macdonald and Ryan Baker, 'Small footprint, small payoff: The military effectiveness of security force assistance', *Journal of Strategic Studies*, 41/1–2, 2018, 89–142.

Black, Jeremy, *Introduction to Global Military History: 1775 to the Present Day* (Abingdon: Routledge, 2005).

Black, Jeremy, 'The Military Revolution II: Eighteenth Century War.' In *The Oxford History of Modern War*, edited by Charles Townshend, 4–54 (New York: Oxford University Press, 2005).

Blankshain, Jessica D. and Andrew L. Stigler, 'Applying method to madness: A user's guide to causal inference in policy analysis', *Texas National Security Review*, 3/3, 2020, https://tnsr.org/2020/07/applying-method-to-madness-a-users-guide-to-causal-inference-in-policy-analysis/

Blanning, Tim, *The Pursuit of Glory: Europe 1648–1815* (London: Penguin, 2007).

Blaufarb, Douglas S., *Organizing and Managing Unconventional War in Laos, 1962–1970* (Santa Monica, CA: RAND Corporation, 1972).

Blom, John David, *Unmanned Aerial Systems: A Historical Perspective* (Fort Leavenworth, KS: Combat Studies Institute Press, 2009).

Bond, Brian, *The Pursuit of Victory: From Napoleon to Saddam Hussein* (New York: Oxford University Press, 2006).

Boot, Max, *The Savage Wars of Peace: Small Wars and the Rise of American Power* (New York: Basic Books, 2002).

Boot, Max, *The Road Not Taken: Edward Lansdale and the American Tragedy in Vietnam* (New York: Liveright, 2018).

Borghard, Erica D., 'Arms and influence in Syria: The pitfalls of greater US involvement', *Cato Institute*, Policy Analysis 734, 7 August 2013, www.cato.org/publications/policy-analysis/arms-influence-syria-pitfalls-greater-us-involvement

Bousquet, Antoine, 'Chaoplexic warfare', *International Affairs*, 84/5, 2008, 915–29.

Bowden, Mark, *Black Hawk Down: A Story of Modern War* (New York: Atlantic Monthly Press, 1999).

Bowden, Mark, 'The Desert One debacle', *The Atlantic*, May 2006.

Boyle, Michael J., 'Do counterterrorism and counterinsurgency go together?', *International Affairs*, 86/2, 2010, 333–53.

Boyle, Michael J., 'The costs and consequences of drone warfare', *International Affairs*, 89/1, 2013, 1–29.

Braithwaite, Rodric, *Afgantsy: The Russians in Afghanistan 1979–89* (London: Profile Books, 2011).

Brands, Hal and Peter Feaver, 'Trump and terrorism: US strategy after ISIS', *Foreign Affairs*, 96/2, 2017, 28–36.

Brands, Hal and Jeremi Suri, 'Introduction: Thinking about History and Foreign Policy.' In *The Power of the Past: History and Statecraft*, edited by Hal Brands and Jeremi Suri, 60–543 (Washington, DC: Brookings Institution Press, 2016, Kindle edition).

Brodie, Bernard, *War and Politics* (London: Cassell & Company, 1973).

Brogan, Hugh, *The Penguin History of the USA* (London: Penguin, 2001).

Brooks, Rosa, 'There's no such thing as peacetime,' *Foreign Policy*, 13 March 2015, http://foreignpolicy.com/2015/03/13/theres-no-such-thing-as-peacetime-forever-war-terror-civil-liberties/

Brooks, Rosa, 'Civil-Military Paradoxes.' In *Warriors & Citizens: American Views of Our Military*, edited by Kori Schake and Jim Mattis, 21–68 (Stanford, CA: Hoover Institution Press, 2016; Kindle edition).

Brooks, Rosa, *How Everything Became War and the Military Became Everything: Tales from the Pentagon* (New York: Simon & Schuster, 2016; Kindle edition).

Brown, Seyom, 'Purposes and pitfalls of war by proxy: A systemic analysis', *Small Wars & Insurgencies*, 27/2, 2016, 243–57.

Bulos, Nabih, W.J. Hennigan and Brian Bennett, 'In Syria, militias armed by the Pentagon fight those armed by the CIA', *Los Angeles Times*, 27 March 2016, www.latimes.com/world/middleeast/la-fg-cia-pentagon-isis-20160327-story.html

Bunker, Robert J. 'Defeating violent non-state actors', *Parameters*, 43/4, 2013/2014, 57–65.

Burgos, Russell A., 'Pushing the easy button: Special operations forces, international security, and the use of force', *Special Operations Journal*, 4/2, 2018, 109–28.

Burke, Jason, *The 9/11 Wars* (London: Allen Lane, 2011).

Burleigh, Michael, *Small Wars, Faraway Places: The Genesis of the Modern World 1945–65* (London: Macmillan, 2013).

Burton, Brian M., 'The promise and peril of the indirect approach', *PRISM*, 3/1, 2011, 47–62.

Bush, George W., 'A period of consequences', Speech at the Citadel, 23 September 1999, www3.citadel.edu/pao/addresses/pres_bush.html

Bush, George W. 'Text: President Bush addresses the nation', *Washington Post*, 20 September 2001, www.washingtonpost.com/wp-srv/nation/specials/attacked/transcripts/bushaddress_092001.html

Bush, George W., *Decision Points* (New York: Crown, 2010).

Byman, Daniel, L., 'Friends like these: Counterinsurgency and the War on Terrorism', *International Security*, 31/2, 2006, 79–115.

Byman, Daniel L., 'Yemen's disastrous war', *Survival*, 60/5, 2018, 141–58.

Byman, Daniel L. and Will McCants, 'Fight or flight: How to avoid a forever war against jihadists', *Washington Quarterly*, 40/2, 2017, 67–77.

Byman, Daniel and Ian A. Merritt, 'The new American way of war: Special Operations Forces in the War on Terrorism', *The Washington Quarterly*, 41/2, 2018, 79–93,

Byman, Daniel, L. and Taylor Seybolt, 'Humanitarian intervention and communal civil wars: Problems and alternative approaches', *Security Studies*, 13/1, 2003, 33–78.

Byman, Daniel L. and Matthew C. Waxman, 'Defeating US coercion', *Survival*, 41/2, 1999, 107–20.

Byman, Daniel L. and Matthew C. Waxman, 'Kosovo and the great airpower debate', *International Security*, 24/4, 2000, 5–38.

Byman, Daniel L., Matthew C. Waxman and Eric Larson, *Air Power as a Coercive Instrument* (Santa Monica, CA: RAND Corporation, 1999).

Cadwalladr, Carole, 'Interview: Jimmy Carter', *The Guardian*, 11 September 2011, www.theguardian.com/world/2011/sep/11/president-jimmy-carter-interview

Call, Steve, *Danger Close: Tactical Air Controllers in Afghanistan and Iraq* (College Station: Texas A&M University Press, 2007).

Callwell, Charles, *Small Wars: Their Principles and Practice* (London: Bison Books, 1996).

Carpenter, Ted Galen, 'Cynical myths and US military crusades in the Balkans', *Mediterranean Quarterly*, 22/3, 2011, 10–25.

Carroll, James, 'Lessons to be learned from the Afghanistan Papers', *The New Yorker*, 12 December 2019, www.newyorker.com/news/daily-comment/lessons-to-be-learned-from-the-afghanistan-papers

Carroll, Rory, 'US chose to ignore Rwandan genocide', *The Guardian*, 1 April 2004, www.theguardian.com/world/2004/mar/31/usa.rwanda

Carson, Austin, *Secret Wars: Covert Conflict in International Politics* (Princeton, NJ: Princeton University Press, 2018; Kindle edition).

Carver, Michael, 'Conventional Warfare in the Nuclear Age.' In *Makers of Modern Strategy*, edited by Peter Paret, 779–814 (New York: Oxford University Press, 1986).

Cassidy, Robert M., *Counterinsurgency and the Global War on Terror* (Westport, CT: Praeger Security International, 2006).

Clark, Wesley, *Winning Modern Wars: Iraq, Terrorism, and the American Empire* (New York: Public Affairs, 2004).

Clausewitz, Carl von, *On War*, translated and edited by Michael Howard and Peter Paret (Princeton, NJ: Princeton University Press, 1984; Kindle edition).

Cockburn, Patrick, *The Rise of Islamic State: ISIS and the New Sunni Revolution* (London: Verso, 2015; Kindle edition).

Cohen, Eliot A., 'The mystique of US airpower', *Foreign Affairs*, 73/1, 1994, 109–24.

Cohen, Eliot A., 'The strategy of innocence? The United States, 1920–1945.' In *The Making of Strategy: Rulers, States, and War*, edited by Williamson Murray, MacGregor Knox and Alvin Bernstein, 428–65 (Cambridge: Cambridge University Press, 2007).

Coker, Christopher, *War in an Age of Risk* (Cambridge: Polity, 2009).

Coker, Christopher, *Barbarous Philosophers: Reflections on the Nature of War from Heraclitus to Heisenberg* (London: Hurst & Company, 2010).

Coker, Christopher, 'Confront and conceal: Obama's secret wars and surprising use of American power', *The RUSI Journal*, 157/6, 2012, 106–7.

Coker, Christopher, *Rebooting Clausewitz: 'On War' in the Twenty-First Century* (New York: Oxford University Press, 2017; Kindle edition).

Colby, William E., 'Public policy, secret action', *Ethics and International Affairs*, 3/1, 1989, 61–71.

Coll, Steve, *Ghost Wars: The Secret History of the CIA, Afghanistan and Bin Laden, from the Soviet Invasion to September 10, 2001* (London: Penguin, 2004).

Conklin, James, 'The theory of sovereign debt and Spain under Phillip II', *Journal of Political Economy*, 106/3, 1998, 483–513.

Constable, Pamela, 'After Taliban assault in Western Afghanistan, allegations of an Iranian role', *The Washington Post*, 6 June 2018, www. washingtonpost.com/world/asia_pacific/days-after-taliban-assault-in-western-afghanistan-allegations-of-an-iranian-role/2018/06/05/a65ec934-605d-11e8-b656-236c6214ef01_story.html

Cooper, Helene, Charlie Savage and Eric Schmitt, 'Navy SEAL killed in Somalia in first combat death there since 1993,' *The New York Times*, 5 May 2017, www.nytimes.com/2017/05/05/world/africa/navy-seal-killed-in-raid-against-islamic-militants-in-somalia.html

Cooper, Helene, Thomas Gibbons-Neff, Charlie Savage and Eric Schmitt, 'Pentagon eyes Africa drawdown as first step in global troop shift', *The New York Times*, 24 December 2019, www.nytimes.com/2019/12/24/world/africa/esper-troops-africa-china.html

Corke, Sarah-Jane, *US Covert Operations and Cold War Strategy: Truman, Secret Warfare and the CIA, 1945–53* (Abingdon: Routledge, 2008).

Cormac, Rory and Richard J. Aldrich, 'Grey is the new black: Covert action and implausible deniability', *International Affairs*, 94/3, 2018, 477–94.

Corn, Tony, 'From Mars to Minerva: Clausewitz, Liddell Hart, and the two western ways of war', *Small Wars Journal*, 21 May 2011, https://smallwarsjournal.com/blog/journal/docs-temp/767-corn.pdf

Cornish, Paul, 'Myth and reality: US and UK approaches to casualty aversion and force protection', *Defence Studies*, 3/2, 2003, 213–26.

Correll, John T., 'Origins of the total force', *Air Force Magazine*, February 2011, 94–7, www.airforcemag.com/article/0211force/

Craig, Campbell and Fredrik Logevall, *America's Cold War: The Politics of Insecurity* (Cambridge, MA: Belknap Press, 2009; Kindle edition).

Craig, Gordon A. 'The Political Leader as Strategist.' In *Makers of Modern Strategy*, edited by Peter Paret, 481–509 (New York: Oxford University Press, 1986).

Craig, Gordon A. and Felix Gilbert, 'Reflections on Strategy in the Present and Future.' In *Makers of Modern Strategy*, edited by Peter Paret, 863–72 (New York: Oxford University Press, 1986).

Cronin, Audrey Kurth, 'Why drones fail', *Foreign Affairs*, 92/4, 2013, 44–54.

Cunningham, Erin, 'In Turkey, soaring support for Syrian offensive and rising anti-Americanism', *The Washington Post*, 4 February 2018, www.washingtonpost.com/world/middle_east/turkish-support-for-offensive-soars-standing-of-longtime-ally-america-tumbles/2018/02/03/0612e970-06a2-11e8-aa61-f3391373867e_story.html

Cusomano, Eugenio, 'Bridging the gap: Mobilisation constraints and contractor support to US and UK military operations', *Journal of Strategic Studies*, 2016, 39/1, 94–119.

Daddis, Gregory, 'Iraq and longing for Vietnam', *War on the Rocks*, 14, July 2014, https://warontherocks.com/2014/07/iraq-and-longing-for-vietnam/

Dallek, Robert, *Franklin D. Roosevelt: A Political Life* (London: Penguin, 2017).

Damon, Arwa and Brent Swails, 'China and the United States face off in Djibouti as the world powers fight for influence in Africa', *CNN*, 27 May 2019, https://edition.cnn.com/2019/05/26/africa/china-belt-road-initiative-djibouti-intl/index.html

Dandeker, Christopher, 'From Victory to Success: The Changing Mission of Western Armed Forces.' In *Modern War and the Utility of Force: Challenges, Methods, and Strategy*, edited by Jan Angstrom and Isabelle Duyvesteyn, 16–38 (London: Routledge, 2010).

De Luce, Dan and Paul McLeary, 'Trump's ramped-up bombing in Yemen signals more aggressive use of military', *Foreign Policy*, 9 March 2017, https://foreignpolicy.com/2017/03/09/trumps-ramped-up-bombing-in-yemen-signals-more-aggressive-use-of-military/

de Young, Karen, 'US indirectly paying Afghan warlord as part of security contract', *The Washington Post*, 22 June 2010, www.washingtonpost.com/wp-dyn/content/article/2010/06/21/AR2010062104628.html

Demmers, Jolle and Lauren Gould, 'An assemblage approach to liquid warfare: AFRICOM and the "hunt" for Joseph Kony', *Security Dialogue*, 49/5, 2018, 364–81.

Deni, John R., 'Security Assistance.' In *Routledge Handbook of Defence Studies*, edited by David J. Galbreath and John R. Deni, 12744–13297 (Abingdon: Routledge, 2018; Kindle edition).

Denselow, James, 'The US departure from Iraq is an illusion', *The Guardian*, 26 October 2011, www.theguardian.com/commentisfree/cifamerica/2011/oct/25/us-departure-iraq-illusion

Deptula, David A., 'Air and space power, lead turning, the future', *Orbis*, 52/4, 2008, 585–94.

Der Derian, James, 'Virtuous war/virtual theory', *International Affairs*, 76/4, 2000, 771–88.

Desch, Michael, C., 'America's liberal illiberalism: The ideological origins of overreaction in US foreign policy', *International Security*, 32/3, 2007/08, 7–43.

Desch, Michael, C., 'Correspondence: Civilians, soldiers and the Iraq War decision', *International Security*, 36/3, 2011–12, 179–99.

Dozier, Kimberly, 'Secret annexes, backroom deals: Can Zalmay Khalilzad deliver Afghan peace for Trump?', *Time*, 15 February 2020, https://time.com/5784103/secret-annexes-backroom-deals-can-zalmay-khalilzad-deliver-afghan-peace-for-trump/

Dueck, Colin, *Reluctant Crusaders: Power, Culture and Change in American Grand Strategy* (Princeton, NJ: Princeton University Press, 2006).

Duffield, Mark, 'Risk management and the fortified aid compound: Everyday life in post-interventionary society', *Journal of Intervention and Statebuilding*, 4/4, 2010, 453–74.

Dunlap, Charles J., 'America's asymmetric advantage', *Armed Forces Journal*, 1 September 2006, http://armedforcesjournal.com/americas-asymmetric-advantage/

Dyer, Gwynne, *War: The Lethal Custom* (New York: Carroll & Graf, 2005).

Echevarria, Antulio J. II, *Clausewitz and Contemporary War* (New York: Oxford University Press, 2007).

Echevarria, Antulio J. II, *Reconsidering the American Way of War: US Military Practice from the Revolution to Afghanistan* (Washington, DC: Georgetown University Press, 2014; Kindle edition).

Echevarria, Antulio J. II, 'Strategic anarchy and the American way of war', *Infinity Journal*, 6/3, 2019, 10–14.

Economist, The, 'The wars in Iraq and Afghanistan have cost most Americans nothing', 9 November 2019.

Economist, The, 'Jihadists in the Sahel threaten west Africa's coastal states', 11 July 2020.

Editors, 'End the war in Afghanistan', *The New York Times*, 3 February 2019, www.nytimes.com/2019/02/03/opinion/afghanistan-war.html

Eichenberg, Richard C., 'Victory has many friends: US public opinion and the use of military force, 1981–2005', *International Security*, 30/1, 2005, 140–77.

Elbagir, Nima, Salma Abdelaziz, Mohamed Abo El Gheit and Laura Smith-Spark, 'Sold to an ally, lost to an enemy', *CNN*, 5 February 2019, https://edition.cnn.com/interactive/2019/02/middleeast/yemen-lost-us-arms/

Elkus, Adam, 'Covert operations and policy', *Infinity Journal*, 2/1, 2011, 13–16.

Elliott, Christopher L., *High Command: British Military Leadership in the Iraq and Afghanistan Wars* (New York: Oxford University Press, 2015).

Erdmann, Andrew N., 'The US presumption of quick, costless wars,' *Orbis*, 43/3, 1999, 363–81.

Eyre, Dana P. and James R. Littleton, 'Shaping the Zeitgeist: Influencing social processes at the center of gravity for strategic communications in the twenty-first century', *Public Relations Review*, 38/2, 2012, 179–87.

Fallows, James, 'The tragedy of the American military', *The Atlantic*, January/ February 2015, www.theatlantic.com/magazine/archive/2015/01/the-tragedy-of-the-american-military/383516/

Farrell, Theo and Michael Semple, 'Making peace with the Taliban', *Survival*, 57/6, 2015, 79–110.

Feaver, Peter D. and Christopher Gelpi, 'A look at ... casualty aversion', *The Washington Post*, 7 November 1999, www.washingtonpost.com/wp-srv/WPcap/1999-11/07/061r-110799-idx.html

Felbab-Brown, Vanda, 'Hurray for militias? Not so fast: Lessons from the Afghan Local Police experience', *Small Wars & Insurgencies*, 27/2, 2016, 258–81.

Felbab-Brown, Vanda, 'The hits and misses of targeting the Taliban', *The New York Times*, 25 May 2016.

Ferguson, Jane, 'In Afghanistan, fighting the Taliban increasingly involves covert operations', *PBS NewsHour*, 14 November 2019, www.pbs.org/newshour/show/in-afghanistan-fighting-the-taliban-increasingly-involves-covert-operations

Ferguson, Niall, *Empire: How Britain Made the Modern World* (London: Penguin, 2004).

Ferguson, Niall, *Colossus: The Rise and Fall of the American Empire* (London: Penguin, 2005).

Fettweis, Christopher J., 'Misreading the enemy', *Survival*, 57/5, 2015, 149–72.

Finlan, Alastair, *Contemporary Military Strategy and the Global War on Terror: US and UK Armed Forces in Afghanistan and Iraq 2001–2012* (New York: Bloomsbury, 2014).

Fox, Robin Lane, *The Classical World: An Epic History of Greece and Rome* (London: Penguin, 2006).

Fraser-Rahim, Muhammad and Mo Fatah, 'In Somalia, Iran is replicating Russia's Afghan strategy', *Foreign Policy*, 17 July 2020, https://foreignpolicy.com/2020/07/17/iran-aiding-al-shabab-somalia-united-states/

Freedman, Lawrence, 'The First Two Generations of Nuclear Strategists.' In *Makers of Modern Strategy*, edited by Peter Paret, 735–78 (New York: Oxford University Press, 1986).

Freedman, Lawrence, *Kennedy's Wars: Berlin, Laos, and Vietnam* (New York: Oxford University Press, 2000).

Freedman, Lawrence, *The Evolution of Nuclear Strategy* (Basingstoke: Palgrave Macmillan, 2003).

Freedman, Lawrence, *The Transformation of Strategic Affairs* (London: Routledge, 2006).

Freedman, Lawrence, *A Choice of Enemies: America Confronts the Middle East* (London: Weidenfeld & Nicolson, 2008).

Freedman, Lawrence, 'The counterrevolution in strategic affairs', *Daedalus*, 140/3, 2011, 16–32.

Freedman, Lawrence, *Strategy: A History* (New York: Oxford University Press, 2013).

Freedman, Lawrence, 'The Possibilities and Limits of Strategic Narratives.' In *Strategic Narratives, Public Opinion, and War: Winning Domestic Support for the Afghan War*, edited by Beatrice de Graaf, George Dimitriu, and Jens Ringsmose, 15–35 (Abingdon: Routledge, 2015; Kindle edition).

Friedrichs, Jorg and Cornelius Friesendorf, 'Privatized security cripples statebuilding; Iraq is a case in point', *The American Interest*, 4/5, 2009, 43–8.

Fukuyama, Francis, *The End of History and the Last Man* (London: Penguin, 1992).

Gaddis, John Lewis, *The Cold War* (London: Allen Lane, 2005).

Gaddis, John Lewis, *On Grand Strategy* (London: Allen Lane, 2018).

Gallagher, M., 'Welcome to the age of the commando', *The New York Times*, 30 January 2016, www.nytimes.com/2016/01/31/opinion/sunday/welcome-to-the-age-of-the-commando.html

Garamone, Jim, 'DOD official cites widening military–civilian gap', *US Department of Defense*, 16 May 2019, www.defense.gov/Explore/News/Article/Article/1850344/dod-official-cites-widening-military-civilian-gap/

Gasbarri, Flavia, 'From the sands of the Ogaden to Black Hawk Down: The end of the Cold War in the Horn of Africa', *Cold War History*, 18/1, 2018, 73–89.

Gat, Azar, *War in Human Civilisation* (New York: Oxford University Press, 2006).

Gates, Robert M., 'The overmilitarization of foreign policy', *Foreign Affairs*, 99/4, 2020, 121–32.

Gentile, Gian P., 'Progress, dissent and counter-insurgency: An exchange', *Survival*, 51/6, 2009, 189–202.

Gelpi, Christopher F., Peter D. Feaver and Jason Reifler, *Paying the Human Costs of War: Public Opinion and Casualties in Military Conflicts* (Princeton, NJ: Princeton University Press, 2009).

Gettleman, Jeffrey, 'The most dangerous place in the world', *Foreign Policy*, 30 September 2009, https://foreignpolicy.com/2009/09/30/the-most-dangerous-place-in-the-world/

Ghazi, Zabihullah and Mujib Mashal, 'US bombs Afghan militia behind insider attack, officials say', *The New York Times*, 11 January 2018, www.nytimes.com/2018/01/11/world/asia/afghanistan-us-militia-insider-attack.html

Gilsinan, Mike, 'The inconvenient truth about ISIS', *The Atlantic*, 14 February 2020, www.theatlantic.com/politics/archive/2020/02/kurdish-leader-isis-conflict-iraq-iran/606502/

Golby, Jim and Peter Feaver, 'Thank you for your lip service? Social pressure to support the troops', *War on the Rocks*, 14 August 2019, https://warontherocks.com/2019/08/thank-you-for-your-lip-service-social-pressure-to-support-the-troops/

Golby, Jim and Peter Feaver, 'It matters if Americans call Afghanistan a defeat', *The Atlantic*, 17 August 2019, www.theatlantic.com/ideas/archive/2019/08/will-americans-call-afghanistan-victory/596188/

Goldberg, 'The Obama Doctrine', *The Atlantic*, April 2016, www.theatlantic.com/magazine/archive/2016/04/the-obama-doctrine/471525/

Goldich, Robert L., 'American military culture from colony to empire', *Daedalus*, 140/3, 2011, 58–74.

Goldsmith, Jack and Matthew Waxman, 'Legal legacy of light-footprint warfare', *Washington Quarterly*, 39/2, 2016, 7–21.

Goldsworthy, Adrian, 'War.' In *The Cambridge History of Greek and Roman Warfare: Volume II*, edited by Philip Sabin, Hans van Wees and Michael Whitby, 76–121 (New York: Cambridge University Press, 2007).

Gopal, Anand, *No Good Men Among the Living: America, The Taliban and the War through Afghan Eyes* (New York: Henry Holt & Co, 2014).

Gray, Colin S., *Modern Strategy* (New York: Oxford University Press, 1999).

Gray, Colin S., *War, Peace and International Relations: An Introduction to Strategic History* (Abingdon: Routledge, 2007).

Gray, Colin S., 'Strategy in the Nuclear Age: The United States, 1945–1991.' In *The Making of Strategy: Rulers, States, and War*, edited by Williamson Murray, MacGregor Knox and Alvin Bernstein, 579–613 (Cambridge: Cambridge University Press, 2007).

Gray, Colin S., *Strategy and Politics* (London: Routledge, 2016).

Greentree, Todd R., 'A war examined: Afghanistan', *Parameters*, 43/3, 2013, 87–97.

Gregg, Aaron, 'Use of military contractors shrouds true costs of war. Washington wants it that way, study says', *The Washington Post*, 30 June 2020, www.washingtonpost.com/national-security/2020/06/30/military-contractor-study/

Grose, Peter, *Operation Rollback: America's Secret War Behind the Iron Curtain* (Boston, MA: Houghton Mifflin, 2000).

Grynkewich, Alexus G., 'Introducing information as a joint function', *Joint Force Quarterly*, 89, 2nd Quarter 2018, 6–7.

Guido, Joseph, 'American way of war in Africa: The case of Niger', *Small Wars and Insurgencies*, 30/1, 2019, 176–99.

Hall, Michael T. and Stanley A. McChrystal, *ISAF Commander's Counterinsurgency Guidance* (Kabul: International Security Assistance Force, 2009).

Halliday, Fred, *The Making of the Second Cold War* (London: Verso, 1986).

Hammes, Thomas X., 'Assumptions – A fatal oversight', *Infinity Journal*, 1/1, 2010, 4–6.

Handel, Michael, *Masters of War: Classical Strategic Thought* (Abingdon: Routledge, 2001).

Hanson, Victor David, 'Land Warfare in Thucydides.' In *The Landmark Thucydides: A Comprehensive Guide to the Peloponnesian War*, edited by Robert B. Strassler, 603–7 (New York: Free Press, 2008).

Hanson, Victor Davis, *The Western Way of War: Infantry Battle in Classical Greece* (Berkeley, CA: University of California Press, 2009).

Hanson, Victor Davis, *Father of Us All: War and History, Ancient and Modern* (New York: Bloomsbury, 2010; Kindle edition).

Hastings, Max, *The Korean War* (London: Pan Books, 2011; Kindle edition).

Hastings, Max, *All Hell Let Loose: The World at War 1939–1945* (London: William Collins, 2011).

Hastings, Max, *Vietnam: An Epic Tragedy 1945–1975* (London: William Collins, 2018).

Hawramy, F., and Emma Graham-Harrison, 'Islamic State using hostages as human shields in Mosul – UN', *The Guardian*, 29 October 2016, www.theguardian.com/world/2016/oct/28/islamic-state-uses-hostages-as-human-shields-mosul-says-un

Haymon, Barin Sultani and Michael Kugelman, 'What's behind the Taliban's major gains in Northern Afghanistan?', *The Diplomat*, 18 May 2017, https://thediplomat.com/2017/05/whats-behind-the-talibans-major-gains-in-northern-afghanistan/

Haynes, Walter, 'The hidden costs of strategy by special operations', *War on the Rocks*, 17 April 2019, https://warontherocks.com/2019/04/the-hidden-costs-of-strategy-by-special-operations/

Headley, Tyler, 'China's Djibouti base: A one year update', *The Diplomat*, 4 December 2018, https://thediplomat.com/2018/12/chinas-djibouti-base-a-one-year-update/

Heltberg, Therese, 'Art, craft, or science: How we think about military leadership', *Modern War Institute*, 29 December 2016, https://mwi.usma.edu/art-craft-science-think-military-leadership/

Heng, Yee-Kuang, 'The continuing resonance of the war as risk management perspective for understanding military interventions', *Contemporary Security Policy*, 39/4, 2018, 544–58.

Hennigan, W.J. 'US special operations forces face growing demands and increased risks', *Los Angeles Times*, 25 May 2017, www.latimes.com/nation/la-na-special-operations-20170525-story.html

Henriksen, Thomas H., *Afghanistan, Counterinsurgency and the Indirect Approach* (Hurlburt Field, FL: The JSOU Press, 2010).

Herman, Arthur L., 'The coming scramble for Africa', *National Review*, 26 December 2018, www.nationalreview.com/2018/12/africa-china-united-states-foreign-policy-economic-development/

Herring, George C., *From Colony to Superpower: US Foreign Relations since 1776* (New York: Oxford University Press, 2008).

Heuser, Beatrice, *Reading Clausewitz* (London: Pimlico, 2002).

Heuser, Beatrice, *The Evolution of Strategy: Thinking War from Antiquity to the Present* (New York: Cambridge University Press, 2010).

Hickey, James E., *Precision-guided Munitions and Human Suffering in War* (Farnham: Ashgate, 2012).

Hiltermann, Joost, 'Iraq: The battle to come', *The New York Review of Books*, 1 July 2017, www.nybooks.com/daily/2017/07/01/iraq-the-battle-to-come/

Hirsch, John L., 'The Black Hawk Down effect', *Foreign Policy*, 12 August 2011, https://foreignpolicy.com/2011/08/12/the-black-hawk-down-effect/

Hogan, Michael, *A Cross of Iron: Harry S. Truman and the Origins of the National Security State, 1945–1954* (Cambridge: Cambridge University Press, 1998).

Hoffman, Frank G., 'Complex irregular war: The next revolution in military affairs', *Orbis*, 50/3, 2006, 395–411.

Holland, Tom, 'America is not Rome. It just thinks it is', *The New York Review of Books*, 5 January 2020, www.nybooks.com/daily/2019/08/06/america-is-not-rome-it-just-thinks-it-is/

Holmes, James, 'Warmaking by remote control is a false choice', *The National Interest*, 25 November 2019, https://nationalinterest.org/blog/warmaking-remote-control-false-choice-99007

Hooker, Richard D., '"The strange voyage": A short précis on strategy', *Parameters*, 42/4, 2003, 59–68.

Hosmer, Stephen T., *Operations Against Enemy Leaders* (Santa Monica, CA: The RAND Corporation, 2001).

Howard, Michael, *Studies in War and Peace* (London: Temple Smith, 1970).

Howard, Michael, *War in European History* (Oxford: Oxford University Press, 1976).

Howard, Michael, *War and the Liberal Conscience: The George Macaulay Trevelyan Lectures in the University of Cambridge, 1977* (London: Temple Smith, 1978).

Howard, Michael, *The Lessons of History* (Guildford: Oxford University Press, 1993).

Howard, Michael, *The Invention of Peace and the Reinvention of War* (London: Profile Books, 2001).

Hudson, Leila, Colin. S. Owens and Matt Flannes, 'Drone warfare: Blowback from the new American way of war', *Middle East Policy*, 18, 2011, 122–32.

Hughes, Geraint A., 'Syria and the perils of proxy war', *Small Wars & Insurgencies*, 25/3, 2014, 522–38.

Human Rights Watch, *"They've Shot Many Like This": Abusive Night Raids by CIA-Backed Afghan Strike Forces* (New York: Human Rights Watch, 2019).

Hummel, Jeffrey R., 'The American militia and the origin of conscription: A reassessment', *Journal of Libertarian Studies*, 15/4, 2001, 29–77.

Ignatieff, Michael, *The Warrior's Honor: Ethnic War and the Modern Conscience* (London: Vintage, 1999).

Ignatieff, Michael, *Virtual War: Kosovo and Beyond* (London: Vintage, 2001).

Ignatieff, Michael, *Empire Lite: Nation-building in Bosnia, Kosovo and Afghanistan* (London: Vintage, 2003).

Jentleson, Bruce W., *American Foreign Policy: The Dynamics of Choice in the 21st Century* (New York: W.W. Norton, 2000).

Jentleson, Bruce W. and Rebecca L. Britton, 'Still pretty prudent: Post-Cold War American public opinion on the use of military force', *Journal of Conflict Resolution*, 42/4,1998, 395–417.

Johnson, Chalmers, *Blowback: The Costs and Consequences of American Empire* (New York: Henry Holt & Company, 2000).

Johnson, Lyndon B., 'Speech at Akron University', 21 October 1964, www.presidency.ucsb.edu/documents/remarks-memorial-hall-akron-university

Johnson, Lyndon B., 'Withdrawal speech', 31 March 1968, https://voicesofdemocracy.umd.edu/lyndon-baines-johnson-withdrawal-speech-31-march-1968/

Johnson, Matthew, 'The growing relevance of special operations forces in US military strategy', *Comparative Strategy*, 25/4, 2006, 273–96.

Johnson, Robert, 'Upstream engagement and downstream entanglements: The assumptions, opportunities and threats of partnering', *Small Wars & Insurgencies*, 25/3, 2014, 647–68.

Johnston, Patrick B., 'Does leadership decapitation work? Assessing the effectiveness of leadership targeting in counterinsurgency campaigns', *International Security*, 36/4, 2012, 47–79.

Johnston, Patrick B. and Anoop K. Sarbahi, 'The impact of US drone strikes on terrorism in Pakistan', *International Studies Quarterly*, 60/2, 2016, 203–19.

Jones, Seth G., *In the Graveyard of Empires: America's War in Afghanistan* (New York: Norton, 2010).

Jones, Seth G., 'It takes the villages', *Foreign Affairs*, 89/3, 2010, 120–7.

Jones, Seth G. and Arturo Munoz, *Afghanistan's Local War: Building Local Defense Forces* (Santa Monica, CA: RAND, 2010).

Jordan, Jenna, 'Heads will roll: Assessing the effectiveness of leadership decapitation', *Security Studies*, 18/4, 2009, 719–55.

Kagan, Donald, 'Athenian Strategy in the Peloponnesian War.' In *The Making of Strategy: Rulers, States, and War*, edited by Williamson Murray, MacGregor Knox and Alvin Bernstein, 24–55 (Cambridge: Cambridge University Press, 2007).

Kagan, Frederick W., 'High-tech: The future face of war? A debate', *Commentary*, January 1998, www.commentarymagazine.com/articles/high-tech-the-future-face-of-war-a-debate/

Kagan, Frederick W., *Finding the Target: The Transformation of American Military Policy* (New York: Encounter Books, 2006).

Kagan, Robert, *Dangerous Nation: America and the World 1600–1898* (London: Atlantic Books, 2006).

Kane, Thomas M., *Strategy: Key Thinkers* (Cambridge: Polity, 2013).

Kaplan, Robert, 'The trap of empire and authoritarianism', *The National Interest*, 5 March 2018, https://nationalinterest.org/feature/the-trap-empire-authoritarianism-24761

Karcher, Timothy, *Understanding the "Victory Disease": From the Little Bighorn to Mogadishu and Beyond* (Fort Leavenworth, KS: Combat Studies Institute Press, 2004).

Karlin, Mara, 'Why military assistance programs disappoint: Minor tools can't solve major problems', 96/6, *Foreign Affairs*, 2017, 111–20.

Karnow, Stanley, *Vietnam: A History* (London: Pimlico, 1994).

Keegan, John, *A History of Warfare* (London: Pimlico, 2004).

Keller, Jared, 'The Pentagon lost track of $715 million in weapons and gear funneled to anti-ISIS allies in Syria', *Task & Purpose*, 18 February 2020, https://taskandpurpose.com/news/syria-weapons-isis-pentagon-inspector-general-report

Kennan, George F. [X], 'Sources of Soviet conduct', *Foreign Affairs*, 25/4, 1947, 566–82.

Kennedy, Caroline, 'The Manichean temptation: Moralising rhetoric and the invocation of evil in US foreign policy', *International Politics*, 50/5, 2013, 623–38.

Kennedy-Pipe, Caroline, 'Nick Rengger and two wars', *International Relations*, forthcoming.

Kennedy-Pipe, Caroline, 'Revisioning Stalin's Cold War.' In *Revisioning Stalin and Stalinism: Complexities, Contradictions and Controversies*, edited by James Ryan and Susan Grant, 113–25 (London: Bloomsbury, 2020).

Kennedy, Caroline and Thomas Waldman, 'Ways of War in the Twenty-First Century'. In *Issues in 2st Century World Politics*, edited by Mark Beeson and Nick Bisley, 92–105 (Basingstoke: Palgrave Macmillan, 2013).

Kennedy, John F., 'Inaugural Address', 20 January 1961, www.jfklibrary. org/learn/about-jfk/historic-speeches/inaugural-address

Kennedy, John F. 'Address before the American Society of Newspaper Editors', 20 April 1961, www.jfklibrary.org/archives/other-resources/john-f-kennedy-speeches/american-society-of-newspaper-editors-19610420

Kennedy, Paul, *The Rise and Fall of the Great Powers* (London: Fontana Press, 1989).

Kibbe, Jennifer D., 'Conducting shadow wars', *Journal of National Security Law & Policy*, 5, 373–92.

Kidd, Andrew H. and Barbara F. Walter, 'The strategies of terrorism', *International Security*, 31/1 2006, 49–80.

Kilcullen, David, *The Accidental Guerrilla: Fighting Small Wars in the Midst of a Big One* (New York: Oxford University Press, 2009).

Kilcullen, David, *Blood Year: The Unravelling of Western Counterterrorism* (New York: Oxford University Press, 2016).

Kilcullen, David and Andrew M. Exum, 'Death from above, outrage from below', *The New York Times*, 16 May 2009, www.nytimes. com/2009/05/17/opinion/17exum.html

Kinzer, Stephen, *Overthrow: America's Century of Regime Change from Hawaii to Iraq* (New York: Times Books, 2006; Kindle edition).

Kiras, James D., *Special Operations and Strategy: From World War II to the War on Terrorism* (Abingdon: Routledge, 2006; Kindle edition).

Kiras, James D., 'A theory of special operations: "These ideas are dangerous"', *Special Operations Journal*, 1/2, 2015, 75–88.

Knowles, Emily and Abigail Watson, *Remote Warfare: Lessons Learned from Contemporary Theatres* (London: Remote Warfare Programme, 2018).

Krauthammer, Charles, 'The unipolar moment', *Foreign Affairs*, 70/1, 1990–1991, 23–33.

Krepinevich, Andrew F., *The Army and Vietnam* (Baltimore, MD: Johns Hopkins University Press, 1988).

Krieg, Andreas, 'Externalizing the burden of war: The Obama doctrine and US foreign policy in the Middle East', *International Affairs*, 92/1, 2016, 97–113.

Krieg, Andreas and Jean-Marc Rickli, 'Surrogate warfare: the art of war in the 21st century?', *Defence Studies*, 18/2, 2018, 113–30.

Krishnan, Armin, 'Controlling partners and proxies in pro-insurgency paramilitary operations: The case of Syria', *Intelligence and National Security*, 34/4, 2018, 544–60.

Krulak, Charles C., 'The strategic corporal: Leadership in the three block war', *Marines Magazine*, January 1999.

Kuperman, Alan J., 'A model humanitarian intervention? Reassessing NATO's Libya campaign', *International Security*, 38/1, 2013, 105–36.

Kyle, Donald G. *Spectacles of Death in Ancient Rome* (London: Routledge, 1998).

LaFeber, Walter, *The American Age: US Foreign Policy at Home and Abroad Since 1896* (New York: W.W. Norton & Co, 1994).

Larson, Eric V., *Casualties and Consensus: The Historical Role of Casualties in Domestic Support for US Military Operations* (Santa Monica, CA: RAND Corporation, 1996).

Lawrence, Mark Atwood, *The Vietnam War: A Concise International History* (New York: Oxford University Press, 2010; Kindle edition).

Layne, Christopher, *Peace of Illusions: American Grand Strategy from 1940 to the Present* (Ithaca, NY: Cornell University Press, 2007).

Lears, Jackson, 'Imperial exceptionalism', *The New York Review of Books*, 7 February 2019, www.nybooks.com/articles/2019/02/07/imperial-exceptionalism/

Ledwidge, Frank, *Losing Small Wars* (New Haven, CT: Yale University Press, 2011).

Leffler, Melvyn P., *A Preponderance of Power: National Security, the Truman Administration, and the Cold War* (Lexington, MA: Plunkett Lake Press, 2018; Kindle edition).

Lembke, Andrew E., *Lansdale, Magsaysay, America, and the Philippines: A Case Study of Limited Intervention Counterinsurgency* (Fort Leavenworth, KS: Combat Studies Institute Press, 2012).

LeoGrande, William M., *Our Own Backyard: The United States in Central America, 1977–1992* (Chapel Hill, NC: The University of North Carolina Press, 1998).

Leonard, Steve, 'That Clausewitz-is-irrelevant "hot take" isn't blasphemous. It's just wrong', *Modern War Institute*, 5 March 2019, https://mwi.usma.edu/clausewitz-irrelevant-hot-take-isnt-blasphemous-just-wrong/

Levering, Ralph B., *The Cold War 1945–87* (Wheeling, IL: Harlan Davidson, 1988).

Levite, Ariel E. and Jonathan (Yoni) Shimshoni, 'The strategic challenge of society-centric warfare', *Survival*, 60/6, 2018, 91–118.

Libicki, M.C., 'Tangled web: Cyberwar fears pose dangers of unnecessary escalation', *RAND Review*, 2013, www.rand.org/pubs/periodicals/rand-review/issues/2013/summer/cyberwar-fears-pose-dangers-of-unnecessary-escalation.html

Lindsay, Jon R., 'Stuxnet and the limits of cyber warfare', *Security Studies*, 22/3, 2003, 365–404.

Linn, Brian M., '"The American way of war" revisited', *The Journal of Military History*, 66/2, 2002, 501–33.

Liptak, Kevin, 'Photos highlight stark differences in Trump and Obama approaches', *CNN*, 30 October 2019, https://edition.cnn.com/2019/10/28/politics/donald-trump-barack-obama-situation-room-photos/index.html

Lissner, Rebecca Friedman, 'The long shadow of the Gulf War', *War on the Rocks*, 24 February 2016, https://warontherocks.com/2016/02/the-long-shadow-of-the-gulf-war/

Lloyd-George, William, 'The CIA's secret war', *The Diplomat*, 25 February 2011, https://thediplomat.com/2011/02/the-cias-secret-war/

Löfflman, Georg, 'America first and the populist impact on US foreign policy', *Survival*, 61/6, 2019, 115–38.

Long, Austin, '"Green on blue": Insider attacks in Afghanistan', *Survival*, 55/3, 2013, 167–82.

Long, Austin, 'Whack-a-mole or coup de grace: Leadership targeting in Iraq and Afghanistan', *Security Studies*, 23, 2014, 471–512.

Long, Austin, 'The limits of Special Operations Forces', *PRISM*, 6/3, 2016, 35–47.

Lujan, Fernando M., *Light Footprints: The Future of American Military Interventions* (Washington, DC: Center for a New American Security, 2013).

Luttwak, Edward N., 'Where are the Great Powers? At home with the kids', *Foreign Affairs*, 73/4 1994, 23–9

Luttwak, Edward N., 'Toward post-heroic warfare', *Foreign Affairs*, 73/3, 1995, 109–22.

Lyckman, Markus and Mikael Weissmann, 'Global shadow war: A conceptual analysis', *Dynamics of Asymmetric Conflict*, 8/3, 251–62.

Lynch, Marc, 'Explaining the awakening: Engagement, publicity, and the transformation of Iraqi Sunni political attitudes', *Security Studies*, 20/1, 2011, 36–72.

Lynch, Marc, 'Belligerent minimalism: The Trump administration and the Middle East', *Washington Quarterly*, 39/4, 2017, 127–44.

Lynn, John A., 'States in Conflict.' In *The Cambridge History of Warfare*, edited by Geoffrey Parker, 167–88 (Cambridge: Cambridge University Press, 2005).

Lynn, John A., 'A Quest for Glory: The Formation of Strategy under Louis XIV, 1661–1715.' In *The Making of Strategy: Rulers, States, and War*, edited by Williamson Murray, MacGregor Knox and Alvin Bernstein, 178–204 (Cambridge: Cambridge University Press, 2007).

Lythgoe, Trent, 'Our risk-averse army: How we got here and how to overcome it', *Modern War Institute*, 9 May 2019, https://mwi.usma.edu/risk-averse-army-got-overcome/

Maass, Matthias, 'From U-2s to drones: US aerial espionage and targeted killing during the Cold War and the War on Terror', *Comparative Strategy*, 34/2, 2015, 218–38.

Machiavelli, Niccolò, *The Prince*, translated by George Bull (London: Penguin, 1999).

Mack, Andrew, 'Counterinsurgency in the third world: Theory and practice', *British Journal of International Studies*, 1/3, 1975, 226–53.

Mahnken, Thomas G., 'The growth and spread of the precision-strike regime', *Daedalus*, 140/3, 2011, 45–57.

Mahoney, Charles W., 'US defense contractors and the future of military operations', *Defense & Security Analysis*, 36/2, 2020, 180–200.

Maley, William, *The Afghanistan Wars* (Basingstoke: Palgrave Macmillan, 2009).

Malkesian, Carter and J. Kael Weston, 'War downsized', *Foreign Affairs*, 91/2, 2012, 111–21.

Malley, Robert and Jon Finer, 'The long shadow of 9/11: How counterterrorism warps US foreign policy', *Foreign Affairs*, 97/4, 2018, 58–69.

Malley, Robert and Stephen Pomper, 'An accounting for the uncounted', *The Atlantic*, 16 December 2017, www.theatlantic.com/international/archive/2017/12/isis-obama-civilian-casualties/548501/

Maltby, William S., 'The Origins of a Global Strategy.' In *The Making of Strategy: Rulers, States, and War*, edited by Williamson Murray, MacGregor Knox and Alvin Bernstein, 151–77 (Cambridge: Cambridge University Press, 2007).

Mandel, Robert, *Security, Strategy and the Quest for Bloodless War* (London: Lynne Reiner, 2004).

Mandelbaum, Michael, *Mission Failure: America and the World in the Post-Cold War Era* (New York: Oxford University Press, 2016; Kindle edition).

Mann, Scott, D., *Game Changers: Going Local to Defeat Violent Extremists* (Leesburg, VA: Tribal Analysis Publishing, 2017; Kindle edition).

Mantello, Peter, 'Playing discreet war in the US: Negotiating subjecthood and sovereignty through Special Forces video games', *Media, War & Conflict*, 5/3, 2012, 269–83.

Mark, Eduard, 'The OSS in Romania 1944–45: An intelligence operation of the early Cold War', *Intelligence and National Security*, 9/2, 1994, 320–44.

Mark, Eduard, 'The war scare of 1946 and its consequences', *Diplomatic History*, 21/3, 1997, 383–415.

Marshall, Jonathan, Peter Dale Scott and Jane Hunter, *The Iran Contra Connection: Secret Teams and Covert Operations in the Reagan Era* (Boston, MA: South End Press, 1987

Maslowski, Peter, 'To the Edge of Greatness: The United States, 1793–1865.' In *The Making of Strategy: Rulers, States, and War*, edited by Williamson Murray, MacGregor Knox and Alvin Bernstein, 205–41 (Cambridge: Cambridge University Press, 2007).

Maslowski, Peter and Don Winslow, *Looking for a Hero*: *Staff Sergeant Joe Ronnie Hooper and the Vietnam War* (Lincoln, NE: University of Nebraska Press, 2004).

Mayer, Michael, 'The new killer drones: Understanding the strategic implications of next-generation unmanned combat aerial vehicles', *International Affairs*, 91/4, 2015, 765–80.

Mayer, Michael, 'Trigger happy: The foundations of US military interventions', *Journal of Strategic Studies*, 42/2, 2018, 259–81.

Mazarr, Michael J., 'The folly of asymmetric war', *Washington Quarterly*, 31/3, 2008, 33–53.

Mazzetti, Mark, 'Former spy with agenda operates a private CIA', *The New York Times*, 22 January 2011, www.nytimes.com/2011/01/23/world/23clarridge.html

Mazzetti, Mark, 'CIA study of covert aid fueled skepticism about helping Syrian rebels', *The New York Times*, 14 October 2014, www.nytimes.com/2014/10/15/us/politics/cia-study-says-arming-rebels-seldom-works.html

Mazzetti, Mark, Adam Goldman and Michael S. Schmidt, 'Behind the sudden death of a $1 billion secret CIA war in Syria', *The New York Times*, 2 August 2017, www.nytimes.com/2017/08/02/world/middleeast/cia-syria-rebel-arm-train-trump.html

McChrystal, Stanley, 'It takes a network', *Foreign Policy*, 21 February 2011, https://foreignpolicy.com/2011/02/21/it-takes-a-network/

McCormick, Thomas J., *America's Half-Century: United States Foreign Policy in the Cold War and After* (Baltimore, MD: Johns Hopkins University Press, 1995).

McFate, Sean, *Goliath: Why the West Doesn't Win Wars. And What We Must Do About It* (London: Penguin, 2019).

McInnes, Colin, *Spectator-Sport Warfare: The West and Contemporary Conflict* (London: Lynne Rienner, 2002).

McInnes, Colin, 'Fatal Attraction? Air Power and the West.' In *Dimensions of Western Military Intervention*, edited by Colin McInnes and Nicholas Wheeler, 28–51 (London: Frank Cass, 2002).

McKelvey, Tara, 'Covering Obama's secret war', *Columbia Journalism Review*, May/June 2011, https://archives.cjr.org/feature/covering_obamas_secret_war.php

McMaster, H.R., 'On war: Lessons to be learned', *Survival*, 50/1, 2008, 19–30.

McMaster, H.R., 'Learning from contemporary conflicts to prepare for future war', *Orbis*, 54/2, 2008, 564–84.

McNeill, William H., *The Pursuit of Power: Technology, Armed Force, and Society* (Chicago, IL: University of Chicago Press, 1984).

Mead, Walter Russell, *Special Providence: American Foreign Policy and How It Changed the World* (New York: Alfred A. Knopf, 2001).

Megerisi, Tarek, 'Libya's hollow victory over the Islamic State', *Foreign Policy*, 28 November 2016, http://foreignpolicy.com/2016/11/28/libyas-hollow-victory-over-the-islamic-state/

Meilinger, Phillip S., 'Busting the icon: Restoring balance to the influence of Clausewitz', *Strategic Studies Quarterly*, 1/1, 2007, 116–45.

Meilinger, Phillip S., *Limiting Risk in America's Wars: Airpower, Asymmetrics, and a New Strategic Paradigm* (Annapolis, MD: Naval Institute Press, 2017).

Melanson, Richard A., *American Foreign Policy since the Vietnam War: The Search for Consensus from Nixon to Clinton* (New York: M.E. Sharpe, 2000).

Melton, Stephen L., *The Clausewitz Delusion: How the American Army Screwed Up the Wars in Iraq and Afghanistan (a Way Forward)* (Minneapolis, MN: Zenith Press, 2009).

Mezran, Karim and Elissa Miller, 'Libya: From intervention to proxy war', *Atlantic Council*, July 2017, www.atlanticcouncil.org/in-depth-research-reports/issue-brief/libya-from-intervention-to-proxy-war/

Michaels, Jeffrey H., 'Managing global counterinsurgency; The Special Group (CI) 1962–1966', *Journal of Strategic Studies*, 35/1, 2012, 33–61.

Michaels, Jeffrey H. and Matthew Ford, 'Bandwagonistas: Rhetorical re-description, strategic choice and the politics of counter-insurgency', *Small Wars and Insurgencies*, 22/2, 2011, 352–84.

Milevski, Lukas, 'Respecting strategic agency: On the categorization of war in strategy', *Joint Force Quarterly*, 86, 3rd Quarter 2017, 35–40.

Millett, Allan R., Peter Maslowski and William B. Feis, *For the Common Defense: A Military History of the United States from 1607 to 2012* (New York: Free Press, 2012; Kindle edition).

Mitchell, Mark E., Zachary Griffiths and Cole Livieratos, 'America's Special Operators will be adrift without better civilian oversight', *War on the Rocks*, 18 February 2020, https://warontherocks.com/2020/02/americas-special-operators-will-be-adrift-without-better-civilian-oversight/

Montgomery, Thomas, 'Ambush in Mogadishu', *PBS Frontline*, September 1998, www.pbs.org/wgbh/pages/frontline/shows/ambush/interviews/montgomery.html#tanks

Moran, Jon, 'Time to move out of the shadows: Special Operations Forces and accountability in counter-terrorism and counter-insurgency operations', *UNSW Law Journal*, 39/3, 2016, 1239–60.

Morefield, Jeanne and Patrick Porter, 'Revenge of the forever wars', *New Statesman*, 10 June 2020, www.newstatesman.com/world/north-america/2020/06/revenge-forever-wars

Morgan, Wesley, 'Behind the US secret war in Africa', *Politico*, 2 July 2018, www.politico.com/story/2018/07/02/secret-war-africa-pentagon-664005

Morris, Ian, *What Is War Good For? The Role of Conflict in Civilisation, from Primates to Robots* (London: Profile Books, 2014; Kindle edition).

Moyar, Mark, *Triumph Forsaken: The Vietnam War, 1954–1965* (New York: Cambridge University Press, 2006).

Moyn, Samuel and Stephen Wertheim, 'The infinity war', *The Washington Post*, 13 December 2019, www.washingtonpost.com/outlook/2019/12/13/infinity-war/?arc404=true

Mueller, John E., 'Trends in popular support for the wars in Korea and Vietnam', *The American Political Science Review*, 65/2, 1971, 358–75.

Mumford, Andrew, *Proxy Warfare* (Cambridge: Polity Press, 2013).

Murphy, Jack, 'US Special Forces sabotage White House policy gone disastrously wrong with covert ops in Syria', *SOFREP*, 14 September 2016, https://sofrep.com/news/us-special-forces-sabotage-white-house-policy-gone-disastrously-wrong-with-covert-ops-in-syria/

Nagl, John A., *Learning to Eat Soup with a Knife: Counterinsurgency Lessons from Malaya and Vietnam* (Chicago, IL: University of Chicago Press, 2005).

Nakasone, Paul M., 'A cyber force for persistent operations', *Joint Force Quarterly*, 92, 1st Quarter 2019, 10–14.

Nealen, Pete, 'The decline of American warmaking Part 2: Risk aversion', *SOFREP*, 4 August, 2014, https://sofrep.com/news/the-decline-of-american-warmaking-risk-aversion/

Nichols, Tom, 'No other choice: Why Truman dropped the atomic bomb on Japan', *The National Interest*, 6 August 2015, https://nationalinterest.org/feature/no-other-choice-why-truman-dropped-the-atomic-bomb-japan-13504

Niva, Steve, 'Disappearing violence: JSOC and the Pentagon's new cartography of networked warfare', *Security Dialogue*, 44/3, 2013, 185–202.

Nixon, Richard M., 'Address to the nation announcing an agreement on ending the war in Vietnam', 23 January 1973, https://millercenter.org/the-presidency/presidential-speeches/january-23-1973-address-nation-announcing-agreement-ending-war

Noetzel, Timo and Benjamin Schreer, 'All the way? The evolution of German military power', *International Affairs*, 84/2, 2008, 211–21.

Nolan, Cathal J., *The Allure of Battle: A History of How Wars Have Been Won and Lost* (New York: Oxford University Press, 2019).

Oakley, David, 'The problems of a militarized foreign policy for America's premier intelligence agency', *War on the Rocks*, 2 May 2019, https://warontherocks.com/2019/05/the-problems-of-a-militarized-foreign-policy-for-americas-premier-intelligence-agency/

Obama, Barack, 'President Obama outlines a new global military strategy', 5 January 2012, https://obamawhitehouse.archives.gov/blog/2012/01/05/president-obama-outlines-new-global-military-strategy

Obama, Barack, 'Address to the nation by the President', 6 December 2015, https://obamawhitehouse.archives.gov/the-press-office/2015/12/06/address-nation-president

Olson, James S. and Randy Roberts, *Where the Domino Fell: America and Vietnam 1945–1995* (Malden, MA: Blackwell Publishing, 2008).

Open Society Foundations and The Liaison Office, *The Cost of Kill/Capture: Impact of Night Raid Surge on Afghan Civilians* (Kabul: Open Society Foundations, 2011).

O'Rourke, Lindsey A., 'The strategic logic of covert regime change: US-backed regime change campaigns during the Cold War', *Security Studies*, 29/1, 2020, 92–197.

Osgood, Robert E. *Limited War Revisited* (Abingdon: Routledge, 2018; Kindle edition).

Overy, Richard, *Why the Allies Won* (London: Pimlico, 1995).

Pamuk, Humeyra and Umit Bektas, 'Turkey fires on US-backed Kurdish militia in Syria offensive', *Reuters*, 26 August 2016, www.reuters.com/article/us-mideast-crisis-syria-turkey/turkey-fires-on-u-s-backed-kurdish-militia-in-syria-offensive-idUSKCN10Z07J

Pape, Robert A., 'The strategic logic of suicide terrorism', *American Political Science Review*, 97/3, 2003, 343–61.

Pape, Robert A., *Bombing to Win: Air Power and Coercion in War* (Ithaca, NY: Cornell University Press, 2014; Kindle edition).

Paret, Peter, *Clausewitz and the State: The Man, His Theories, and His Times* (Princeton, NJ: Princeton University Press, 1985).

Parker, Geoffrey, 'The Making of Strategy in Habsburg Spain: Philip II's "Bid for Mastery", 1556–1598.' In *The Making of Strategy: Rulers, States, and War*, edited by Williamson Murray, MacGregor Knox and Alvin Bernstein, 115–50 (Cambridge: Cambridge University Press, 2007).

Pastor, Robert, *Exiting the Whirlpool: US Foreign Policy toward Latin America and the Caribbean* (Princeton, NJ: Princeton University Press, 1993).

Paul, Christopher, Isaac R. Porche III and Elliot Axelband, *The Other Quiet Professionals: Lessons for Future Cyber Forces from the Evolution of Special Forces* (Santa Monica, CA: RAND Corporation, 2014).

Payne, Andrew, 'Presidents, politics, and military strategy: Electoral constraints during the Iraq War', *International Security*, 44/3, 2019–2020, 163–203.

Payne, Kenneth, 'Fighting on: Emotion and conflict termination', *Cambridge Review of International Affairs*, 28/3, 2015, 480–97.

PBS, 'Bin Laden's fatwa', 23 August 1996, https://web.archive.org/web/20140419014901/http://www.pbs.org/newshour/updates/military-july-dec96-fatwa_1996/#

Penney, Matthew T., 'The Anbar awakening in context ... and why it is so hard to replicate', *Military Review*, 95/2, 2015, 106–17.

Perry, David, 'Blackwater vs bin Laden: The private sector's role in American counterterrorism', *Comparative Strategy*, 31/1, 2012, 41–55.

Polk, William, *Violent Politics: A History of Insurgency, Terrorism and Guerrilla War, from the American Revolution to Iraq* (New York: HarperCollins, 2007).

Porch, Douglas, 'Imperial wars: From the Seven Years War to the First World War.' In *The Oxford History of Modern War*, edited by Charles Townshend, 94–116 (New York: Oxford University Press, 2005).

Porch, Douglas, 'Expendable soldiers', *Small Wars & Insurgencies*, 25/3, 2014, 696–716.

Porter, Bernard, *The Lion's Share: A Short History of British Imperialism 1850–1995*, Third Edition (Harlow: Pearson, 1996).

Porter, Bernard, *The Absent-Minded Imperialists: Empire, Society, and Culture in Britain* (New York: Oxford University Press, 2004).

Porter, Patrick, 'The Weinberger doctrine: A celebration', *Infinity Journal*, 3/3, 2013, 8–11.

Porter, Patrick, *The Global Village Myth: Distance, War, and the Limits of Power* (London: Hurst & Company, 2015).

Porter, Patrick, 'Soldiers fighting alone: The wars of the market-security state', *Parameters*, 45/3, 2015, 5–11.

Porter, Patrick, 'Why America's grand strategy has not changed: Power, habit, and the US foreign policy establishment', *International Security*, 42/4, 2018, 9–46.

Porter, Patrick, 'Afghanistan and the lies we tell ourselves', *The Critic Magazine*, March 2020, https://thecritic.co.uk/issues/march-2020/afghanistan-and-the-lies-we-tell-ourselves/

Powers, Thomas, *Intelligence Wars: American Secret History from Hitler to al-Qaeda* (New York: The New York Review of Books, 2002).

Poznansky, Michael, 'Revisiting plausible deniability', *Journal of Strategic Studies*, published online, 2 March 2020, 1–23.

Prados, John, *Safe for Democracy: The Secret Wars of the CIA* (Chicago, IL: Ivan R. Dee, 2006).

Prados, John, 'The continuing quandary of covert operations', *Journal of National Security Law and Policy*, 5/2, January 2012, 359–72.

Press, Daryl, G., 'The myth of air power in the Persian Gulf War and the future of warfare', *International Security*, 26/2, 2001, 5–44.

Press, Daryl, G., *Calculating Credibility: How Leaders Assess Military Threats* (Ithaca, NY: Cornell University Press, 2005).

Price, Bryan C. 'Targeting top terrorists: How leadership decapitation contributes to counterterrorism', *International Security*, 36/4, 2012, 9–46.

Purkiss, Jessica, Abigail Fielding-Smi and Emran Feroz, 'CIA-backed Afghan unit accused of atrocities is able to call in air strikes', *The Bureau of Investigative Journalism*, 8 February 2019, www.thebureauinvestigates.com/stories/2019-02-08/cia-backed-afghan-unit-atrocities

Raitasalo, Jyri, 'Moving beyond the "western expeditionary frenzy"', *Comparative Strategy*, 33/4, 2014, 372–88.

Rashid, Ahmed, *Descent into Chaos: The World's Most Unstable Region and the Threat to Democracy* (London: Penguin, 2009).

Rasmussen, Mikkel Vedby, *The Risk Society at War: Terror, Technology and Strategy in the Twenty-First Century* (New York: Cambridge University Press, 2006).

Rauta, Vladimir, 'A structural-relational analysis of party dynamics in proxy wars', *International Relations*, 32/4, 2018, 449–67.

Rauta, Vladimir, Matthew Ayton, Alexandra Chinchilla, Andreas Krieg, Christopher Rickard and Jean-Marc Rickli, 'A symposium – Debating "surrogate warfare" and the transformation of war', *Defence Studies*, 19/4, 2019, 410–30.

Recchia, Stefano, 'Pragmatism over principle: US intervention and burden shifting in Somalia, 1992–1993', *Journal of Strategic Studies*, 43/3, 2020, 341–65.

Recchia, Stefano and Thierry Tardy, 'French military operations in Africa: Reluctant multilateralism', *Journal of Strategic Studies*, 43/4, 2020, 473–81.

Record, Jeffrey, 'Force protection fetish: Sources, consequences (?) and solutions', *Aerospace Power Journal*, 14, 2000, 4–11.

Reid, Rachel and Sahr Muhammedally, *'Just Don't Call It a Militia': Impunity, Militias, and the 'Afghan Local Police'* (New York: Human Rights Watch, 2011).

Reiter, Dan, 'FDR, US entry into World War II, and selection effects theory', *International Security*, 35/2, 2010, 176–81.

Reiter, Dan and Allan C. Stam, *Democracies at War* (Princeton, NJ: Princeton University Press, 2002).

Rempe, Dennis, M., 'An American Trojan horse? Eisenhower, Latin America, and the development of US internal security policy 1954–1960', *Small Wars and Insurgencies*, 10/1, 1999, 34–64.

Rempfer, Kyle, 'Special operations launches "secret surrogate" missions in new counter-terrorism strategy', *Military Times*, 8 February 2019, www.militarytimes.com/news/your-army/2019/02/08/fighting-terrorism-may-rely-on-secret-surrogate-forces-going-forward/

Renic, Neil C., 'A gardener's vision: UAVs and the dehumanisation of violence', *Survival*, 60/6, 2018, 57–72.

Reuters, 'Arms supplied by US, Saudi end up with Islamic State, researchers say', 15 December 2017, www.reuters.com/article/us-mideast-crisis-iraq-arms/arms-supplied-by-u-s-saudi-ended-up-with-islamic-state-researchers-say-idUSKBN1E82EQ

Reynolds, David, *America, Empire of Liberty* (London: Penguin, 2010).

Ricks, Thomas, *Fiasco: The American Military Adventure in Iraq* (New York: The Penguin Press, 2006).

Ricks, Thomas E., 'General failure', *The Atlantic*, November 2012, www.theatlantic.com/magazine/archive/2012/11/general-failure/309148/

Rissen, James and Mark Mazzetti, 'Blackwater guards tied to secret CIA raids', *The New York Times*, 11 December 2009, www.nytimes.com/2009/12/11/us/politics/11blackwater.html

Rizer, Arthur, 'Lawyering wars: Failing leadership, risk aversion, and lawyer creep – Should we expect more lone survivors?', *Indiana Law Journal*, 90/3, 2015, 935–74.

Roberts, Andrew, *Storm of War: A New History of the Second World War* (London: Allen Lane, 2009).

Roberts, J.M. and Odd Arne Westad, *The Penguin History of the World*, Sixth Edition (London: Penguin, 2013).

Robinson, Linda, 'The future of Special Operations: Beyond kill or capture', *Foreign Affairs*, 91/6, 2012, 110–22.

Rogers, James and Caroline Kennedy-Pipe, *Drone Warfare: Concepts and Controversies* (Manchester: Manchester University Press, 2019).

Rose, Gideon, 'Generation Kill: A conversation with Stanley McChrystal', *Foreign Affairs*, 92/2, 2013, 2–8.

Ross, Jay, 'Time to terminate escalate to de-escalate – It's escalation control', *War on the Rocks*, 24 April 2018, https://warontherocks. com/2018/04/time-to-terminate-escalate-to-de-escalateits-escalation-control/

Roth, Jonathan P., 'War'. In *The Cambridge History of Greek and Roman Warfare: Volume II*, edited by Sabin, Philip, Hans van Wees and Michael Whitby, 368–98 (New York: Cambridge University Press, 2007).

Runkle, Benjamin, 'The lost lessons of "Black Hawk Down"', *War on the Rocks*, 3 October 2013, https://warontherocks.com/2013/10/the-lost-lessons-of-black-hawk-down/

Ryan, Alan, *On Politics: A History of Political Thought from Herodotus to the Present* (London: Allen Lane, 2012).

Ryan, Maria, '"War in countries we are not at war with": The "war on terror" on the periphery from Bush to Obama', *International Politics*, 48/2–3, 2011, 364–89.

Ryan, Missy and Sudarsan Raghavan, 'Special Operations troops aiding Libyan forces in major battle against Islamic State', *The Washington Post*, 10 August 2016, www.washingtonpost.com/news/checkpoint/ wp/2016/08/09/u-s-special-operations-forces-are-providing-direct-on-the-ground-support-for-the-first-time-in-libya/

Salehyan, Idean, 'The delegation of war to rebel organisations', *Journal of Conflict Resolution*, 54/3, 2010, 493–515.

Sanger, David E., *Confront and Conceal: Obama's Secret Wars and Surprising Use of American Power* (New York: Broadway Paperbacks, 2013; Kindle edition).

Sanger, David E., *The Perfect Weapon: War, Sabotage, and Fear in the Cyber Age* (London: Scribe, 2018; Kindle edition).

Savage, Charlie and Mark Landler, 'White House defends continuing US role in Libya operation', *The New York Times*, 15 June 2011, www. nytimes.com/2011/06/16/us/politics/16powers.html

Savage, Charlie, Eric Schmitt and Thomas Gibbons-Neff, 'US kept silent about its role in another firefight in Niger', *The New York Times*, 14 March 2018, www.nytimes.com/2018/03/14/world/africa/niger-green-berets-isis-firefight-december.html

Scahill, Jeremy, 'Blowback in Somalia', *The Nation*, 7 September 2011, www.thenation.com/article/archive/blowback-somalia/

Scales, Robert, *Scales on War: The Future of America's Military at Risk* (Annapolis, MD: Naval Institute Press, 2016; Kindle edition).

Scales, Robert, 'The great duality and the future of the army: Does technology favour the offensive or the defensive?', *War on the Rocks*, 3 September 2019, https://warontherocks.com/2019/09/the-great-duality-and-the-future-of-the-army-does-technology-favor-the-offensive-or-defensive/

Scheipers, Sibylle, 'Auxilliaries at war in the Middle East', *Survival*, 57/4, 2015, 121–38.

Schmitt, Eric and Mark Mazzetti, 'Secret order lets US raid Al Qaeda', *The New York Times*, 9 November 2008, www.nytimes.com/2008/11/10/washington/10military.html

Schmitt, Eric and Rod Norland, 'Amid Turkish assault Kurdish forces are drawn away from US fight with ISIS', *The New York Times*, 28 February 2018, www.nytimes.com/2018/02/28/world/middleeast/syrian-kurds-isis-american-offensive.html

Schneider, Jacquelyn G., 'Persistent engagement: Foundation, evolution and evaluation of a strategy', *Lawfare*, 10 May 2019, www.lawfareblog.com/persistent-engagement-foundation-evolution-and-evaluation-strategy

Schooner, Steven L., 'Why contractor fatalities matter', *Parameters*, 38/3, 2008, 78–91.

Schreer, Benjamin and Thomas Waldman, 'Strategy on Autopilot: Resolute Support and the Continuing Failure of Western Strategy in Afghanistan.' In *Terrorism and Insurgency in Asia: A Contemporary Examination of Terrorist and Separatist Movements*, edited by Benjamin Schreer and Andrew T.H. Tan, 58–71 (Abingdon: Routledge, 2019).

Schroden, Jonathan, 'There was no "secret war on the truth" in Afghanistan', *War on the Rocks*, 16 December 2019, https://warontherocks.com/2019/12/there-was-no-secret-war-on-the-truth-in-afghanistan/

Scott, Ridley, *Black Hawk Down* (Los Angeles, CA: Sony Pictures Releasing, 2001).

Senate Select Committee on Intelligence, 'Committee Study of the Central Intelligence Agency's Detention and Interrogation Program', 3 December 2014, www.intelligence.senate.gov/sites/default/files/press/findings-and-conclusions.pdf

Shapiro, Jeremy, 'Ask not what your country can do for foreign policy', *War on the Rocks*, 7 July 2020, https://warontherocks.com/2020/07/ask-not-what-your-country-can-do-for-foreign-policy/

Shaw, Martin, *Post-Military Society* (Cambridge: Polity, 1991).

Shaw, Martin, *The New Western Way of War: Risk-transfer War and Its Crisis in Iraq* (Cambridge: Polity, 2005)

Shy, John and Thomas W. Collier, 'Revolutionary War.' In *Makers of Modern Strategy*, edited by Peter Paret, 815–62 (New York: Oxford University Press, 1986).

Sidey, Hugh, 'The lessons John Kennedy learned from the Bay of Pigs', *Time*, 16 April 2001, http://content.time.com/time/nation/article/0,8599,106537,00.html

Simpson, Emile, *War from the Ground Up: Twenty-First Century Combat as Politics* (New York: Oxford University Press, 2013).

Slayton, Rebecca, 'What is the cyber offense–defense balance? Conceptions, causes, and assessment', *International Security*, 41/3, 2016–2017, 72–109.

Smith, Hugh, 'What costs will democracies bear? A review of popular theories of casualty aversion', *Armed Forces & Society*, 31/4, 2005, 487–512.

Smith, Michael, *Killer Elite: Inside America's Most Secret Special Forces* (London: Cassell, 2011; Kindle edition).

Smith, Rupert, *The Utility of Force: The Art of War in the Modern World* (London: Penguin, 2005).

South, Todd, 'The Battle of Mogadishu 25 years later: How the fateful fight changed combat operations', *Army Times*, 2 October 2018, www.armytimes.com/news/your-army/2018/10/02/the-battle-of-mogadishu-25-years-later-how-the-fateful-fight-changed-combat-operations/

Sperber, Amanda, 'Inside the secretive US air campaign in Somalia', *The Nation*, 7 February 2019, www.thenation.com/article/archive/somalia-secret-air-campaign/

Sperber, Amanda, 'The "collateral damage" of the US's unofficial war in Somalia', *In These Times*, 16 December 2019, http://inthesetimes.com/features/us-air-strikes-somalia-al-shabab-ISIS-pentagon-civilian-casualties.html

St Clair, Jeffrey and Alexander Cockburn, 'Armies, addicts and spooks: The CIA in Vietnam and Laos', *Counterpunch*, 29 September 2017, www.counterpunch.org/2017/09/29/armies-addicts-and-spooks-the-cia-in-vietnam-and-laos/

Stanger, Allison, *One Nation under Contract* (New Haven, CT: Yale University Press, 2009; Kindle edition).

Stanger, Allison and Mark Eric Williams, 'Private military corporations: Benefits and costs of outsourcing security', *Yale Journal of International Affairs*, 2/1, 2006, 4–19.

Stanik, Joseph T., *El Dorado Canyon: Reagan's undeclared War with Qaddafi* (Annapolis, MD: Naval Institute Press, 2016).

Stapleton, Bradford Ian, 'The problem with the light footprint', *Cato Institute*, Policy Analysis 792, 7 June 2016, www.cato.org/sites/cato.org/files/pubs/pdf/pa792_1.pdf

Stein, Aaron, 'The trouble with Tanf: Tactics driving strategy in Syria', *War on the Rocks*, 12 June 2017, https://warontherocks.com/2017/06/the-trouble-with-tanf-tactics-driving-strategy-in-syria/

Strachan, Hew, *European Armies and the Conduct of War* (Kings Lynn: Routledge, 2006).

Strachan, Hew, *Carl von Clausewitz's On War: A Biography* (New York: Atlantic Monthly Press, 2007).

Strachan, Hew, *The Direction of War: Contemporary Strategy in Historical Perspective* (New York: Cambridge University Press, 2013).

Strachan, Hew and Andreas Herberg-Rothe, 'Introduction.' In Hew Strachan and Andreas Herberg-Rothe (eds), *Clausewitz in the Twenty-First Century*, 1–44 (New York: Oxford University Press, 2007).

Strassler, Robert B. (ed), *The Landmark Herodotus: The Histories*, translated by Andrea L. Purvis (London: Quercus, 2008).

Summers, Harry, *On Strategy: The Vietnam War in Context* (Hawaii: University Press of the Pacific, 2003).

Thomas, Jim and Chris Dougherty, *Beyond the Ramparts: The Future of US Special Forces Operations* (Washington, DC: Centre for Strategic and Budgetary Assessments, 2013).

Thomas, Raymond, 'SOCOM: Policing the world', *The Aspen Institute*, 21 July 2017, https://aspensecurityforum.org/wp-content/uploads/2017/07/SOCOM_Policing-the-World.pdf

Tierney, Dominic, *How We Fight: Crusades, Quagmires, and the American Way of War* (New York: Hachette Book Group, 2010; Kindle edition).

Tierney, Dominic, 'The legacy of Obama's "worst mistake"', *The Atlantic*, 15 April 2016, www.theatlantic.com/international/archive/2016/04/obamas-worst-mistake-libya/478461/

Tierney, John J., *Chasing Ghosts: Unconventional Warfare in American History* (Washington, DC: Potomac Books, 2007).

Treverton, Gregory F., 'Covert action and open society', *Foreign Affairs*, 65, 1986–87, 995–1014.

Truman, Harry S., 'Address before a Joint Session of Congress', 12 March 1947, https://avalon.law.yale.edu/20th_century/trudoc.asp

Trump, Donald, 'Remarks by President Trump on the killing of Qasem Soleimani', 3 January 2020, The White House, www.whitehouse.gov/briefings-statements/remarks-president-trump-killing-qasem-soleimani/

Tucker, Robert W., 'Reagan's foreign policy', *Foreign Affairs*, 68/1, 1988/89, 1–27.

Turse, Nick, 'Pentagon's own map of US bases in Africa contradicts its claim of "light" footprint', *The Intercept*, 27 February 2020, https://theintercept.com/2020/02/27/africa-us-military-bases-africom/

Turse, Nick and Sean D. Naylor, 'Revealed: The US military's 36 code-named operations in Africa', *Yahoo News*, 17 April 2019, https://news.yahoo.com/revealed-the-us-militarys-36-codenamed-operations-in-africa-090000841.html

Twain, Mark, 'Mark Twain home, an anti-imperialist', *New York Herald*, 15 October 1900.

Ucko, David H., 'Systems failure: The US way of irregular warfare', *Small Wars and Insurgencies*, 30/1, 2019, 223–54.

Ucko, David H. and Robert C. Egnell, 'Options for avoiding counterinsurgencies', *Parameters*, 44/1, 2014, 11–22.

United States Army and Marine Corps, *FM 3-24: Counterinsurgency* (Washington, DC: US Department of Defense, 2006).

United States Government, 'NSC 162/2 – Basic National Security Policy', 30 October 1953, https://fas.org/irp/offdocs/nsc-hst/nsc-162-2.pdf

United States Government, 'National Security Decision Directive Number 207', 20 January 1986, https://fas.org/irp/offdocs/nsdd/nsdd-207.pdf

United States Senate Armed Forces Committee, 'Report of the Inquiry into the Role and Oversight of Private Security Contractors in Afghanistan', 28 September 2010, https://fas.org/irp/congress/2010_rpt/sasc-psc.pdf

United States Special Operations Command, *Command History*, 2007, https://fas.org/irp/agency/dod/socom/2007history.pdf

Valeriano, Brandon and Benjamin Jensen, 'The myth of the cyber offense: The case for restraint', *CATO Institute*, Policy Analysis 862, 15 January 2010, www.cato.org/publications/policy-analysis/myth-cyber-offense-case-restraint

van Creveld, Martin, *Command in War* (Cambridge, MA: Harvard University Press, 2002).

van Creveld, Martin, *The Art of War: War and Military Thought* (New York: Smithsonian Books, 2005).

van Creveld, Martin, *The Culture of War* (New York: Ballantine Books, 2008).

van Creveld, Martin, *More on War* (New York: Oxford University Press, 2017; Kindle edition).

van Wees, Hans, 'War and Society.' In *The Cambridge History of Greek and Roman Warfare: Volume II*, edited by Philip Sabin, Hans van Wees and Michael Whitby, 273–99 (New York: Cambridge University Press, 2007).

Vlahos, Michael, 'Fighting identity: Why we are losing our wars', *Military Review*, 87/6, 2007, 2–12.

Vos, Klaas, 'Plausibly deniable: Mercenaries in US covert interventions during the Cold War, 1964–1987', *Cold War History*, 16–1, 2016, 37–60.

Votel, Joseph L. and Eero R. Keravuori, 'The by-with-through operational approach', *Joint Force Quarterly*, 89, 2nd Quarter 2018, 40–7.

Vrolyk, John, 'Insurgency, not war, is China's most likely course of action', *War on the Rocks*, 19 December 2019, https://warontherocks.com/2019/12/insurgency-not-war-is-chinas-most-likely-course-of-action/

Waldman, Matt, 'System failure: The underlying causes of US policy-making errors in Afghanistan', *International Affairs*, 89/4, 2013, 825–43.

Waldman, Thomas, 'Politics and war: Clausewitz's paradoxical equation', *Parameters*, 40/3, 2010, 1–13.

Waldman, Thomas, '"Shadows of uncertainty": Clausewitz's timeless analysis of chance in war', *Defence Studies*, 10/3, 2010, 336–68.

Waldman, Thomas, *War, Clausewitz and the Trinity* (London: Routledge, 2013).

Waldman, Thomas, 'Reconciliation and research in Afghanistan: An analytical narrative', *International Affairs*, 90/5, 2014, 1049–68.

Waldman, Thomas, 'Vicarious warfare: The counterproductive consequences of modern American military practice', *Contemporary Security Policy*, 39/2, 2018, 181–205.

Waldman, Thomas, 'Strategic narratives and US surrogate warfare', *Survival*, 61/1, 2019, 161–78.

Waldman, Thomas, 'Buy now, pay later: American military intervention and the strategic cost paradox', *Defence Studies*, 19/1, 2019, 85–105.

Walt, Stephen M., *The Hell of Good Intentions: America's Foreign Policy Elite and the Decline of US Primacy* (New York: Farrar, Straus & Giroux, 2018).

Walt, Stephen, M., 'The great myth about US intervention in Syria', *Foreign Policy*, 24 October 2016, https://foreignpolicy.com/2016/10/24/the-great-myth-about-u-s-intervention-in-syria-iraq-afghanistan-rwanda/

Walt, Stephen M., 'Everyone misunderstands the reason for the US–China Cold War', *Foreign Policy*, 30 June 2020, https://foreignpolicy.com/2020/06/30/china-united-states-new-cold-war-foreign-policy/

Ward, Robert Hunter, 'Fewer civilian casualties: Trending toward a constraint on the use of force', *Comparative Strategy*, 39/1, 2020, 29–40.

Washington Post, The 'US–Taliban peace deal', 1 March 2020, www.washingtonpost.com/context/u-s-taliban-peace-deal/7aab0f58-dd5c-430d-9557-1b6672d889c3/

Wax, Emily and Karen DeYoung, 'US secretly backing warlords in Somalia', *The Washington Post*, 17 May 2006, www.washingtonpost.com/wp-dyn/content/article/2006/05/16/AR2006051601625.html

Weaver, Mary Anne, 'Lost at Tora Bora', *The New York Times*, 11 September 2005, www.nytimes.com/2005/09/11/magazine/lost-at-tora-bora.html?_r=0

Webb, Jim, 'Congressional abdication', *The National Interest*, 1 March 2013, https://nationalinterest.org/print/article/congressional-abdication-8138

Weigley, Russell F., *The American Way of War: A History of United States Military Strategy and Policy* (Bloomington, IN: Indiana University Press, 1977).

Weinberger, Caspar, 'The uses of military power', 28 November 1984, www.pbs.org/wgbh/pages/frontline/shows/military/force/weinberger.html

Weiner, Tim, *Legacy of Ashes: The History of the CIA* (London: Allen Lane, 2007).

Wertheim, Stephen, 'The price of primacy: Why America shouldn't dominate the world', *Foreign Affairs*, 99/2, 2020, 19–29.

Westad, Odd Arne, *The Cold War: A World History* (London: Penguin, 2017).

Western, Jon, 'Sources of humanitarian intervention: Beliefs, information, and advocacy in the US decisions on Somalia and Bosnia', *International Security*, 26/4, 2002, 112–42.

White House, 'A National Security Strategy of Engagement and Enlargement', February 1995, https://history.defense.gov/Portals/70/Documents/nss/nss1995.pdf?ver=2014-06-25-121226-437

Williams, Paul D., 'Subduing al-Shabaab: The Somalia model of counterterrorism and its limits', *Washington Quarterly*, 41/2, 2018, 95–111.

Williams, Paul D., 'Building the Somali National Army', *Journal of Strategic Studies*, 43/3, 2020, 366–91.

Woods, Chris, 'The story of America's first drone strike in Afghanistan', *The Atlantic*, 30 May 2015, www.theatlantic.com/international/archive/2015/05/america-first-drone-strike-afghanistan/394463/

Woodward, Bob, *Obama's Wars* (London: Simon & Schuster, 2010).

Xuetong, Yan, 'The age of uneasy peace: Chinese power in a divided world', *Foreign Affairs*, 98/1, 2019, 40–9.

Yates, Lawrence A., *Power Pack: US Intervention in the Dominican Republic, 1965–1966* (Fort Leavenworth, KS: Combat Studies Institute, 1988).

Zakaria, Fareed, 'New China scare: Why America shouldn't panic about its latest challenger', *Foreign Affairs*, 99/1, 2020, 52–69.

Zalman, Amy and Jonathan Clarke, 'The global war on terror: A narrative in need of a rewrite', *Ethics and International Affairs*, 23/2, 2009, 101–13.

Zelikow, Philip, 'Why did America cross the Pacific?', *Texas National Security Review*, 1/1, 2017, 36–67.

Zenko, Micah, 'The true forever war', *Foreign Policy*, 24 January 2014, https://foreignpolicy.com/2014/01/24/the-true-forever-war/

Zenko, Micah, 'Trump is America's first contradiction-in-chief', *Foreign Policy*, 12 February 2019, https://foreignpolicy.com/2019/02/12/trump-is-americas-first-narcissist-in-chief/

Index

blowback 108, 171, 184, 192, 195
see also consequences of vicarious
warfare
Bolivia 97
bombing
in Iraq 142
in Kosovo 143
precision 141
public attitudes to 142
in Second World War 74–5, 76
in Vietnam 93, 94, 95–6
see also airpower; weapons
Bosnia 142, 143
Boxer Rebellion 65–6
Boyd, John 141
Bradley, Omar 221*n*24
Brezhnev, Leonid 99, 108
Britain *see* Great Britain
British Empire 41–2, 43, 44, 45, 46, 47
Brzezinski, Zbigniew 98, 238*n*123
Bundy, McGeorge 93, 94
bunkerization 153, 184–6
Burke, Edmund 211
Burma 73
Bush, George W. 120, 137, 146, 149,
152
Butler, Smedley 231*n*70
'by, with and through' 157, 163, 176

C
Cambodia 95, 96
carpet bombing 76, 94
Carter, Jimmy 98–9, 238*n*119, 238*n*124
Carthage 26
Casey, William 99–100, 103, 104
Castro, Fidel 89
casualties
civilians 44, 126, 134, 178, 180, 189
historically 26, 36, 37, 61
public attitudes to 126–7
in Vietnam 94
Central Intelligence Agency (CIA)
and Afghanistan 161
Cold War 81, 82, 86–9, 91, 92, 95,
97, 99–100, 102, 108, 109
Counterterrorism Center 104
formation of 86
and Iraq 155

militarization of 190
Second World War 73, 74
and SOF 190–1
Special Activities Center (SAC)
190
and Special Operations Command
(SOCOM) 150
and Syria 156–7
and Vietnam 92, 95
China 65–6, 215–16
citizens/civilians
as casualties of war 44, 126, 134,
178, 180, 189
citizen-soldiers (historically) 24,
26–7, 42, 48, 49, 58, 59
in classical history 23–7
conscription 24, 26, 44, 45, 50, 57
early American 58–9, 60–1
and elite monopolization of warfare
31–3, 36
and empire 42–3, 47
see also public attitudes to war
city-states 23–5
Civil War 64
civilians *see* citizens/civilians
Clark, Mark 72
Clark, Wesley 143
Clarridge, Duane 103–4
Clausewitz, Carl von 2, 6, 11, 27, 34,
36, 59, 141, 165–75, 204, 213,
259*n*32
culminating point of victory 170–4
and politics of force 167–70
Cleveland, Grover 70
Clinton, Bill 138, 140, 145
coercive airpower 93, 172
coercive diplomacy 85, 93, 96
cognitive domain 169
Cold War 79–110
accountability 105–6
assessment of 106–12
containment strategy 81, 87, 98, 105
dénouement 97–101
nuclear weapons 83–5
origins of 80–3
Second Cold War 99
Southeast Asia 90–7
vicarious approaches 85–104
war frame of 173–4